Jesus

THE EXPLOSIVE STORY OF

THE THIRTY LOST YEARS AND

THE ANCIENT MYSTERY RELIGIONS

TRICIA McCANNON

for the evolving human spirit

HAMPTON ROADS
PUBLISHING COMPANY, INC.

Cover design: Adrian Morgan.
Cover photograph: © Corbis/Fine Art/The Gallery Collection
Text design: Dutton and Sherman Design
Unless otherwise noted, all figures are illustrated or photographed by the author.
Editor: Greg Brandenburgh
Production Editor: Michele Kimble
Copy Editor: Laurel Warren Trufant, Ph.D.
Proofreader: Carol Marti

Hampton Roads Publishing Company, Inc.
Charlottesville, VA 22906
www.hrpub.com

Library of Congress Cataloging-in-Publication Data

McCannon, Tricia.
      Jesus : the explosive story of the thirty lost years and the ancient mystery
   religions / Tricia McCannon.
            p. cm.
      Includes bibliographical references.
      Summary: "An account of Jesus' life during his many missing years, where he
   was and what he learned before beginning his public ministry in Palestine"—
   Provided by publisher.
      ISBN 978-1-57174-607-8 (6 x 9 tc : alk. paper)
      1. Jesus Christ—Biography—Apocryphal and legendary literature. 2. Jesus
   Christ Miscellanea. I. Title.
   BT520.M33 2009   232.⁹—dc22

10 9 8 7 6 5 4 3 2
Printed in Canada
TCP

DEDICATION

To the great spiritual Masters and Initiates throughout all the centuries who have kept the torch of the Mysteries alight. May the Spirit of the Christ and the Spirit of Ma'at (Cosmic Truth) inspire each generation to remember and embrace our own divine natures in their search for the Way.

CONTENTS

Part III
Jesus among the Essenes

Part IV
Jesus in the Land of the Celts

Part V
Jesus in the East

Part VI
Jesus in Egypt

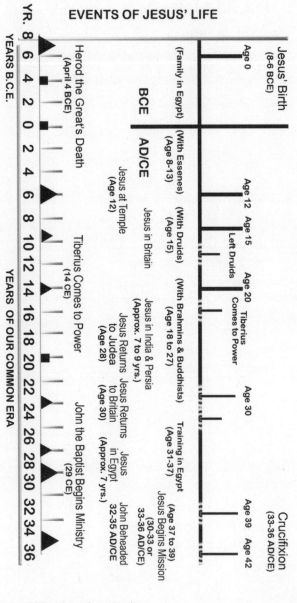

FIGURE 1. Jesus' life and travels—a timeline.

The Invitation

There lives a Master in the hearts of men,
maketh their deeds, by subtle pulling strings,
dance to what tune He will.
With all thy soul trust Him, and take Him for thy succor, Prince![1]

The Bhagavad-Gita

I never intended to write this book.

I have long been a teacher of the spiritual path, an international speaker, and a mystic trained in the Mysteries of many ancient streams of wisdom. I have researched and written books about world prophecy and the profound events facing our world today, and about the secret teachings of the ancients. I included a discussion of Jesus in my second book because I saw in him a key example of how beautiful teachings can negatively impact the world when perverted by the power elites. In the course of my inquiries, my own beliefs transitioned from a simple Christian perspective to a far broader knowledge of the Mysteries—the secret teachings of the ancients. And this led me to a deeper investigation of the true history of Jesus.

Yet I never intended to write this book.

I was raised in the Deep South in a fundamentalist Christian family, but my own spiritual path was always different from theirs. As a child, I experienced many clairvoyant episodes that involved everything from communi-

cating with animals to seeing fairies and devas in the woods. I was visited by
angels and spirit guides, and accessed information about other people's past
and future lives clairvoyantly. Neither my family nor the Christian church we
attended could explain my experiences. And many of the Christian doctrines I
was taught didn't make any sense to me—especially the idea that we only have
one short life in which to become enlightened, and the mystifying notion that
a noble, loving Creator could condemn us to eternal suffering if we didn't "get
it right."

Rather than struggle to find logic in Christian teachings, I began to study
spiritual beliefs that seemed more coherent, more loving, and more uplifting
than the religion of my youth. I studied Jesus' hidden teachings from the "lost
books" of the Bible and learned the history of his travels to other lands. I became a student of Buddhism, Theosophy, Hinduism, shamanism, Celtic mysticism, Native American spirituality, and the Egyptian Mysteries. For over three
decades, I worked with many different spiritual masters and became an initiate
in several profound paths. As the years passed, I gained control of my strong
spiritual gifts through meditation and prayer, and started helping others connect with their own divine essence. I began to do readings for people to help
them heal their wounds and re-empower themselves.

Ultimately, I became a "headliner" at conferences around the world. I took
groups of like-minded pilgrims on sacred journeys to Egypt, England, Peru,
Italy, Mount Shasta, the Four Corners, and Greece. I began to investigate the
Earth's energetic history. I traveled the Nile, spent time in the temples, and
slept inside the Great Pyramid. I spent years in Magical England and visited
the gardens of Chalice Well, where Joseph of Arimathea set up the first Christian church a few years after the Crucifixion. I followed the journey of Mary
Magdalene through southern France, tracking the path of the refugees from
Israel as they fled from the tyranny of Jerusalem. And with each new discovery,
I drew nearer to unraveling the Mysteries of the ages. My clairvoyant readings
deepened. I began tracking souls back to their place of origin, discovering the
higher worlds of countless angels and spirit guides, and learning how we are
connected to these realms. I was visited by masters who taught me about the
celestial origins of us all.

Of course, not everyone shared my expanded views. When I visited my
fundamentalist family, they kept me apart from my young nieces and nephews
lest they become contaminated by a desire for a broader base of knowledge. After twenty years of this painful dynamic, I finally turned to Jesus for answers.

Yet I never intended to write this book.

TALKING WITH JESUS

Christmas 2006. I was deep in the throes of writing. I had been hard at work on the computer all day and had just decided to take a break. I stretched out in my office, surrounded by sacred images of the masters and angels I had worked with for decades. The incense from my prayer altar wafted through the room. My eyes were closed, yet I slowly became aware that Jesus was standing over me. I could see his gold-white aura through my eyelids as clearly as if my eyes were open. His radiance seemed to penetrate my forehead.

"I want you to write a book about my lost years and secret teachings," he said telepathically. "There has been enough struggle—enough war and bloodshed in my name."

Stunned as I was by the radiance of his joyful, brilliant presence, it took me a moment to respond. "Well," I thought, "I'm in the middle of writing some other books right now. Maybe when I finish these . . ."

Jesus' light grew stronger and, somehow, this radiance made the idea of writing another book seem effortless and easy. He was smiling down upon me. He waved his hand as if to say that what he required of me would only take a moment. I realized that I could write this book for him, and then go back to my other projects. Right?

An image of my dysfunctional family flashed through my head. I groaned as I thought of the effect this book would have on my relationship with them. And there were millions of people like my family out there—those more committed to the letter of Christianity than to the Spirit behind it. If I wrote this book, what might the consequences be?

Jesus hovered above me, letting me take my time to work through my own thoughts.

Then I thought of the many people like me—people who love Jesus with all their hearts, who have seen the negative impact of the social, political, and emotional control exercised in the name of dualistic religion. Like me, they are trying to find a more inclusive vision. Like me, they see a world divided, torn apart by people arguing about God. Like me, they seek a path of unity that can integrate Jesus into a larger reality. Like me, they know that, if we can truly live this path, it will bring a lot more unity into the world.

"But why me?" I wondered. Perhaps it was because I had explored how these pieces fit together and because I had been studying the Mysteries my whole life.

I knew about the documented records of Jesus in India and the stories of Jesus among the Buddhists. I had done ceremony at Glastonbury and walked the same hills of Priddy that the songs tell us he walked. I had felt the quiet calm of Joseph of Arimathea's spirit in the gardens of Chalice Well. I had been ordained as a bishop of the Madonna Ministries in the now-abandoned Chapel of Mary at Glastonbury Abbey. From my studies of the Anunnaki gods of the Middle East, I knew about the teachings of the *neteru*. I had studied Zoroaster and the solar lord Mithra. I knew about the illuminated savior gods of ancient Egypt—Horus, Osiris, and Thoth—who had come to lift mankind from darkness. I had heard the Egyptian legends of the phoenix, the divine and radiant being that descends periodically from the higher realms and sings its song of beauty, only to be destroyed by darkness and then reborn in light.

A single unifying thread must be woven through all these Mysteries. I just knew it. There is a plan that runs through everything—all the spiritual teachings, all the esoteric paths. Each of the masters was a part of something far larger, something orchestrated at a higher level. And Jesus stood at its center. He traveled across the world, following the golden thread through the wisdom of many lands, then returned to the land of his birth and distilled his vast knowledge into a few simple precepts that everyone can understand: love your neighbor as yourself; turn the other cheek; judge not lest you be judged; the kingdom of Heaven is within us all.

But what about the other things Jesus taught? The writings of the Dead Sea Scrolls and the Nag Hammadi texts are slowly being published, and a few of the Lost Gospels have been released. But there are still so many things that most people don't know. Could I connect the dots between these sources and bring them forward? If I did, would it bring some sanity into the world? Would people really listen? Or were they simply too committed to conflict and separation?

Jesus still stood above me, waiting, hovering in a golden light. I felt the ancient power of his presence and the infinite patience he had for all living beings who were caught up in conflict and turmoil. When I concentrated on him, all my doubts disappeared and there was only the Light.

I thought of all that Jesus had faced in his life. The world into which he was born was torn apart by the religious tyranny of the Pharisees and Sadducees on one hand and the military power of the Romans on the other. One group wanted to stone him; the other crucified hundreds in the name of obedience. Only the bravest of souls would have confronted these powerful forces. But Jesus had done so, even to the point of death, even going against members of his own family, who did not understand that he was teaching a higher law until after he was resurrected.

Suddenly, all the pieces of my life seemed to fall into place—my dysfunctional family, my clairvoyance and clairaudience, my travels throughout the world in search of answers, my studies with the Great White Brotherhood and the Vairagi masters, my twenty years as a writer and teacher.

My heart melted, and I knew what I had to do.

Seeking a New Perspective

The hidden life of Yeshua ben Joseph, better known to us as Jesus Christ, may be among the greatest mysteries of all time. Certainly, over the past 2000 years, there has been no more beloved or controversial figure. Yet no teacher's words of peace and brotherhood have ever been more misused to create division, war, and persecution.

Over the last three millennia, hundreds of books have been written about Jesus by theologians, lay people, and scholars alike. Yet certain key questions remain: Who was Jesus? Where was he trained in the esoteric wisdom he taught? Where did he live during the nearly thirty years that are unaccounted for in the Bible? Did he travel? Who were the mysterious Wise Men who suddenly appeared in Bethlehem after his birth, and what did they have to do with his mission? Why do we hear no more of these spiritual masters after their brief appearance at the Nativity? What secret teachings did Jesus share with his apostles? Are they written down? Why do we not have access to them? What were his attitudes toward women, marriage, and the Divine Feminine? What happened to Mary and Martha? And what about Lazarus, whom Jesus resurrected from the dead? Was Jesus ever married?

Jesus' life is very much a mystery story. We all know the beginning of the tale, when the Magical child is born; and we all know its ending, complete with its pain and sorrow, suffering and ultimate victory. But a vast portion of the middle chapters is missing. Jesus' whereabouts and activities for nearly three decades are not recorded in the Bible. Where did he live before the age of twelve? And what about the decades before his ministry began? Did he have teachers who helped him to prepare for his deeper mission?

Today it is time for a larger perspective on Jesus—one that is inclusive and loving, not exclusive and territorial; one that honors the Prince of Peace for who he truly was, not our dualistic version of who we have been told he was. A lifetime of research has convinced me that Jesus' birth, life, teachings, and death were all part of a larger plan, set in motion long ago by a divine intelligence in answer to the calls of a suffering world. His life was an event planned by a larger spiritual hierarchy, supported by this hierarchy, and foreshadowed by the teachings of other masters who came before him. His birth was foretold by the masters of at least five spiritual traditions, including the teachers Buddha and Zoroaster. Both the Egyptians and the Druids saw Jesus as part of a larger plan to heal world consciousness—in his own age and in ours. And these traditions all participated in a central illuminating body called the Great White Brotherhood, an ancient wisdom order also known as the Melchizedek Order, the Fellowship of Light, and the Great Mystic Lodge.[2]

This book explores how Jesus was connected with the Great White Brotherhood and the secret schools of initiation. It draws on records from the Vatican, Tibet, India, Israel, and Egypt. It references Greek, Aramaic, and Pali texts and a book of wisdom brought to Britain by Joseph of Arimathea shortly after the Crucifixion that contains accounts of Jesus and Joseph's meetings with the Druids. It explores oral legends of Jesus' time in Britain and written records of his teachings in Persia, India, Chaldea, and Egypt. It also links the mystical teachings of the Druids, the Essenes, the Brahmins, the Persian Magi, the Egyptian Therapeutae, and the Buddhists to Christian thought. The essential nexus between these various paths lies in the spiritual teachings of the Great White Brotherhood, with whom Jesus had profound connections.

This book seeks the real reason why Jesus has remained such a powerful and pivotal figure in world consciousness for nearly two millennia, and will remain so for thousands of years to come. It tells the story of the unrevealed miracles of our past and the coming of age in our present. It also identifies the long line of spiritual initiates who continue to work toward enlightenment—masters who recognized Jesus as "the long awaited one," and the "master of masters."

The 2160-year cycle of the Age of Pisces is almost complete; the Age of Aquarius is at hand. We see its markers all around us—from electronics to space travel, from computers to iPods, from the Information Revolution to the Hubble telescope. Our world is moving at light speed. We can no longer maintain the illusion that the people on the other side of the planet are strangers. We no longer have the option of blowing each other to bits lest we render our planet uninhabitable. We cannot pretend that the destruction of the rainforests in South America does not change the weather patterns in England, Canada, or the Pacific Rim. The coming age will be about discovering what unites us as a world, not what divides us. And Jesus is a perfect teacher of this path.

It is my hope that this book will reveal the profound being who was Jesus Christ, and the sacrifices of all the great avatars who have come into this world to serve humankind. It is my hope that it will awaken your heart, illumine your mind, and allow your spirit to penetrate into the mysteries of the eternal One.

Yet I never intended to write this book.

PART I

The Mysteries of the Ages

CHAPTER 1

The Wisdom Orders

That which is called the Christian religion existed among the ancients, and never did not exist, from the beginning of the human race until Christ came in the flesh, at which time the true religion which already existed began to be called Christianity.[1]

—Saint Augustine, *Retractions*

There are many perspectives from which one can write a book about Jesus: agnostic, evangelical, fundamentalist, channeled, historical, or atheist. This book is none of these, although it is based in history, mystical spirituality, and Christianity.

You are about to embark on a journey of miracles and masters. Most people today have no awareness of the profound Mystery traditions that existed in our historic past at the time that Jesus lived. These philosophic and practical traditions had been in full swing some 4000 years before Jesus was born and continued for 400 years after his death and resurrection. Deeply influential in philosophic thought, these Mystery traditions were developed in antiquity by the sages of many lands. They provided guideposts for individuals who sought the deeper truth behind the tumultuous, often violent, materialism of everyday political and economic life. They addressed the deeper questions of existence— Who am I? Where have I come from? Where am I going?—and gave every seeker a chance to discover their own eternal answers.

Because the existence of these ancient mystery orders has been largely un-acknowledged by mainstream history, it is difficult to decipher how they are re-

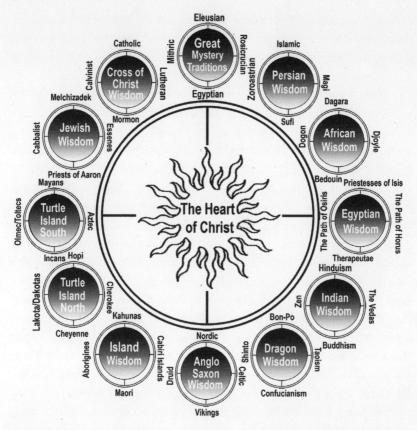

FIGURE 2. The sacred wheels of the Mystery Schools—twelve world traditions inspired by the masters.

lated to the historical and spiritual figure of Jesus. To do so, we must have three key things: a knowledge of the organizing body called the Great White Brotherhood that stood behind the traditions; an orientation to the great Mystery traditions, what they taught, and which chapters were active as Jesus was growing up; and a familiarity with the language of hermetics, the means through which these Mysteries were passed on.

THE GREAT WHITE BROTHERHOOD

The overarching mystical body that supported Jesus' mission and helped prepare to him for it was the Great White Brotherhood. These keepers of wisdom, these profound light beings, have overseen the rise and fall of countless civilizations. From time to time, one of these enlightened souls has incarnated on

Earth to bring a greater balance to the world. This enlightened order is comprised of teachers, adepts, masters, holy sages, and avatars of every race and nationality, and from higher realms as well. Their mission is, quite simply, to uplift world consciousness and awaken humans from their slumber.

These enlightened beings—lost in legend and whispered about in rumor—have been the inspiration behind significant revolutions in the arts, sciences, and humanities. The noble Buddha of India; the wise Lao Tzu of China; the honorable Zoroaster of Persia, Greek philosophers like Plato, Socrates, and Aristotle, who fathered much of our Western philosophy; Pythagoras, the father of mathematics; Herodotus, the father of history; Hippocrates, the father of modern medicine; Euclid, the father of geometry; and Democritus, the father of the atom—all were initiates of the Mystery traditions. All established streams of wisdom that nourished their civilizations and prepared Jesus for his all-important mission. In the ancient world many of our greatest minds were initiates of these mysteries: Pindar, Percales, Plutarch, Hypatia, Parmenides, Zeno, Thales, Empedocles, Anaxagoras, Plotinus, Cicero, Solon, and Heraclitus. In more recent history, we find many learned initiates from the ancient mystery schools: Leonardo da Vinci, Botticelli, William Blake, Sir Isaac Newton, Johannes Kepler, Sir Walter Raleigh, John Milton, Daniel Defoe, Victor Hugo, Thomas More, Roger Bacon, Copernicus, William Shakespeare, and John Dee.[2] All trained in the great schools of Egypt, Greece, Britain, or Europe.[3]

The Great White Brotherhood chose the color white as one of its primary symbols, because it represented purity and illumination. Thus, in many traditions, the Sun, the most visible manifestation of illumination in our world, became the symbol of the Creator itself, synonymous with the Christed spirit that lies dormant within every human heart. The Brotherhood tells us that "Each living being contains within itself a centre of life, which may grow to be a Sun," a metaphor for the light within.[4] According to 33rd degree Mason Manly P. Hall, "This glorious, radiant orb of day . . . this Supreme Spirit of humanitarianism and philanthropy is known to Christendom as Christ, the Redeemer of worlds."[5] Thus the Sun became linked to various expressions of God's power, externalized as the great solar lords Ra, Horus, Mithra, and Jesus—all symbols for the inner Christ.

The ancients saw the Sun as three separate, but co-joined, expressions: the spiritual Sun, which is the spirit of God itself; the "soular" Sun, which is expressed in the human incarnations of the Sons of God who periodically descend to Earth to teach mankind; and the material Sun that we see rising in our skies each day, which acts as a vehicle for the Holy Spirit, sending its light rays down to coax forth life.[6] "Light is the subtlest, most intangible of things which man can register by means of one of his five senses," Hall tells us. "This divine irradiation shines upon all from the outside just as the Sun illuminates every object with its rays."[7]

The Great White Brotherhood, or mystical Fellowship of Light, awaited the arrival of Jesus as the "soular Sun," or representative of God. This divine being bore many names throughout the ancient world: the Messiah, the Saoshyant, the Horus-king, HU-Hesus, and the Adam Cadman, the living expression of a fully enlightened god-man. This Brotherhood was completely committed to welcoming Jesus—the "soular" Sun—into the world and supporting his mission. Their Magi designed his course of study and helped him to develop his spiritual and physical gifts until they pushed the limits of what one can accomplish in a mortal body.

Over the millennia, the Brotherhood has had at least seventy-two separate chapters throughout its long and illustrious history, including the mystical Essenes, the mysterious Magi, the contemplative Buddhists, the Celtic Druids, and the obscure college of the Egyptian Therapeutae. These various chapters can be represented as a twelve-rayed circle. These were the traditions in which Jesus was trained and this twelve-fold geometry is reflected in the twelve apostles.

Some of the better-known chapters of the Great White Brotherhood include the esoteric Rosicrucians; the Eleusinian Mysteries of Greece; the oracle centers at Delphi, Ephesus, Sais, and Buto; the egalitarian Freemasons; the gentle Theosophists; the courageous Knights Templar; the holy Cathars; the Knights of the Round Table; the Order of the Golden Dawn; and the ancient Order of King Solomon. Over time, many of these orders have been exterminated by secular or religious authorities, but the spirit that inspired them and the desire to bring their truths to men's hearts and minds remains and is being reborn in our time.

The many chapters of the Great White Brotherhood that have flourished around the world follow many different paths. Yet students at the higher levels of these orders realize that each path leads to the same essential goal: a reconnection with the source of life itself. In the ancient world, this quest for perfection ran like a golden thread through all the great spiritual traditions. The uninitiated—stuck at the lower levels of spiritual development and caught in their limiting paradigms of dogma, fear, and power—often believe that these paths are in conflict, but this is a great misperception. Such limited thinking can never offer true enlightenment or world peace, and can only result in isolated groups being at odds with the rest of humanity.

Indeed, all these streams of wisdom flow into the same sea of enlighten-ment. The drumbeats of Mother Earth, the prayer chants of the Tibetans, the beauty of a Catholic Mass, the wisdom of the Jewish Kabbala, the dervish danc-ing of the Sufis, the stillness of the Zen Mind, the celebrations of the Goddess—they all seek a loving and sacred intercourse with the Divine and eventually lead to the same great truth. At this level of understanding, all paths are sacred. And this was the central teaching of the Brotherhood—that, behind the many faces of the gods and goddesses, there is only one Supreme Being, the Great Architect of the universe.

The Mystery Schools were overseen by legendary masters who existed on the subtle planes of vibration—enlightened figures like Saint Germaine, Serapis Bey, Lin Wa, Yablu Sacabi, Sudar Singh, Lantos, Shamus I Tabriz, Kabir, Rumi, Sai Baba, Tawart Managi, and Rebazar Tarz. Many of these masters can only be accessed now through focused meditation or a heightened dream state, since they serve in the temples of Golden Wisdom on the higher planes. Behind them are an even more select group of Supreme Masters who are emanations of God-realized beings from the higher realms—Jesus, Thoth, Lakshmi, Krishna, Babaji, Buddha, Quan Yin, Isis, Osiris, and Horus.

Among these Supreme Masters are the four great solar lords who are direct expressions of the Divine Father himself. The Upanishads tell us that these four eternal "Sons of God" were known as the four great *Kumaras*, a Sanskrit word that means "son." In Sanskrit, *Khu* is the ancient name for the higher self; *Ma* is a name for the Divine Mother; *Ra* is the name for the Sun god, or father of light. Thus *Kumara* combines the three key concepts of mother, father, and holy child into one direct emanation. Jesus—also known as Sananda Kumara—is one of these four great Sons of God who periodically return to our world.

The Three-step Throne

The Mystery schools were based on three grades of initiation that built upon one another: the Lesser Mysteries, the Greater Mysteries, and Mastery. These grades are symbolized in the three-step throne of Isis, a metaphor for achieving "the throne" of enlightenment. A similar three-step process was also adopted by early Christian mystics in the three stages of purification, illumination, and perfection.[8]

At the simplest level, the Mystery Schools taught honesty, morality, kind-ness, honor, and the virtue of compassion for all living creatures. They focused on the eternal nature of the soul, the mechanics of the universe, and our con-

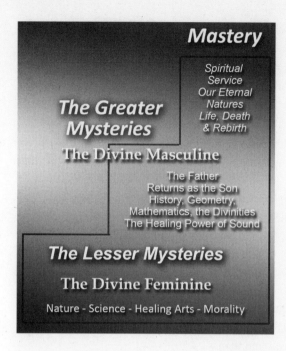

FIGURE 3. The three steps of Isis. The Foundational or Lesser Mysteries of the Divine Mother taught the study of nature. The Greater Mysteries taught the secrets of the Divine Father who comes to Earth periodically as the Divine Son. In Mastery, initiates finally committed to a life of integration and service to all of humanity.

nection to God. Their curriculum encompassed the sciences, mathematics, geometry, history, the movement of the stars and planets, and the energetic pathways of the human body and of the Earth. They also addressed the proper balance of mind, body, and spirit as a pathway to healthy living. Their healing methods included herbology, naturopathy, hands-on healing, and meditation. They taught initiates to work within the subtle energy realms, encouraged them to remember their own divine natures, and urged them to transcend this world while still living in their earthly bodies. Jesus employed these practices when he healed the sick, cast out demons, calmed the elements, performed distance healing, and had foreknowledge of his own death and resurrection.

The Mystery Schools communicated these sacred truths through what they called the Right and Left Eye of Horus, another way of describing the left and right sides of the brain. The right eye, representing the masculine, taught the grounded laws of cause and effect through mathematics and the physical sciences. The left eye, symbolizing the feminine, taught students to create a direct experiential connection with their own eternal natures. Within the Mystery Schools, this was done through meditation, ritual, and the use of ceremonial mystery dramas.

The first step toward enlightenment, the Lesser Mysteries, was dedicated to the Divine Feminine as it is expressed in nature. The Lesser Mysteries taught biology, botany, herbs, medicine, astronomy, and a keen observation of the natural world and all the observable ways in which the Great Spirit of the Divine Mother moves through it. By coming into right relationship with the Divine Feminine, initiates began to experience nature as a teacher and to discover the mysteries of nature herself.

The Lesser Mysteries also established the moral foundations of honesty, nobility, and responsibility, stressing the importance of the Golden Rule, a wisdom that Jesus also taught. They taught about the subtle worlds and the eternal laws of karma that govern the cosmos, and revealed the purpose of man's existence, using parable, allegory, and proverbs to teach the history, evolution, and cosmology of the human race.

The second grade of initiation, the Greater Mysteries, explored the secrets of the Divine Masculine and revealed how the Divine Father periodically returns to the world of form as the Divine Son. In this grade, initiates learned the importance of dying to the ego, epitomized in the sacrificial figure of Osiris, who returned to life as Horus, the bringer of truth. In Christianity, we call this being "born again," although the ancients' comprehension of this life-and-rebirth cycle was far more profound than ours.

The Mystery Schools actively cultivated symbolic near-death experiences overseen by trained adepts who had already transversed this life-altering path. Initiates were carefully prepared for the spiritual journey into non-ordinary states of reality by a thorough course of study that included fasting, meditation, yogic exercises, and prayer. In the advanced degrees, writes Paul Brunton, initiates "were brought into personal communion with the Creator; they stood face to face with the Divine."[9] The purpose of this spiritual catharsis was to shed attachments to old ways and to let go of the ego—the "little self."

In the Eleusinian Mysteries, a cycle of Greek Mystery dramas originally based on the Egyptian Mysteries, initiates were deliberately led through a death-and-rebirth process symbolized by passage through a series of dark caves, where they were forced to confront their deepest fears. Through this passage, aspirants had a chance to glimpse the eternal flame that lay within their souls, a flame that cannot be diminished or extinguished, even in death. Initiates then crossed to the other side and peered beyond the veils of mortal life, encountering the higher-dimensional beings that today we call angels, celestial messengers, or gods and goddesses. Here, Brunton tells us, initiates "solved the mystery of death. They learned that it was really disappearance from one state of being, only to reappear in another; that it affected the fleshly body, but did not destroy

the mind and the self. They learned too, that the soul not only survived the destruction of its mortal envelope, but progressed onwards to higher spheres."[10]

While the Lesser Mysteries taught the consequences of our actions after
death, the Greater Mysteries revealed through out-of-body journeys how our
negative beliefs and actions can prevent us from reaching the heavenly worlds.
The Lesser Mysteries concentrated on methods for controlling our animal-
driven passions while the Greater Mysteries developed the initiates' mental and
spiritual bodies with specific yogic techniques.[11] In the Greater Mysteries, initiates learned about the seven dimensional levels of reality, explored the vast
cycles of time that govern human evolution, and gained knowledge of the chain
of worlds nested within the universe.[12] Physicists today are just rediscovering
these multi-dimensional realms that lie beyond our physical senses, but they
were known to the mystics of virtually every spiritual tradition in the world
long ago.

In the third step of initiation, Mastery, an awareness of both the male and
female aspects of the Divine brings integration and personal balance. This balance is foundational to becoming enlightened. After achieving integration and
balance, initiates then committed themselves to the enlightenment of others.
These Knowers or Twice Born, as they came to be known, died to their old ways
of life. They passed beyond surface illusions to the heart of their own divine essence and returned transformed. This is what Jesus meant when he said: "Most
assuredly, I say to you, unless one is born again, one cannot see the kingdom of
God" (John 3:3).

Unfortunately, we have largely lost the ability to achieve this integration
and balance because our culture denigrates the Divine Feminine. Most Christians today don't realize that Jesus honored both the Divine Father and the
Divine Mother, whom he called the Abba/Amma. In the Gospel of Philip, Jesus
teaches: "Truth is the Mother; knowledge is the Father . . . " but this reference
disappeared from Catholic liturgy almost 1800 years ago.[13] Our world has thus
been completely out of balance for many centuries.

Over the course of several years, initiates of the Mystery Schools crossed
from a world of theory to one of experience. They discovered for themselves
the secrets of life, death, and rebirth. Once they accomplished this, they had
nothing to fear from death. They realized that, during our limited time here on
Earth, we must celebrate our lives from the depths of our being and use them
to make a difference for ourselves and others. This profound realization is what
lies at the heart of the ancient Mystery Schools and explains why they were held

in such high regard by the most learned individuals and faithfully protected by initiates for over 4000 years.

So great, in fact, was the respect these sacred schools inspired that none of their numberless initiates ever revealed their secret rituals. Today, we have but scattered clues about what transpired along the path to initiation, although archaeologists continue to find tombs whose inscriptions indicate that those interred had "renewed their lives" and thus were likely students of the Mysteries.[14] The Greek historian Plutarch (46-120 C.E.), himself an initiate and a near contemporary of Jesus, writes: "While we are . . . encumbered by bodily affections, we can have no intercourse with God . . . But when our souls are released [by the Mysteries] and have passed into the region of the pure, invisible and changeless, this God will be their guide and king . . . ."[15] Plato also writes of a "divine initiation" through which aspirants "become spectators of single and blessed visions, residents in a pure light, and [are] made immaculate and liberated from this surrounding garment which we call the body . . . ." Likewise, the Syrian philosopher Iamblichus observes: "The essence and perfection of all good are comprehended in the gods . . . [and] accompanied with a conversion to, and knowledge of ourselves . . . [T]his is the aim . . . in the priestly lifting of the soul to divinity."[16]

JESUS AND THE TRANSMISSION OF THE MYSTERIES

So what evidence do we have that Jesus was trained in the Mysteries? First, we need only look at his life and his miracles, which were performed in accordance with natural law, to know that he had discovered the invisible secrets behind the world of form. He clearly knew how to employ the many gifts of the yogis, masters, and Magi. Whether he was born with these gifts or acquired them through study does not matter. Only a highly advanced soul could have achieved this level of balance and integration in 10,000 lifetimes.

Moreover, we know Jesus was trained in the Mysteries because he tells us so. In the Gospel of Matthew, he tells his disciples that to them "it has been given to know the secrets of the kingdom of heaven." Here, the word "secrets," or *mysteria*, translates literally as "the Mysteries."[17] In the New Testament alone, the word *mysteria* is used specifically in regard to Jesus' teachings twenty-two times. In the Gospel of Thomas, he tells his apostles, "It is to those who are worthy of my mysteries that I tell my mysteries," clearly revealing himself as a Master of these traditions. In the apocryphal Acts of John, he holds a private conversation with John shortly after the Crucifixion, in which he reveals the very mystery of his death and resurrection: "Therefore ignore the many and despise those who are outside the mystery; for you must know that I am wholly with the Father, and the Father with me."[18]

The Gospel of Philip, a collection of Jesus' sayings that focus on the four great sacramental mysteries of Christianity—baptism, anointing, the Eucharist, and the Bridal Chamber—reports Jesus as saying, "Those above, revealed to those below, so that we could know the mysteries of Truth." In fact, Philip writes: "The Master did everything in a mystery: [his rites of passage were] baptism, chrism, Eucharist, redemption, and bridal chamber,"[19] referring to the Mysteries' initiatory rites of being born, committing to the Divine, sacrificing to unconditional love, surrendering to grace, and finally embracing the "sacred marriage" between the inner male and the female. Victoria LaPage, author of *Mysteries of the Bridal Chamber*, relates why much of this deeper mysticism may have been hidden in the early years of the Church:

> [I]t is highly probable that originally the four canonical gospels were chosen from among many others for inclusion in the Christian scriptures because of their suitability for the lowest, most numerous and most exoteric of the three initiatory grades. More esoteric texts, such as the Gospel of Thomas, the book of Clement, and the Gospels of Barnabas, Peter, Mary and Philip, which we now refer to as apocryphal, may well have been regarded as suitable only for the higher grades and reserved for private readings.[20]

The Gospel of Matthew describes how Jesus often spoke in parables, one of the prime methods of teaching within the Mystery Schools. Herod Antipas also refers to this in a letter to the Roman Senate: "He [Jesus] resorted to the allegorical method of the Egyptian Hebrews [in his teachings]."[21] Jesus used phrases like, "Let those who have the ears to hear, let him hear," recalling a similar phrase used within the Mystery traditions to announce stories with multiple levels of meaning—in other words, stories encoded with a meaning known only to initiates. This use of parable, story, and myth was a powerful teaching device employed by the Egyptian Schools, whose initiates even encoded their hieroglyphic writings on three different levels so they could be understood by all, delivering different meanings depending on the reader's level of esoteric training.

Indeed, it quickly becomes clear that there are many levels to Jesus' life and teachings that have been suppressed, destroyed, or left out of Western Christianity altogether—among them his participation in the Mystery traditions. Morton

Smith, a scholar of ancient history at Columbia University, discovered a letter written in 200 C.E. by Clement of Alexandria, an early church father, that describes a secret Gospel of Mark. "[It is] a more spiritual gospel," Clement writes, "read only to those who are being initiated into the Great Mysteries." This intriguing letter, written long before Eusebius, speaks of a secret mystical tradition without national borders. That Jesus taught and participated in this tradition proves that he was no slave to regional agendas and that he moved beyond symbols of relative good and evil.[22]

INITIATION IN EARLY CHRISTIANITY

Like the ancient Mystery religions, the early Christian Gnostics taught a three-step initiatory process. Their communities were organized into three ranks: the hylics or catechumens, the psychics, and the pneumatics.[23] Initiation into a Gnostic community began with baptism, which represented the acolytes' rebirth into a new life and a cleansing away of the old one. In the second stage of initiation, which took place at the Paschal Vigil (an all-night baptismal service preceding Easter Day), certain elements of Mark's secret tradition were shared with the aspirant. In the third stage, reserved for the pneumatics or true Gnostics, an unwritten tradition was passed on. This transmission of an unwritten secret reserved for private instruction was a classic element of the Mystery Schools.[24]

Elaine Pagels writes about the Gnostics' initiatory process in her classic book *The Gnostic Gospels*:

> Gnostic teachers usually reserved their secret instruction, sharing it only verbally, to ensure each candidate's suitability to receive it. Such instruction required each teacher to take responsibility for highly select, individualized attention to each candidate. And it required the candidate, in turn, to devote energy and time, often years, to the process.[25]

Pagel speculates that the effort required by Gnostic Christianity of its initiates may, in fact, explain the slow spread of the sect, leaving the Roman Church, which did not require this slow initiatory process, free to take control of the masses. "For two to three hundred years this triune initiatory structure prevailed in Gnostic circles, until it was denounced as heresy and eradicated," Pagels observes. "As long as it survived," she argues, "there is evidence that the Church possessed a high wisdom tradition no less rarefied than that of any Roman Mithraic cell or Egyptian Serapion."[26]

In the apocryphal text *The Apocalypse of Peter*, the apostle whose name was co-opted by the Roman Church to sanction its formation, Peter calls the bishops and deacons of the early Church "waterless canals," decrying their pretension to teach the doctrine of Jesus without really knowing the substance behind it. Peter declares that the truly enlightened "neither attempt to dominate others nor do they subject themselves to the bishops and deacons." Instead, he claims, they participate in the "wisdom of the brotherhood that really exists," in spiritual fellowship "with those united in communion."[27] Clearly Peter refers to the teachings of the Great White Brotherhood here.

One of the most brilliant fathers of the early Christian Church, Origen, writes again of secret Mysteries some 200 years after Jesus' death, calling the ignorant faith of the masses "somnatic Christianity." He separates this common faith from a higher wisdom founded on a genuine experience of the inner planes and a knowledge of cosmic law. Likewise, the Gospel of Philip tells us that many people " . . . go down into the water [meaning baptism] and come up without having received anything."[28] And Paul described how he was "caught up in the third heaven," where he was told of certain "hidden mysteries" he could only share with Christians that he considered to be "more mature" (I Corinthians 2:6).

All this makes it clear that there was once a legacy of Mystery teachings within the early Christian movement and that these Mysteries were more than likely taught by Jesus. It is also clear that this tradition has been lost to us for nearly 1600 years. So, although many of us proudly proclaim today that we are Christians, we know little of the ancient wisdom that lies at the core of our faith.

CHAPTER 2

The Language
of the Mysteries

Nature speaks in symbols and in signs.[1]

—John Greenleaf Whittier

The Mystery Schools taught that God, or the divine Spirit that animates the universe, can be most purely observed in nature. Thus many of their greatest initiates became scientists, poets, and artists who excelled in biology, astronomy, mathematics, music, painting, and art. And, just as today some scientists are drawn to the realm of the mystical through awe of their own scientific discoveries, the great philosophers and scientists of the Mysteries believed that, in observing the principles of nature, they could begin to understand the cosmological "language of God." They encoded these discoveries in symbols based on the natural world. Thus the esoteric language of hermetics was born.

Hermetics can be called the language of the soul, for it leads us to the deepest mysteries of the cosmos, allowing us to enter the realm of the sacred. Hermetics is a language of symbol codes that directs us to a deeper truth about the universe and our relationship to it. Those trained in the Mysteries hold the keys to this symbolic code; those who do not see only the surface meaning. To penetrate the hidden legacy of Jesus and to understand his associations with the Mystery traditions, we must learn this hidden language, which holds the key to our ancient past—a key that opens the door to the heart of the Mysteries themselves.

Egyptologist and symbolist John Anthony West writes:

The symbol . . . is a scrupulously chosen pictorial device designed to evoke an idea or concept in its entirety. It is a means of bypassing the intellect and talking straight to the intelligence of the heart, the understanding. The heart synthesizes; the mind analyzes. A true symbolism is neither primitive nor subconscious. It is a deliberate means of evoking understanding, as opposed to conveying information.[2]

While many of us are familiar with the concept of using symbols to convey meaning, most of the symbols we use today are exoteric, or outwardly directed. They tell us to stop the car, find a restaurant, or quit smoking. Hermetics, on the other hand, is a language of esoteric, or inwardly directed, instructions that can be contemplated at multiple levels over time. They direct us to something deep within ourselves that our souls already know, but that our personalities have forgotten. Today, many of these symbols are found carved into our churches and synagogues, but few really understand what they mean.

The Mystery Schools of the Great White Brotherhood used the language of hermetics to convey their teachings, endowing their symbols with multiple levels of meaning. Today, some speculate that the meaning of these symbols may be intrinsic to human nature, or to Creation itself. Many hermetic symbols are woven into the Christian faith: the cross, the dove, the lion, the eagle, the trinity, the Sun, the Tree of Life. In fact, these symbols may be part of a great cosmic language used to transmit the secrets of the universe and to activate portals of human awakening.

THRICE-GREAT HERMES

The word "hermetics" comes from the name of the Greek god of wisdom, learning, and truth—Hermes. Hermes Trismegistus, or Thrice-Great Hermes, is the Egyptian god Thoth, the Lord of Divine Words, who bestowed on humanity almost the entire spectrum of knowledge—geometry, architecture, astronomy, astrology, herbs, healing, mathematics, and spiritual philosophy.[3] Egyptian archaeologists attribute to Thoth the establishment of the first common tongue.[4] In fact, Thoth and his wife, Seshat, are credited with creating the sacred hieroglyphics of ancient Egypt, as well as the twenty-six-letter alphabet used in English and all the Romance languages today.[5]

Clement of Alexandria writes, in the first century after Jesus, that, in his day, the Royal Library of Alexandria housed forty-two books written by Thoth

FIGURE 4. Thrice-Great Hermes, whose Egyptian name was Thoth, the god of wisdom and writing, and the father of the language of hermetics.

that contained all the wisdom of the ancient world on subjects as diverse as law, medicine, science, astronomy, astrology, geography, physics, writing, cosmology, and Magic.[6] And it was well acknowledged by the ancients that Thoth's vast wisdom inspired the writings of *The Hermetica* and the *Book of Poimandres* referred to in the early Christian gospels of the Gnostics.

Thoth was also one of the four great Kumaras, or Sons of God—Sanaka Kumara. Like Jesus, he was one of the greatest masters. And like Jesus, he was called the Logos, for he contained within himself the divine blueprint from which the universe is continually reborn. Thoth endowed humanity with a knowledge of the natural laws of the physical world and inspired the creation of the first great Mystery Schools, giving human beings a deeper knowledge of the spiritual worlds.[7] His teachings and principles of Hermetic law are the bedrock upon which the Mystery tradition was laid.

Did Jesus know about these symbols and teach them to his students? Yes. We know he was aware of the transmission of wisdom through these symbols, because in the Gospel of Philip, Jesus says, "Truth did not come into the world naked, but it came in types and images," adding, "One will not receive truth in any other way." Jesus even tells us that, "The exiled will return to unity and be fulfilled . . . through these symbols."[8] And in the apocryphal Acts of John, we read: "The Lord had performed everything as a symbol and a dispensation for the conversion and salvation of man."[9]

In fact, Jesus was well versed in the symbolic language of the Mysteries, and he carefully encoded his teachings into very specific hermetic symbols. The icon of the fish, the *ichthys*, for example, had far deeper meanings than the simple statement, "I will make you fishers of men." This one simple symbol went right to the heart of Jesus' message, since its shape represents the *Vesica Piscis*, or the union of male and female, and the All Seeing Eye of God long revered in Egypt.

FIGURE 5. The ichthys fish, or *Vesica Piscis* is an early symbol of Christianity, and similar to the *omphalos*, or great Cosmic Egg, was considered the "Seed syllable" that emanated out of the universe.

The Cross and the Honeybee

The cross and the honeybee are two more examples of symbols that have many levels of meaning across many spiritual traditions. The cross is thought by most Christians to signify Jesus' death at Golgotha. Yet this sacred symbol has a deeper and more ancient meaning as it represents the x-y axis of space and time, as well as the Tree of Life. Even the *Catholic Encyclopedia* tells us that "the cross . . . greatly antedates, in both East and the West, the introduction of Christianity. It goes back to a very remote period of human civilization."

In fact, veneration of the cross goes back thousands of years to Tammuz, a Babylonian version of the great sacrificial Sun god or king whose death regenerates the world. We know the cross also appears in the iconography of the great solar lords Mithra, Krishna, and Quetzalcoatl, savior gods who were said to have been crucified upon the Tree of Life.[10] The cross is also linked with the Egyptian god Osiris, the Druid god HU, and the Greek Dionysus or Roman Bacchus—all earlier versions of a resurrected savior god—as well as the divine Purusha, the Hindu savior archetype whose love for humanity regenerates the world.[11]

The cross was also a common symbol among Tibetans, who laid out heaven in the shape of a swastika or a cross. The swastika, misused by Hitler to represent an anti-life principle, originally related to the turning or cycles of the universe. It can be seen in Buddhist mandalas and Native American medicine wheels. At the time of Jesus, initiates of the Eleusinian Mysteries in Greece were given a cross suspended on a chain or a cord to wear around their necks upon completion of the initiation ritual.[12] And the Tau cross, a symbol that looks like a capital letter T that was used for centuries within Christianity, was inscribed on the foreheads of all initiates admitted into the Mysteries of Mithra.

The Egyptian Rot-n-no priests, who charted the movement of the stars, wore garments with crosses sewn on them. For them, the cross represented the fundamental axis of time and space. Crosses were also found on the hats of Zoroastrian Magi many centuries before Jesus was born, representing mastery over the material world.

The cross is also part of the Egyptian ankh, an ancient symbol of eternal life. The ankh, which brings together the flat-headed Tau cross and the feminine oval of the womb or great Cosmic Egg, represents balance between male and female energies, as well as the finite world that descends from the infinite World of First Causes, the seed from which all creation sprang. After 391 c.e., the Coptic Christian Church of Egypt adopted the ankh in lieu of the traditional Christian cross.[13] Later, Christianity appropriated the cross, retaining

FIGURE 6A. Tammuz cross headband. Tammuz was an agricultural god of Egypt and Mesopotamia, who brought the arts of animal husbandry to mankind. Later linked to the cycles of fertility and rebirth, the rites of Tammuz go back thousands of years before Jesus. Illustrated by Sylvia Laurens.

FIGURE 6B. The Rot-n-no Priests of Egypt carry the ancient symbol of the cross on their robes, demonstrating that it was used in religious symbology thousands of years before Christianity.

FIGURE 6C. The ankh, the Egyptian symbol for eternal life, is a fusion of the T-shaped Tau cross, representing time and space, and the *Vesica Piscis* or womb from which Creation sprang.

FIGURE 6D. The base of the Cavalry Cross also reflects the three steps of initiation known within the Mystery Schools, and the mastery of our physical, emotional, and mental natures, which leads to our victory over the "cross" of time and space.

some of its symbolic elements that pertained to the Mysteries. In the Calvary cross, for example, we see the three steps of initiation from the Mystery traditions at the base of the design.

While Jesus did not suggest that his followers use the cross as a symbol of either his life or death, he most certainly did reenact the cosmic drama of the savior god upon the cross, just as many savior gods had done before him. Thus it is natural that the cross, a hermetic emblem of the Tree of Life, came to be viewed as an affirmation of Jesus' victory over the wheel of life, death, and rebirth. The Gospel of Philip confirms this: "The Godhead will retire, not to the Holy of Holies . . . it will rest beneath the arms of the cross. . . ."[14] Furthermore, since the ancient Mystery Schools saw the cross as an icon of our victory over time and space, this powerful hermetic symbol can certainly be attached to Jesus, who transcended the mortal wheel of death with his resurrection.

The honeybee is another hermetic symbol with a long history and many-layered meanings. The beehive, for example, refers to the many-dimensional layers of creation, as well as to the practice of collecting golden nectar (another name for wisdom) and preserving it for future generations. Since honey and salt were the only two preservatives known to the ancient world, honey became a symbol of resurrection or reincarnation. Honey was also linked to the pharaohs of northern Egypt, whose symbols meant "He who belongs to the bee."[15] Bees were called "the tears of the Sun god, Ra." The dead were sometimes embalmed in honey and placed in fetal positions in large *pithoi*, or burial vases, to await rebirth.[16] In religious rites, honey was used as a symbol of immortality, representing birth, death, and resurrection, a theme consistent with all the great Mystery Schools.[17]

Bees are also linked to the Hindu gods Krishna and Indra, who were also incarnations of the solar power, or "Sons of God." Krishna is an incarnation of Vishnu, the ultimate preserver of the universe in the trinity of creation, destruction, and preservation. He is often symbolized as a blue bee sitting on a lotus. In the *Rig Veda*, Vishnu, Krishna, and Indra are known as the *madhavas*, or the "nectar born ones," meaning those whose essence is of the highest celestial realms.[18]

The shape of the honeycomb reflects the field of light that many traditions believe surrounds the human body. This field, called the *Merkaba*, is a six-pointed, six-sided shape that echoes the six-sided geometry of the honeycomb, as well as the six-petalled lily often inscribed at the top of Egyptian temples and depicted in the Flower of Life.[19] Egyptian Magi conveyed this esoteric teaching to Moses, who transformed the hexagonal honeycomb into the six-pointed hexagram known as the Star of David.

More than 300 golden bees were discovered in the tomb of a Merovingian king, whose lineage many believe can be traced back to Jesus.[20] The fact that Jesus' Merovingian descendants used the bees as a symbol of kingship tells us that Jesus and his line knew the true meaning of the bee and saw themselves as heirs of the pharaohs, the Egyptian keepers of wisdom (and the Mystery Schools) who had so honored the hermetic symbol.

The Mystery traditions tell us that bees were originally brought to Earth from the planet Venus—a hermetic myth connecting them with the goddess of love.[21] Bees are also linked to the goddesses Isis, Demeter, and Aphrodite—all

Figure 7. This image reveals how the honeycomb can be overlaid with the Flower of Life and the Star of David, each reflecting the six-sided Mer-ka-ba field of the human body used in advanced states of meditation.

expressions of the Divine Mother who represent the potency of nature. According to the Greek philosopher Porphyry, the priestesses in Aphrodite's temple at Eryx were also called *melissae*, a term which can be translated as "bees," or as "one who serves the goddess." The goddess herself was called Melissa.[22]

The emblem of the mother bee originally belonged to Isis, the Egyptian goddess of civilization. Isis was known as Demeter in Rome, the "pure Mother Bee" who governed the cycles of life. It was to Isis and her daughter Kore (also Kernel or Persephone) that the first level of the Eleusinian Mysteries was dedicated. Where Isis/Demeter represented the benevolent Mother God, Kore represented the daughter, a soul that had descended to Earth and fallen into darkness and forgetfulness. These Mysteries thus represented a return to the light and ascension into heaven. The bee was later adopted by the Catholic Church as a symbol for the Virgin Mary, who became a substitute for Isis, the Divine Mother.[23] Medieval hymns refer to her as "a nest of honey" and a "dripping honeycomb."[24]

In ancient Egypt, one of the names and emblems for the pharaoh was "Beekeeper."[25] The Roman Papacy later adopted the symbols of the bee and the beehive—symbols that had long been known by the Sarmoung Society of Persia, who sent at least one of the three Wise Men to attend Jesus' birth. Mithraism also used the beehive to represent the multilayered dimensions of reality, so, by adopting these symbols, the Catholic Church was acknowledging, through the language of hermetics, that it and its leaders were the heirs to an ancient wisdom that derived from both the Egyptian and Persian worlds.

Bees appear in many papal coats of arms—etched into shields with the keys to the kingdom, often with a beehive at the top as the crowning point. There are three bees on the crest of Pope Urban VIII, as well as a three-tiered crown derived from the Mithraic and Zoroastrian crowns known within the Mystery Schools. This emblem was adapted into the crown of the papacy that is still worn by popes at public ceremonies. The bee symbol was later disguised as the fleur-de-lis—the head and two wings of the flower representing the Trinity. Bees also grace a 17th-century fountain in Rome—the Fontana delle Api designed by the famous sculptor Bernini to honor the pope.[26]

While the symbols of the bee and the cross predate Jesus' life by thousands of years, they are completely relevant to his history and his message. Jesus was trained in the Egyptian and Mithraic Mysteries. Throughout his travels Jesus collected the wisdom of the ages and transmitted that wisdom to later generations. As Charles Francis Potter, author of *The Lost Years of Jesus Revealed*, says:

Jesus [is not] the uneducated faith-healer and miracle monger of Galilee alleged . . . to have spoken only colloquial Aramaic (the first Yiddish), to have written only on the ground with his finger, and to have been quite ignorant of the wonderful Greek paideia and Roman civilization of his time. Careful study of the Essene scrolls . . . confirmed by the Egyptian Gnostic codices from Nag Hammadi, reveals him to have been not only well-versed in the knowledge and culture of Rome, Persia, Athens, and Alexandria, a wide traveler, and a great teacher, but also an original independent thinker and a dedicated existential empiricist.[27]

FIGURE 8. This Freemasonry drawing of Isis with a beehive and a book shows the goddess as the original Beekeeper, the one who keeps the wisdom of the ages. Notice as well the hermetic symbols of the two columns, the cross, the trinity, and the vine, all of which are found in Egyptian mysticism and are reflected in Christian symbology. Illustrated by Sylvia Laurens.

FIGURE 9A. Crest of Pope Urban VIII. On his shield are three bees representing the trinity, and a beehive crown similar to the pineal gland that must be activated to open the Third Eye. The keys to the Kingdom of Heaven are crossed like the crook and the flail of Osiris in ancient Egypt.

FIGURE 9B. Papal beehive crown. This multi-layered hat reveals the three steps of Isis, and was intended to mark the Pope as the next Bee Keeper of the Mysteries. Illustrated by Sylvia Laurens.

THE LOGOS AND THE GODDESS OF NATURE

While the great mystic schools mimicked nature in much of their hermetic symbolism, they also sought to penetrate nature's mysteries at every possible level: scientifically, metaphorically, and hermetically. In the more advanced levels of training, Mystery School initiates were taught ways to communicate with the forces of nature and control them, much as Jesus did when he commanded the winds and waters to be still. As Timothy Wallace-Murphy and Marilyn Hopkins point out in their book *Custodians of the Truth*, "the incredibly sophisticated levels of gnosis attained through such initiations were never used by the initiates for personal gain . . . [I]t was for the benefit of the entire community."[28] Henry L. Drake concurs:

> With the growth of social consciousness, these secret societies became the custodians of the highest cultural concepts. Before [an initiate] could be entrusted with the divine powers of mind and will, he must accept knowledge as a responsibility to his Creator and his world, rather than an opportunity for the advancement of personal ambitions.[29]

The ancients realized that, if the mastery of natural forces like magnetism, electricity, and atomic structure fell into the wrong hands, the effects on the world could be devastating. We can observe some of those negative effects today in our misuse of the atomic bomb, our polluted atmosphere, and the harmful effects of nuclear radiation.

So the masters took great pains to protect these scientific secrets. They chose their students carefully and strove to ensure the purity, discretion, and moral responsibility of all candidates. Paul Brunton describes how the Egyptian masters guarded their knowledge "with the utmost secrecy and kept [these teachings] so exclusive that Egypt's name became synonymous in classical times with mystery. . . . Many knocked at the doors of the Mystery Temples in vain, [and] . . . every man who emerged through those doors belonged ever after to a secret society which moved and worked with higher purpose and profounder knowledge among the profane masses."[30] The Greek historian Diodorus Siculus (ca. 90–30 B.C.E.) claims that "those who have participated in the Mysteries become more spiritual, more just and better in every way,"[31] while Iamblichus observes that "to unite one's soul to the Universal Soul requires a perfectly pure mind."[32]

The sages understood that, when they approached their studies with the idea of helping nature and working with her, nature would "open wide . . . the portals of her secret chambers, lay bare before thy gaze the treasures hidden in the very depths of her pure virgin bosom." Thus did one become a "Magician," in the truest sense of the word. Iamblichus insists that the priests and priestesses of the great Mystery Schools did not gain their knowledge of the divine realms "by mere reason alone," but rather, by means of a priestly theurgy, which he defines as the practice of "working with the divine forces directly," as opposed to theology, which is merely "talking about" them.[33] This approach is quite different from the one science uses today. Yet, in the last hundred years, since the discovery of the subatomic quantum field, more and more scientists have rediscovered the underlying principles that were once taught in the Mysteries, and have begun to stand in awe of nature's handiwork.

Adepts of the Mysteries knew that, beneath the world of the senses, there is a higher intelligence. They called this the *Logos*, or the divine blueprint. Christians later translated this term as "the Word," an apt reference to the breath of God, or Holy Spirit, that creates the universe. Today, scientists call this intelligence the unified field. Physicist Michio Kaku calls it "a knowledge of the implicate and explicate orders," meaning an ability to see beyond the visible world of the senses to the underlying causes behind it. Throughout Earth's history, only a few individuals have attained a complete merger with the Logos, or the highest divine intelligence. Among them are Jesus, Thoth, Osiris, Horus, and Isis.

THE DEATH AND RESURRECTION OF THE MYSTERIES

While the Mysteries were widely practiced throughout the ancient world, once the monotheistic religions of Christianity, Islam, and Judaism took hold—with their penchant for dualism, separation, and judgment—knowledge of these elevated realities and access to the principles behind them was suppressed, and those who transmitted that wisdom were exterminated or forced to go underground. Thirty-third degree Mason, C. W. Leadbeater, describes the process:

> Even before the destruction of the Roman Empire the withdrawal of the Mysteries as public institutions had taken place; and this fact was mainly due to the excessive intolerance displayed by the Christians. Their amazing theory that none but they could be "saved from the hell" which they themselves had invented naturally led them to try all means, even the most cruel and diabolical persecutions, to force people of other faiths to accept their particular shibboleth. As the Mysteries were the heart and stronghold of a more rational belief, they of course, opposed them bitterly, quite forgetful that in the earlier days of their religion they had claimed to possess as much of the inner knowledge as any other system.[34]

Over the past 2000 years, established religions have so distorted the knowledge of the Mysteries that many good-hearted people who have earnestly sought the truth have come to believe erroneously that the ancient Mysteries are not compatible with Jesus' teachings. In order to consolidate its political, financial, and religious power, the Roman Church deliberately maligned all other paths to salvation. It plundered the ancient temples, adopted their rituals, stole, destroyed, or conscripted all vestiges of truth, and murdered those who dared object.[35] And it did these things in the name of the Prince of Peace. Even though Jesus' journey was deeply woven into these sacred paths—even though he reflected the wisdom of the ancient Mysteries and was a master initiate of them all—it deliberately erased Jesus' connections to the ancient Mystery traditions so that others could not follow in his footsteps.

The Roman Church knew the power behind the liberation of the human spirit. It knew that spiritual awakening could radically diminish its grip on secular power structures. So it used a variety of tactics to prevent that awakening and to ensure that the ancient Mysteries could not resurface. It cast aspersions on the truly self-aware to generate fear and scandal, and redirected the public's energies to suit its own agenda. Since their primary purpose was to control all of humanity's financial and energetic resources, it had to destroy those with the ability to "walk between the worlds."

Yet through all these centuries of upheaval, the masters of the Great White Brotherhood have continued to keep alight the flame of knowledge. Sometimes this wisdom was passed on orally because it was not safe to commit it to paper. Sometimes the wisdom appeared to die with the adepts who sought to transmit it. But still it has flourished, inspiring life-expanding movements like the Renaissance, Romanticism, Theosophy, and the awakening age of science.

Today, with the Age of Aquarius at hand, the Mysteries are flourishing once again, rediscovered by modern-day initiates who find that the wisdom of the ancient Schools is reflected in the life and teachings of Jesus—and in their own Christed spirits.

PART II

Birthday of a King

CHAPTER 3

Herod and the Magical Star

And God said let there be lights in the firmament of the heavens to
divide the day from the night; and let them be for signs, and for seasons,
and days, and years.

—Genesis 1:14

To understand the story of Jesus' life, we must start with his birth and with the
pivotal events that mark him as a master of the great Mystery religions. That
means exploring some of the non-canonical accounts of the Nativity, including
the sequence of events that propelled the Holy Family into Egypt, the astrological forces in play at the time of his birth, the experiences of the shepherds who
were tending their flocks the night Jesus was born, reports of the unusual star
that appeared over Bethlehem, and Herod's own description of the arrival of
the Magi at his court—an account that gives us a rare glimpse into the political
climate of Judea at the time. These extraordinary records—all of which, ironi-
cally, come straight out of the Vatican archives—provide a much fuller picture
of the tumultuous events surrounding the Nativity than is traditionally known
from the New Testament.

HEROD'S EYEWITNESS ACCOUNT

Herod the Great is the traditional antagonist of our story. He is portrayed as the
ruthless leader who created the social and political climate into which Jesus was
born and as the catalyst for the Holy Family's flight into Egypt.

The Jewish historian Flavius Josephus tells us that Herod Antipater, better known as Herod the Great, ruled Judea from 37 to 4 B.C.E., a period of roughly thirty-three years.[1] Herod was a charismatic, persuasive, and powerful leader who was feared and loathed by his contemporaries. He came from the southern region of Idumaea, so he was not from the Jewish line of Jacob, which had traditionally ruled Judea.[2] Biblical scholar Martin A. Larson tells us that Herod was, in fact, only half Jewish.[3] A competent soldier, resourceful politician, and capable administrator, he was also a bully. Josephus describes him thus:

> [W]hen one looks upon the punishments he inflicted, and the injuries he did not only to his subjects, but to his nearest relations, and takes notice of his severe and unrelenting disposition there, he [the reader] will be forced to allow that he was brutish, and a stranger to all humanity . . . a man ambitious of honor, and quite overcome by that passion. . . .[4]

Author Adrian Gilbert adds: "A terrifying mixture of Macbeth and Othello, he, unlike the other monarchs in the region, had no hereditary legitimacy."[5] To gain power, Herod persuaded the Roman general Mark Antony to place an army under his command. He used it to besiege Jerusalem for five long months, capturing the city in 37 B.C.E.

Once in power, Herod beheaded Antigonus, the last remaining Jewish king, and assassinated forty-five members of the Sanhedrin, the Jewish religious body that governed the country, thereby eliminating all opposition to his reign. To gain legitimacy, he married Mariamme, a princess of the royal blood, then had her brother, the high priest Aristobulus, drowned in a swimming pool "accident" in Jericho.[6] In the course of his reign, he methodically executed all remaining members of the royal dynasty of Israel, later even murdering Mariamme and his two grown sons, Alexander and Aristobulus.[7] Today, Herod's reign is remembered for three important events: the birth of Jesus, the rebuilding of the temple in Jerusalem, and the famous Massacre of the Innocents recorded in the Gospel of Matthew.

It is this massacre, perhaps more than any other event, that reveals Herod's concern to establish his own legitimacy. His hostility and suspicion extended to every member of the Jewish royal bloodline, including the small infant whom Jewish prophecy promised as the long-awaited Messiah—the "anointed one" who would take back the throne of Judea. Increasingly fearful for his crown, Herod ordered all male children born within a two-year span in Bethlehem to be executed in an attempt to destroy any male child who might usurp his power and become the new king of the Jews.

Various versions of this story appear in Christian literature. Today it is unclear exactly how many children were actually murdered. Byzantine records say that 14,000 innocents were slaughtered. An early Syrian list states that 64,000 children died. Other sources tell us that only six to twenty children died—a figure that may be closer to the truth, since Bethlehem was not a large town.[8] Since the edict applied to all male children born within a two-year period, however, the actual count may lie somewhere in the middle. Despite the desperation that Herod's act reveals, this massacre went unrecorded in the histories of Josephus, so we do not know the year of the killings and thus cannot use them to establish more closely the year of Jesus' birth.

Some historians believe that Josephus may have omitted this event because it actually took place some seventy years earlier. Yet Josephus' histories claim to go back as far as Moses. And there may be another reason Josephus failed to report the event, since he himself was ensconced in luxury in the palace of the Roman emperor Vespasian when he wrote. Surely he would have been aware that any of his writings that reflected badly on the Roman Empire and its leadership—like the massacre of innocent children—would not have pleased his patron. Other historians wonder whether the massacre was simply a dramatic narrative device inserted into the biblical book of Matthew to "spice up" the story of Jesus' birth. Yet a letter discovered in the Vatican archives—a letter written by Herod himself—makes clear reference to these events, so we know that they actually took place.[9]

The letter is one of many documents discovered in the Vatican Library by W. D. Mahan, an American minister who, in 1856, became aware through a series of divinely inspired events that many intriguing documents were hidden in the Vatican Library. Reverend Mahan spent the next ten years researching these records for information about the life of Christ, traveling to Rome, Constantinople, and Damascus. He finally chose eleven crucial documents from the nearly 560,000 manuscripts held in the Vatican archives and had them translated by scholars from their original Greek or Aramaic. In 1887, he published his discoveries in a slender book called *The Archko Volume*. Today, these documents are known as *The Acts of Pilate*. It is most revealing that, shortly after Mahan's book appeared, Pope Leo XIII closed the Vatican archives to scholars, thus prohibiting any other academics from following up on Mahan's research.[10]

A letter headed "Herod Antipater's Defense to the Roman Senate" was among Mahan's discoveries. The letter gives us a rare insight into Herod's personality, the politics of the day, and his relationship with the Hillel Court and the Jewish Sanhedrin. In it, Herod writes to the Roman Senate of three Magi who arrived at his court on the night that the mysterious star appeared over Bethlehem. Herod shares the prophecy of the birth of the long-awaited Messiah and uses it to justify his edict ordering the children's death. The letter contains many details of the events, including descriptions of the Magi, one of whom came from Egypt. Despite the lavishness of Herod's own court, he found that the "wise men" dressed in ways that he called "fantastic." The following excerpt picks up at the point where the Magi have just entered his palace:

> As to this great excitement in Bethlehem, three strange, fantastic looking men called on my guards at the gate. . . . One of them said he was from Egypt. I asked, what was their business? He said they were in search of the babe that was born to rule the Jews. I told them that I ruled the Jews under Augustus Caesar. But he said this babe would rule when I was gone. . . . I asked him how he knew of this babe. He said they had all had a dream the same night about it. I told them that the devil played with their brains when they were asleep.[11]

Herod goes on to describe his interactions with the Hillel Court, whom he calls "the most learned body of talent in Jerusalem," and speaks of an unease, "a sort of deriding and mocking spirit among the lower classes in regard to the Roman authority." He dismisses the phenomenon of the star as "nothing more than a meteor traveling through the air, or the rising vapor from the foot of the mountains out of the low marsh ground."

Herod warns however, that although this may have been "nothing but a phenomenon of nature, and the whole thing a delusion," it did not better the condition he was in. "A man will contend for a false faith stronger than he will a true one," he observes. "The truth defends itself, but a falsehood must be defended by its adherents: first to prove it to themselves and secondly, that they may appear right in the estimation of their friends." He then enumerates the political conditions that were undermining his power, predicting "an insurrection brewing fast and nothing but a most bloody war as the consequence." He uses these circumstances to justify his decision to "pluck the undeveloped flower in its bud lest it should grow and strengthen," revealing his determination to maintain a position that could, at any moment, be taken away from him by the Roman Senate on one hand, and by the rambunctious Jews on the other. He finishes thus: "These are the grounds of my action in this matter. I am satisfied I did the best that could be done under the circumstances."[12]

ANGELS AND SONS OF THE LIGHT

We learn of the Star of Bethlehem from the three synoptic gospels in the New Testament that report the events surrounding the birth of Jesus. In Luke, the Magi tell Herod, "We have seen His star in the East and have come to worship Him. . . . Then Herod, when he had secretly called the wise men, determined from them what time the star appeared. . . . When they heard the king, they departed; and behold the star which they had seen in the East went before them, until it came and stood over where the young Child was. . . ." (Luke 2:8–20).

Luke's account seems to indicate that a bright light appeared in the heavens, moved as if directing the Wise Men where to go, and finally parked itself over the manger, as if to say, "X marks the spot." This mystery has puzzled astronomers for centuries. Scientific-minded researchers have long questioned what kind of star could behave in this way, since the movement of this light does not match the behavior of a meteor, a normal star, an asteroid, or even a supernova. Colin Humphreys warns of the difficulties associated with treating the star as a real astronomical object: "[A] star that rose in the East, appeared over Jerusalem, turned south to Bethlehem, and then came to rest over a house would have constituted a celestial phenomenon unparalleled in astronomical history: yet it received no notice in the records of the times."[13]

In truth, the appearance of the star over Bethlehem has been one of the most mysterious events of the Bible for over 2000 years, especially since any star the Magi had been following would have been visible in the night sky over Judea for at least several weeks for everyone to see. The distance from Persia to Bethlehem is around 500 miles. The distance is approximately the same from Egypt. Traveling at the rate of ten miles per day, the Magi would have needed at least two months to reach Jerusalem on camel. This means that the star would have been in the sky for at least two months. This indicates that, based on the accounts in the Bible, this star was no ordinary celestial object.

Moreover, on the night of Jesus' birth, the brilliant star was also seen by people all over Bethlehem. A wonderful, little-known version of this story that predates the one told in Matthew is found in *The Acts of Pilate*.[14] This very detailed account was given immediately after the actual event in response to an inquiry made by none other than the Sanhedrin High Council, which sent one of its own "investigators" into the field to determine the truth behind the purported celestial event. In it, Jonathan, son of Heziel, reports the following:

> I met with two men, who said they were shepherds, and were watching their flocks near Bethlehem. They told me that while attending to their

sheep, the night being cold and chilly, some of them had made fires to warm themselves, and some of them had laid down and were asleep; that they were awakened by those who were keeping watch with the question, "What does all this mean? Behold, how light it is!"; that when they were aroused it was light as day. But they knew it was not daylight, for it was only the third watch. All at once the air seemed to be filled with human voices, saying, "Glory! Glory! Glory to the most High God!" And "Happy art thou, Bethlehem, for God hath fulfilled his promise to the fathers; for in thy chambers is born the King that shall rule in righteousness.

I asked him how they felt, if they were not afraid; they said at first they were; but after awhile it seemed to calm their spirits, and so fill their hearts with love and tranquility that they felt more like giving thanks than anything else. They said it was around the whole city, and some of the people were almost scared to death. Some said the world was on fire; some said the gods were coming down to destroy them; others said a star had fallen; until Melker the priest [from Bethlehem] came out shouting and clapping his hands, seeming to be frantic with joy.[15]

Jonathan then reports that he went to see Melker, a priest from Bethlehem, "who related to me much the same as the shepherds had reported. He told me that he had lived in India, and that his father had been a priest at Antioch; that he had studied the sacred scrolls of God, all his life, and that he knew that the time had come, from signs given." The next day, three strangers from a great distance called on him

> ... and they went in search of this young child; and they found him and his mother in the mouth of the cave, where there was a shed projecting out for the sheltering of sheep; that his mother was married to a man named Joseph, and she related to them the history of her child, saying that an angel had visited her, and told her that she should have a son, and she should call him Jesus, for he would redeem his people from their sins; and he should call her blessed forever more.[16]

When I first read this account, I was astonished! This is clearly a far more complete version than that related in the New Testament. Furthermore, Jonathan's reference to a chilly evening seems to indicate that the event took place in the spring, summer, or fall, when, in those desert latitudes, shepherds were known to watch their flocks at night.[17] Jonathan also describes a phenomenon that lit up the skies in such a way that even people in the village came out of their homes amazed and frightened—not unlike reports of modern-day UFO encounters. While this analogy may seem a bit outrageous, it is clear from Jonathan's account that some sort of luminaries, or angels, or extraterrestrials, or higher-dimensional beings who knew of Jesus' impending birth were involved and may have heralded his coming.

Certainly, in the ancient world, the appearance of celestial emissaries was not unknown. Roman historian Pliny the Elder (23–79 c.e.) tells us that there had long been a popular belief that the birth of an important king, or "son of God," was signaled by the appearance of a new star in the heavens. Rabbinical literature reported similar celestial events associated with the births of Moses and Abraham. Other historians claim that celestial heralds were sighted at the birth of Alexander the Great, and a few months before the birth of Octavian Augustus Caesar.[18] Sometimes these celestial chariots or "stars" were associated with the descent of divine or semi-divine beings, much as today we might report a remarkable UFO sighting.

Virtually every culture has its "myths" of gods and goddesses visiting our planet, inspiring religions and the arts of higher civilization. And while monotheistic religions have conditioned us to believe that Jehovah is "the One, the Only Universal God Himself," the first commandment makes it clear that, 1400 years earlier, Jehovah was concerned about competition.

The Book of Genesis speaks clearly about the "sons of God" who came down from the sky to mate with the daughters of men (Genesis 6:1–4). Historically, the semi-divine children of these "gods" were thought to have been sent to Earth as savior-kings, and their births were heralded by celestial phenomena. In Celtic mythology, comets were an aspect of Lugh, the god of light, and it was believed that they brought with them "sons of the living light" to incarnate in human form.[19] As "sons of the Sun," many half-divine ancient heroes like Gilgamesh, Hercules, Achilles, and Perseus were also said to have been born under celestial omens.

While merging the concept of angels, higher-dimensional celestials, and gods may be a bit of a stretch for some readers, let us just take a moment to consider the possibility. While most of what we hear about extraterrestrials is focused on abductions by strange gray aliens, thousands of people around the world report uplifting contact with beings that, 1000 years ago, might have been called angels. These celestial beings are usually described as having luminous skin and radiant eyes, and sometimes the power to fly. Luke tells us that "an angel of the Lord stood before [the shepherds], and the glory of the Lord shone around them." After Jesus' birth, Joseph had "dreams" of angels counseling him to flee to Egypt for safety. After the Crucifixion, two radiant men, or angels, appeared beside Jesus' tomb, telling Mary Magdalene that he had risen. So clearly, whoever or whatever was behind Jesus' ministry was from beyond this world in both a physical and a spiritual sense. If, indeed, Jesus was known to the spiritual hierarchies, then it stands to reason that these luminous beings had knowledge of his purpose and had been sent to announce his arrival and to reassure his followers after his death. The real question is where do these beings come from?

As most serious investigators have come to realize, the study of UFOs is not simply a study of metallurgical samples and space engines. It is a manifestation of a deep multi-dimensional aspect of our experience. Conceiving of a world that includes these phenomena requires that we broaden our modes of thought to include a multi-dimensional universe. In fact, physicists like Michio Kaku tell us that there may be as many as ten different dimensional realities.[20] These realities may include beings like angels, ghosts, spiritual guides, and even life forms from other planets that, on occasion, appear to give us a hand. These beings exist at higher frequencies than we do, and yet they are able to interact with us. Whether we call them angels, masters, or extraterrestrial beings, their purpose is to further world illumination and world peace.

THE ESSENES AND THE STAR

In her remarkable book *Jesus and the Essenes*, Dolores Cannon shares the transcripts of hypnosis clients who have past-life memories as Essenes. Much of the information from the transcripts has been corroborated by biblical researchers, archaeologists, and other hypnotherapists working independently. Cannon's work reveals some very interesting information given by people who knew Jesus personally in their past lives. Whether you believe in past lives or not, the information in Cannon's books gives us a window into what may have happened at the time of Jesus' birth.

One of Cannon's past-life sessions was with an Essene named Suddi who was a legal scholar at the time of Jesus. Suddi lived in Qumran some fifty miles from the city of David, yet he witnessed the appearance of the star over Bethlehem from the hills of his monastery. In his account, Suddi describes four separate stars that came together over the fields to create the phenomenon known as the Star of Bethlehem. Each of these stars led one of four Magi, who came from four different countries to meet in Bethlehem. Three of them—Gasper, Balthazar, and Melchior—are the ones we know from Christian lore. The fourth, we are told by Suddi, never arrived. Even though Suddi's account is a bit fragmented, it conveys the sense of wonder and magnificence he felt witnessing this event:

> It is the beginning of everything . . . to be able to see this for myself. . . .
> It is all that I could ask . . . to know that the prophecy is being
> fulfilled. . . . It is said that from four corners that [four] starts will rise
> together and when they meet, it will be the time of His birth. . . . It is like
> the heavens themselves have opened up and all the light is just shining
> down upon us. . . . It is like the sun of day! It is so bright![21]

Before they joined, these four stars created a cross in the sky, a powerful initiatic symbol known throughout the ancient world that represented the great Tree of Life in the ancient Mystery traditions. These four royal stars were well known in Jesus' time by their actual names: Aldebaran, Regulus, Antares, and Fomalhaut. Each was located in one of the four fixed signs of the zodiac: Taurus (the bull), Leo (the lion), Scorpio (the eagle), and Aquarius (the man).[22] They have long been related to biblical lore, their symbols painted in countless churches over the last 2000 years. Long before Jesus was born, they were named in the Old Testament and connected with the chariots of fire that came down from the sky (Ezekiel 11–13).

While it is not logical to believe that these four stars actually moved out of their orbits to merge in the sky, obviously something spectacular did happen. The event would have had enormous spiritual importance in the ancient world—symbolizing, perhaps, that angels from the four corners of the universe bowed down to this new king.

Suddi's thought-provoking account is enough to make us wonder what may actually have happened in the skies over Bethlehem. "There are many who try to explain it in many different manners," Suddi reports.

> They tried to say that it was a warning of the gods that Rome was about
> to fall. That it was a comet. It is said that there were points of light where
> the heavens opened up and shone through. There have been many explanations for it. But it was God showing that this was His son, and giving
> us a way to know. There are many people who say that these things are
> impossible, and all things are impossible without faith. But when one
> believes, all things are possible.[23]

CHAPTER 4

Signs in the Heavens

Oh King, you are this great star, the companion of Orion, who transverses the sky with Orion, who navigates the Duat with Osiris.[1]

—Ancient Egyptian Pyramid Texts

While many people know that December 25 may not be the real date of Jesus' birth, most do not realize that scholars do not even know the exact year he was born. Some adamantly claim it to be 3 or 4 B.C.E., but the latest possible date is actually 4 B.C.E., since Herod the Great died in April of that year. Others argue that Jesus was born as far back as 12 or 13 B.C.E. The consensus lies somewhere in between—around 6 to 8 B.C.E. For the purposes of our timeline, we will use the conservative 6 to 8 B.C.E. date range.

Even the Bible gives conflicting dates for Jesus' birth. The Gospel of Luke, for example, tells us that he was born when Quirinius was governor of Syria: "And it came to pass in those days that a decree went out from Caesar Augustus that all the world should be registered. This census first took place while Quirinius was governing Syria" (Luke 2:1–2). Yet history records that Quirinius was not appointed governor of Syria until 6 C.E., ten years after Herod died. On the other hand, we know from the Roman historian Tertullian that the first Roman census in Judea took place between 5 and 8 B.C.E.[2] To more accurately determine the date of Jesus' birth, we turn to the celestial alignments of the heavens, looking for events that may have created the phenomenon of the star.

SUPERNOVAS AND COMETS

The Jews referred to astronomy as *Mazzaroth*, from the two Hebrew words *mazzara*, meaning "to consecrate", and *nasal* or *naw-zal*, meaning "to distill" or "to flow out." Applied to the heavens, *Mazzaroth* refers to the river of stars that flows out from the center of the galaxy, emphasizing the twelve consecrated astrological signs that encircle our solar system. Because this imagery reminded the ancients of the flowing rivers of bounty, they named it the Milky Way, or Mother's Milk.

The appearance of celestial signs has long been associated with the incarnation of avatars, masters, and kings. The great Buddha is said to have been born upon the arrival of a comet, as were Krishna in India and Confucius in China.[3] The Persian savior Mithra and the Greek god Apollo (the Egyptian Horus) are also said to have been born beneath such a "star." Alexander the Great, who was declared semi-divine by an oracle in Egypt shortly before he was crowned pharaoh in Thebes, claimed this honor as well.[4]

Over the centuries, many great minds have attempted to solve the riddle of the star over Bethlehem. Astronomers argue that this brilliant light may have been a comet, a nova, or some type of extraordinary conjunction between planets. Some have even speculated that it was a supernova that appeared for a few months in the sky and then dissipated. This hypothesis, which was first made by Johannes Kepler in 1614, has received considerable support from various Biblical scholars in recent decades.[5] Chinese astronomers recorded a nova in the constellation of Capricorn that was visible for over seventy days between March and April of 5 B.C.E. While this timeframe is certainly close enough to the Nativity to be considered, we can't say whether this nova and the Star of Bethlehem were one and the same. Astronomers have calculated that this supernova would only have been visible some forty degrees off the horizon, which means that it could never have behaved as eyewitnesses reported; it could not have moved in the sky or hovered over the manger, and it certainly could not have come together from four stars into one. In fact, it would have appeared at a very low angle and remained stationary in relation to the celestial background.[6]

Astronomer F. J. Tipler suggests that the star may have been a Type Ia supernova or a Type Ic hypernova located in the Andromeda Galaxy.[7] This event occurred on March 22 of 8 B.C.E., the morning after the spring equinox, during a conjunction of the planet Mars with the Sun. Yet this supernova would have been only faintly visible in the sky and only for a period of about two weeks. This is hardly long enough for the Magi to have traveled across several countries to reach Jerusalem. Furthermore, the faint appearance of this nova would not have constituted the kind of profound celestial event reported by the people of Bethlehem.

Others believe the Bethlehem star was a comet, a theory first proposed by Origen, a third-century church father.[8] Many great painters, including the Italian artists Giotto di Bondone, Francesco d'Antonio, Antonio Busca, Gentile da Fabriario, Juan de Flandes, and Jean de Saint-Igny, were inspired by this possibility.[9] We know that Halley's Comet did pass over Jerusalem in 12 B.C.E., making it a possible contender, yet this would place Jesus' birth much earlier than biblical scholars believe.[10] Chinese astronomers have recorded only two other comets around the same time: one in 5 B.C.E. and one in 4 B.C.E. Astronomers tell us that the comet of 5 B.C.E. had an observable tail, while the comet of 4 B.C.E. did not. Religious investigator Colin Humphreys feels the former could have been the Bethlehem star:

> Evidence from the Bible and astronomy suggests that the Star of Bethlehem was a comet which was visible in 5 B.C.E., and described in ancient Chinese records. A comet uniquely fits the description in Matthew of a star which newly appeared . . . traveled slowly through the sky against the star background and which "stood over" Bethlehem. The evidence points to Jesus being born in the period of March 9th to May 4th, 5 B.C.E., probably around Passover time.[11]

There are some genuine logistical problems with this theory, however. While the Chinese believed that comets are "broom stars" that sweep away the old and bring in the new, the astronomers of Persia and Rome believed exactly the opposite. They saw comets as harbingers of doom and disaster, and linked them to legends of the Flood. Therefore, it is highly unlikely that a comet would have inspired the Magi of Sumeria, Syria, or Egypt to journey to Bethlehem. Moreover, 5 B.C.E. is only one year before Herod's death. Even if Herod had decreed the Massacre of the Innocents shortly before his death, and then hurriedly written his letter of explanation to the Roman Senate virtually on his deathbed, he would certainly have remembered the Magi's recent visit. In other words, a decree that looked back two entire years would have been (pardon the pun) overkill. No, even if the Star of Bethlehem were actually a comet, 5 B.C.E. seems a little late for Jesus' birth.

The Divine Conjunctions

Another possible explanation for the star is a divine conjunction of celestial bodies. A conjunction is the meeting of two planets in the sky at roughly the same degree—a meeting that strengthens the power of them both. The resulting brilliance would have been visible for only a few days and would then have vanished as the planets separated. While these events might have seemed extraordinary to the common people, conjunctions were familiar to astronomers of the time, so they could easily have been predicted by the Magi. During the decade when Jesus was born, only two astronomical conjunctions occurred that could have given the appearance of a single, exceptionally bright star: a conjunction of Venus and Mercury, and a conjunction of Jupiter and Saturn. Both had deep significance within the ancient Mystery traditions.

The conjunction of the bright planets Venus and Mercury, which occurred just before the Sun appeared on the horizon, was seen as a harbinger of blessings. It was referred to by the Jews as the *Shekinah*. Venus, known as the Morning Star and the Evening Star, is associated with the goddess of love, the Egyptian Isis, Queen of Heaven. Mercury is sacred to Thoth or Hermes, the god of wisdom. Thus, the hermetic significance of this conjunction unites the male and female energies in a perfect harmony that would foretell the coming of an illumined messenger with the radiance of the Sun behind him—in this case, Jesus. Since the event took place just before dawn, it would have occurred in the section of the eastern sky that astrologers call the first house, implying that the god of light had arrived on Earth to proclaim a message of unconditional love and wisdom.

Robert Lomas and Christopher Knight, authors of *The Book of Hiram*, were the first to rediscover the significance of the *Shekinah* in Jewish history. While investigating archaeological sites among the neolithic Grooved Ware people of the British Isles, they stumbled upon references to this alignment in many of the ancient temple sites, particularly those that held the Goddess in high esteem. Their investigations led them to Hebrew writings that confirmed that this rare celestial event was awaited, not only by the Jews of Judea, but by Druid priests in Britain, astronomers in Egypt, and—more than likely—Magi in Persia.

According to Lomas and Knight, this astronomical event also coincides with pivotal dates in Jewish history, marking windows of great change for the Hebrew people like the biblical Exodus and the building of King Solomon's temple. In the timeframe of Jesus' birth, the Shekinah rose three times, each time just before dawn: December 25, 8 B.C.E., April 18, 8 B.C.E., and

FIGURE 10. The merger of two bright planets in the sky is called a conjunction, and could have been seen for a period of a few weeks as the bright Star of Bethlehem. Illustrated by Sylvia Laurens.

November 11, 7 B.C.E. We'll consider the significance of each of these dates and their esoteric associations in the next chapter.

The second possibility for the Star of Bethlehem is the conjunction of Jupiter and Saturn, the two largest, most brilliant planets in our solar system. This conjunction was rediscovered by Johannes Kepler in the early 1600s, but it had been known to the ancients for many centuries. These two giant planets rendezvous like clockwork every twenty years, but a sequence of three conjunctions in a row between these two planets occurs only once every 139 years. And triple conjunctions in the sign of Pisces happen only once every 900 years![12] It is significant that a series of such conjunctions took place in Pisces between 7 and 8 B.C.E., just as our planet was entering the 2160-year Age of Pisces, whose symbol is the fish—the very symbol that Jesus chose for key aspects of his teachings.

FIGURE 11. Rediscovered by Johannes Kepler in the 16th century, the sacred conjunction of Jupiter and Saturn is repeated in the sky every twenty years, and was well known to Persian, Indian, and Egyptian sages.

The conjunction of Saturn and Jupiter represents the union of the worlds of spirit and matter, and it has long been called the Renewal of Time.[13] Saturn represents secular kingship and the structure of time itself—its laws, its rules, and its expressions in form. Saturn is the ancient of ancients, the king of the physical world. Jupiter's significance is altogether different. Jupiter represents the king of the celestial realms, ruling travel, truth, learning, and teaching within the domain of the higher mind. Jupiter is the planet of spiritual kingship, the consummate spiritual initiate and teacher. This archetype fits well with Jesus, who spent much of his life traveling the world to perfect his mastery. In hermetic terms, this auspicious conjunction represents the "king of the world of form" merging with the "spiritual king" to herald the new Age of Pisces. This merger would have easily lasted several months.

A Saturn-Jupiter conjunction began in late May of 7 B.C.E. and was exact on July 29 of that year. This last date was a most significant day in Persian, Chaldean, and Egyptian culture, since it heralded the helical rising of Sirius, a star long associated with Isis, the Divine Mother, in the esoteric Mysteries. It was the wisdom of Isis and the strength of her son, Horus, that delivered Egypt from the tyranny of the oppressor god Set. Isis is the redeeming presence of love that restores all things; Horus is the returning Lord of Light who saves the world from darkness. Thus, the star Sirius represented not only Isis, the Divine Mother, but also Horus, the returning king who was born of the Virgin Mother. The Egyptians believed that all their pharaohs were Horus-kings, who when they died, became one with Osiris, the Egyptian version of Christ.[14]

RISING STARS

Two significant stars and three constellations rose in the night sky over Bethlehem around the time of Jesus' birth: the stars Sirius and Regulus and the constellations Orion, Leo, and Canis Major. Sirius, long called *Spdt* by the Egyptians (Sothis by the Greeks), lies in the constellation of Canis Major, the great dog, and had always been associated with Isis, the Vigin Mother. Osiris, her husband, was known as the Redeemer; he is represented by the constellation Orion, whose light guides the way into heaven; and finally Regulus, the bright star in the chest of the constellation of Leo, the Lion, has long been known as "the heart of the king."

The helical rising of Sirius each year coincided with the annual rising of the Nile, the harbinger of fertility not only for Egypt, but for most of the Mediterranean world, which depended on Egypt for bread. Like most stars, Sirius has a period when it disappears below the horizon and cannot be seen. At the time when Jesus was born, Sirius had just returned to visibility on July 29 after a seventy-day disappearance.[15] In the ancient world, this reappearance heralded a new cycle of prosperity and hope. In Egypt, the return of Sirius to the night sky signaled the Egyptian New Year.

Adrian Gilbert tells us that, in the Zoroastrian tradition, Sirius also represented the spirit of wisdom.[16] The Tibetans called this star Rishi-Agastya, after the holy *rishis* or priest-kings. In Tibet, the star's rising marks the annual festival of "setting free the waters of spring," drawing strong parallels between the birth of an avatar who nourishes the world and the Persian savior Mithra, who began creation by releasing the waters of life from the Great Cosmic Egg. To the Hebrews, Sirius was known as the Star of Jacob, who was the progenitor of the twelve tribes of Israel—one for each of the twelve signs of the zodiac. In Persian, Arabian, and Syrian astrology, Sirius was simply called the Messiah, or *Messaeil*, the "anointed one."[17]

The second celestial force that played a role in the sky over Bethlehem at the time of Jesus' birth was Osiris, the Redeemer, whose three stars form the belt of Orion. The Mayans called Orion "the First Father." They believed that it is through this particular "star gate," *Xibalba* (pronounced She-bul-ba), that souls enter "the place of creation,"[18] perhaps another name for heaven. The role of the Redeemer or Lord of Light has also been ascribed to Jesus, who, like Osiris, is continually linked to the balance scales of life. It was Osiris who received the souls of the dead into heaven.[19]

Researchers Robert Bauval and Graham Hancock have documented many significant alignments in ancient cultures—Mayan, Peruvian, Indian, Egyptian—related to the constellation of Orion. In their acclaimed book *The Orion Mystery*, they present evidence that the three large pyramids of Giza were deliberately modeled after the three stars in the belt of Orion, revealing the enduring importance of this constellation to our ancestors. Osiris was "*neb tem*, the Universal Master, who was human yet mysterious, suffering and commanding." In myth and scripture, his is the voice that calls for things to be put right when the order of the world is threatened. Osiris, perhaps an earlier incarnation of Jesus, came into the world "with the purpose of protecting the earth, priests, gods, saints, the Scripture, righteousness and prosperity," says Hancock.

> In India the reincarnated Messiah comes as Rama and later as Krishna and, in the last of days, will appear again as Kalki, "the Fulfiller." The same figure is also found in Mexico as Quetzalcoatl, the once and future king, and in Britain as King Arthur. He appears again in Egypt, manifest-

ing from the beginning of dynastic history in the form of the man-god Osiris—"the Far Strider," the Universal Lord—who dies, but who will be eternally reborn.[20]

On July 29, 7 B.C.E., as Sirius rose in the dark sky of early dawn, it met with the bright star Regulus, heralding the spiritual king who returns to Earth from age to age to change the world. Regulus, known as "the little king," is hardly little, weighing in at five times the size of our own Sun.[21] The Arabs called this star *Qalb Al Asad*, meaning the "heart of the lion," for it sits in the chest of the constellation of the great solar lion, Leo—a symbology particularly sacred to the Persians, the Hebrews, the Mayans, and the Egyptians, and long associated with Jesus as well. Regulus is also one of the four Watchers of Persian astrology, and one of only fifteen *Behenian* stars—Magical stars associated with generating the motion of the entire zodiac, a wisdom attributed to the god Thoth.[22] July 29, the date of the Sun's conjunction with Regulus, was known in the ancient world as the Lion's Gate—a hermetic doorway through which the spirit of a new king might enter the world.[23] To the Jews, this king was represented by the long-awaited Lion of Judah, the prophesied Messiah, the anointed priest/king from the line of David.

Since Leo is governed by the Sun, there is an immediate link between Jesus as a solar Lord, and the luminous "sons of God" long honored throughout the ancient world. Jesus emphasizes this connection many times by connecting himself with the light. In the Gnostic gospel *The Sophia of Jesus Christ*, Jesus even tells us, "I came from that Primordial, self-originated, primal boundless light that I may tell you all."[24]

The iconic lion also lay deep at the heart of the Egyptian and Persian Mysteries, whose savior heroes Osiris, Mithra, and Hercules were all linked to this same feline symbology. This association goes back to the spiritual initiates of Egypt, whose most advanced group was called the Panthers—*Pan thera* meaning "the All God (or Goddess)." The Sphinx—half man, half lion, the "Keeper of the Mysteries" who faces the rising Sun—is the emblem of this theme. Between his paws, at the center of his chest—right where the bright star Regulus is found in the constellation of Leo—lay the entrance to the underground chambers of initiation. Thus the lion was a short-hand glyph for the solar energies of the Lion King whose heart was the portal to the Mysteries. The lion is at once a hermetic symbol for the Sun god whose light illuminates the world, the will of the First Logos, the Word or the "divine utterance" of the Father, and the Son of God.

Regulus is also known as "the heart of the king," a reference to the solar lord Horus, and to Osiris, his father. Like Jesus, Osiris rose from the dead.

FIGURE 12. The Lion of Judah has long been connected with the royal House of David and prophecies of the Jewish Messiah. Yet the lion was also linked to the Persian Mithra and the Egyptian Osiris, as well as a group of high-level initiates within the Mystery traditions known as "Panthers," of which Jesus was an initiate. Illustrated by Sylvia Laurens.

Horus, his son, was conceived through the love and healing arts of his mother, Isis. Horus ultimately grew to manhood and defeated the tyrant Set, thus returning balance and justice to the world after the horrendous murder of his father. Horus—Apollo in Greece—became the Sun god of healing and music, and the overseer of all shepherds.[25] Thus, the astrological alignment of Sirius and Regulus, celestial symbols for Isis and Horus/Osiris, would have been seen as an announcement that a new Horus-king had arisen to redeem the Earth from darkness.[26]

The Sun (and thus the lion) is also the seat of creative power, the source of heat and light that brings about life. To the ancients, the powerful meeting of these two stars, Sirius and Regulus, occurring at the same time as the conjunction of Saturn and Jupiter, would have symbolized the birth of Horus the Younger. In hermetic terms, this meant that the new Horus—a king who was both secular and spiritual, the bringer of truth for the new age, a new Osiris—had arrived.

On the morning of July 29, 7 B.C.E., Mercury, a planet long dedicated to the wise master Thoth, hovered close to Regulus. Thoth was the protector of Isis and Horus in their darkest hours, as well as the perennial counselor to the pharaohs. An Egyptian drawing shows Horus seated on the lap of his mother, Isis, who wears the crown of *Hat-hor*, a term that means "house of Horus," or the throne of the king. In the drawing, Thoth, as the initiator of the Mysteries, stands to one side with a jar of anointing oil, ready to "christen" the boy. Amon, the Holy Spirit, stands on the other side, blessing Isis with the symbol for eternal life. If Jesus were born on this day, and thus with this astrological chart, it would signify that the god and goddess of wisdom and love, along with the Holy Spirit, had given their blessings to the new Horus-king. Just as Mercury and the Sun met Regulus at the Lion's Gate of Leo, Thoth blessed the birth of a new spiritual and secular king (Saturn and Jupiter conjunct in the sign of Pisces, the fish).

By mid-January of 6 B.C.E., the planet Jupiter had moved out of phase with Saturn, and the brilliance of this conjunction had passed. January 6, 6 B.C.E. is the last possible date that these two planets could have been seen together. Ancient documents found among the possessions of the famous Hebrew statesman Rabbi Abravanel (1437–1508) reveal that, during the course of the year 7 B.C.E., Hebrew astrologers in Chaldea were intensely tracking the movement of these two planets. They knew there would be at least three important conjunctions during this period. This was further substantiated in 1925, when the Star Calendar of Sippar was excavated from among the ruins of the Sumerian city of Sippar. This calendar revealed Jewish astrologers' many detailed calculations

FIGURE 13. The birth of Horus in the papyrus swamps. The goddess Isis suckles her young son Horus, an archetype for Mary and Jesus. They are attended by Thoth, the god of wisdom, who offers Horus the ankh as a key to eternal life, and by Amon, the Egyptian personification for the Holy Spirit, who touches the ankh to her lips. Illustrated by Sylvia Laurens.

for 7 B.C.E., indicating that these portents in the heavens had marked that as the year the Messiah would return.[27]

So it appears that two known astronomical events, the conjunction of Venus and Mercury, called the Shekinah, and the conjunction of Saturn and Jupiter, known as the Renewal of Time, could have been seen over Bethlehem and interpreted as the prophetic star. Of the three dates on which the Shekinah occurred between 6 and 8 B.C.E., the most synchronistic, at least in the context of the Mysteries, is December 25, 8 B.C.E. And of the three possible dates when Saturn and Jupiter were conjunct in the heavens, the most powerful and auspicious is July 29, 7 B.C.E., when the lion star Regulus joined with the goddess star Sirius to meet the Sun in the sign of Leo, the sign of the returning king. But this still doesn't give us a definitive date for Jesus' birth. In the next chapter, we'll discuss the esoteric meanings of these dates and explore just what the early Christian followers believed.

CHAPTER 5

Birth Chart of a King

The heavens declare the glory of God; and the firmament sheweth his handy work. Day unto day uttereth speech, and night unto night sheweth knowledge. There is no speech nor language, where their voice is not heard.

—Psalms 19:1–3

In the last chapter, we narrowed the likely dates of Jesus' birth to December 25, 8 B.C.E. and July 29, 7 B.C.E. The first would make Jesus a Capricorn; the second would make him a Leo. A case can also be made for October 3 and October 10-13 of 7 or 8 B.C.E., which would make him a Libra. In the ancient Mystery traditions, each of these dates has spiritual associations appropriate to the birth of a priest-king.

In the early centuries of Christianity, some groups celebrated Jesus' birth on May 20, while others insisted the correct date was actually April 19 or 20. All three of these fall in the spring and would have made Jesus either a Gemini or a Taurus in the Julian calendar. The only evidence to support any of these dates, however, is that Venus and Mercury were conjunct on April 18, 8 B.C.E., forming a "bright star" that could have been seen over Bethlehem. None of these dates holds any symbolic significance for the ancient Mystery traditions, however.

Some researchers reason that Jesus must have been born in the spring, since he, like the great god Osiris, was seen as the regenerating power of nature itself. Moreover, they argue, that was the season of taxation. Yet it was not the paying of taxes that drew Joseph and Mary to Bethlehem, but the registration of a new census. "And it came to pass in those days that a decree went out from Caesar Augustus that all the world should be registered . . . and Joseph also went up from Galilee, out of the city of Nazareth, into Judea, to the city of David, which is called Bethlehem, because he was of the house and lineage of David" (Luke 2: 1–4). In truth, this registration could have taken place at any time during the year.

Astrologically, if Jesus were born in March, he would have been a Pisces. And in fact, if Jesus is the herald of the emerging Age of Pisces, this has some logic to it. Pisces is the sign of "he who swims in the celestial waters" and is traditionally connected with the visionary or mystic, one who is able to travel in the mind of God. Early Christians used the sign of the fish as a secret emblem for their brotherhood. First-hand accounts of the Essenes who knew Jesus tell us that he was "enormously powerful and loving . . . [with] the energy of a high priest . . . ."[1] Certainly this kind of personality would be in line with the archetype of an evolved Pisces.

If, on the other hand, Jesus were born in April, he would be an Aries, a sign ruled by Mars, a planet long associated with the energies of war. Aries are known for their volatile personalities and fiery tempers, a profile far more in line with the outspoken John the Baptist, who, the Bible tells us, was born a full six months before Jesus (Luke 1:24-27). On the other hand, if Jesus were born under Taurus, the bull (April 21 to May 21), he would be ruled by a "fixed" earth sign, signifying stability and stubbornness. Taureans are not normally thought of as revolutionaries standing on the front lines of change, however. They are traditional and often content to work within conventional systems rather than shaking up the world.

So, of these three possible signs, only Pisces (February 18 through March 19) is a likely possibility for Jesus' birth, given what we know of his personality and mission. Yet this earlier March date was not proposed by the early Christian groups, nor did it align with the important conjunctions of the time.

RETURN OF THE LORDS OF LIGHT (DECEMBER 25)

Evidence for December 25, 8 B.C.E. as the day of Jesus' birth is somewhat stronger. As we know, there was a major conjunction of Venus and Mercury on that day and, within the Mystery religions, this day had great significance. December 25 was also the birthday of other world saviors, including Horus, Osiris, Mithra, Adonis, and Attis—all earlier incarnations of the Lord of Light who

FIGURE 14. The constellation of Pisces the Fish has long been associated with Jesus because he was born as the Age of Pisces began. The fish was also used as a secret symbol of initiation among the early Christians, and Jesus' disciples called themselves "Fishers of Men." Illustrated by Sylvia Laurens.

were called the sons of God and who, in their respective ages, changed world consciousness. If Jesus were born on December 25, he would immediately be aligned with these avatars who had changed the course of humanity. So perhaps it is not surprising that, in the fifth century, the Roman Church, in one of its famous councils, chose this as the true date of Jesus' birth in an attempt to lay the controversy to rest.[2]

In the language of the Mysteries, December 25 represents the return of the great solar light. This date falls just four days after the winter solstice, the shortest day and longest night of the year, and is therefore linked to the annual cycle of renewal. Darkness is a metaphor for the slumbering consciousness of mankind. Exactly three days after the solstice, the Earth begins to awaken, to turn back toward the illuminating radiance of the Sun—a change that visibly associates December 25 with the planetary return of the Lord of Light. On the solstice, the ancients declared, God's Sun died. He remained dead for three days and was born again on December 25. It is also interesting to note that the two solstices and two equinoxes create a perfect cross in the circle of our solar year, causing the ancients to claim that the Sun was hung upon the cross at the spring equinox.[3] Thus the symbology of crucifixion is also attached to this high holy day. In Egypt, December 25 and the four days that follow it were considered most sacred. December 25 was the birthdate of Horus and Osiris, who were both earlier incarnations of the four great Kumaras who come periodically to redeem the world. Because of the deep significance of this day in the Mystery religions, and the brilliant Shekinah that occurred on December 25, 8 B.C.E., we must consider it a logical candidate for Jesus' birthdate.

RETURN OF THE AION AND THE SIGN OF CAPRICORN (DECEMBER 25 AND JANUARY 6)

Some early Christian sects celebrated Jesus' birthday on January 6. This would make Jesus a Capricorn, usually symbolized by a goat with a fish's tail. Capricorns, ruled by the kingly planet Saturn, are usually considered to be old souls. With their tails in water and their feet on the ground, their purpose is to bring spiritual wisdom into the world of form. The higher aspect of this sign is the pure, unblemished unicorn, a Magical animal with great healing gifts—a symbology well suited to Jesus. January 6, 6 B.C.E. was also the last possible date when Jupiter and Saturn's conjunction could have been seen in the early morning hours over Bethlehem, giving the date some astronomical significance as well.

The ancient world had long associated January 6 with the coming of a new world savior, referred to in many cultures as the Aion (or Aeon), the Lord of Eternity. The Aion, like Mithra and Jesus, was said to have been born of a Virgin Mother and existed outside of time. He was seen as the Lord of Light who arrived at the threshold of each new age to usher in the new cycle. Later, the Roman Church chose this date to mark the visit of the Magi and dubbed it the Epiphany, meaning the "shining forth." Yet the Greek Orthodox and Armenian churches kept January 6 as the date of Jesus' birth (the coming of the new Aion), creating what we now call the twelve days of Christmas that stretch between December 25 and January 6.[4] In fact, many early church fathers insisted on January 6 as Jesus' actual birthday. "For Christ was born in the month of January . . . at the beginning of January sixth."[5] And January 6 also marked Egyptian festivals to the great god Ptah or Hephaestus, the "first father" of civilization, and to Horus, the divine savior-god who is often depicted carrying the torch of knowledge. Both Ptah and Horus were seen as catalysts for new eras of human enlightenment.[6]

This date was also sacred to the goddess Kore, an aspect of Isis, the Great Mother to whom the Greek Mystery religions were dedicated. It was Demeter or Isis who gave birth to Kore, and the Virgin Kore who gave birth to Aion, "the Son of God," making Kore and Aion earlier incarnations of the same Virgin

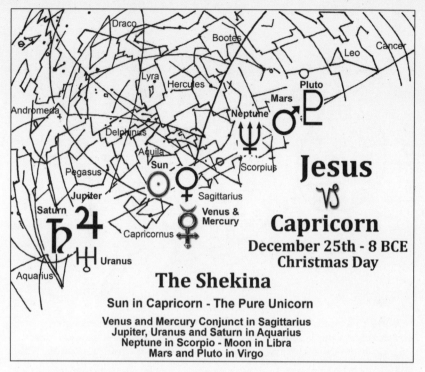

FIGURE 15A. Birth chart for December 25, 8 B.C.E. The conjunction of the Shekinah, the meeting of the planets Venus and Mercury, occurred just before the helical rising of the Sun, making this a prime candidate for the star that rose over Bethlehem.

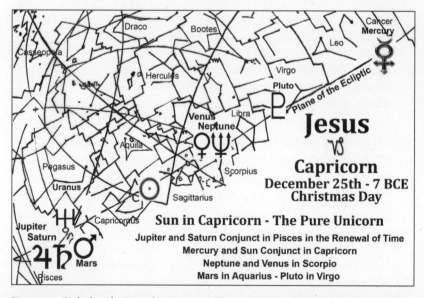

FIGURE 15B. Birth chart for December 25, 7 B.C.E. The conjunction of Saturn and Jupitor, heralding the merger of the secular and spiritual "King of the World," would have had great meaning within the ancient mystery religions, particularly occurring on Decemer 25th, the birthdate of other earlier world saviors.

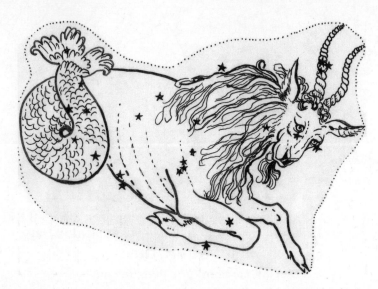

Figure 16. The constellation Capricorn is sometimes depicted as a fish-goat, and as the sign of the Christ Child, the unblemished one, whose foundation is in the world of Spirit, and whose feet are in the world of matter. Its secondary symbol is a pure white unicorn. Illustrated by Sylvia Laurens.

Mother and Son we have come to know in Christianity.[7] Some 400 years after the birth of Jesus, Epiphanius writes about the similarities between these far more ancient pagan celebrations and the Christian symbols:

> [On this night the people] stay up the whole night singing songs and playing the flute, offering these to the images of the gods; and [then] . . . after cock-crow, they go down with torches into a subterranean sanctuary and bring up a carved wooden image, which is laid naked on a litter. On its forehead it has the sign of the cross, in gold, and on both its hands two other signs of the same shape, and two more on its knees; and the five signs are all fashioned in gold . . . [And] if you ask them what this mysterious performance means they answer: "Today, at this hour, the Kore, that is to say the Virgin, has given birth to the [new] Aeon."[8]

THE BALANCE IN THE HEAVENS (OCTOBER 10–13)

The hermetic associations between Jesus and the balance scales also place October 10 through 13 among the strongest candidates for his birthday. These dates correspond with the report from Suddi the Essene, who claimed that the

Nativity was close to the Jewish New Year (October 1). Arab legends affirm that Jesus was born in mid-October, a week or two after Rosh Hashanah, which is followed ten days later by Yom Kippur.[9] The Hebrews believed that on Yom Kippur each soul must pass before the Creator to be judged, just as sheep must pass before the shepherd for inspection. If Jesus were born at this time, it would make him a Libra, drawing a natural parallel between him and Osiris as the Lord of Judgment in heaven. This parallel may explain why the balance scales were first adopted as a symbol by the early Christian church.

If Jesus were indeed born in October, he would have been a Libra and John the Baptist, born some six months earlier, would have been an Aries. There are several excellent reasons to consider this birth date for John. On April 4 of 6 B.C.E., Jupiter and Mercury were conjunct in the sign of Aries (the expansive spiritual communicator) ahead of the Sun and Mars (the fiery warrior). Saturn (representing old structures), along with the planets Uranus and Venus, had moved into Pisces. These planetary movements represent the breaking up (Uranus) of old structures through a gospel of love (Venus). These planetary positions would symbolize a personality who leads the way (Aries) aggressively (Mars) for the king (Saturn) of the new age (of Pisces), who is the lover (Venus) and awakener of others (Uranus). This configuration fits John the Baptist well.

To explore the possibility of these October dates, I ran the astronomical alignments for the years 6, 7, and 8 B.C.E. On October 3, 7 B.C.E., I found the conjunction of Saturn and Jupiter, which signified the union of the celestial and terrestrial kings, just as it did for July 29 and January 6. In both years, I found that the Sun appears to swing around the Ecliptic and come to rest exactly on the apex of the scales around October 12 or 13. In the language of the Mysteries, this configuration represents the great solar lord (the Sun) presiding over the scales of truth. At the center of the scale is a single pole, representing the Tree of Life. The Sun presides at the top of this Tree, illuminating everything below it. This symbology could easily be ascribed to Jesus. In John 23:35–36, Jesus says: "A little longer the light is with you. Walk while you have the light, lest darkness overtake you; he who walks in darkness does not know where he is going. While you have the light, believe in the light, that you may become sons of the light." And ten verses later, he tells us, "I have come as a light into the world, that whoever believes in Me should not abide in darkness."

In 7 B.C.E., the position of the Sun at the apex of the scales was complemented by Mercury in Libra, representing fairness of speech and mind. Neptune and Venus were also in Scorpio (planets representing the archetypes of the visionary and the lover). Fiery Mars was in Sagittarius, a warrior and pilgrim for truth. All of these qualities seem appropriate to Jesus, a visionary lover of the Mysteries and a pilgrim for higher truth.

This same solar apex occurred again in October of 6 B.C.E., but this time, Mercury, Venus, and the Sun were all conjunct in Libra, forming a triad of love and wisdom grounded in the sign of fairness. Neptune (the mystic) was passing through Scorpio, representing the Mysteries, and almost perfectly aligned with the galactic center.

In esoteric terms, October 3, and 10–13 are all flawless matches for the spiritual energies of the Lord of Light who illumines the halls of heaven.

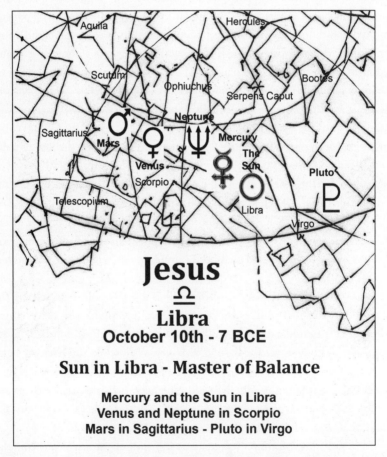

FIGURE 17. Birth chart for October 10, 7 B.C.E. Every year between October 10th and 13th, the Sun comes to rest at the top of the balance scales, creating a perfect symbol for the Lord of Light who oversees the weighing of the hearts of humanity. An October birth date is in keeping with Islamic reports of Jesus' birth, and matches up with the accounts of the Essene teacher Suddi.

Figure 18. The balance scales of Libra with the Sun, symbolically representing the Lord of Light who sits at the top of the Tree of Life. Illustrated by Sylvia Laurens.

The Lion of God (July 29)

Our last credible possibility for Jesus' birthday is July 29, 7 b.c.e. This date is aligned not only with Leo, the sign of the regal lion, but with the stars Sirius and Regulus, symbolizing the queen and king in their celestial dance. This important date also includes the meeting of Jupiter and Saturn in Pisces, the sign of the fish. Since the impending Age of Pisces was breaking at the time that Jesus was born, this conjunction would have been seen by sages around the world as highly significant. In the language of the Mysteries, it would indicate that Jesus embodied the qualities of both the spiritual and worldly ruler. In its own way, this dramatic conjunction of energies is one of the strongest possibilities we have considered.

Each of the four dates discussed here as possibilities for Jesus' birth is supported by strong astronomical alignments, any of which could have created the effect of the star over Bethlehem, if indeed that was an astronomical event. Each holds great esoteric meaning, and each is astrologically aligned with Jesus' mission. With their deeper connotations within the Mysteries, they are also dates that the Magi of many countries would have known about and considered in their search for the new Messiah.

For myself, I lean toward either July 29 (Leo) on the October dates (Libra). The case for Jesus as a Libra, and for John the Baptist as an Aries six months earlier, seems to ring most true, supported by the Arabic legends, the eyewitness testimony of Suddi the Essene, and the powerful astronomical evidence. Moreover, the profound similarities between Jesus and Osiris as masters who hold "our soul in the balance" also strongly support the October dates.

In the end, however, we may never know the exact date that Jesus was born. And perhaps, in a way, this is part of the message—that all people, no matter

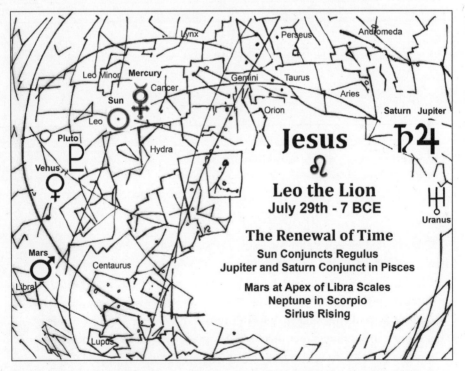

Figure 19. Birth chart for July 29, 7 b.c.e. Co-joining with the return of the bright star Sirius, and rising in the sign of Leo the Lion-hearted king, this July date is a strong contender for the birth of Jesus, and is linked to legends of the return of the king, as well as the conjunction of Jupiter and Saturn, called the Renewal of Time.

FIGURE 20. The astrological sign of Leo the Lion reveals the star Regulus, "the little king," at its heart. This was the doorway within the great Mystery traditions, through which the initiate must pass, opening his heart to the redeeming power of love. Illustrated by Sylvia Laurens.

what their astrological gifts or limitations, have the ability to transcend the circumstances of their birth by aligning with their highest selves. While the power of the stars and planets and the conditions of our upbringing may influence us, each of us has the power to transcend the outside world and become enlightened by aligning to the light within. Therein lies the path to the divine heart.

PART III

Jesus among the Essenes

CHAPTER 6

Journey into the Mysteries

There is an earthly sun, which is the cause of all heat, and all who are able to see may see the sun; and those who are blind and cannot see him may feel his heat. There is an Eternal Sun, which is the source of all wisdom, and those whose spiritual senses have awakened to life will see that sun and be conscious of His existence; but those who have not attained spiritual consciousness may yet feel His power by an inner faculty which is called Intuition.[1]

—Paracelsus, quoted in Manly P. Hall, *The Secret Teachings of All Ages*

Most people who have read the Bible know that Jesus spent his early years in Egypt, where he remained until he was five, six, or even seven years old. The Gospel of Matthew reports that "[a]n angel of the Lord appeared to Joseph in a dream saying, 'Arise, take the young Child and His mother and flee to Egypt . . . stay there until I bring you word; for Herod will seek the young Child to destroy him'" (Matthew 2:13-15). Joseph did as he was told, not returning to Galilee until after the death of Herod the Great.

Stories of Jesus' early life with his family have come to be known as the Infancy Gospels. Traditional versions of the Holy Family's flight to Egypt come from only one historical source: the early Christian patriarch Theophilus, who lived in Alexandria from 384 to 412 c.e., shortly after the formation of the Roman Orthodox Church in 325 c.e. The story goes that, one day while praying, Bishop Theophilus received "a personal revelation" from Mary herself. According to Theophilus, on the eve of the sixth day of Hathor, a time corresponding

FIGURE 21. The flight into Egypt. The belief in a trinity lay at the core of Egyptian theology, honoring the divine Mother, divine Father, and divine child. Today it has been transmitted to us in the beautiful stories of the Nativity, with Mary, Jesus, and Joseph representing these virtues.

to our modern month of November, Mary revealed to him all the details of the Holy Family's journey to Egypt and bade him write down her words.

Theophilus' account tells of the Holy Family's overland journey to Egypt, where Mary and Joseph visited thirty or more sites before returning home to Palestine some years later. As astonishing as his story may sound, it is even more astonishing that the newly forming Christian church accepted it *prima facia* and never questioned its accuracy! Theophilus' revelation became the official version of the Holy Family's journey.

Theophilus received his revelation around the time of the Theodosian Decrees, a series of papal dictates that closed all ancient temples and conscripted them for use by the emerging Christian church. These decrees also demanded that all pagan feast days be subsumed under Christian holidays and celebrated accordingly.[2] By the fourth century, Manly P. Hall tells us, this self-righteous intolerance had become the hallmark of the early church fathers, who consciously promoted a program of condemnation and hatred in the name of the Prince of Peace.[3]

Despite the violence and hatred they incited, the Theodosian Decrees accomplished several important things for the early church. They destroyed the ancient centers of learning and dismantled age-old universities. They obliterated written records from the past, making whole blocks of human history untraceable. They destroyed the sacred images and symbols that people had worshipped for centuries and replaced them with a new iconography. And they

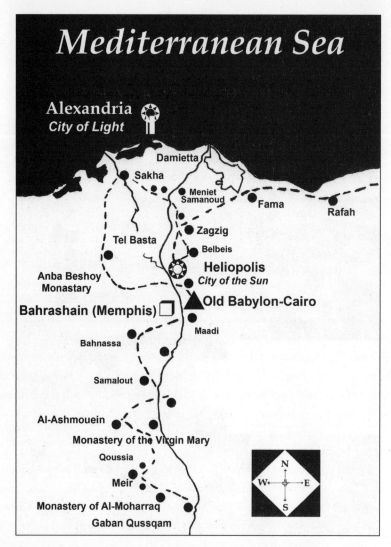

FIGURE 22. Theophilus' version of the route the Holy Family took through Egypt.

used the faith in older beliefs to propagate a new, more limiting theology—one that allowed no religious freedom whatsoever. Bishop Theophilus' "vision" was used to justify the takeover of ancient wisdom sites, harnessing the devotional energies of those sacred spots and producing a steady source of income for the Roman Catholic Church—income that has continued to support the church for the past 1500 years. During the Middle Ages, Christian knights used this purported vision to challenge the Muslim occupation of Egypt.

Bishop Theophilus chronicled his vision in a manuscript called the *Mimar*, a document that may still be hidden in the Vatican today. Some historical reports say, however, that his account was not written down until 700 years later, in the eleventh or twelfth centuries. This, of course, leads many scholars to question whether this story was simply fabricated by the early church out of whole cloth. Michael Baigent, author of *The Jesus Papers*, concludes, therefore, that it cannot be " . . . an accurate account of any such journey, although it may very well contain some elements of a real journey."[4]

THE INFANCY GOSPELS

The official version of Mary and Joseph's journey to Egypt is printed in a pamphlet put out by the Egyptian Ministry of Tourism. It goes like this: "In those far off days, there were three routes which could be followed by travelers transversing Sinai from Judea to Egypt, a crossing which was usually undertaken in groups, for without the protection of well-organized caravans, the ever-present dangers, even along these known and trodden paths, were ominously forbidding."[5] This much of the story may be true. Caravans were a normal way for people to travel, but many also traveled by sea. And given Joseph's connections with the Essenes, sea travel may have been a far more likely choice for the Holy Family.

The booklet then paints the picture of a journey that sounds both solitary and perilous. Joseph and Mary "picked their way, day after day, through hidden valleys and across uncharted plateaus in the rugged wastelands of Sinai, enduring the scorching heat of the sun by day and the bitter cold of the desert nights, preserved from the threat of wild beasts and savage tribesman, their daily sustenance miraculously provided, the all-too-human fears of the young Mother for her Infant allayed by the faith that infused her with His birth."[6]

Although this version implies that the couple traveled alone with Jesus, we know that the Holy Family included not only Joseph, Mary, and the infant Jesus, but Joseph's older children as well. Greek Orthodox records reveal that Joseph already had four sons and three daughters from a previous marriage—James, Jose, Jude, Simon (or Simeon), Esther, Martha, and Salome.[7] And despite the bleak description of Egypt given in the pamphlet, Egypt was, at the time, a profoundly cultured civilization that had been at the peak of its artistic, philosophic, and material abundance for thousands of years. While the official version would have us believe that the Holy Family went unprotected into the Egyptian wilderness, there is strong evidence that they stayed in the monasteries of the Great White Brotherhood while they were there.

In fact, according to Suddi, the Holy Family sheltered with the Essene order in Qumran for many days while they gathered supplies for their journey. Because of Herod's edict, it was suddenly dangerous to be seen on the road with an infant. The fact that Joseph trusted his family's life to the Essenes implies that he was on intimate terms of friendship with the order and may well have been a member of it. The Brotherhood realized that it must find a way to get the family safely out of Judea. After all, they understood only too well the importance of this child. They knew that Jesus was the one for whom they had been waiting. So they sent the Holy Family to their sister monastery in Egypt.[8]

An informed portrait of Egypt at that time reveals a country quite different from the generalized notion of a desolate, poverty-stricken land. Alexandria, the nation's capital, where the Holy Family first arrived, was a bustling, cosmopolitan city and the nexus of the Hebrew, Greek, Mesopotamia, and Egyptian worlds. It was founded in 331 B.C.E., a good three centuries before Jesus was born, by Alexander the Great, the famous Macedonian general who dreamed of fashioning a world united by peace. Alexander envisioned his city as a place where all spiritual, religious, and philosophical traditions could be shared in open exchange. Although he didn't live to see this dream fulfilled, Alexandria did, in fact, become the center of learning for the entire Middle East and remained so for almost 700 years.[9] At the time when the Holy Family arrived, the city had a population of some 300,000 free men and women, and two or three times as many servants, bringing the population to over a million people.

There were more than 300,000 Jews living in the Egyptian communities of Alexandria, Khnum, Heliopolis, and Memphis, and there were major Jewish temples in Khnum, Bubastis, and Alexandria. "Jewish immigration into Egypt was extensive, encouraged particularly by the removal of all boundaries between Egypt and Israel from 302 B.C.E. until 198 C.E., a period when Israel formed part of the Ptolemaic empire."[10] These immigrants quickly became absorbed into the prevailing Greek culture. Alexandria was thus a teaming multi-national metropolis, and an easy place for the Holy Family to get lost in, especially if they didn't want to be found.

SERAPIS, THE ARCHETYPE OF JESUS

Squarely in the middle of Alexandria stood the huge Serapeum, an enormous temple to Serapis, the great solar lord who foreshadowed Jesus. The worship of Serapis is thought to have originated in India and been brought back to Greece, Rome, and Egypt by seafaring traders. Plutarch tells of the pharaoh

Ptolemy Soter, who had a dream in which a colossal statue appeared to him and asked to be brought to Alexandria. No one knew of such a statue until a traveler named Sosibius declared that he had seen such an image at Snope. Immediately, Ptolemy sent his men to bring the god back to Egypt. Plutarch writes, "Three years elapsed before the image was finally obtained, the representatives of the Pharaoh finally stealing it and concealing the theft by spreading a story that the statue had come to life and, walking down the street leading from its temple, had boarded the ship prepared for its transportation to Alexandria."[11]

In the Egyptian world, Serapis melded easily into Osiris, thus becoming a bridge between the Greek and Egyptian cultures. Serapis, known as the long-suffering or "weeping god," was an archetypal figure of the great world savior who came periodically to Earth and gave his life to help mankind.[12] Like Osiris and later Jesus, Serapis was willing to sacrifice himself for the love of humanity. This archetype is akin to the Indian concept of the divine Purusha, a being who is said to be the "eternally existent Self that permeates the Universe" and who, in his compassion, descends to Earth from age to age to uplift humanity.

Clues to the true identity of Serapis can be gleaned from a close examination of his name. Serapis is a combination of two words: *soros*, meaning "a stone coffin," and *apis*, meaning the "bull of heaven," the pure white bull sacred to the followers of Osiris, the benevolent savior lord who traveled the world after the Flood to bring food, grains, wine, and the arts of civilization to the starving masses, while his queen and counterpart, Isis, ruled Upper Egypt in his stead. When he returned to Egypt, however, his evil half-brother Set deceitfully imprisoned him in a stone coffin and threw him into the river to die. Serapis was thus deeply connected to the Osirian legends.

In Hebrew, Serapis, or *seraph*, meaning "to blaze out" or "blaze up," is synonymous with fire, linking him, like Jesus, to the Sun. *Seraph* is also the root of the word "seraphim," used for angelic beings said to be made of pure fire.[13] In many spiritual traditions, fire was considered the element closest to the Source, the great central Sun of life. So Serapis became the icon of the Christed solar God-man who sacrifices himself for humanity.

The depictions of Serapis extant today look surprisingly like Jesus. They show him as a handsome young man with shoulder-length hair, kind eyes, and a pensive face. Manly P. Hall describes him as conveying "the twofold impression of manly strength and womanly grace."[14] Serapis is often shown wearing a wreath of golden wheat upon his head reminiscent of medieval paintings of a haloed Christ with rays of light coming from his head, and of the famous crown of thorns. This shining wreath also links Serapis to the solar lords Mithra,

Zoroaster, and Horus/Apollo, each of whom was depicted wearing a similar blazing crown. Serapis was, in many ways, a composite of many of these solar lords: Osiris, the Egyptian lord of the dead; Zeus, the high god of the Greeks; and even Asclepius, the human father of healing. He also foreshadowed Jesus himself and depictions of him may actually have been forecasts of Jesus' birth.

By 6 or 7 B.C.E., the worship of Serapis had spread throughout much of the Greco-Roman world. Aside from Alexandria, his most notable center of worship was in Delos, Greece, a community founded by an Egyptian priest in the third century before Christ. The Roman emperor Hadrian so loved Serapis that, even 200 years after Jesus, he spent a decade building a splendid replica of Egypt's Serapeum in the city of Tivoli. Other temples of Serapis can be found across the Mediterranean, as far north as the Roman settlement of York in Britain, and as far east as India.

SERAPIS AND THE LOGOS

According to the Greek historian Phylarchus (third century B.C.E.), the word *serapis* meant "the power that disposed the universe into its present beautiful order."[15] This power was also known as the Logos, a word long associated with Jesus that means "the template for creation." Until the time of Christ, only the great lords Osiris and Thoth had been called the Logos, although there is some evidence that Serapis was also included in this elite group. Like Thoth, Serapis was often shown holding a ruler, implying that he held the measure of

FIGURE 23. Images of Serapis look remarkably similar to later images of Jesus. Serapis was often known as the "Weeping God," who wept tears for the suffering of humanity. Illustrated by Sylvia Laurens.

the world in his hands. He is usually depicted with either a dove or an eagle resting on his head—initiatic symbols of the Holy Mother Spirit and the Father God—and with a lamb-faced serpent at his side. Serapis' hand rests on it to symbolize his mastery of the kundalini life force and his role as the sacrificial lamb. He wears a wreath of wheat, or sometimes a measuring cup (like the chalice of the Holy Grail), on his head, to symbolize that, as the "green god of regeneration," he, like Osiris and Jesus, brings abundance to all.

The symbology of Serapis is deep and rich. He is sometimes shown standing on a crocodile, telling us that, like Mithra, Horus, Isis, and later Mother Mary and the Archangel Michael, he has conquered his lower nature.[16] The

FIGURE 24. Serapis with crocodile, ruler, lamb, dove, and wreath. This complex hermetic statue gives insight into the many sacred aspects of Serapis, the archetype for the coming Jesus. Here Serapis stands upon a crocodile, representing his mastery of his reptilian nature. Beside him rises the kundalini forces of the serpent, shown with the face of the sacrificial lamb; on his head is a dove of peace, and a golden wreath of wheat, symbolizing abundance, and his link to the Sun. From *Mossaize Historie der Hebreeuwse Kerke* (taken from the 1923 Manly P. Hall book *The Secret Teachings of all Ages*)

crocodile epitomizes Osiris' eternal enemy, the evil serpent Set or Satu from whom we get the name Satan. Set represented our negative reptilian qualities—anger, lust, greed, vanity, attachment, and worldly ambition. And just as Horus (Osiris' son) eventually overcame the chaos of Set and restored order to the world, so do all great solar lords teach the mastery of the egoic nature and the subjugation of the inner demons.

Records of the statues of Serapis reveal that they were made of various precious materials, including gemstones and metals, to represent the concept of totality, or the one god who contains all things within himself. One such statue was composed of four different metals—gold, silver, bronze, and lead—representing the four ages of the world. Clement of Alexandria, an early church father, describes one exquisite statue that was a compound of gold, silver, lead, tin, sapphire, hematite, emerald, and topaz, all mixed with ashes from the temple of Osiris to create a figure of azure blue, a color that, for 2000 years, has been associated with Jesus. Indigo is also the vibrating color of the *nuri sarup*, or astral body, and is associated with inner sight. One labyrinth sacred to Serapis held a colossal thirteen-foot statue carved from a single emerald. Green was associated with Osiris, the Egyptian god of vegetation, and was also used for the Davidic kings of Jesus' line. Later, it was adopted by the Merovingian kings, who were said to be descendants of Christ.

Serapis was known as "the god of the seven letters" (S-E-R-A-P-I-S), linking him to the seven days of creation, the seven planetary spheres, the seven visible rays of light, the seven vowels, and the seven divine intelligences that manifest through the solar light.[17] The number seven, often used in the Mystery Schools to represent the seven subtle energy bodies and seven chakras of the physical body, can also be seen in the Jewish menorah's seven branches. The central shaft of the menorah represents the Tree of Life upon which the Lord of Light hangs, surrounded by six lights that represent the seven lanterns of the body that must be lit to travel the path back to heaven. Jesus speaks directly of these energetic pathways and their connection with the Tree of Life in the apocryphal Essene Gospel of Peace: "Yea, I tell thee truly, the paths are seven through the Infinite Garden, and each must be traversed by the body, the heart and the mind as one . . . to soar above the abyss to the Tree of Life."[18]

The Greek philosopher and geographer Strabo tells us that the Serapeum, the Alexandrian temple of Serapis, stood in the western district of the city, in the Greek quarter. It housed a library of 40,000 to 50,000 volumes that were available to the general public. Today, tragically, no trace of the temple remains. Manly P. Hall relates how it was destroyed:

When the Christian soldiers, in obedience to Theodosius' order, entered the Serapeum at Alexandria to destroy the statue of Serapis that had stood there for centuries, so great was their veneration for the god that they dared not touch the image lest the ground should open at their feet and engulf them. At length, overcoming their fear, they demolished the statue, sacked the building and finally, as a fitting climax to their offense, burned the magnificent library which was housed within the lofty apartments of the Serapeum.[19]

In the foundations of the temple, below the ruins, the soldiers found Christian symbols from Jesus' own teachings—the icthys, the iconic fish, or the *Vesica Piscis*—a symbol whose true meaning was woven into the very fabric of the Mystery Schools. An early church historian of the fifth century declared that "after the pious Christians had razed the Serapeum at Alexandria and scattered the demons who dwelt there under the guise of the gods, beneath the foundations was found the monogram of Christ."[20] This profoundly sacred symbol, representing the union of opposites, is found above the entrances of many European cathedrals. Its petal-like shape can be seen in the six petals of the Flower of Life, the ancient hermetic symbol that holds the mathematical equation for divine order itself.

FIGURE 25. Here, the menorah is shown atop the Star of David and the icthys symbol.

FIGURE 26. When 4th-century Christians destroyed the visible levels of the Serapeum under the orders of the Holy Roman Church, they discovered the Christian symbols of the fish inscribed upon its pavement stones when they reached the lower levels. Illustrated by Sylvia Laurens.

Some even claim that *Christus*, or *Chrestus*, was another name for Sera-pis, since the names can both be translated as "the Messiah" or "anointed one." Thus, the emperor Hadrian wrote: "The worshipers of Serapis are called Chris-tians, and those who are devoted to the god Serapis, call themselves Bishops of Christ."[21] One historian was moved to write: "After the crucifixion of the Light of the World, the religion of the Cross of Light, the seed of Gnostic mystic Christianity, arose from the ashes of the Library of Alexandria and Egypt."[22]

In truth, Serapis was the cosmic archetype of Jesus himself, honored cen-turies before Christ arrived in the flesh. It is a great shame that the early Chris-tian popes were so blinded by their quest for power that they missed what was right before their eyes: Jesus, their savior god, had been prophesied and fore-shadowed in cultures around the world. Saint Augustine alone sensed the truth: "That which is called the Christian religion existed among the ancients, and never did not exist, from the beginning of the human race until Christ came in the flesh, at which time the true religion which already existed began to be called Christianity."[23] Certainly, when Jesus first visited Egypt as a child and later, when he studied there as an adult, the belief in a divine savior god who comes into the world to uplift mankind was in full flower in the temples of Serapis and among his followers.[24]

THE GOLDEN AGE OF WISDOM

The Holy Family first arrived in Alexandria at a time of great intellectual and spiritual exchange. It was in Alexandria that Eratosthenes first measured the diameter of the Earth, more than fifteen centuries before Copernicus or Gali-leo were born.[25] It was here that Euclid provided an analysis of geometry and proportion and a comprehensive theory of numbers, and where Archimedes invented a pump that is still in use after 2300 years. The royal library of Al-exandria, with its 700,000 books and scrolls, and the temple of Serapis were both recognized as international centers of spiritual, philosophical, and sci-entific knowledge, and sages from all the great cultures—India, China, Syria, Phoenicia, Greece, and Egypt—flocked there to teach and to learn, along with thousands of Jews from Palestine.

Each of these civilizations erected temples to whatever god or goddess they worshipped, and virtually everyone understood that all these gods were merely aspects of the same Great Creator who designed the universe. The multitude of gods and goddesses merely represented archetypes within that creation, aspects of the one divine, unknowable deity described in the Hebrew Kabbala.[26]

Jewish scholars tell us that this was the period when Jewish scriptures were first translated into Greek. "The most famous version of the Old Testament was produced in Alexandria about the year 280 B.C.E.," writes Manly P. Hall. "Apparently, Demetrius of Phaleron, who was librarian during the time of Ptolemy Philadelphus, convinced the Pharaoh that a transcription of the books of Moses should be included in the royal collection."[27] In Alexandria, Jews studied the philosophy of Socrates and Plato and read Greek mythology and literature. Some even adopted Greek ideas about democracy and freedom, a system of governance completely different from Jewish patriarchy.

The Jews were also drawn to the teachings of Pythagoras (ca. 569-475 B.C.E.), which were based on the earlier writings of Thoth/Hermes and explored the world through the disciplines of science, mathematics, harmonics, and philosophy. Thoth, one of the prime architects of the Mysteries across the world, influenced the philosophies of the Therapeutae of Egypt, the Essenes of Israel, and the Druids of Britain. Pythagoras, a Greek master, united Hellenic humanism with Thoth's teachings on numbers, music, and sacred geometry to create a powerful effect on Mediterranean cultures and on the Essenes of Palestine.

Pythagoras was born in Samos, Ionia, some 500 years before Christ, but around the same time that Buddha and Zoroaster were born. He is considered by many historians to be the first pure mathematician of the Western world. Trained in the Mystery Schools of ancient Egypt, Pythagoras set up his own Mystery School in Crotona, on the southern edge of Italy, patterning it on the three-step initiation rites of the traditional schools. Although much of what he taught was kept in strict secrecy by initiates, we do know that he emphasized a balance between science, philosophy, and spirituality—a balance illustrated by a "golden triangle" that forced cooperation between the three. Religion and philosophy had to reflect the observable principles of science; science strove to discover the unified consciousness of the divine and apply it to practical rules of governance.

Pythagoras spent much of his life in search of truth. He studied with the Druid masters of Britain, was initiated in the Eleusinian Mysteries of Greece, and became a pupil of the Magi of Persia during his captivity in Babylon. Clement of Alexandria even claims he was a pupil of Zoroaster and a disciple of the Brahmans in India.[28] But the foundations of Pythagoras' knowledge, like Plato's, came from Egypt, where he studied for twenty-two years in the temples of Diospolis.[29] The Egyptian Mysteries, based on the sacred rites of life, death, and rebirth, were the wellspring from which other world traditions were born, and many of the greatest thinkers of the ancient world—Socrates, Plato, Euclid, Homer, Solon—journeyed to Egypt to partake of this wisdom.

FIGURE 27. The great sage Pythagoras was known for his extensive teachings on the nature of number, geometry, music, and sacred forms. Pythagoras set up his school in Crotona, Italy with his wife.

Pythagoras, like Jesus, was known as a son of God. He taught that there is one overarching God—a supreme mind expressed in both the seen and unseen worlds. Pythagoras regarded the planets as magnificent deities or souls subservient to the One First Cause. He taught that both man and the universe were made in the image of God, and that there was a divine congruence between the macrocosm of the universe, and the microcosm of man.[30] Initiation into the Pythagorean Mysteries involved a carefully choreographed Mystery drama, enacted over several days and nights, during which the initiate experienced egoic "death" and was reborn as a realized being. These dramas were usually conducted in an underground labyrinth that symbolized the intricate twists and turns of life, the passage through death, and the process of rebirth. The physical passage through darkness was a metaphor for man's blindness and ultimate emergence into the light. These same inner processes were known to the Gnostic Christians and were what lay, in part, behind Christ's words: "Most assuredly, I say to you, unless one is born again, he cannot see the kingdom of God" (John 3:3).

Pythagoras' teachings were highly revered, not only by the Druids and the Greeks, but by the Essene sect of which Jesus and his family were a part. In fact, early Christian sects recognized Pythagoras as a true prophet and Herald of the

The Mystical Triangle of Wisdom

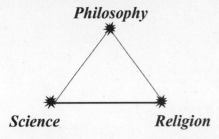

Philosophy

Science   *Religion*

FIGURE 28. Within the ancient Mystery religions, the mystical triangle of wisdom symbolized the checks and balances necessary between science, spirituality, and philosophy, which must corroborate one another.

Good Realm, and drew on the philosophy, science, and metaphysics taught in the ancient Orphic, Pythagorean, Platonic, and Neo-Platonic Mystery schools.

It was an incredible time, a golden age of art, science, and philosophy that lasted for over 700 years, bringing some of the finest minds in the world to Alexandria. What might our world be like if this rich flower of wisdom had not been destroyed, but had been allowed to blossom for 2000 years? IMagine taking the best of every wisdom tradition, every human art or science, and finding the commonalities between them, thus creating a unified philosophy of life based on the finest attainments of the human mind.

It was in the midst of just such an age that Jesus—the ultimate democrat and a true champion of truth—arose. The knowledge of the divine solar lords who return to Earth from age to age had been well established for thousands of years, and the dream of Jesus and what he stood for was already known by the sages of many lands. And it was Egypt that opened her arms to embrace him.

CHAPTER 7

The Secret Brotherhood in Egypt

The face of truth is hidden by thy golden orb, O Sun.
That do thou remove, in order that I,
Who am devoted to truth, may behold its glory.[1]

> —Isha Upanishad, XV (thought to be written by Issa, or Jesus)

Coptic Christian sources claim that the Holy Family's sojourn in Egypt lasted only four years, yet Arabic sources tell us that the Holy Family remained in Egypt for nearly seven, a period that fits seamlessly with other stories of young Jesus' travels.[2]

Jesus' family most likely encountered two occult spiritual groups during their years abroad—both of which would have been well known to Joseph, who was a highly respected member of the Essenes. The first was the Jewish Zadokite priesthood, direct descendants of the lines of Aaron, who were established in Egypt at the Jewish temple of Bubastis. The second was the Order of the Therapeutae, the Egyptian branch of the Great White Brotherhood whose main centers were in Alexandria and Heliopolis, the ancient city of the Sun.

THE ZADOKITES AND THE THERAPEUTAE

The Jewish temple at Bubastis stood some twenty miles north of Cairo, south of the city of Alexandria. It was established around 170 B.C.E. by the descendants of the original Zadokite priesthood after the Syrian invader Antiochus invaded Israel and took over the temple of Jerusalem.[3] When the temple in Jerusalem fell, Onias III, a Zadokite high priest, asked Ptolemy VI for permission to establish a Jewish temple at Bubastis. Ptolemy agreed. The temple became one of the major strongholds for the Jewish people.[4] Its priests, hereditary Zadokites, believed that they represented the legitimate teachings passed down from the time of Moses.

The Zadokites strictly maintained the traditional faith while awaiting the birth of the "chosen one," the true messianic king who would arrive to overthrow the usurpers and take back Israel. While the legitimacy of this Jewish temple as the "real" initiatic stronghold of Judaism in Egypt is still being argued by scholars, it is clear that this temple would have been fully established and functioning when Joseph, Mary, and Jesus first arrived in Egypt.

The history behind the Bubastis temple may explain the resistance of the Sanhedrin in Jerusalem to Jesus and his teachings. Jesus, as scion of the kingly line of David, would have been seen as a threat to the council's authority. Jesus' wisdom, age, and bloodline would have marked him as a possible claimant to the throne, making him a danger to Herod as well. Supported as he was by the Zadokites, the Nazoreans, the Zealots, and the Essenes, Jesus was the single most powerful threat to both Herod and the Sanhedrin.

This may also explain why the more aggressive apostles—Simeon the Zealot, or even Judas Iscariot—were drawn to Jesus. They expected him, based on his background, to take on both the Roman Empire and Herod—to reinstate the Zadokite priesthood, return the bloodline of King David, and bring Judea back to the true teachings of Moses. Thus an understanding of the significance of the Egyptian Jewish temple at Bubastis is crucial to an understanding of the politics of Jesus' time. Without this background, it is difficult to appreciate just how far Judaism had strayed from its illumined, spiritual roots. It also explains why Jesus, as an adult, upbraided the priests of the temple at Jerusalem, calling them "[b]lind guides, who strain at a gnat and swallow a camel! . . . Woe to you, scribes and Pharisees, hypocrites! For you are like white-washed tombs which indeed appear beautiful outwardly, but inside are full of dead men's bones and all uncleanness. Even so you also outwardly appear righteous to men, but inside you are full of hypocrisy and lawlessness" (Matthew 23:24, 27–28).

The second temple that figures largely in the story of the Holy Family's stay in Egypt belonged to the Therapeutae, the Egyptian branch of the Great White Brotherhood. It is likely, in fact, that the Holy Family spent much of its stay in Egypt with this order. Although the Therapeutae had centers in many parts of the ancient world, including Greece, Britain, Damascus, Galilee, Persia, the Himalayas, and among the masters of the Far East, its main academy lay in mighty Egypt, the motherland of the world.[5] Because the city of Alexandria was the great intellectual and spiritual center of its time, it is not surprising that this mysterious order chose to have a visible presence there.

The word *Therapeutae* means "physicians of souls" and reminds us of our modern word "therapy." These wise light workers were committed to a life of spiritual devotion, and they brought healing to those they touched. Philo Judaeus, the famous Jewish philosopher and historian who lived in Alexandria at the time of Jesus, writes that the Therapeutae were ancient even in his time. While the Essenes were primarily confined to Palestine, the Therapeutae were known in many parts of the world, but were especially prominent in Egypt.[6] Their headquarters lay on the shores of Lake Mareotis, an artificial lake 360 miles in circumference that lay outside the city of Alexandria. Lake Mareotis, the most westerly of the lakes in the Nile delta, was a place where the Mysteries of Osiris had been celebrated for hundreds of years.[7]

Our knowledge of the mysterious Therapeutae comes almost entirely from the historian Philo, who spent most of his life in Alexandria. He claimed to be a high initiate of the Mysteries of Moses, which, he tells us, resembled what we now call the pagan Mysteries. This connection means that Philo was more than likely a member of the Zadokite line, which followed the true teachings of Moses. Philo compares the community of the Therapeutae to the followers of Dionysus, the Greek version of Osiris, describing them as an order that became the template for all later Christian monasteries.[8]

Timothy Freke and Peter Gandy tell us that the Therapeutae were actually Jewish Pythagoreans, learned in hermetic and spiritual wisdom. Like the initiates of all the ancient Mystery Schools, they believed that the ancient myths held encoded secrets to deeper mystical truths. The fourth-century Christian father Eusebius was so struck by the likeness of the Therapeutae to the early Christian monks that he actually claimed they were Christians who had been converted by the apostle Mark, even though the Therapeutae had existed centuries before Jesus was born.

When aspirants joined the Therapeutae order, they were said to "die" to the outside world. They voluntarily gave up their property to their heirs so that all things in the community were owned in common. This was also true of the Essene communities, and later of the Knights Templar and the Cathars of France, who brought all their possessions into the order as part of the common wealth.

The Therapeutae believed that, behind the many faces of the gods and goddesses, there was a single God, the architect of the universe. They welcomed both men and women into their order and lived together in communities where initiates occupied houses clustered around a central lodge that represented the Sun, a visible symbol for the light of knowledge. This gave each initiate a sense of both seclusion and community. They met together for meals and for fellowship and ritual, but most of their daylight hours were spent in solitary occupations like writing, contemplation, study, or worship.

We are just beginning to uncover the many links between the Essenes, the early Gnostic Christians, and the far more ancient order of the Therapeutae, all of which are connected through the Great White Brotherhood. Some believe that this deep hermetic order originated with the Egyptian god Thoth, also known as the Greek god Hermes. One of Thoth's lesser-known names was Theutates, and it is from the name Hermes that we get the modern words "hermit" and "hermitage."[9] These devoted men and women became models for later Christian nuns and monks. Like the more secluded and ascetic factions of the Essenes in Palestine and the hillside hermits of the Druids in Britain, the Therapeutae were deeply devoted to lives of quiet study and prayer. These devoted men and women became models for later Christian nuns and monks. They were not given to painful ascetic practices, but rather cultivated laughter and optimism, and enjoyed simple luxuries.[10] Like their brothers and sisters in other Great White Brotherhood communities, they dressed primarily in white, prayed to the Creator at sunrise and sunset, and practiced a life of dedicated simplicity. They studied the teachings of Pythagoras and encoded their truths in deep mystic rites and parables. Philo writes of them: "They assembled together with glad faces and in white garments, and the proceedings were begun with prayers, in which they stood and stretched their eyes and hands to heaven."[11]

Philo placed the origin of the Therapeutae in Jewish Hellenism. Others agree:

> The name, "Therapeutae," was a Greek cultic term for worshippers . . .
> of an Hellenistic Egyptian god, Serapis. An association of this god, on an
> inscription in Delos, calls its members Therapeutae. . . . Eusebius, in the
> fourth century A.D., concurred, regarding Philo's book as referring to a
> Christian order, and it certainly influenced Christianity.[12]

Yet there are others who believe this sect to be far older than the Jewish religion. Manly P. Hall writes: "Even in Philo's day the cult seems to have been considered ancient, and some historians think it to be the same as the school of Egyptian scientist-philosophers mentioned by Strabo and which Plato and Eudoxus are said to have consulted."[13]

Philo tells us of a most curious tradition among the mysterious order:

> They are accustomed to pray twice a day, at morning and at evening.
> When the sun is rising, entreating God that the happiness of the coming
> day may be real happiness, so that their minds may be filled with heav-
> enly light. And when the sun is setting they pray that their soul, being
> entirely lightened and relieved of the burden of the outward senses, and
> of the appropriate object of these outward senses, may be able to trace
> out trust existing in its own consistory and council chamber.[14]

This ritual of gazing at the Sun in the first and last hours of the day was
practiced in virtually every chapter of the Great White Brotherhood, and it was
certainly practiced among the Essenes, the Therapeutae's spiritual brothers. In
the Essene Manual of Discipline, found among the Dead Sea Scrolls, we read:
"With the coming of day I embrace my Mother, with the coming of night I join
my Father, and with the outgoing of evening and morning I will breathe Their
Law, and I will not interrupt these Communions until the end of time." Likewise, in the Essene Gospel of Peace we read:

> The first Communion is with the Angel of the Sun, She who cometh
> each morning as a bride from her chamber, to shed her golden light on
> the world. Oh thou immortal, shining, swift-steeded. . . . There is no life
> without thee. . . . Through thee is opened the flower in the center of my
> body. Therefore will I never hide myself from thee. . . . Enter the holy
> temple within me and give me the Fire of Life![15]

WORSHIP OF THE SUN

This veneration of the Sun appears in all the ancient Mystery Schools and is
depicted in countless paintings, sculptures, stained-glass windows, and icons.
As an emblem of illumination and light, the Sun was recognized as the most
visible center of the universe, the outward symbol of the invisible Creator God.
This principle was expressed by the Greek Helios, the Incan Inti, the Aztec To-
natiuh, the Celtic Lugh, the Indian Surya, and the Mayan Hunab Ku. As a symbol of beauty, truth, and immortality, the Sun was personified in the Egyptian
gods Ra, Horus, and Osiris, each identified as "falcons of the horizon." Thus, the
glyph of the all-seeing eye of Horus bespoke the solar nature of these beings
whose light illuminated the world.

The Sun established itself as "the most perfect symbol of the ineffable First
Cause," observes David Fideler, author of the superb book *Jesus Christ, Sun of*

God. Philo described God as "the Sun of the sun, the intelligible object behind the object comprehensible by sense," while Plato observed that "The Sun's body can be seen by any man, but his soul by no man."[16] Two hundred years into the Christian era, the neo-Platonic philosopher Plotinus (205–270 C.E.) still echoes these thoughts: "No eye ever saw the Sun without becoming sun-like, nor can a soul see beauty without becoming beautiful. You must become first all-godlike and all-beautiful if you intend to see God and beauty."[17]

And thus we come to the presence of the Sun in Jesus' teachings.

CHAPTER 8

The Sun and the Power of Twelve

Be Thou praised, oh Lord, for all Thy creation,
More especially for our Brother the Sun, who bringeth forth the day.
Thou givest light thereby, for he is glorious and splendid in his radiance
    to Thee....[1]

—Saint Francis of Assisi, *Hymn of the Sun*

The Sun, which was connected with the concept of an ultimate divinity of illumination thousands of years before Jesus was born, was also woven into the earliest Mysteries of Christianity. Symbols of this occult wisdom were inscribed by the early church fathers into the innermost sanctuaries of the Vatican as promises of enlightenment. Historian Norman H. Baynes reports: "It was to the rising sun that Christians alike in East and West turned in prayer, whether in congregational worship or in private devotion."[2] And Clement of Alexandria wrote of "the Sun of the soul...; through Him alone, when He has risen within the depth of the mind, the soul's eye is illuminated."[3]

Christian iconography teaches that Jesus passed from the cross of suffering to the cross of glory, which is depicted with the Sun's rays radiating from its center. Priests proclaim a "celestial radiancy," as they light the Paschal Taper and, during the Eucharist, the wafer representing the holy host is placed in a monstrance created in the likeness of a Sun. The early church father Origen even taught that the Sun, Moon, and stars worshipped Christ, and that he died for them as well as for mankind: "He did not die on behalf of men only, but on behalf of all other rational beings...such as the stars."[4]

Almost from the beginning, Christian liturgy has symbolized Jesus as the son, or Sun, or "son of the Sun." The choice of Sunday as the Christian Sabbath, for example, was not accidental; it was the day dedicated to the Sun in the ancient world. Many early Christian customs—the Yule log and the fiery pudding of the English Christmas, the crown of candles of the Swedish Saint Lucia festival, and the lighted Christmas tree of many cultures—invoked the concept of *Sol Invictus*, or unconquered Sun, and underscored the theme of returning light to a time of darkness.[5]

Today, a walk through the exquisite rooms of the Vatican tells us that the Sun is still a central symbol of Christianity. In the center of the dome of Saint Peter's Basilica, images of the Sun and Moon are inscribed into the vault of the heavens, surrounded by a canopy of stars. And in the sanctuary below the dome, at the high altar of Saint Peter himself, behind the canopied dais of the Triumph of the Chair that is its central focus, is a glorious Sun through which the Holy Spirit of the dove descends.[6] At the center of Saint Peter's Square stands a 150-foot obelisk, a symbol associated with the Sun and connected with the phoenix and the Tree of Life. And in the middle of the Piazza del Campidoglio is a large motif of a twelve-pointed Sun, a clear representation of the twelve signs of the zodiac, with the Sun at its center.[7] Jacquette Hawkes, in his book *Man and the Sun*, describes the earliest known Christian mosaic, which shows "Christ as [the] Sun driving a chariot with a flying cloak and rayed nimbus behind his head."[8]

The Sun, as the most powerful source of light in our world, was also a hermetic symbol for the spiritual power of light itself. Without the Sun, our entire universe would be in darkness. Psychologist Carl Jung writes that the Sun, ". . . . is the truly 'rational' image of God, whether we adopt the standpoint of the primitive savage or of modern science. In either case, [it is] the Father-God from whom all living things draw life . . . the creator, the source of energy into our world. . . . Therefore the sun is perfectly suited to represent the visible God of this world, i.e., the creative power of our own soul. . . ."[9]

David Fideler presents a different perspective: "Like God," he notes, "the sun eternally gives forth from itself without ever being diminished, thus establishing itself as the most perfect symbol of the ineffable First Cause. Yet . . . among the learned, the sun itself was never taken to represent the First Cause, and was merely seen as its image and manifestation on a lower level of being, within the confines of space and time."[10] Mathematical cosmologist Brian Swimme agrees, explaining in clear scientific terms how the daily sacrifice of

Figure 29. The Piazza del Campidoglio (Capitol Square) was designed by Michelangelo as a courtyard in the Vatican. When seen from above, we see the twelve rays of light at the center of the Sun, surrounded by the web of the universe.

the Sun, which transforms four million tons of itself into light every second, could be used as an accurate symbol for the sacrifice of Christ:

> In the case of the Sun, we have a new understanding of the cosmological meaning of sacrifice. The Sun is, with each second, giving itself over to become energy that we, with every meal, partake of. We so rarely reflect on this basic truth from biology, and yet its spiritual significance is supreme. The Sun converts itself into a flow of energy that photosynthesis changes into plants that are consumed by animals. So for four million years, humans have been feasting on the Sun's energy stored in the form of wheat or maize or reindeer as each day the Sun dies as Sun and is reborn as the vitality of Earth. . . . In the cosmology of the new millennium the Sun's extravagant bestowal of energy can be regarded as a spectacular manifestation of an underlying impulse pervading the universe.[11]

The Sun and the Great White Brotherhood

The Therapeutae and the initiates of the ancient Mystery Schools knew that the Sun exuded luminous frequencies that could open their minds and hearts to the higher worlds. The Egyptians believed that "in the red glow of twilight which precedes the dawn," the gates of the afterlife realm swung open.[12] Thus, they used the art of Sun-gazing to link themselves with the heavenly realms and attain gnosis, or inner knowing. They believed that, by standing on the earth barefooted and gazing at the Sun for only five or ten seconds at sunrise and sunset, they could receive its life-giving illumination.

Scholars speculate that Sun-gazing began with the so-called heretic pharaoh of the Eighteenth Dynasty, Akhenaton. Certainly images from Akhenaton's reign (believed to be from 1353 to 1336 B.C.E.) reveal his long and abiding adoration of the Sun. These images often show the pharaoh with his wife, Nefertiti, drawing life energy from the Sun's rays. Students of Freemasonry will recognize the small hands at the end of the sunbeams in these images as the "Paws of the Lion," which raise all things to life.[13] Like the symbols of the lion and the heart, the Sun was a key emblem in Christianity as well as in the teachings of the ancients. At the core of the pagan philosophies was the concept of the universal savior god who came from the heavenly realms to lift the souls of regenerated men to heaven through his own nature—an idea very much like the belief that Jesus lifts us into the light.

Akhenaton, like Moses and later Jesus, was trained by the priests of Heliopolis, a spiritual sanctuary known in the Bible as the city of On.[14] His decision

Figure 30. Akhenaton, referred to as "the Heretic King," attempted to cut through the many facets of the divine, epitomized by the gods and goddesses, to elevate the one God behind the many. His attempt caused great political ripples within the kingdom, and destabilized the existing hierarchy of the temples. Here Akhenaton and Nefertari are Sun-gazing, receiving the life-giving energies of the Sun. Illustrated by Sylvia Laurens.

to devote himself to the "one God," Aten, who was an aspect of the wise or setting Sun, would thus have grown out of his knowledge of the centuries-old teachings of that priesthood. In an effort to bring simplicity to the complex teachings of Egypt for the common man, Akhenaton turned to the "Great and living Aten . . . our father . . . our reminder of eternity, our witness of what is eternal; who is established in rising and setting each day ceaselessly. Whether he is in heaven, or on earth, every eye beholds him without hindrance, whilst he fills the land with his rays and enables everyone to live."[15]

Like followers of many other spiritual traditions, Akhenaton revered the Sun as the spiritual center of the world. He believed that it was through the Sun's life-giving rays that physical life existed—a belief now seconded by modern science. "How much Akhenaton understood," Egyptologist Flinders Petre notes, "we cannot say, but he had certainly bounded forward in his views and symbolism to a position, which we cannot logically improve upon at the present day."[16]

The concept of the trinity may have also originated with the Sun, grounded in its daily pattern of sunrise, high noon, and sunset. The Egyptians, in fact, gave the sun three different names: at dawn, it was Khepri, the new Sun, the scarab beetle that pushes the solar disc across the sky; at noon, it was Ra or Ra-Horakhty, the victorious Sun; at sunset, it was Aten, the wise or learned Sun that reveals its wisdom only to the sages. Manly P. Hall carries this over into Christian symbology:

> God, the Father, the Creator of the world, is symbolized by the dawn. His color is blue, because the sun rising in the morning is veiled blue mist. God the Son, the Illuminating One sent to bear witness to His Father before all worlds, is the celestial globe at noonday, radiant and magnificent, the maned Lion of Judah, the Golden haired Savior of the World. Yellow is His color and His power is without end. God the Holy Ghost, is the sunset phase when the orb of day, robed in flaming red, rests for a moment upon the horizon line and then vanishes into the darkness of the night to wander in the lower worlds and later rise again triumphant from the embrace of darkness.[17]

JESUS, THE SUN, AND THE POWER OF TWELVE

"It was while Akhenaton was Pharaoh," H. Spencer Lewis tells us, "that the children of Israel dwelt in Egypt and the leaders of those tribes became initiates of the Great White Brotherhood. It was at this time that Moses, as one of the initiates, became acquainted with the fundamentals of the religion, which he afterward modified to present to those who followed him out of Egypt into Palestine." Manetho, the Egyptian high priest and historian of Heliopolis from the third century B.C.E., lends support to this account with his own well-preserved records, which reveal that Moses was, in fact, a student of Heliopolis, one of the centers of the Great White Brotherhood where Jesus also studied. "When Jesus was ready for his entrance into the supreme college and monastery of the Brotherhood at Heliopolis," Lewis tells us, " . . . the records show that he was surrounded, as we have stated, with every comfort and convenience, and that for his study he was given many of the rarest manuscripts containing the texts of ancient doctrines and creeds."[18]

Jesus clearly identified himself with the spiritual light of the Sun, and the Sun was intrinsic to the devotions and communions of the Essenes. In fact, in *The Essene Gospel of Peace*, Jesus himself tells us: "Thou shalt seek the Angel of the Sun, and enter into that embrace which doth purify with holy flames."[19] In the traditional canons of the New Testament, Jesus declares: "I have come as a light into the world, that whoever believes in Me should not abide in darkness"

(John 12:47). "I am the light of the world," he claims. "He who follows me shall not walk in darkness, but have the light of life" (John 8:12). Jesus repeated this connection between himself and the Sun throughout his ministry in order to make clear who he was and from whence he came. While Jesus was undoubtedly talking about the radiant, divine spark of life that exists within every living thing—a spark that comes from the power of God—he chose to invoke the physical symbol of the Sun as a metaphor for this light. Furthermore, his gathering of twelve disciples reveals his knowledge of the ancient solar and stellar theology—the twelve constellations of the zodiac that circle the central point of the Sun.

The number twelve is intrinsic to the geometry of the universe. Scholars of ley lines claim that the Earth itself is put together like a giant dodecahedron, a twelve-sided sphere. Twelve celestial gods ruled the heavens in the Greek, Roman, and Mesopotamian worlds. "The ancient philosophers understood the structure of number to be analogous with the structure of creation," writes British symbologist John Michell, "and they realized also that number is basically duodecimal, being naturally governed by the number twelve." Michell goes on to say:

> The number 12 . . . is the symbol of the Universe and the measure of tone. In expressing myself thus, I speak simply as the interpreter of the ancient philosophers and modern theosophers . . . [this] is a scientific and sacred dogma accepted among all nations from the north of Europe to the most eastern parts of Asia. Pythagoras, Timaeus of Locris, Plato, in giving the dodecahedron as a symbol for the Universe, were expounding the ideas of the Egyptians, the Chaldeans, and the Greeks. [20]

The number twelve is embedded deep in our consciousness. The Hebrews acknowledged twelve tribes; we mark our lives through the twelve months of the year and the twelve hours of the day and night. In the human body, there are twelve cranial nerves and twelve energy meridians. There are twelve elemental letters in the *Sefer Yetzirah*, the Hebrew book of esotericism.[21] Knowledge of the sacred Sun and the iconic significance of twelve was passed on within the ancient Mystery Schools, and within the Great White Brotherhood in particular. In the shorthand language of hermetics, certain symbols came to represent this solar power: the color gold, the lion, leopard, and puma, and the astrological sign of Leo—all emblems of Jesus.

The Sun was woven into the deepest fabric of the Mystery traditions as the most visible symbol of the divine, and was honored by scholars, philosophers, and thinkers the world over. Emperor Julian I (331–363 C.E.), the last of the great philosopher-mystics of the late Roman Empire, writes of a solar trinity that echoes the symbology found in Egyptian lore: "The Threefold Sun represents the transcendental Source of all good that dispenses beauty, existence, perfection and oneness."[22] The first Sun was God, the invisible power behind it all. The second Sun was Helios, a solar power expressed by the solar lords Mithra and Jesus that rules the gods and goddesses of the many planes. The third Sun was the visible disc we see in the sky each day.[23] Later, this concept of the three-fold Sun was expressed in Christian mysticism as the tri-fold flame found within the Christed heart.

Jesus would have been trained in these teachings by the Essenes and the Therapeutae, and by the Great White Brotherhood itself. And he would have shared these teachings with his disciples. We see clues to this in the Christian community set up by Joseph of Arimathea in Britain. Joseph, Jesus' uncle and disciple, chose to inscribe this same celestial geometry into the design of his community at Avalon. This early "church" consisted of twelve circular thatch-and-wattle huts built around a central temple, duplicating the geometry of the zodiac and placing Jesus, as the Sun, at the center. Later, this same symbology appears in the mosaic floor of Saint Mary's Chapel at Glastonbury Abbey. We know from excavations of the abbey grounds that the diameter of each of these huts was exactly 21.6 feet, the overall structure thus yielding a miniature version of the great 2160-year celestial cycle that marks each astrological age in the 26,000-year precession of the equinoxes.

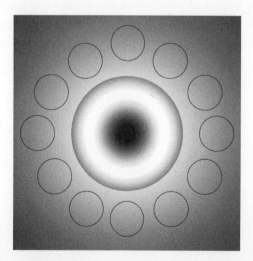

FIGURE 31. The symbology of the twelve around the One represents the twelve signs of the Zodiac around the Sun. It is seen in Jesus' twelve apostles, and in the twelve tribes of Israel. Joseph of Arimathea also used it in the formation of the first Christian community in Britain in 37 C.E.

In hermetic terms, Joseph was revealing that Jesus—like Mithra, Ra, Horus/Apollo, and other world saviors—represented the Sun itself. He was identifying Jesus as a direct incarnation of celestial light. This hermetic symbology clearly links the teachings of Jesus with those of the ancient Mystery Schools and a long line of spiritual initiates who preceded him by thousands of years.[24]

Moreover, as the central figure around which the twelve revolved, Jesus marks himself as the thirteenth—the center of the light. The number thirteen has always been associated with the Divine Mother—the Goddess, the Earth Mother, the Virgin of the World, the Turtle Woman upon whom human existence depends. All turtle shells are divided into thirteen segments, thus the turtle was used in the Mysteries to represent the Earth. This number also links Jesus with the lunar cycle, for there are thirteen twenty-eight-day lunar cycles in every year; thus the Essenes divided their year into thirteen equal cycles.[25] This link between Jesus and the lunar cycles is yet another link to the god of wisdom, Thoth, whose symbol was the Moon.

By deliberately establishing a connection between himself and the numbers twelve and thirteen, Jesus reveals to all initiates who know the language of hermetics that he encompassed both the radiance of the Sun and the wisdom of the Moon, merging male and female energies in a perfect androgynous balance. These core teachings are shared in the Gnostic Gospel of Thomas, in which Jesus tells us that, by merging and balancing our male and female aspects, we may gain the power to enter the kingdom of heaven.

Later, this same solar symbology emerged in the early Christian Church. Clement of Alexandria proclaimed Jesus to be "Christ the True Sun." Origen and Cyprian, both initiates of the ancient Mystery Schools, echoed these sentiments.[26] Bishops like Zeno of Verona elaborated at great length on "Christ as the Eternal Sun." The depth and breadth of Jesus as a great solar lord will become increasingly apparent as we move further into our story and the teachings of the Great White Brotherhood.

CHAPTER 9

The Infancy Gospels

So that is what I remember. And his eyes looking at you, like great pools of love, understanding and forgiving all you may have done. All your weaknesses were somehow forgiven, as if he were your best friend who understood all about you. Ah, wonderful eyes, yes.[1]

—Joseph, from Stuart Wilson and Joanna Prentis,
The Essenes: Children of the Light

Biblical scholars tell us that, in the early centuries of Christianity, there was a deep hunger for information about Jesus' early years and the years after he returned to Judea. The Infancy Gospels, a collection of accounts supplied by the early Church in the second century C.E., were an attempt to satisfy that hunger. Whether they are factual accounts of those years or merely allegories, the Infancy Gospels reflect the belief that Jesus embodied redemption and healing. While none of them was accepted into the New Testament canon, these stories have remained popular for nearly 1800 years.

There are five Infancy Gospels. The Gospel of the Infancy of Jesus Christ is the longest of the group. Widely influential in the early centuries of the church, this gospel is believed to have been used by Mohammed in compiling the Koran.[2] It was also the only Infancy Gospel honored by the early Christian Nestorians.

The Protevangelium of Jacobi, also known as The Infancy Gospel of James, is generally attributed to Jesus' younger brother James (Jacob). Since this gospel was not written until 150 C.E., however, James cannot possibly be the author. Moreover, scholars generally agree that it was written by a gentile, rather than a Jew, for it makes no references to either Passover or any Jewish customs. The gospel is, however, a beautiful, poetic telling of the story of Mary's birth, childhood, and betrothal to Joseph, of their journey to Bethlehem accompanied by Joseph's sons, and of Jesus' birth in the cave.[3] The gospel ends as Jesus' cousin John (the Baptist) and John's mother, Elizabeth, flee to the mountains for safety, and the soldiers of Herod slay John's father, Zacharias, for not revealing the whereabouts of his son. This gospel was the inspiration for much of the early Christian imagery of Mary during the Middle Ages.

The Infancy Gospel of Thomas, which has nothing to do with the apostle Thomas, but is rather attributed to Thomas the Israelite, was extremely popular in the first centuries after Christ and has been translated into many languages. It is thought to have been written in Greek around 150 C.E. and appears in the writings of the early Christian father Irenaeus around 185 C.E. Biblical scholar Willis Barnstone writes: "For modern apologists, the work is an ethical embarrassment, for the little Jesus is not only a child prodigy but a child terror, performing nasty miracles. The author was probably Gentile, since the work betrays no knowledge of Judaism."[4] Manly P. Hall tells us that, "like many other early sacred books, the Book of Thomas was fabricated for two closely allied purposes: first, to outshine the pagans in miracle working; second, to inspire all unbelievers with the 'fear of the Lord.'"[5] It covers the period between Jesus' birth and his appearance in the temple at age twelve. For me, it is one of the most intriguing accounts, for it tells the stories of Jesus' use and misuse of power.

The Gospel of Pseudo-Matthew, also known as The Infancy Gospel of Matthew, was originally named The Birth of Mary and Infancy of the Savior. Scholars believe this work to be a fabrication created by the church in the eighth or ninth centuries. This gospel is another retelling of young Mary's virginal pregnancy and is the first gospel to claim Jesus was worshipped in a manger by a donkey and an ox. Then, as if to fulfill Old Testament prophecy, Jesus goes on to charm lions, leopards, wolves, and dragons who come to honor him.

Finally, there is the Arabic Infancy Gospel, compiled in the sixth century. Drawn from the gospels of Thomas and James, it claims to have come from a much earlier Syrian source. This gospel was translated into Arabic about the time that Christianity began to spread into the Arabian peninsula, and some of its stories are found in the Koran.[6]

Overall, the Infancy Gospels tell the tale of a brilliant, Magical child with many uncanny gifts—a child known for curing the sick and raising the dead, speaking in full sentences from the day of his birth, and driving out demons

FIGURE 32. Jesus holding a dove as a young boy around eight. Illustrated by Sylvia Laurens.

that looked like serpents and snakes, creatures feared by the later Christian church, but symbolic of more positive concepts to most of the ancient world. Some of the stories found in these gospels contain elements that make them suspect, yet there are nuggets of truth scattered among them. They tell of the gentle Mary and baby Jesus extending themselves to rich and poor alike and being showered with gifts along the way.

MIRACLES AND MAGIC

While there is evidence that, during their four to seven years in Egypt, the Holy Family may have stayed with the Therapeutae in Alexandria, Heliopolis, or Memphis (a city close to Heliopolis), or even with the Jewish community in Bubastis, there are also indications in the apocryphal Infancy Gospels that they traveled. The stories contained there tell of miracles and Magic spread across a number of regions and lands.

There is the story of the priest whose son is afflicted with spirit possession—a problem that appears to have been common in Judea, given the number of exorcisms recorded in the New Testament. The half-crazed boy, who is prone to seizures, pulls the baby Jesus' newly washed swaddling clothes off the clothesline and puts them on his head. Immediately, snakes and crows begin to fly out of his mouth and the boy is cured of his madness.[7]

Another story finds the Holy Family passing through a particularly dangerous area known for its thieves and outlaws, who robbed travelers and then took them captive for ransom. The brigands are lying in wait as the Holy Family approaches, when suddenly they hear the beating of horses' hoofs in the distance and the thunderous sound of an approaching army. The robbers flee in terror, leaving behind not only their loot, but their prisoners.[8] When Joseph and Mary arrive with their family, they free the captives and everyone is saved.

In one account, the Holy Family enters a town just as a wedding is about to start. The young bride is deaf and mute. During the wedding reception, she stretches out her hands to hold the baby Jesus, and suddenly her hearing and speech are restored. In joy, the girl begins to sing praises. Impressed with this amazing healing, the village residents quickly spread word of the miracle

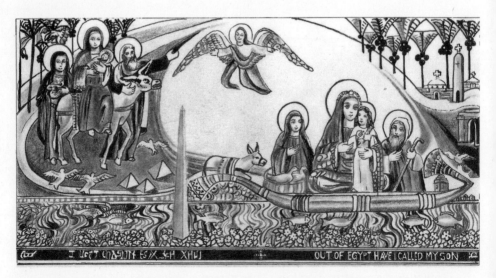

FIGURE 33. The Holy Family in Egypt. The images of the three pyramids, the obelisks, and the Nile alerts us to a location near Heliopolis, twelve miles north of the Great Pyramid complex of Giza. Overhead hovers a protective, guiding angel.

throughout the town and, the next day, another young woman brings a gift of perfumed bathwater to honor the holy child. As she leaves, she happens to sprinkle some of the used bathwater onto a girl who has leprosy. Within days, the girl's leprosy vanishes.[9] The grateful girl offers her services to the Holy Family as a nanny—a strange turn of events, since, with all of Joseph's older children around, young Mary should already have had ample support. Nonethless, the story tells how the girl accompanies them to a city that is home to a great king whose wife is in a sorrowful and mournful condition. The girl asks the princess the reason for her tears, upon which the wife confesses to having born a leprous son by a previous marriage. The child's father disowned him because of his disease and cast the mother out. The girl replies:

> "I have found a remedy for your disease, which I promise you, for I also was leprous, but God hath cleansed me, even he who is called Jesus, the son of the Lady Mary." . . . "But how can this be?" says she. "Where is he?" "Behold," replied the girl, "Joseph and Mary; and the infant who is with them is called Jesus; and it is He who delivered me from my disease and torment."

The next day, the prince's wife takes perfumed water to wash the baby Jesus, then pours the same water on her son, who is instantly cured.

In one tale, the young Mary goes to see a dyer of cloth and takes Jesus with her. While the adults are visiting, Jesus wanders into the room where the dye vats are kept. In curiosity, he places all the clothes in the dyers' workroom in the black-dye vessel. When the shopkeeper reenters his shop and sees what Jesus has done, he is furious and demands that Mary pay for all of the clothes. When Mary lectures Jesus, he walks over to the vat and pulls out the clothes—all of which are the same color they were when they went in.[10]

In one odd account, Jesus and some friends are playing on the rooftop of a house when one of the children accidentally falls off and dies. The other boys flee, afraid of being blamed, but Jesus remains. The boy's family come out of the house and see their young son lying dead in the dirt. In their anger and despair, they accuse Jesus of pushing him off the roof. Jesus vehemently denies this accusation, then stands over the dead boy and calls out, "Zeinunus, who threw you down from the housetop?" The dead boy answers, "You did not throw me down, but someone else did." Flabbergasted by the miracle, the family picks up their dead son and goes on their way, apparently not expecting that someone who can make the dead talk can also bring them back to life.

A more serious story tells of a neighbor's child who is bitten by a poison-
ous snake. Seeing the grownups carrying the dead child, Jesus asks them what
has happened. When they explain, Jesus tells them to return the child to the
place of the accident. He calls the serpent out, instructing it to suck all the poison out of the child's wound. According to this account, the snake slithers onto
the child and does as it is told, taking away all its poison. Jesus then touches the
child and immediately restores the boy to health. As the boy begins to cry, Jesus
comforts him and says, "Cease crying, for hereafter thou shalt be my disciple."
The child is said to have become Simon the Canaanite.[11]

One last example tells how Joseph, Jesus' father, is commissioned to build a
new wooden throne for a local king. Joseph works on this project for two long
years and, when it is time to install the throne, Jesus accompanies him to the
palace. When they arrive, Joseph realizes that the throne is not large enough for
the king. The king is angry. When Jesus asks his father what is wrong, Joseph
replies, "I am afraid that I have lost my labor in the work which I have been
about these two years." Jesus reassures Joseph and tells him to grasp one side of
the throne, then himself grasps the other. They each pull and the throne seems
to grow beneath their hands, adjusting itself to the proper size. Everyone is
astonished.[12]

POLITICS AND PROPAGANDA

While many of the stories in the Infancy Gospels bring hope and Magic to
the heart, some of them seem to serve a more manipulative function for the
church. Two such stories have been repeated down through the centuries. The
first concerns two sisters who, on the death of their father, decided to marry
their only brother off to a suitable wife. But the brother has been cursed by
a jealous woman and transformed into a mule. The sisters are in a dreadful
predicament, because their brother controls the family's resources. Rachael,
the young traveling companion and maid-servant of the Holy Family, sees the
women weeping and asks what saddens them. When they explain their problem, Rachel replies: "Take courage and cease your fears, for you have a remedy
for your afflictions near at hand, even among you in the midst of your house
. . . " She then appeals to young Mary for help. Mary places Jesus on the mule's
back, and the mule immediately turns back into a human. The sisters celebrate
their brother's transformation and decide that Rachel should be his wife.[13]

There are a number of points to consider in this rather strange and unlikely account. The text refers to "the Lady Saint Mary," instead of simply Mary.

Since "saints" did not exist in early Christianity, but were created only later by the Catholic Church, these references indicate that this text was written several centuries after Jesus' time. In addition, Mary calls her young son "My Lord Jesus Christ," another unlikely turn of phrase for someone writing in the early years of the faith. And finally, the whole story seems to be a clumsy retelling of the famous story of the Golden Ass with a Christian twist.

Lucius Apuleius wrote *The Golden Ass* between 150 to 170 C.E., only about thirty years before the Infancy Gospels were written. An immensely popular story throughout the ancient world, it was based on an even older Greek tale dedicated to Isis. It tells the story of Lucius, who is turned into a donkey by an incompetent Magician girlfriend. Before she can turn him back, Lucius the donkey is stolen by bandits. After a series of hilarious mishaps, Lucius is redeemed by the goddess Isis. In gratitude, he devotes himself to her Mysteries.

For anyone familiar with the Mystery traditions, this tale is an allegory of the soul's descent into the world of folly and its redemption through the transformative power of love. The Sufis use this same symbolism, comparing the ego to a stubborn donkey. Yet the story of Jesus and the mule claims the sisters could get no help from any other "Magicians or wise men," and that only Jesus could redeem the brother—a clear implication that there are no other paths to salvation, a message the church would most certainly have endorsed.

A story from the Protoevangelium of Jacobi relates how a statue falls as the Holy Family passes through an Egyptian town. The statue allegedly declares: "The unknown God is come hither, who is truly God; nor is there anyone besides him who is worthy of divine worship; for he is truly the Son of God. At the fame of him this country trembled, and at his coming . . . we ourselves are affrighted by the greatness of his power." This is a clear example of the church advancing a political agenda under the guise of religious truth. While it is certainly possible that some kind of seismic event caused a statue to topple, the story goes on to claim, "the idol was broken, and all the gods fell down and (were) destroyed by a greater power. Then was fulfilled the prophecy which saith, 'Out of Egypt I have called my son.'"[14] This passage clearly brands the tale as an allegorical version of "my god is bigger than your god."

Since the Infancy Gospels were not written until 200 years or more after Jesus' death, it is likely that many of them were created by the church to support their attempts to "topple the competition." Jesus tells us: "I did not come to judge the world, but to save the world" (John 12:47). In The Essene Gospel of Peace, he says: "In the Garden of the Brotherhood, each shall follow his own path, and each shall commune with his own heart. For in the infinite Garden there are many and diverse flowers. . . ."[15] But that was clearly a message that the church could not endorse.

The Infancy Gospel of Thomas, which may be more authentic than that of James, contains stories that portray the young Jesus misusing his power and describe the difficulties this created for his family. In one, Jesus is playing with some Hebrew boys by a running stream just after it has rained. He makes the water go into little lakes and puddles "by word alone," completely clears it of mud so that it sparkles, and takes some soft clay from the bank and forms twelve sculptured sparrows. A passing Jewish elder, frowning on these creative activities because it is the Sabbath, goes to tell Jesus' parents. Joseph asks the child, "Why do you do on the Sabbath what it is not lawful to do?" Jesus claps his hands and cries to the sparrows, "Be gone." And the sparrows fly off chirping. The Jew is amazed and goes to tell the leaders of the temple what he has seen.[16]

This story has a moral aspect to it, seeming to say that the power of the divine is unlimited beside the more repressive "laws" of man. The old Jewish man represents the "old law of limitation," while Jesus represents the new law—that through the power of love, we can create life around us. It goes on to relate how Jesus reacts in anger to another boy who destroys the arrangement Jesus has made of the waters: "[W]hat did the pools and the water do to harm you? Behold you shall also wither as a tree, and shalt not bear leaves or roots or fruit." And immediately the boy becomes withered and shriveled.[17] His parents bear him away, bemoaning his lost youth and reproaching Joseph: "What kind of child do you have who does such things?" Prompted by his father, Jesus restores the child, leaving only a small part of him withered to remind him of his actions.

This story is followed by another that tells of Jesus striking a child dead for accidentally bumping into him. The parents of the dead boy go to Joseph and demand that he and his family leave the village. Joseph confronts Jesus and asks him why he does such things. Jesus responds by immediately blinding the offending villagers. "Those who saw were very frightened and puzzled, and they said about him, 'Every word he speaks, whether good or evil, happens and is a miracle.'"[18]

These stories present a poignantly human picture of Jesus as a child. While the idea that Jesus, as a child, could respond in anger is not what we have come to expect of him as an adult, it is entirely within reason that he may have been frustrated by the callous nature of other children. We all recall the casual cruelty of those early years when bullies ran amuck. Would any of us not have wished to have such power in a moment of anger? Perhaps if we can believe in the honorable, God-like nature of Jesus, we can also accept his human nature—

the nature of a child struggling to use his gifts wisely, to walk the middle path that leads to peace. The fact that Jesus came to master such power and to teach the path of forgiveness to those around him is perhaps the true miracle.

While we may never know whether any of these tales have any basis in truth, they still give us insight into the times in which they were written. They provide a window into the expectations of a populace that saw Jesus, not so much as a man, but as a mythic figure who could wish away any problem. "No great figure has ever appeared in history without an abundance of myths and stories growing up around them," observes Dr. Frank Crane, "It is impossible that a man representing so great a force as Jesus of Nazareth should have appeared in the world without finding many echoes of His personality in contemporary literature."[19] At the end of the day, each reader must decide for him or herself what to believe about these tales.

CHAPTER 10

The School of the Prophets

> It was such a joy to listen to him. . . . It was as if he had stepped out of his own focus into the Light of the Spirit, and from that focus all was simple, all things so clear. Ah, yes, many a learned teacher almost despaired after hearing him, wondering how he could ever reach that level.[1]
>
> —Stuart Wilson and Joanna Prentis, *The Essenes: Children of the Light*

The Gospel of Luke tells us that, by the age of twelve, Jesus was safely back in Galilee with his family. We learn in this gospel of the Holy family's visit to Jerusalem. Joseph was commanded to bring Jesus to the temple for a review before the priests—perhaps an early version of the bar mitzvahs of today, in which young men are tested on their knowledge of the faith at around the age of thirteen. This occurred at the time of Passover, a seven- or eight-day festival of celebrations and religious services that included the annual examination of the coming generation's knowledge of the scripture. The biblical accounts tell us that the Holy Family stayed only a few days in Jerusalem, then traveled north with a caravan of families without realizing that Jesus had stayed behind. Mary and Joseph return to Jerusalem to find Jesus at the temple in conversation with the high priests, who are deeply impressed by the depth of the boy's knowledge.

I have always been curious about what may have transpired during this conversation in the temple that could have impressed these learned men so profoundly. The following excerpt from Robert Siblerud's *The Unknown Life of Jesus* draws from at least five different apocryphal sources to help fill in the details:

All that heard Jesus were astonished at His understanding and His answers. A certain astronomer was present at the gathering and asked Jesus whether He studied astronomy. Jesus responded by telling him the number of heavenly bodies, and the trines, squares, and sextile aspects of the planets. Jesus told him about the progressions and retrograde motion of planets, their size and several prognostications associated with them . . . . Jesus also talked about philosophy, physics, and metaphysics to the elders. He explained the principles of the physical body and how the soul operated within it. A philosopher arose saying, "Oh Lord Jesus, from henceforth I will be your disciple and servant."[2]

Now this exchange, which is quite astonishing considering that Jesus is only twelve years old at the time, clearly reveals that he had already received an extensive education that included an advanced knowledge of astrology, astronomy, physics, physiology, history, philosophy, and metaphysics. While Jesus may have been a profoundly enlightened person, or even a divine being, his mind and body still had to be educated, just as geniuses like Mozart or da Vinci, who "received" their symphonies or visions at early ages, still had to learn how to play the piano or paint. Somehow, at the early age of twelve, Jesus had already acquired a thorough knowledge of the Jewish scriptures, as well as the cosmological and earth sciences. Indeed, it appears that his training exceeded even that of the temple priests.

Where had Jesus received this knowledge? There are three possibilities: in Egypt, in Britain, or from the Essenes. This means that he would have been taught by the Therapeutae, the Druids, or the Essenes—or perhaps by all three.

THE MYSTICAL ESSENES OF PALESTINE

If the Holy Family lived with the Therapeutae of Egypt for a time, Jesus was more than likely exposed to some of these deeper concepts, either formally or informally, at the temple of Heliopolis or in the city of Alexandria. The details of the family's stay in Egypt are not, however, generally known. There are no clear records of when the Holy Family returned to Galilee, although we know it was after Herod's death in 4 B.C.E. The Coptics tell us that they lived in Egypt for only four short years, but the Muslims claim they remained there for seven.[3] Jesus would have been at least four or five if the Holy Family returned to Galilee shortly after Herod's death.[4] But the family may well have taken some time settling their affairs in Egypt before returning home and, as we shall see later, Joseph, Mary, and the young Jesus are known to have visited the British Isles when Jesus was only seven. And historical evidence supports a longer stay by the family in Egypt.

Historians tell us that there were thousands of Jews in Egypt at that time; these Jews had moved there to escape the oppressive tyranny of Roman and Jewish rule in Judea. Even though Egypt was a Roman province, its populace enjoyed religious freedom. In fact, Egypt had always been a haven for all those who thought beyond the confines of orthodox religion. "As far back as the New Kingdom (c. 1567–1080 B.C.), when Egypt commanded a vast empire that included Syria and northern Mesopotamia, Asiatic and Greek gods were worshipped alongside the Egyptian ones . . . and in the city of Memphis, Phoenicians, Syrians and Jews were allowed to build temples to their gods. Egypt has always been an open multi-cultural society," writes Manly P. Hall.[5]

If Jesus did begin his education in the heady cosmopolitan atmosphere of Egypt, what might he have learned? Certainly Egyptian wisdom had included a sophisticated knowledge of mathematics, astronomy, philosophy, and all the esoteric and physical sciences for well over 3000 years, even in the decades of Egypt's waning greatness. Alexandria flourished for another 400 years after Egypt began its decline, not reaching the end of its golden age until the first two centuries after Christ.[6] And even though the Caesars had come to power in Jesus' time, Egypt was still a formidable nation.

We know that the Therapeutae, brothers to the Essenes, lived in Egypt and had centers in Alexandria and Heliopolis, and that the Essenes traveled to Egypt on a regular basis.[7] Prentis and Wilson's past-life regressions give glimpses into the Essene wisdom school based in the teaching library in Alexandria, a place Jesus most likely visited. One of their subjects, an Essene scholar named Daniel whose main base was in Qumran, frequently traveled to other Essene communities both inside and outside of Israel. He describes the library of the Therapeutae community at Lake Mareotis near Alexandria as even larger than the library at Qumran. "[A]ll along the south wall were tables for the scholars to sit at. . . . The other three sides of the building were occupied with shelving, right up to the ceiling. There were special ladders, with broad platforms instead of rungs, so you could stand comfortably at any height . . . The shelves were divided off so that five or six scrolls could be stored in each compartment. All the compartments were labeled and numbered and a central index told you where the scroll you wanted was to be found."[8]

Suddi, the Essene teacher who reported seeing the star over Bethlehem, tells us that Jesus and John the Baptist began their training in Qumran around the age of eight.[9] Children traditionally began school at age seven in Israel; this was also the starting age for the wisdom traditions of Egypt and Greece, who taught their students in cycles of seven years, graduating them from their first levels at around thirteen or fourteen.[10] Suddi describes the initiation for young students who had reached the age of consent within the Essene Order, a ceremony in which they were "cleansed in the waters":

> And it is said that they are washing away their past and from this point they shall start anew. There are different ways of doing it. Some pour the water over and some make them lie down upon the water . . . [they wear] either a robe made out of flax or none at all. It is part of the purification, the stripping bare of the soul.[11]

This passage indicates that the rite of baptism was already known and practiced among the Essenes—giving an insight into the origins of the teachings of John the Baptist.

H. Spencer Lewis describes another aspect of initiation into the wisdom traditions:

> [I]t was considered absolutely necessary for the student of religion or philosophy to journey to the very seat of each of the ancient religions, where he (or she) might have access to copies of the authentic versions of each religion and an opportunity to live among the peoples, thus becoming intimately acquainted with the rituals, rites, and practices of the tenets. Many of the great avatars in the past had journeyed to distant places for this purpose, and it was in this way that knowledge of the various ancient teachings had become universally disseminated.

Lewis also tells us that, after the Magi had traveled to see Jesus at his birth, they journeyed to the monastery at Mount Carmel and left instructions with the heads of the Essene order regarding the instruction that Jesus was to receive. These directives, Lewis says, "were sent by the Supreme Temple at Heliopolis, and instructed that the young avatar was to complete his education by a thorough study of the ancient religions and teachings of the various sects and creeds most influential in the development of civilization."[12] In other words, after his Essene training, Jesus was to become familiar with the higher principles and creeds taught within the Mystery Schools of India, Persia, Britain, and Egypt—chapters of the Great White Brotherhood that the traditional Judaic patriarchy would have called "pagan."

MEETINGS WITH JESUS AND JOHN

When Suddi was living at Qumran, the stronghold of the Essene community, he was directly involved with both Jesus and John. He knew them as children and then, later, as his students. While he never refers to his two prize students by name, he refers to them through their father's names, Benjoseph and Benzacharias (literally "son of Joseph" and "son of Zacharias"), respectively.

Suddi describes Jesus as a calm child with beautiful eyes and sandy-red-blonde hair who looked at you "as if he knew all the secrets of the universe and just gloried in them. . . . It was as if he watched everything . . . to learn of it, to experience all at once." John he describes as very red-headed and "fierce like a lion. He is strong and lets everyone know exactly what he is thinking. They don't have to agree, but they are sure to know his point of view." They are two very different personalities, Suddi tells us. Benzacharias (John) is exuberant and joyful and celebrates life, while Benjoseph (Jesus) is quiet and delights in everything. Jesus "has knowledge . . . [and] a very calm acceptance. ..He knows perhaps what shall be shall be.[13] It is said, Suddi claims, that Jesus "shall spread the word and he shall take the suffering of the world upon his shoulders. And through his suffering we shall be saved." To attain this perfection of the soul and to attain heaven, Suddi tells us, "a man must again be born. This is in some of the prophecies."[14]

Suddi reports that Jesus and John came to him as students when they were eight and remained with him for four or five years, or until the age of thirteen. Before that, he says, Jesus Benjoseph had lived in Egypt and had traveled "far off from there to learn"—that he "went with his uncle to see many places farther away."

Evidence from other past life hypnotherapy sessions corroborate Suddi's information. In one account, Jesus is described as "much better balanced" than most, and exceptional "because he was very quick at getting to the heart of things, but in a very quiet way. . . . He had a great range in his character . . . and sometimes it would seem that he looked right through you, and that could be challenging for some people and make them feel uneasy.[16]

The channeled Essene legal scholar Daniel, who traveled between the Qumran and Hebron communities, describes Jesus thus:

> There was a great clarity, a searching in the eyes, but the love was strong
> and his manner so gentle. He had clear eyes, all-seeing eyes, but much
> love in them and he spoke with great gentleness: great strength and great
> gentleness. It is said that many ones who had been Essenes for many years

and thought they knew what it was to be an Essene, when they encountered Jesus, only then did they begin to realize what it was like to be an Essene to your fingertips.[17]

NAZARETH AND GALILEE

The Essene school at Mount Carmel, where Jesus and John studied as boys, lay close to the little town of Nazareth, a small village in the northwest corner of Palestine. This is where the gospels tell us that Jesus' family settled when they returned to Galilee. In recent years, researchers have questioned whether Nazareth actually existed in Jesus' time, since it does not appear in any scrolls, books, maps, or military records—indeed, does not appear until the fourth century of our common era. There was a small village named en Nazareth in the western part of Galilee and many believe this village was renamed Nazareth by the church to attract pilgrims and lend credibility to scriptural accounts of Christ's life.

The past-life accounts examined by Wilson and Prentis in their book, *The Essenes: Children of the Light,* tell us that the village was surrounded by green pastures and hills and had a spring in the middle called "Mary's well" that was ancient even before Jesus was born.[18] Yet in the decades before the Holy Family settled there, this tiny town was a place of brigands and cutthroats, its reputation giving rise to the adage that "nothing good ever comes from Nazareth." Is it not ironic, and even appropriate, that Jesus would be raised in a town whose very name needed to be redeemed?

It is significant that Jesus' father, Joseph chose to resettle his family in Galilee, an area known to be quite independent in its observance of Jewish rabbinical law. We know that both Jews and gentiles lived there, although most of the settlers were forced to become Jewish around 100 B.C.E. Because it had long been settled by gentiles, Galilee was far more liberal in its approach to spirituality than its more orthodox neighbors. There are even direct references to this in the Bible. Matthew refers to "Galilee of the Gentiles" (Matthew 4:15), as does the Old Testament book of Maccabbees found in the Apocrypha (Maccabbees 5:15). In this account, the ruler of Israel, Judas Maccabaeus, gives his brother Simon 3000 men to rescue the Jews in Galilee. Simon "fought many battles with the 'heathens,'" bringing the Jews safely back into Judea.[19] Afterward, Galilee continued as a nation of gentiles until 103 B.C.E., when Aristobulus, grandson of Simon and first official king of the Maccabee line, forced all those living in Galilee to adopt circumcision and Mosaic Law.

The Gentiles living in Galilee which included the parents of Jesus were Aryans by blood, Gentiles by natural religious classification, mystics by philosophical thought and Jews by forced adoption. In other words the Gentiles of Galilee after 103 B.C.E. were forced to adopt circumcision and respect the Mosaic Law, and in accordance with this, by law all children at a certain age had to accept the Jewish faith in a formal way by appearing at the synagogue for probationary admission to the church.

This passage indicates that Jesus' appearance at the temple at age twelve was required by law. As mystical Essenes, this ceremony would have been of little interest to Mary and Joseph. As advanced souls with rather extensive esoteric training, the competitive posturing of the traditional rabbis would probably not have appealed to them.

As Essenes and ex-gentiles, the people of Galilee were far more liberal than their southern neighbors. They were farmers, shepherds, and craftsmen—country folk with country accents. Even their dialects were different from those of the city people, and this difference may have caused Judea's rabbinical circles to have a general contempt for all things Galilean. Galilee was, in fact, looked down upon by the Jerusalem priests, particularly by the Sanhedrin, who considered themselves superior to their Judean countrymen. This distain was so marked in the Sanhedrin's records that they mention only four great Galilean rabbis.[20]

The Galileans are historically described "as people of generous spirits, with warm, impulsive hearts, and intense nationalism, (and) beside the stiff rigidity of Jerusalem, they had simple manners of earnest piety. The Talmud accused them of being quarrelsome, but admits that they cared more for honor than for money."[21] The priests even claimed that these "Galileans" leaned more toward mystical Kabbalistic pursuits than toward simple blind obedience to the "law." And it is precisely because of these more open attitudes that the Holy Family settled in Galilee, where they could be far from the interfering influences of Jerusalem's Pharisees. And, of course, this allowed them to send their children to school at Mount Carmel, away from the eyes of the priests.

THE SCHOOL AT MOUNT CARMEL

Both modern Nazareth and the ancient Essene school of Mount Carmel lie in Galilee, a two-day journey on foot from the monastery of Qumran, which lay to the south, closer to Jerusalem. While Mount Carmel is not mentioned in the New Testament, in the Hebrew Bible it is referred to as *Hakkarmel*, or "the garden-land." In later Hebrew texts, it is known simply as *Karmel*, and in modern Arabic as *Kurmul*, or more commonly as *Jebel Mar Elias* (Mountain of Saint Elias, for the prophet Elijah). Most of the ridge on which it sat is, even today, covered with rich thickets of evergreens, and with prickly oak, myrtle, lentisk, carob, and olive trees. In Jesus' time, deer and leopard roamed through its forests, and it was well known for its profusion of aromatic plants and wild flowers. Mount Carmel's location on the shores of the Mediterranean Sea also ensured that it enjoyed benevolently cool breezes and a constant source of moisture.

Most of us have been conditioned to believe that the people of Jesus' times were poorly educated and unsophisticated. However, Mount Carmel and Qumran were both excellent centers of learning with deeply educated instructors and extensive libraries. There were also the great libraries in Alexandria and Damascus, all of which were connected to the Great White Brotherhood.[22] Several Jewish historians give us insight into the demanding education required of the children of that time:

> There can be no reasonable doubt that at that time such schools existed throughout the land. We find references to them at almost every period; indeed, the existence of higher schools and Academies would not have been possible without such primary instruction . . . . Tradition ascribes to Joshua, the son of Gamla, the introduction of schools in every town, and the compulsory education in them of all children above the age of six. It was even deemed unlawful to live in a place where there was no school. Such a city deserved to be either destroyed or excommunicated.[23]

Living in Galilee, Jesus' parents would logically have sent Jesus to the school at Mount Carmel, for it had a long and impressive history. Daniel, the Essene, tells us that Mount Carmel "had a large library. But this was a teaching library and not a research and copying center, so I did not consider it to be a main Essene library as the other three were (in Alexandria, Damascus and Qumran)."[24]

Surprisingly, a great deal is known about the history of the mountain itself. "In prehistoric days, it was covered in forests, and hermits and prophets dwelt within its caves," writes John Michell. "And on its peak stood temples and altars to a succession of ruling gods, Jehovah, Baal, and Zeus, as well as the god Carmel, who presided over an oracle there. The name [Carmel] means a garden, an image of paradise." In the 15th century B.C.E., Thutmosis II of Egypt refers to Carmel as "the Holy Head," while the neo-Platonic philosopher Iamblicus says that Mount Carmel was "sacred above all mountains and forbidden of access to the vulgar," telling us that it was once dedicated to the gods. Iamblichus notes that, in his youth, the Greek master Pythagoras traveled to Mount Carmel after completing his initiation into the Phoenician Mysteries in Sidon: "On his way to Egypt to study, Pythagoras stopped to take solitude at the Temple of Zeus that once stood atop this mountain."[25]

Legends from earlier times tell of the Grotto of Elijah, so named for the famous prophet who lived and taught at Mount Carmel. This "Cave of the Sons of the Prophet" was said to have been inhabited by none other than Elijah himself and was famous for its healing properties even in ancient times.[26] It had once been a retreat for women who hoped to conceive, and for lunatics who spent three nights there to be cured. The Muslims called this cave *el Khadr*, which means "becoming green," and to the Carmelites it was known as the School of the Prophets. This ancient and holy mountain would certainly have been an appropriate site for Jesus and John's formal education, especially since John was said to have been the reincarnation of the Jewish prophet Elijah.[27]

Later, tenth century crusaders on a pilgrimage to Mount Carmel discovered a small monastery on the mountain occupied by Byzantine priests, who said that, when their predecessors first arrived at the mountain, the site was already occupied by a community of early Christians who were conducting "a house of studies." This sounds surprisingly like the Gnostics, the inheritors of at least some of the Essene wisdom. In fact, the Gnostics claimed to be the spiritual heirs of an ancient Jewish monastic order that had lived and studied at Mount Carmel since the days of Elijah and his school of the prophets— perhaps the very Essene school that Jesus and John attended.[28] Archaeological finds from the late Roman period of Justinian (482–527 C.E.) also confirm the existence of the school.

While the cave itself appears to have been created originally as an artificial grotto, it has been used for centuries in rituals of renewal. An Essene group currently active in the area tells us:

> The ancient vegetarian Nazoreans are said to have had a Holy Temple and Monastery on [Mount] Carmel where they worshipped both God and Goddess in the sacred groves, vineyards, high places, before stone altars, within caves and in constructed tents and shrines where they burned incense and prayed according to the movements of moon, sun and stars. It is likely that the site of the original caves, holy springs and structures used by the ancient Essene Nazoreans of Carmel lies in the Siah canyon. . . .[29]

While it may surprise some to learn that the Essene order honored both the Divine Mother and Father, we find echoes of this teaching in the words of Jesus prior to their editing by the established church. In The Essene Gospel of Peace, Jesus speaks often of the importance of honoring both the male and female aspects of creation:

> Blessed is the Child of Light who is pure in heart, for he shall see God. For as the Heavenly Father hath given thee His holy spirit, and thy Earthly Mother hath given thee Her holy body, so shall ye give love to all thy brothers. And thy true brothers are all those who do the will of thy Heavenly Father and thy Earthly Mother.[30]

The modern Order of Monastic Carmelites, now living atop Mount Carmel, claim an unbroken line of succession that stretches back to these times. Their church stands on the peak north of the site they call Stella Maris, a peak named after a woman known as Mary the Magdala. Yet it may surprise many to learn that this name, Stella Maris, goes back to even more ancient times, when Isis, the Queen of Heaven, was revered throughout much of the world by the very same name.[31]

CHAPTER 11

The Teacher of Righteousness

From beginning to end
Of beginning less and endless Samsara
I will live a life devoted to the benefits of beings,
In the presence of the Lord of the World
I form an enlightened attitude.[1]

—Tibetan Buddhist prayer

The social, political, and religious climate in Judea at the time when the Holy Family returned there was complex. Three very distinct religious groups were in power in Jerusalem: the Pharisees, the Sadducees, and the Essenes. Judea itself was divided into provinces and, while Jerusalem was densely populated with the traditional Pharisees and Sadducees, Galilee, to the north, had a far more mystical spiritual climate.

The Sanhedrin, the governing body for the entire country, was located in Jerusalem. It was composed of seventy-one Jewish patriarchs who, acting as a cross between our modern legislative bodies and judicial courts, set the religious regulations for everyday life. They were the highest authority in the land on all matters except those that pertained to the Roman Empire; they created the religious interpretations of the laws and judged all who broke the rules. Much like the U.S. Supreme Court today, the Sanhedrin made all final decisions on the enforcement of religious and social laws, yielding only military jurisdiction to the Romans.[2] The patriarchs that composed the high council were Pharisees or Sadducees, who held most of the social, political, and financial power in the country. While the more metaphysically oriented Essenes did not have an official presence on the council, there were covert Essene members, like Joseph of Arimathea and Nicodemus, who were sympathetic to Jesus. But, by necessity, they kept their true alliances secret. Members of the Sanhedrin were appointed, not elected, and there is every reason to believe that these appointments were for life.[3]

The Sanhedrin met in a large stone building called the Temple of Hewn Stones, which stood within the giant citadel palace built by Herod around 20 B.C.E. that was considered one of his greatest accomplishments. The entire complex was destroyed by the Roman emperor Vespasian in 68 C.E., in response to the continued uprisings of the Zealots.

The term Sanhedrin comes from the Greek word *sunédrion*, meaning "to sit together," as in a legislative assembly.[4] The council was ruled by a chief justice called the *Kohen Gadol*, or "high priest," who was also called a *Nasi*, a Hebrew term derived from a word meaning "to separate." In post-Biblical times, this type of assembly has been called the *Beth-Din*, or the "house of judgment," giving us a clue as to how the assembly saw its role in the community and the way it wielded its religious power.[5] Purported by some Hebrews to have been established as far back as the time of Moses, and by others to have been created only after the Jewish captivity in Babylon some 900 years after Moses, the great Sanhedrin was steeped in oppressive and judgmental dogma.

RELIGIOUS LAW AND SOCIAL CONTROL

When Jesus was a youth, the wisdom behind the purer teachings of Moses had moved far beyond the simple Ten Commandments to a complicated mass of scriptural regulations. The Midrash Halakha, for example, was a complex book of 613 rules created by Jewish priests when the Hebrews were captive in Babylon (587–536 B.C.E.). Since the Jews were not allowed to have a physical temple of their own, the rabbis created "a highly legalistic code that impinged on every aspect of its adherents' behavior" to bind the people together.[6] Thus, not only were the Jews bound by the military rules of the Roman Empire, they were also subject to hundreds of socio-religious regulations based on a very literal interpretation of Mosaic law. Of every nation in the Middle East, the Jews were perhaps the most dogmatic and stubborn in their ways, and it was in part to throw off these shackles that Jesus incarnated among them.

Daily Jewish law was based on 248 positive and 365 negative commandments (mitzvot) that regulated almost every aspect of Jewish life.[7] While some

FIGURE 34. Moses with the serpent staff and the tablets of initiation. Illustrated by Sylvia Laurens.

of these rules may once have been pragmatic, others were patently absurd: do not walk more than 2000 paces on the Sabbath; do not buy meat or curdle milk on the Sabbath; do not make anything on the Sabbath; do not heal anyone on the Sabbath; do not carry anything on the Sabbath. Then there were laws that would challenge even the most conservative of us. The Law of Nail Clippings, for example, commanded that you must always burn your nail-clippings. The Law of Tassels declared that, if you happened to tread on a portion of the fringe of your gown while going up a ladder, you must stop where you are and wait for the tear to be repaired before continuing. The Law of the Hedgerow stated, that "Whoso pulleth down a hedge a serpent shall sting him." There were also dire warnings against those who gave authority to anyone other than the Pharisees, since "a teacher of the Law is more important than even a man who is 'an uprooter of mountains.'"[8]

Understandably, this kind of oppressive regulation was a burden for those who just wanted to live happy, loving, spiritually fulfilled lives. Moreover, to transgress in any of these matters, even in the smallest way, ensured destruction. It is clear from this heavy-handed leadership that the Pharisees and Sadducees were hardly spiritual men. Their concept of religion had grown out of the military victories of King Saul, King David, and King Solomon. They believed in the law of obedience or punishment, and they believed that, in order for their religion to continue, they had to create a glorious physical temple that was a direct reflection of their own prosperity as a country. Such an impressive structure took money to run and, to this end, they taxed their people heavily. The double taxation by Rome and the Sanhedrin was a heavy burden to the people and one of the major social and political problems of Jesus' day.

Naturally, the Sanhedrin felt threatened by anything that might change this status quo, including the mystical ideas of the Essenes, the military might of the Romans, and the more liberal democratic philosophies of the Greeks. Even the ascetic Zealots, who wanted to overthrow Roman rule, were a threat. Thus, the Sanhedrin colluded with both Herod Antipater and Herod Antipas to destroy any rising leaders who might undercut their authority.

The elitist Sadducees and the powerful Pharisees disliked one another intensely. Scholars have theorized that the term Sadducee comes from the Hebrew word *tsadiq*, meaning "righteous," and the Sadducees were, in fact, known for their strict, superior attitudes toward others. They were materialists who believed in the power of the physical world and were well known for their cruel and unusual punishments. They did not believe in angels, reincarnation, or eternal life.

The Pharisees, on the other hand, came from both the middle and upper classes. They advocated extending Jewish law into every facet of daily life. Their name is believed to derive from the Hebrew word *perusim*, which means "separated ones." However, it has been suggested more recently that the word may come instead from the Hebrew term *parosim*, meaning "specifier," since they sought to specify the correct meaning of God's law to the people.[9] Like the Sadducees, the Pharisees were wealthy and adamant about their beliefs. They believed in reincarnation and the return of the soul, and they wanted to educate the masses in their dogma. Perhaps not surprisingly, the Pharisees were far more open to Greek influence than their counterparts, the Sadducees. Herod Antipater claimed to be a Pharisee, but was said to have been equally swayed by Roman theology. The apostle Paul was also a Pharisee and, until his conversion, most adamant in the persecution of Jesus' followers.

One of the clearest descriptions of the difference between the Pharisees and the Sadducees is found in the Book of Acts when Paul stands trial before the Sanhedrin in Jerusalem. Paul very cleverly turns the two factions against one another and thus avoids the wrath of both:

> But when Paul perceived that one part were Sadducees and the other Pharisees, he cried out in the council, "Men and brethren, I am a Pharisee, the son of a Pharisee; concerning the hope and resurrection of the dead I am being judged!" And when he had said this, a dissension arose between the Pharisees and the Sadducees; and the assembly was divided. For the Sadducees say that there is no resurrection, and no angel or Spirit; but the Pharisees confess both. Then there arose a loud outcry. And the scribes who were of the Pharisee's party arose and protested, saying, "We find no evil in this man; but if a spirit or an angel has spoken to him, let us not fight against God" (Acts 23:6–9).

The third faction in Judea was the mysterious Essenes. Biblical scholars suspect that the Essenes moved their school and intellectual center to Qumran in response to a social, political, and spiritual rupture between the public rulers of Israel and the true heirs of the line of David—between the original line of Levitical priests and the House of Maccabee that came into power around 160 B.C.E. The Dead Sea Scrolls refer to a "Teacher of Righteousness" who broke away from the powerful elite and led the Essenes into the hills around Qumran. References to the Teacher of Righteousness also appear in the mysterious Damascus Scroll, written around 100 B.C.E.—a text that expresses a fervent hope for the restoration of a Davidic monarchy.

These scrolls speak of a teacher "to whom God made known all the mysteries of the words of his servants the prophets."[10] It is intriguing, however, that, at the time the Damascus Scroll was written, the Essenes seemed to expect that another Teacher of Righteousness would be born to redeem the people from the misguided rulers who had assumed power. Clearly, the Essenes were awaiting the arrival of a teacher whom many within their inner circle would recognize as Jesus.

THE TEACHER OF RIGHTEOUSNESS

The Damascus Scroll places the Essenes' origin some 390 years after the Babylonian exile, which began in 587 B.C.E.—or around 197 B.C.E. According to the scroll, the Essenes, better known as the Nazoreans, had been leaderless for some twenty years, "groping blindly for the way," and then "God... raised for them a Teacher of Righteousness to guide them in the way of His heart."[11] This teacher was the first prophet born since the time of Elijah, and was said to have the proper understanding of the Torah and to be the one through whom God would reveal to the community "the hidden things in which Israel had gone astray."[12] While biblical scholars have not yet identified this Teacher, it is clear that he had access to knowledge that was either unknown or unaccepted by the traditional priesthood.

The early church father Epiphanius, writing in the fourth century, described the inner workings of the Essene order:

> The Nasorean were Jews by nationality. . . they acknowledged Moses
> and believed that he had received laws, not this law, however, but some
> other. And so, they were Jews who kept all the Jewish observances, but
> they would not offer sacrifice or eat meat. They considered it unlawful
> to eat meat or make sacrifices with it. They claim that these Books [the
> Midrash, etc.] are fictions, and that none of these customs were instituted
> by the fathers. This was the difference between the Nasoreans and the
> others.[13]

Thus the Essenes had knowledge of special laws—laws transmitted to Moses but not honored by the Jerusalem temple, laws that had perhaps been brought to them by the original Teacher of Righteousness. These laws may have been practiced, not only by the Essenes in Palestine, but also by the Zadokite community in Egypt.

Some speculate that this Teacher was an advanced member of the Great White Brotherhood who sought to lay the groundwork for Jesus' coming. Some claim he was the Egyptian adept Serapis Bey, one of the ancient masters known to initiates of the Therapeutae in Egypt. Others link him to immortal Thoth, who is said to appear from time to time in various civilizations to guide men's paths when they have lost their way. While we may never know the true identity of this mysterious wisdom keeper, there are clues we can consider. We know he lived roughly 200 years before Jesus was born, confirming our date of 197 B.C.E. as the approximate date the Essenes appear on the scene. He made his connection with the Essenes around 150 B.C.E., inspiring their move into the desert fastness of Qumran and the establishment of other hidden centers of Essene philosophy.

When the Jewish high priest Onias III set up the alternate temple in Egypt (170 B.C.E.), this temple was overseen by members of the house of Aaron, who were awaiting a messiah from the house of David. This prophesied king was also thought by the Essenes to be the second Teacher of Righteousness, Jesus.

So the Essenes may have been the only spiritual group in Israel at that time who taught true Mosaic Law. Indeed, we know that they believed that what was being taught in Jerusalem was not aligned with the higher spiritual precepts of their religion. As noted earlier, the temple in Jerusalem was captured by Syrian invaders in 175 and 200 B.C.E., and then taken over by Pharisees loyal to those invaders. Then it was converted briefly to a temple dedicated to Zeus. The Maccabbee rebellion finally expelled the invaders, but only with the help of the Roman military. That's why the Romans were in Judea in the first place.

But 150 years later, by the time Jesus was born, even the courageous Maccabbee leaders had passed into history and Herod the Great had come to power, crushing any remaining resistance within the Sanhedrin to solidify his power. This was the state of affairs in Judea when Jesus was born.

CHAPTER 12

The Mystical Essenes

They are eminent for fidelity and are the perfect,
Ministers of Peace. . . . They also take great pains in studying
The writings of the Ancients and choose out of them
That which is most for the advantage of their Soul and body.[1]

—Josephus, *The Works of Flavius Josephus: Antiquities of the Jews*

The Essene Order was a key part of the Great White Brotherhood and, therefore, instrumental to the success of Jesus' mission. Although the Essenes' most famous sanctuary in Qumran was destroyed by the Romans around 68 C.E., it is significant that many of the Essenes' most important manuscripts were spirited away to sister communities in Damascus, Alexandria, and Mount Carmel long before that destruction occurred.[2]

From the recent discoveries of the Dead Sea Scrolls (1947) and the Nag Hammadi Texts (1945) in Egypt, we know that many of the documents that did survive were hidden by the Essenes in nearby caves. And while it is likely that more of these precious manuscripts exist than is currently known, it may be that we will never see them. The Christian edicts of destruction that swept the world from the end of the fourth century C.E. robbed us of enormous chunks of human history. Entire libraries in great centers of learning were burned and their owners tortured or killed.

Michael Baigent reveals several documents that have come to light on the black market in the past few decades. Some of these papyri date to Old Testament times, while others relate directly to Jesus in the years before or after the Crucifixion. Baigent shares the story of a British cleric who, in the 1930s, was often consulted on the translation of medieval French documents. He was summoned by colleagues at the Seminary at Saint Sulpice in France to translate a document once held by the French Cathars during the 12th and 13th centuries. The book, a collection of Jesus' teachings called the Book of Love, was one of the treasures that caused the Cathars to be purged by the Roman Church.[3] Indeed, much of the written evidence of the Essene order and, later, of the the Gnostic Christians, has simply "vanished." Today scholars are still trying to piece together exactly what the Essenes believed and how they functioned. Yet we know that the Essenes held a unique place in history, for we know they were connected with the mystical, even more ancient, Great White Brotherhood, which had centers around the world.

Political and Philosophical Differences

Traditional archaeology confirms that the Essene community at Qumran flourished from around the second century B.C.E. to the destruction of Jerusalem in 68 C.E., a period of about 300 years. We know that the Essenes "separated" from mainstream Judaism because of differences between their core philosophies and those of the Pharisees and Sadducees. These differences were exacerbated by the political turmoil in Judea and by the political murders of the high priests that occurred between 190 and 150 B.C.E., when the Syrians invaded Palestine.

What distinguished the Essenes most clearly was that they did not believe in any animal sacrifice, while the Pharisees and Sadducees routinely required supplicants to sacrifice lambs, pigeons, doves, bulls, and other animals to the temple at Jerusalem. To the Essenes, the killing of any animal to appease God was an abomination and, as we shall see, many Essene followers were vegetarians.[4]

Another small but important detail reveals an even deeper philosophic difference: the Essenes used a calendar different from that used by the Pharisees and the Sadducees. While this may seem minor to us, in the days of Jesus, the keeping of time was an extremely important indication of cultural and religious values. Like the early Egyptians, the Essenes honored both a solar and a lunar calendar, revealing that they still taught a balance between the male and the female aspects of the Divine, a philosophy that is well represented in the Essene Gospels of Peace. The use of a solar calendar comes directly out of Egypt, where the highest visible symbol of God was Atum-Ra. The center of this worship lay at Heliopolis, the sacred "city of the Sun," the symbol for the invisible Creator behind all things. This symbolism lay at the center of both the Therapeutae and the Essene worldview, and the practice of Sun-gazing was taught in both these orders, as it was in many orders of the Great White Brotherhood. Jesus reflects this reverence for the Sun in his teachings when he says, "Let thy love be as the sun which shines on all the creatures of earth. . . ."[5]

Yet both the Essene and Egyptian cultures also honored the Moon and the thirteen twenty-eight-day lunar cycles of each year that expressed the energies of the Divine Feminine.[6] In Egypt, the Moon was associated not only with the Divine Feminine, but also with Thoth, the wise architect-teacher who taught the seven hermetic principles of creation. Thoth was known as a "master of time," for it was he and his father, Enki/Ptah (and Thoth's older brother, Marduk) who first charted the heavens, determining the great 26,000-year (25,920 to be exact) year precession of the equinoxes that affects the rising and falling ages of mankind.[7]

Conversely, the patriarchal Sanhedrin of Jerusalem refused to honor the Divine Feminine and knew only a solar calendar, cutting itself off from the balance of male and female that is inherent in all of nature and that keeps a culture in equilibrium. While the Goddess, under the name of Ashtoreth or Ashera, was still worshipped in Jerusalem at the time of King Solomon, by the time Jesus was born, the patriarchy had successfully obliterated all traces of female power.[8] The Jewish Book of Jubilees, in fact, forbade the honoring of a lunar calendar, linking it to the centuries-old worship of the Divine Feminine, which they denied.[9]

Because of this difference in calendars, the Essenes celebrated their festivals at different times than the traditional Sadducees and Pharisees. This tells us that they were either celebrating entirely different events or principles, or that they had knowledge of a far older tradition than the wealthy, politically entrenched Sanhedrin.[10] Yet the real reason behind this discrepancy in holidays lies with Moses.

MOSES: INITIATE PRINCE OF EGYPT

The Old Testament book of Exodus tells the story of the baby Moses who was found in the bulrushes and adopted by the pharaoh's daughter. The story then skips forward many years to find Moses murdering an Egyptian guard who was abusing a Hebrew slave. Moses then flees Egypt and ends up in the deserts of Midian for forty years. There, he marries Zipporah, one of the daughters of

Jethro, the black Midian priest (Exodus 2:5–21). Upon returning to Egypt, Moses gathers his disenfranchised people and begins his forty-year exile.

Jewish scholar Karl Abraham and psychologist Sigmund Freud (who wrote *Moses and Monotheism*), both believed that Moses was descended of Egyptian royalty. Freud claimed that the story of Moses' humble origins was a fabrication to disguise the fact that this great Jewish prophet was a full member of the Egyptian royal family. Philo Judaeus and Flavius Josephus support this assertion. And as the second son of the Egyptian pharaoh, Moses, whose name derived from *mos*, the common Egyptian term for "child," would have been instructed in all the wisdom of the Egyptian Schools.[11]

Although the Bible conveniently leaves out Moses' many years of formal training in the ancient Mystery traditions, Chaeremon, a first-century B.C.E. Egyptian high priest and chief librarian of the Serapeum in Alexandria, says that Moses was educated as a sacred scribe, a highly sought-after position requiring years of training. Manetho, historian and high priest of Heliopolis, claimed that Moses was trained at Heliopolis and was versed in the solar worship of Egypt.[12] Historical records confirm that Moses studied in the temples of Heliopolis, the oldest and most sacred of all Egyptian universities. Manetho produced these records for Ptolemy II, revealing that Moses was trained in the Heliopolan temples of On. Thus the entire foundation of Moses' knowledge came from the Mystery Schools of ancient Egypt—the same Egyptian Schools where Jesus was later to prepare for his mission before returning to Galilee.

From these records, we know that Moses' childhood name was Moüses, signifying a person who is "preserved out of the water." His adult name, however, was Osarseph, (or Osarsiph), a derivative of Asar or Osar, two names used for Osiris himself.[13] These names mark Moses as a possible heir to the Egyptian throne. Ralph Ellis confirms that "the priest who framed . . . [the Jewish] constitution and their laws was a native of Heliopolis, Osarseph, named after the god Osiris [who was] worshipped at Heliopolis, but when he joined his people, he changed his name and was called Moses."[14]

Accounts of Moses' birth found in Christian and Hebrew scripture were not written down until almost 1000 years after the Jews left Egypt—a span of time that may have obscured historical fact. While traditional biblical lore tells us that Moses was entirely of Hebrew stock, evidence suggests this is not completely true. Suddi, the Essene teacher of the law, says the Essene order taught that Moses' mother was a princess of Egypt who had an affair with a Hebrew man of noble descent, a man from the house of Joseph. Knowing that her father would never accept a child from this liaison, the princess created the fiction of finding the child among the rushes, thus mimicking the ancient story of the baby Horus who was born amid the rushes of Philae Island. So Moses may well have been born of royalty on both sides of his bloodline. Suddi reports that only when Moses grew into a man did he discover his father's true identity, and then he deliberately sought out the teachings of his Hebrew heritage.[15]

As the second son of the pharaoh, Moses would have been educated with all the privilege, luxury, and discipline of the royal house. He was most certainly well trained in Egyptian statesmanship, military strategies, and theology, and thus in Egyptian rituals and beliefs that honored both the solar and lunar aspects of the Divine.

Furthermore, in the New Testament we read that, during the Israelites' forty years in the desert, "Moses placed a veil over the scriptures of Israel" so that they could not be read by the uninitiated (II Corinthians 3:13–18). This strange comment reveals that the Hebrew scriptures were encoded so that ordinary people could not understand or interpret them correctly. "Even to this day, when (the word of) Moses is read, a veil lies on their heart. . . ." (II Corinthians 3:15). And later, the apostle Paul says, "But even if our gospel is veiled, it is veiled to those who are perishing, whose minds the God of this age has blinded. . . ." (II Corinthians 4:3–4).

Paul Brunton believes that this veil was the encoded information of the higher initiates of Egypt that Moses had written down for the tribes of Israel. Yet, because Moses was bound by the vows of secrecy of the ancient Egyptian Mystery Schools, he could only reveal this information to his fellow Israelites in a way that could be understood by other initiates.

Now Moses, as an Adept, knew and used the sacred writing of the initiates, i.e. the hieroglyphs in their third or secret spiritual meaning.[16] When he completed the Pentateuch, he wrote the text in Egyptian hieroglyphs. Access to these texts was available to his initiated priests, who (at that time) understood hieroglyphs.

But when the Israelites had settled down in Palestine and centuries had rolled over their heads, the knowledge of the meaning of the hieroglyphs had grown vague. . . . When nearly a thousand years after the great exodus of the Israelites from Egypt, the elders of Israel put together that collection of books which we now call the Old Testament, the difficulties which faced them in trying to translate Moses' writings into Hebrew were immense. For Moses wrote as an Adept, but these elders, however learned, were not Adepts.[17]

This difference in initiated and secular understanding created a tremendous gap between the Pharisees and Sadducees and their Essene counterparts in Jesus' time. Many Essenes were practicing mystics who "maintained the same doctrine as 'the sons of Greece'; [referring] perhaps to the Pythagoreans or the later Platonists in that they too viewed humans as housing an immortal soul within a mortal, perishable body."[18] The Essenes thus had a deep understanding of the spiritual worlds and had attained many spiritual abilities. Josephus writes: "There are also those among them who undertake to foretell things to come . . . and it is but seldom that they miss in their predictions."[19] The Sadducees and Pharisees of Jerusalem, on the other hand, were pragmatists, grounded in the law and in the political realities of the time.

The split between the Sadducees and Pharisees of Jerusalem and the Essenes of Galilee was not only philosophic and practical, but also deeply spiritual—the first, members of the power elite who self-righteously pretended to be initiates; the second, genuine learned mystics. Jesus himself speaks of this difference: "The scribes and Pharisees sit in Moses' seat. Therefore whatever they tell you to observe, that observe and do, but do not do according to their works; for they say, and do not do. For they bind heavy burdens, hard to bear, and lay them on men's shoulders; but they themselves will not move them with one of their fingers. . . . Woe to you, scribes and Pharisees, hypocrites! For you pay the tithe of mint and anise and cumin, and have neglected the weightier matters of the law; justice and mercy and faith. These you ought to have done, without leaving the others undone" (Matthew 23: 2–4, 23). Jesus thus acknowledged the Essenes as the true inheritors of Moses' wisdom.

Much of what traditional scholars know about the Essenes is based on the written testimonies of four men, two Jews and two Romans: Philo, Flavius Josephus, Pliny the Elder, and Pliny the Younger. Philo's accounts of the Essenes are of particular interest, since he was a philosopher himself and an initiate of the Mysteries. He lived in Egypt in the same era that Jesus did (20 B.C.E. to 50 C.E.) and visited Jerusalem at least once during his lifetime.

Philo writes that the Essenes "use a three-fold rule and definition: love of God, love of virtue and love of mankind."[20] He describes them as an industrious people who live in the towns and villages of Judea, avoiding the cities. "They do not enlist by race," he tells us, "but by volunteers who have a zeal for righteousness and an ardent love of men." They deny animal sacrifice and place no great value on material possessions, but rather "live without goods and without property, not by misfortune, but out of preference." They bore no arms, did not keep slaves, and avoided commerce.

> They live together in brotherhoods, and eat in common together. Every-thing they do is for the common good of the group. . . . With respect to philosophy, they dismiss logic but have an extremely high regard for vir-tue. They honor the Sabbath with great respect over all the other days of the week. They have an internal rule which all learn, together with rules on piety, holiness, justice and the knowledge of good and bad.[21]

While it is clear from this description that the Essenes were a highly devout spiritual group, for centuries biblical scholars treated them as eccentric ascet-ics living on locusts and honey at the edge of the wilderness. This perception changed radically, however, with the discovery of the Nag Hammadi texts and the Dead Sea Scrolls. Today, many scholars recognize the Essenes as the earliest true Christians, and acknowledge that the sect likely evolved into the Gnostic Christians and may have emerged centuries later as the Cathars of France. Jo-sephus writes that, in Palestine alone, there were over 4000 male members of this sect.[22]

THE ESSENES AND THE GREAT WHITE BROTHERHOOD

Thirty-three Degree Masonic teacher H. Spencer Lewis tells us that the Essenes "were a branch of the illuminated brotherhood or Great White Lodge, which had its birth in the country of Egypt during the years preceding Akhenaton, pharaoh of Egypt and the great founder of the first monotheistic religion, who supported and encouraged the existence of a secret brotherhood to teach the mystic truths of life." The name Essene is derived from the Egyptian word *kashai*, which means "secret." "There is a Jewish word of similar sound," Lewis observes, "*chsahi*, meaning 'secret' or silent; and this word would naturally be translated into *essaios* or Essene, denoting 'secret' or mystic . . . the Egyptian symbols of light and truth are represented by the word chosen, which translit-erates into the Greek as *essen*."[23]

The Latin transliteration of *esseni* means "the pious ones."[24] In Aramaic, *esseni* can also be translated as "healers" or "holy ones," English words that are derived from the Hebrew words *hasayya* and *hasin*.[25] This meaning is similar to that of the Cathars, the highly evolved medieval Christian sect that was destroyed by the Catholic Church. Cathar means "the pure." This meaning is also linked to the terms Nazorean or Nazarene, which are translated as "people of the Truth" or "those with secret knowledge."[26]

For centuries, scholars did not realize that the Essenes were students of many different streams of wisdom, including Egyptian, Buddhist, Zoroastrian, and Pythagorean.[27] Their contemporaries regarded them as the heirs to Chaldean and Egyptian astronomy and to the medicines of the ancient Persians. Josephus, writing between 75 and 85 C.E., tells us that many of the Essene beliefs were similar to those of the Greeks.[28] They believed in the immortality of the soul, the impermanence of the body, and the return of the soul to a higher, more ethereal region—similar to the Isles of the Blessed spoken of by the Egyptians and the Greeks (the Elysian Fields of Heaven), or to a place of darkness and punishment, similar to the concept of Hades or Hell.[29]

The Essene lifestyle was also highly Pythagorean, dedicated to the nature of truth and the scholarship of all the sciences. They were learned in the teachings of numbers, sacred geometry, the study of the planets and their movements, and the power of harmony, music, and healing—all studies sacred to Thoth, the Egyptian god of wisdom. Josephus writes: "The sect of the Essenes maintains that Fate governs all things and that nothing can befall man contrary to its determination and will. These men live the same kind of life which among the Greeks has been ordered by Pythagoras," whose school was dedicated to Horus/Apollo, the god of light and healing.[30][31]

Others, including biblical scholars Gordon Strachan, Martin Larson, and Martin Hengel, have commented on the important role that Pythagorean thought played in the development of Essene thought. Jewish historian Heinrich Graetz has even called early Christianity "Essenism with foreign elements," believing that the Essenes taught many of the same practices as Buddhism today, including a focus on vegetarianism, communal living, and meditation. So great, in fact, are the similarities in philosophy, spiritual practices, and training between Buddhist and Essene thought that Yale professor of Sanskrit and comparative philology E. Washburn Hopkins was moved to write: "Finally, the life, temptation, miracles, parables, and even the disciplines of Jesus have been derived directly from Buddhism."[32]

The Essenes called themselves the Children of the Light, clearly aligning themselves with the Great White Brotherhood, who used the Sun as one of its most sacred symbols.[33] We know from Philo that they deliberately cultivated a regimen of raw and natural foods, clean air, clean water, clean sunlight, and daily exercise. They were a long-lived people, often attaining the age of 100 or more. Edmond Bordeaux Szekely, translator of *The Essene Gospel of Peace*, writes that "it was very rare for them to die before their hundredth or hundred and twentieth year, and most of them lived still longer," a fact that is echoed by Josephus.[34]

The Essenes believed in karma, the laws of reincarnation, and the teachings that Jesus passed on when he said, "What you sow is what you reap." They worked daily with the angelic kingdoms, the unseen powers of inner realms, cultivating these relationships in their meditations, healing work, and the acquisition of wisdom. Jesus names fourteen of these angels in his teachings to his fellow Essenes, whom he addresses as "Sons of the Light."[35] The seven female angels are the Angel of the Sun, the Angel of the Water, the Angel of the Air, the Angel of the Earth, the Angel of Life, the Angel of Joy, and the Earthly Mother herself. The seven male angels are the Angel of Power, the Angel of Love, the Angel of Wisdom, the Angel of Eternal Life, the Angel of Work, the Angel of Peace, and the Heavenly Father himself.[36] Szekely writes, "All authors agree that they had secret traditions, practices and teachings, which were transmissible only by initiates. . . . Above and before all, they had their traditional secrets based on angelology, the fundamental science of all their teachings."[37]

In *The Unknown Life of Jesus Christ*, Robert Siblerud writes that the Essenes "practiced telekinesis, clairvoyance, levitation, restoring the dead to life and laying-on-of-hands." Like the gurus of ancient India, members of this order were acquainted with the spiritual powers that come from years of intense practice. "They were learned in the arts of healing, gemstones, roots, languages, esoteric philosophy and writing."[38] Certainly, this kind of education was perfect for Jesus in the early years before his travels began, and it would explain, at least in part, how he came to dazzle the rabbis at the Jerusalem temple. While Jesus clearly possessed his own deep reservoir of innate wisdom, he was also privy to a pool of esoteric knowledge well beyond the traditional schools of Jerusalem—a knowledge transmitted through the Great White Brotherhood.

THE ESSENES AND THE MESSIAH

For centuries, there have been claims that Jesus was an Essene—that they knew of his coming and supported his mission. In fact, their own prophecies foretold that such a teacher would be born. From the beginning, the Essenes were linked with the coming of "the anointed one," the returning solar lord who would become the Christ. This may explain why the Essenes simply vanished shortly after the Crucifixion. Fearing that certain aspects of Jesus' ministry would be traced back to them, they fled, taking with them their most treasured records. In fact, we know that, once the Essene community's purpose had been fulfilled, they left as mysteriously as they had come, leaving only a minimal presence in Qumran until its final destruction in 68 C.E.

Many Christian rituals derive directly from Essene teachings—for example, baptism, a rite representing spiritual rebirth. Jesus tells us: "Most assuredly, unless one is born of water and the Spirit, one cannot enter the kingdom of God" (John 3:5). This ritual cleansing was also practiced in Egypt and India with full-body immersion in the Nile and the Ganges.[39] Likewise, the Essenes passed around a cup of wine during their weekly rites of renewal, just as the Persian devotees of Mithra and the Egyptians devotees of Osiris had done for centuries. This clearly pre-figures the Christian Eucharist. And, as we have already discussed, the Essenes greeted the Sun each day at dawn, earning their name "the Sons of Light."[40] These three rituals—baptism, communion, and Sun-gazing—all link the Essenes to their Therapeutae brothers in Alexandria and Heliopolis, the Egyptian priests in Egypt, the Druids of Britain, the Buddhists of India, the Magi of Persia, and a dozen or more other religious sects around the world who had practiced these age-old rites of purification and renewal for centuries.

Twenty-first-century excavations in Palestine revealed that the monastic community of Qumran was composed primarily of men; however, the bones of women and children have also been found in the surrounding community, telling us that Essene families played some part in the domestic life of the order. Josephus describes an order that thinks "that by not marrying they cut off the principal part of the human life, which is the prospect of succession; nay rather that if all men should be of the same opinion, the whole race of mankind would fail."[41] Szekely tells us that the Essenes lived in perfect equality between men and women, contrary to the customs and social structures of their time.[42]

Like the Buddhists, these mystical scholars sought an inner peace through the balance of their bodies, minds, and spirits, which they reflected in their simple, clean diets and their contact with the Earth. They believed that the process of enlightenment was a daily practice, and that the ego pulls us back into the world of selfishness through greed, anger, lust, vanity, fear, or undue attachment. Thus, they actively sought to cultivate their own inner gnosis, or self-knowledge, acknowledging the famous inscription over the Temple of Delphi—"Know thyself"—as the heart of the human journey.[43]

Like the Druids and Therapeutae, the Essenes wore white robes inside their own communities, but deliberately dressed to blend in when they went into the world. Aspiring initiates underwent a three-year initiation before finally being accepted into the order.[44] Only after the seventh year of training did the Essenes admit their students into their greater secrets, eventually taking them through all three initiatic stages to bring them to the highest degree of comprehension. These three stages were marked by colored headbands: green for healers, the lowest grade of mastery; blue for teachers, the second degree of mastery; and white for master teachers, the third degree of initiation. This system is identical to that used by the Druids and the Egyptians, which is not surprising—linked as they all were through the Great White Brotherhood.[45]

CHAPTER 13

Children of the Light

They are eminent for fidelity and are the perfect ministers of Peace . . .
They also take great pains in studying the writings of the Ancients and
choose out of them that which is most for the advantage of their Soul
and body.[1]

—Flavius Josephus, *The Works of Flavius Josephus: The Wars of the Jews*

The Essenes formed the base of spiritual guidance for Jesus' mission in Palestine. Their community was divided into four main groups, each with its own social habits, interests, and skills. These were the monastic scholar-priests, the more social lay Essenes, the inner core of the deeply spiritual Nazarenes, and the militant Zealots.[2]

The monastic scholar-priests made up the inner level of the Essene community. These priests were all male, unmarried, and celibate, and they lived apart from the world, as many orders of ascetic monks do today. The aim of this group was self-purity and righteousness. One of their primary goals was the collection, transmission, and protection of all the ancient knowledge they could gather in their extensive libraries. They taught the original precepts of Moses, and were intent on transcribing and preserving old records of Earth's wisdom, including records of the great ages of mankind from before the Flood. This included knowledge of the sunken continent of Atlantis, Enoch's hidden books of discourses with the gods, and aspects of spiritual principles reflected in the original Hebrew teachings.[3] It also encompassed the Pythagorean traditions, the hermetic wisdom of Egypt, and the Greek philosophers whose teachings were opening the minds of many across the world.[4] They apparently also studied ancient books on Magical cures and exorcisms—volumes that were "the reputed works of Solomon, who composed treatises on miraculous cures and driving out evil spirits."[5]

In his *Antiquities of the Jews*, Josephus writes:

> They are scrupulous students of the ancient literature. They are ardent students in the healing of diseases, of the roots offering protection, and of the properties of stones. . . . They are sworn to love truth and to pursue liars. They must never steal. They are not allowed to keep any secrets from other members of the sect; but they are warned to reveal nothing to outsiders, even under the pain of death. They are not allowed to alter the "books" of the sect, and must keep all information secret, especially the names of the angels.[6]

This group of monastic scholar-priests is probably best represented in the traditional writings of the Torah, the Temple Scroll, the Community Rule, and the Damascus Document—all found among the Dead Sea Scrolls.[7]

The lay Essenes called themselves lay monks. They often had families, lived in a state of communal cooperation, and shared everything as common property. "The aim of this brotherhood was social harmony and peace through Universal Law," write Stuart Wilson and Joanna Prentis. "They respected human culture and the natural world, and . . . followed a strict vegetarian diet."[8] They remained focused on the esoteric Mysteries. Some of their members traveled widely, while others became scribes or researchers. Still others worked in the community. "There are also some among them who undertake to foretell future events," Josephus writes, "having been brought up from their youth in the study of the sacred Scripture, in divers purifications, and in the sayings of the prophets; and it is very seldom that they fail in their predictions."[9]

Where the scholar-priests focused primarily on the Hebrew scriptures, the lay Essenes were spiritually diverse, studying Buddhist, Egyptian, Greek, and Persian thought, as well as Hebrew and Druidic knowledge.[10] They formed the perfect nexus of wisdom, blending six of the twelve major streams of spiritual understanding into one. Their skills included teaching, research, and the arts of psychic self-defense. They had knowledge of gemstones, plants, and hands-on healing, and they understood the power of heat, light, sound vibration, numbers, sacred geometry, and color.

They recognized three different classifications of beings: humans, star beings (or extraterrestrials), and angelics, or beings from the spiritual dimensions. In fact, all of their fourteen major communion rituals worked with the seven female and seven male angels described above, each of whom oversaw a particular aspect of nature. It was part of the lay Essenes' practice to connect deliberately with these angels during the course of their day. They understood that, in the world of vibration, the divine life energy of the Creator can emanate from the Earth or the Sun, or from other stellar kingdoms.[11]

The third group of Essenes were the Nazoreans, a sub-sect of the monastic scholar-priests and lay Essenes that was linked to the royal Jewish bloodlines of the house of David.[12] Josephus wrote that the Nazorean sect lived on the banks of the Jordan River and the eastern shores of the Dead Sea about 150 years before Jesus was born. Contemporary scholars tell us that the heart of the Nazorean sect was located in Cochaba, a town in the Galilean-Damascene region, east of the Sea of Galilee.[13] They were called the "keepers of the covenant," or the *Nazrie ha Brit*, a name thought to derive from *Nazir*, meaning "a guardian of the truth," and *Essene*, meaning the "pious ones."

Assyriologist Heinrich Zimmern believes that the term Nazarene may even have entered the Hebrew language when the Jews were in exile in Babylon, perhaps created by the inner circle of the esoteric Jewish orders to protect the perennial truths of Moses that were being corrupted by time. Zimmern cites references to the Babylonian words *nasaru* or *nasiru*, meaning "keepers or pre-servers of divine secrets," telling us that this was the esoteric lineage most likely to have carried on the hidden wisdom of Moses' true teachings.[14]

In the Near and Middle East, the Nazoreans were associated with esoteric fraternities dedicated to safeguarding sacred knowledge. These initiatory fraternities were believed to have descended from the highly respected prophetic orders that were once influential throughout the ancient world. From this line, we get the books of the prophets in the Old Testament. Nazoreans were, in fact, Jesus' crucial link to the Mysteries, marking him as "the true heir of an age-old religious line."[15]

Certainly there are many reasons, not the least of which was his bloodline, to believe that Jesus was born into the Mystery traditions of the Nazoreans. Matthew 2:23 tells us plainly that Jesus was "a Nazarene," a member of this sect of prophets and "knowers of divine secrets." And yet Josephus, writing some eighty-nine years after the Crucifixion, says that the tradition of true prophetic succession had lapsed in Judea, and that it was dangerous for any Hebrew prophet from the north to preach in Jerusalem, which was under the jurisdiction of the Levitical and corrupted priests.[16]

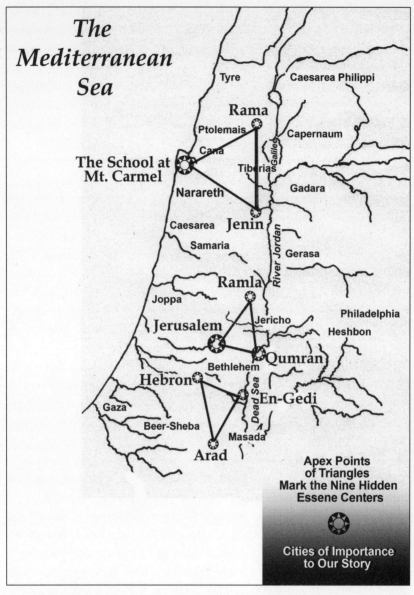

The Mediterranean Sea

Tyre

Caesarea Philippi

Rama

Ptolemais

Capernaum

Cana

The School at Mt. Carmel

Tiberias

Narareth

Gadara

Caesarea

Jenin

Samaria

Gerasa

River Jordan

Ramla

Joppa

Jericho

Philadelphia

Jerusalem

Heshbon

Bethlehem

Qumran

Hebron

Dead Sea

En-Gedi

Gaza

Beer-Sheba

Masada

Arad

Apex Points
of Triangles
Mark the Nine Hidden
Essene Centers

Cities of Importance
to Our Story

FIGURE 35. Map of Essene centers throughout Israel at the time of Jesus, taken from accounts of Essenes who lived at that time.

The rank of chief Nazarite high priest was traditionally held by the Davidic crown prince of Israel, who, like the ancient priests of Isis, wore ceremonial black, while other members of the order wore white. This role would have fallen naturally to Jesus, casting him in the role of prophet and inheritor of the crown. LaPage tells us, "The four initiatory grades of the Order appear to have been the equivalent of the four sacerdotal grades that once governed Hebrew society: that of priest, prophet, king, and messiah or avatar."[17] In the course of his lifetime, Jesus was to assume all these roles.

LaPage also explores the connection between the Nazoreans and the Mandaeans, a branch of the Semitic lineage who claim to be the last Gnostic sect in existence. They teach that John the Baptist was their preeminent teacher, and that Jesus, one of John's initiates, broke away from the original sect to form his own school, taking many of John's followers with him. This much is consistent with accounts in the New Testament, where John openly tells his students, "He must increase and I must decrease" (John 3:30). The Mandaeans also claim that Jesus violated their oath of secrecy by openly teaching their doctrines. This violation caused resentment among the members. Yet this open, democratic approach is consistent with Jesus' philosophy, which portrayed spiritual enlightenment as open to all, not just to the well-born or the elite.

The importance of the Nazorean sect is made clear when we understand the two major philosophical positions in Jewish thinking that were in contention at the time of Jesus' birth. On one hand, the dualistic Zoroastrian concept of heaven and hell, Satan and God, created a philosophical tension like a lethal tug of war. This tradition was taught by the Levitical priests and the great Sanhedrin in Jerusalem. On the other hand, the original esoteric teachings of Moses remained true to a wisdom that had come out of Egypt, honoring both the feminine and masculine aspect of God in balance with one another.

These two philosophies, alternately known as "Persian Judaism" and "Egyptian Judaism," can be loosely compared to fundamentalism and Gnosticism in Christian doctrine. The former is convinced that the world is going to end in a showdown between "us" and "them," and that God is going to punish all unbelievers with fire and brimstone. The latter believes in making a direct and living connection with the divine, and working to become more spiritually attuned to and responsible for our own words, thoughts, and actions. They practice kindness to all living things, including animals, and try not to participate in judgmental or dualistic thinking—a difficult task in the world in which we live. Those Christians trained in the ancient Mysteries traditions fall in the Gnostic camp.

As we can see in the Old Testament, Egyptian Judaism engendered a long line of prophets who claimed a direct connection with the source of Creation itself, and who acted as a check and balance for the secular Jewish kings, who were involved with everything from building cities and planning military strategies to ensuring food supplies and making laws. For centuries, these prophets acted as unacknowledged elders for the Jewish community and maintained hallowed repositories of knowledge in towns like Jericho, Bethel, and Sinai-Kadesh, and at the school at Mount Carmel in the north. As had been the tradition in Egypt, the high priest of this Nazorean order was traditionally a prophet whose office had been passed down for hundreds of years through the house of Zadok, a house that had been given its royal status by King Solomon himself.[18]

Yet this hidden priesthood was seen by the Levitical priests in Jerusalem as a threat. In fact, they were so afraid of the Nazorean influence that they passed laws saying that any man, after Ezra, who assumed the role of a prophet—by writing scripture, for example, or instructing the people—was "to be thrust through by his own mother and father" (Zechariah 13:3). They were forbidden to exercise their spiritual gifts and hereditary rites under pain of death. If they did not obey, they were forced into exile in the Syro-Palestinian wilderness, like John the Baptist. These "prophets were bitterly and increasingly at odds with the Levitical priesthood of the Temple, [thus] . . . the eclipse of the prophetic tradition and the rise to power of the Levites in the period of the second Temple must be regarded as the sign of some kind of Levitical power seizure."[19]

This knowledge throws considerable light on why Jesus chastised the Pharisees, saying, "You who shut up the kingdom of heaven in men's faces, neither going in yourselves nor allowing others to go in who want to." He upbraids the Pharisees for their censorship with these biting words: "Woe to you, scribes and Pharisees, hypocrites! Because you build the tombs of the prophets and adorn the monuments of the righteous, and say, 'If we had lived in the days of our fathers, we would not have been partakers with them in the blood of the prophets.' Therefore are you witnesses against yourselves that you are sons of those who murdered the prophets. Fill up, then, the measure of your father's guilt. Serpents, brood of vipers! How can you escape the condemnation of hell?" (Matthew 23:13, 29–34).

Michael Larson lends support to this theme of abuse by the priests and lawmakers from within their temple strongholds.

Under Alexander Jannaeus, who ruled [Judea] from 103-78 B.C., this hostility and persecution [against the Essenes by traditional Jewish sources] intensified. The Essene documents written during this period are filled with the fiercest denunciations of the Jewish priests and authorities, who not only raided the communes of the Holy Ones and decimated their membership, but were also guilty of constant acts of aggression against their innocent and unoffending neighbors. I know of no other literature more replete with comparable condemnations of acts of violence committed without provocation. . . .[20]

These politics were highly relevant to Jesus, because he was a prophet who, in his own country, could be put to death for teaching a higher wisdom. It was unsafe for him, as the Davidic crown prince, a high initiate of the Mystery orders of the Nazarite Essenes, and a truly advanced spiritual being, even to remain in his own country for most of his life. Although he did eventually return to his people to free them from the tyranny of a corrupt priesthood, it would not have been prudent for him to remain in Judea until he was ready to start his mission.

Modern esotericist Julius Evola writes that the role of sacred kingship is essentially a unifying one that correlates all the different belief systems and faiths in the world under one primordial spiritual tradition. This leader's task is to discover and then harmonize the many spiritual viewpoints. This is possible because the higher the initiate goes, the less important are the outer forms; this is the true criterion of kingship. Mystics, say the Muslim writers, meet in a spiritual world that is above form. Some members of the Nazorean community sought a more priestly king like Jesus, one who was a true avatar. Others hoped for a warrior king who would rise like David and lead them in battle. Yet it is clear that Jesus' teachings transcended even the doctrines of this special sect and became his own unique philosophy that encompassed the wisdom of the world.

THE ZEALOTS

The fourth group of Essenes were the Zealots—a feisty, difficult group considered by some to be fringe members of the sect. Unlike their vegetarian brothers, the Zealots were strong political activists who ate meat and sought the downfall of the Roman Empire through open rebellion and violence. They believed that only a militant response to the Roman occupation would solve their problems, and they looked for a Messiah who would overthrow Roman rule. The Zealots saw themselves as part of a holy "army of God" and frequently lived apart in the wilderness.

Like the Zoroastrians, the Zealots held an apocalyptic view of the future. In other words, salvation must ultimately come through a great confrontation between the forces of good and evil, dark and light. This polarized attitude grew out of their intense frustration with both the Roman military and the corrupt Sanhedrin, who had usurped the power of Jerusalem. The Zealots believed that they were the "good guys," and that the Romans and Sanhedrin council were enemies that needed to be destroyed. This dualism was grafted onto earlier forms of Judaism through their exposure to the Persian teachings of Zoroaster during the years of the Hebrews' captivity in Babylon. The Zealots believed they were moving toward a final Armageddon—an event that came to pass when Herod's temple was wiped out by the Romans in 68 C.E.

The Zealots were looking for a secular leader who would rise like King David to lead them in battle. But Jesus was not a Zealot, and the Zealot philosophy cannot be reconciled with his Buddhist values of love and peace. Jesus taught: "Those who live by the sword will die by the sword" (Matthew 26:52). He urged all men to "render unto Caesar those things that are Caesar's and unto God those things that are God's." He fought injustice with words and understanding, deliberately choosing not to lead a violent uprising, but rather to encourage a spiritual revolution in the world.[21]

Simon the Zealot, one of Jesus' disciples, took his name from this sect, and it is quite possible that Judas Iscariot was also a member. This may help explain Judas' disappointment with and betrayal of Jesus. He may have hoped to convince Jesus to take some political or military action against the Romans and the Sanhedrin.[22]

The Zealots wanted a warrior king who could deliver them from Roman rule. "They lived only for the day when a Messiah would emerge . . . and lead them in a victorious war against the Romans and their puppet kings and high priests, . . . so that once again there might be a pure line of high priests and kings of the Line of David in Israel."[23] Others longed for a spiritual Teacher of Righteousness to liberate their souls. Some expected a priest/king like Solomon who would restore Judea to its pre-conquest glory. Still others believed that the Messiah would come as two separate people—one from the priestly house of Aaron, the other from the secular house of David, mirroring the ancient relationship of Jewish kings and "holy prophets."[24] Thus, when John the Baptist first arose, many believed that the secular king's arrival was at hand. They hoped this "Christed one" would take up arms and lead them with Elijah at his side.[25]

And in the Damascus Document, a collection of rules and practices found among the Dead Sea Scrolls, we see these two figures being brought into one man—a true messiah or world avatar who would combine the priestly gifts of enlightenment with the secular power of kingship. Jesus was this very person. His path was not to engage the world in more bloodshed or suffering, but to pave the way for a new kind of freedom based on the lasting principles of illumination and heart—a message that has endured throughout the savagery of the 2000-year reign of Pisces.

Part IV

Jesus in the Land of the Celts

CHAPTER 14

The Holy Family in Britain

Did those feet in ancient time
Walk upon England's mountains green?
And was the holy lamb of God
On England's pleasant pastures seen?[1]

—William Blake, "Jerusalem"

Among the Great White Brotherhood, there are many stories of how Jesus spent his early teenage years—among them tales of his travels to the Druids, the Brahmins, the Buddhists, the Magi, and the Egyptians. All these groups had academies where the Mysteries were taught, and it was here that Jesus expanded his wisdom during his nearly three decades of growing mastery.

Over the past 200 years, a number of researchers have corroborated aspects of these stories, documenting Jesus' passage through various lands. Legends of his sojourn in the British Isles, for instance, seem to frame his life, culminating in the hauntingly beautiful stories of the Arthurian legends and the quest for the Holy Grail. There are reports of Jesus visiting Britain on at least four separate occasions: first as a young child around the age of seven visiting Cornwall and Scotland with his uncle, Joseph of Arimathea, and his mother, Mary; then around the age of fifteen, when he lived on the mysterious Isle of Avalon and studied with the Druids; then on a visit at around the age of thirty, after returning from India; and finally in 37 c.e., shortly after the Crucifixion.[2] The British historian Gildas writes that Jesus returned to Britain after he was resurrected to dedicate the Chapel at Avalon to his mother Mary.

There are many reasons why Jesus might have chosen to establish a powerful, long-lasting relationship with Britain—among them a certain spiritual kinship with the Druids, many of whose beliefs are reflected in Christianity. Many of the legends of his travels there come from Cornwall, the western geographic "boot" of England, where, for centuries, stories have been told of Joseph of Arimathea's involvement with the tin trade. One Cornish story reports that Joseph "came in a boat to Cornwall, and brought the boy Jesus with him, and the latter taught him how to extract tin and purge it from its wolfram. Even today the miners shout 'Joseph was in the trade!' when the tin is flashed."[3]

Legends of Jesus as a youth persist in Somerset as well, a region once known as the Summerland. These tales come from the villages of Priddy, Pilton, and Glastonbury, slightly south of the Mendip Hills where Joseph is said to have mined tin. This ancient site was once called Avalon, a mystical island of three gentle hills known as the Isle of the Blessed, whose history is rich with the legends of King Arthur and the Holy Grail. On the island, there is an area called Paradise, intricately tied to the Mystery rites of the Druids. Reverend Lionel Smithett Lewis, author of *St. Joseph of Arimathea in Glastonbury* tells us of Jesus traveling through Land's End in the far west of Cornwall, Saint Ives in the north, and Penzance in the south, as well as through the Ding Dong Mines at Penwith. "Saint Joseph, the foster father of Our Lord, used to come as a ship's carpenter there frequently to get tin, and . . . on one occasion he brought [with him] Our Lord."[4] This supports the Cornish legends of Jesus as a child under the loving care of his mother and his uncle.[5] Lewis cites evidence that, "as a youth Jesus traveled as a shipwright aboard a trading vessel of the Tyre, and that he was stormbound on the shores of west England throughout the winter."[6] Arthurian scholar Geoffrey Ashe and British historian Gordon Strachan both explore the legends of Jesus in England, citing over twenty ancient places in the English countryside that are called Issa, the Aramaic rendering of Jesus' name.

So strong, in fact, is the mark young Jesus made in those early years that, over 2000 years later, legends of his visits to the British Isles persist. A tinsmith foreman in Cornwall at the turn of the 20th century wrote: "We workers in metal are a very old fraternity, and like other handicrafts we have our traditions among us. One of these is that Joseph [of Arimathea] . . . made voyages to Cornwall in his own ships, and that on one occasion he brought with him the child Christ and his mother and landed them at Saint Michael's Mount"—a holy island off the southwest of Cornwall that is easily accessed from the coastal town of Penzance, whose name means "holy headland," perhaps referring to these same ancient legends.[7]

Dobson claims, "Our Lord not only visited Britain when a boy in the care of Joseph of Arimathea, but later, when a man, came and resided for some time at Glastonbury immediately prior to the beginning of His ministry at the age of 30, during which visit He preached here, contacted the Druids, and sowed the seeds of a future Christian Church in our land."[8] This legend is found in Cornwall, Somerset, Gloucestershire, Priddy, Pilton, and the west of Ireland.

Moreover, Dobson's claim is supported by an abundance of place names that bear the name Jesus used during his travels—*Issa*, or *Isa*, meaning "first-born." This name was also used by the Egyptian Coptic churches of the first century, who spelled Jesus' name as *Essa*. In India, Jesus was called Saint Issa, and *Isa* is the Aramaic spelling for Jesus found in the Koran, denoting him as the direct ambassador of the Divine. In Scotland, the name is linked to the Scottish Isle of Skye, close to Eilean Isa—an island that lies just off the coast of Dunvegan Bay. Eilean Isa translates as "the Isle of Jesus."[9]

Is the appearance of all these place names merely coincidental? Perhaps, but these English legends are supported by other evidence as well, like the legends uncovered by Henry Jenner in the Outer Hebrides and the story told by an old Falmouth woman, who claimed "Jesus passed by and blessed these parts."[10]

There is also a place in the north of Cornwall called Saint Issey, along with a spring named, appropriately, the Jesus Well.[11] And in the county of Limerick, Ireland, is a place called Cathair Essa, meaning the "chair of Essa," a throne where Jesus is said to have sat.[12]

Gildas, in fact, confirms that "We certainly know that Christ, the True Sun, afforded His light, the knowledge of His precepts, to our Island in the height of the reign of Tiberius Caesar," making Jesus somewhere between twenty-seven and thirty at the time of this visit—a time that coincides perfectly with reports that place him in Britain around the age of thirty.[13]

THE SACRED GEOMETRY OF THE DRUIDS

Few people realize today that, 2000 years ago, the nobility of Greece, Rome, and other countries throughout the Mediterranean sent their sons and daughters to study abroad, particularly in the British Isles. The influence of Druidic culture on Greek, Roman, and Jewish thought is thus a well-established fact in Roman records, and was even mentioned by Julius Caesar, who calls the British schools "colleges." Records reveal that, at the time of Jesus, some of the finest universities in the world were in the Celtic lands, and that the rich and noble of Greece and Rome sent their children there to study.[14] These schools were revered for their extensive knowledge of science, law, and religion—studies extremely important to the Essenes. At the time of Jesus, Druidic philosophy had been taught in Britain for over 2000 years, and Britain boasted "over sixty Universities and some 60,000 students." Scottish historian David Hume (1711–1776) wrote: "No religion has ever swayed the minds of men like the Druidic."[15]

The Druids welcomed students and teachers from every land. Their moral codes were high and their discipline strong—both tenets in keeping with the philosophy of the Essenes. In fact, the Druids, like the Essenes, were but another chapter of the Great White Brotherhood and displayed many of the same philosophic and social customs as their southern counterparts. For example, the Druids, like the Therapeutae and Essenes, wore only white clothing and taught healing, the laying on of hands, herbology, numerology, astronomy, astrology, mathematics, and angelic and star lore.[16] They were advanced in the arts of healing and prophecy and believed in the concept of a single God with many sub-divinities. Like the Egyptians and Essene Kabbalists, they based their philosophy on the concept of a trinity and the mystical Tree of Life.[17]

All of these sects embraced the teachings of Pythagoras and there is evidence that Pythagoras himself once studied with the Druids.[18] We know that Pythagoras was an initiate of virtually every Mystery tradition in the world—including the Greek, Persian, Egyptian, and Druid traditions—and we know that his wisdom was later incorporated into both the Essene and Druidic schools.[19] He was taught by the Archdruid Abaris, who was trained in the wisdom of Atlantis and is said to have had the power to fly.[20] The second-century Christian author Hippolytus writes: "The Celts honor them [the Druids] as prophets and seers because they foretell matters by the ciphers and numbers according to Pythagorean skill . . . [and] the Druids also practice the Magic arts."[21] To the untrained, science is often called "Magic," just as to the uninitiated, advanced gifts of the spirit seem to be miracles of God or even witchcraft. Later, in Jerusalem, Jesus himself would be accused of witchcraft by the Sanhedrin for his many miracles, which they called "Magic."

In his book *The Holy Land of Scotland*, Barry Dunford writes:

> The megalithic tradition in the British Isles can apparently be traced
> back to at least 3000 B.C., if not earlier. This tradition seems to have been
> based on a very sophisticated philosophy of sacred science such as was
> taught centuries later by the Pythagorean School. This ancient sacred
> science revolved around an awareness of the microcosmic energy systems
> of the earth being interconnected to a vast macrocosmic stellar matrix

encompassing the heavenly firmament. This is clearly portrayed by the geomantic and astrological alignments of numerous megalithic stone circles and other ancient sites throughout the world.[22]

Later, we will explore the Druids' geomantic knowledge and how this same system of heaven-and-earth alignments was reflected in Egyptian lore.

In fact, the Druids and the Essenes both had their roots in ancient Egypt and were probably connected through a common ancestry from the original Atlantean migrations.[23] Historians have documented the migration of Egyptian leadership into the British Isles around 1500 B.C.E. led by the mysterious Queen Scota, an Egyptian princess from the era of Akhenaton.[24] Later, her descendant, another Queen Scota, helped establish Egyptian customs and language among the local people. This historical link to Egypt is underscored by the discovery of Egyptian inscriptions and faience beads throughout Ireland and Scotland (286 to date)—artifacts identical to those found in the tombs of Egypt, thus establishing a clear connection between the cultures of the British Magi and the Egyptian Mystery Schools.[25]

There also seems to have been a large migration of Hebrews into Britain around 723 B.C.E., around the time that Samaria was conquered by the Assyrians. This was almost 150 years before King Solomon's palace in Judea fell to the Babylonians. All this provides evidence that Phoenicia, Egypt, and Israel had strong ancestral ties to Britain and that there were large integrated settlements of Hebrew immigrants occupying Celtic lands.[26]

Why does this matter in a book about Jesus? Because the sea-faring traffic between the Mediterranean cultures of Rome, Greece, Israel, and Egypt allowed commerce with the Celtic lands of the north. All of these cultures influenced the mystical lore of the Druids, which, in turn, helped to shape the education of Jesus. And they were all connected through the Great White Brotherhood. "It little matters what we call the members of those priesthoods," writes Barry Dunford, "Belites, Pastophori, Levites, Curetes, Magi, Brahmins or Druids; they were connected by secret ties and intercommunicated from the Indus to the Tiber, from the Nile to the Thames."[27]

Certainly by the time of Jesus, Druid teachers, like their Essene counterparts, practiced a critical balance between the physical, mental, emotional, and spiritual bodies, and cultivated the gifts of prophecy, healing, and opening the third eye. Like the Essenes, they believed in the coming of a world teacher who would reform the hearts of mankind, and they predicted that his name would be Yesu.[28] The Celts taught that there had been two such teachers in the past:

Beli, meaning "light," and *Taran*, the controlling providence of the present age.[29] Moreover, they believed in the coming of a world savior named Yesu, who would be the overseeing teacher of the future age.[30] This name is astonishingly close to Yeshua, the Hebrew rendering of Jesus' name, from the Hebrew word *yeshu'ah*, meaning "to save."

JOSEPH OF ARIMATHEA

The New Testament tells us that Joseph of Arimimathea was "a rich man ... who counted himself among Jesus' disciples" (Matthew 27:57–60). In the Gospel of Mark, we learn that he was "a prominent [Sanhedrin] Council member, who was himself waiting for the kingdom of God" (Mark 15:42–43). Likewise, Luke describes him as "a Council member [of the Sanhedrin], a good and just man, who had not consented to their counsel and deed [of the Crucifixion]" (Luke 23:50–51).

As his name implies, Joseph came from a place called Arimathea, a site that historians believe to be the little seaside town of Ramla, only eight miles north of Jerusalem.[31] Ramla, or Rama, was one of the nine Essene centers of wisdom and was linked in a triangle with the larger communities of Qumran and Jerusalem, and the birthplace of the biblical prophet Samuel. It was there that Joseph resided when he was in Judea conducting business with the Sanhedrin. Before he was known as Joseph of Arimathea, however, he was called Joseph of Marmore. *Mar* is an eastern term for lord, thus signifying "great," so this title may have meant "Great Lord Joseph." Marmore is also the name of an island just off of Smyrna, or Marmorica, the coastal district west of Egypt, so this name may also link Joseph to Egypt, suggesting more clues about his enigmatic past with the Egyptian brotherhood.[32]

The early Christian scholar Saint Jerome (347–420 C.E.) writes that Joseph was also a *Nobilis Decurio*, a recognized officer of rank within the Roman Empire. Gildas tells us that "a Decurion was established in every little mining centre, being charged with the care of the farms, the water supply, the sanitary arrangements and the local fortifications." Lewis reports that the office of a Decurion was of such importance that "it was easier to become a Senator of Rome than a Decurion in Pompeii."[33]

Joseph was also a legislative member of the provincial Roman Senate, earning him respect among the more established members of the Sanhedrin. This position was doubtless linked to his well-known tin-mining operations in Britain. As an essential ingredient of bronze, tin was crucial to the production

FIGURE 36. Joseph of Arimathea.
Illustrated by Sylvia Laurens.

of weapons for the Roman Empire, and Britain was the only major source of tin in the ancient world. Because Joseph's family had a virtual monopoly in the tin-mining industry, it is not surprising that Joseph was one of the richest and most influential men of his day, in both secular and religious circles.

In addition, many scholars believe that Joseph's family owned one of the largest private fleets in the world and traveled constantly between Cornwall and the many harbors of the Roman Empire. Such mobility would have given Jesus access to many ports of call, and allowed both Jesus and Joseph to stay in contact with other branches of the Great White Brotherhood throughout Europe, Africa, and Asia.[34]

We know that Joseph was likely a member of the Essene or Egyptian Therapeutae. A man who chose to keep his spiritual alliances to himself for social, political, and financial reasons, Joseph seems to have led a double life—as a servant of a higher spiritual order and as a man who was both wealthy and well connected. His position on the Sanhedrin High Council and his ability to travel widely by sea also gave him access to many powerful people, allowing him to wield influence in places where more monastic Essenes could not.

Only such a position of authority could have enabled Joseph to meet with Pontius Pilate on the eve of the Crucifixion, as described in the Gospel of Matthew (27:57–58). It was at Joseph's request that Jesus' body was released just hours after his death, to be buried in Joseph's own tomb. Dobson writes: "Both the Roman and Jewish law laid it down as a duty for the nearest relatives to dispose of the dead irrespective of how they had died. . . . Joseph, if a relative, would be obeying the law, both Jewish and Roman, and fulfilling a duty, and Pilate could give ready consent without fear of giving offense."[35]

ANNA, MARY, AND CHRIST

Once Jesus graduated from the Essene school at Mt. Carmel, it was natural his parents would send him to Britain to continue his education, since there were already strong links between Jesus' family and the Celtic nobility. In fact, Anna, Mary's mother, came from Cornwall.[36]

> Anna was born of Cornauaille [Cornwall], of royal blood. Brutally treated by a jealous husband, when with child, she fled towards the sea; an angel caused her to enter a vessel, and took her to Asia and then to Jaffa, where she landed, and whence she reached Nazareth. There she gave birth to a little girl, whom she named Mary. When the child was fifteen years old, she was married to a carpenter, named Joseph, and Anna then prayed to God to take her back to Cornouaille. The same angel again took her over the waves. Anna found that her husband [in Britain] was dead, divided her property among his vassals, and ended her days beside the bay of Palue near the well, which is still to be seen there, in a little cot, where Jesus came several times to visit her. When she died, her body vanished.[37]

Elsewhere, Anna is described as "a princess from a Celtic family in Britain. She was a very wise and graceful person, but also a person of authority. We recognized her as someone of real ability, a high initiate." This report confirms Anna's arranged marriage to an Essene husband, her return to Britain after his death, and young Mary's later marriage to Joseph.[38]

In Cornwall, there are a number of place names that seem to support this story, specifically an island off the coast of Cornall called Lammana (Lam Anna), which means "Church of Anna." Legend says that Jesus visited here with his uncle, and the island is home to a 2000-year-old well called Saint Anna's Well.[39] Near it are chapels named Saint Anna's Chapel and Lan Anna, both dedicated to Jesus' grandmother.[40]

On the mainland across from the island, excavations in the 1930s uncovered 2000-year-old Mediterranean artifacts brought by sea-faring traders who once visited these shores. At this ancient community is another well dedicated to Anna, and a single rock called "Essa's Bed," a place where Jesus may have slept when he visited his grandmother. Close by is Saint Just in Roseland, and another Saint Just sits on the western edge of Cornwall. These names may well refer to visits by Joseph of Arimathea.

Mary Caine, author of *The Glastonbury Zodiac*, writes that Anna's family "was known as the Gewissae, which surely means the Knowers or the Wise Ones, perhaps [even the] Gnostics."[41] The Gewissae harken back to an ancient matriarchal past when Celtic power was passed through the bloodlines of the mother, just as it was in early Hebrew times. The Indo-European word *gwen*, which means "woman," appears in the name Guinevere, which means "woman or wife." Eventually, the name came to mean queen, or an empowered female sovereign.[42] Gewissae also contains the word Issa, the Aramaic rendering of the Hebrew name Joshua, meaning "firstborn son."[43] In ancient Sanskrit, the creator God of the universe and architect of the visible world is Issara. Since Ra is the name of the Egyptian Lord of Light, Issara means literally "the first born Son of Light," the creator of the visible worlds.[44]

It is from the ruling clan of the Gewissae that the great Celtic kings of legend originated—Bran, Berlin, and Gwydion. Caine adds, "It is not surprising to find then that Merlin came from the land of the Gewissae."[45] Merlin, the Magician of Arthurian legend, is believed to be descended from a line of Druid Magi well versed in the Mysteries. If Caine's history is accurate, it suggests that Anna, Jesus' grandmother, came from a Celtic line of priest-kings with great mystical powers—the same royal bloodline that later birthed Merlin. This explains why Britain has long been at the center of the Grail Mysteries and means that Jesus had a royal Druidic heritage, as well as being of the royal Davidic bloodline.

THE PROTEVANGELION

The Protevangelion is an apocryphal gospel that emerged during the second century of our common era. It relates a rather sanitized version of the story of Anna put out by the Catholic Church. In this version, the story picks up when Anna is married to Joachim, a man of Hebrew descent. She has already borne the child of her Celtic husband that she was carrying when she fled. The Protevangelion claims that, when Anna conceived Mary, she was past her best childbearing years—perhaps as young as thirty or forty. Joachim is reprimanded by the Jewish high priest for not having produced any Jewish children—a man's worth being determined by his ability to produce heirs (Luke 2:23). The de-

FIGURE 37. Like the legendary sage Merlin, Druids often carried Ogham staffs upon which they wrote their teachings in the sacred language of the trees, largely lost to the modern world. Illustrated by Sylvia Laurens.

spairing couple goes into seclusion to pray and Anna promises to dedicate any child she bears to the temple. In answer, "An angel of the Lord stood by her side and said, 'Anna, Anna, the Lord hath heard thy prayer; thou shalt conceive and bring forth, and thy progeny shall be spoken of in all the world.'"[46]

Mary is consecrated to the temple at the age of three, growing up in a pure environment, completely dedicated to God. This explains how and why Mary remained a vestal virgin. When she is almost thirteen, she is betrothed by the high priest to the carpenter Joseph.

Joseph is portrayed in the Protevangelion as a well-respected older member of the community, a member of the Essenes or Great White Brotherhood, and a builder by trade. The Hebrew word for carpenter is *nagger*, but it is significant that it can also mean "scholar," or "man of learning."[47] This second meaning was eventually lost and Jesus simply became "the carpenter" in Christian tradition—a metaphor for one who builds the temple of God within himself.

The Protevangelion describes Joseph as a widower who owns his own house and has already raised one family. Joseph objects that he is too old for Mary, but he is admonished not to go against the "will of the Lord." So reluctantly, Joseph accepts the betrothal, leaving the young maiden to live in his house alone while he finishes a six-month construction project in another village. When Joseph returns home, he finds that Mary is pregnant. Understandably, he is very upset. But Mary tells him she has been visited by "an angel of the Lord."

> And she took a pot and went out to draw water, and heard a voice saying unto her, "Hail thou, who art full of grace, the Lord is with thee; thou art blessed among women." And she looked around to the right and to the left [to see] whence that voice came, and then trembling, went into her house . . . And behold, the angel of the Lord stood by her, and said, "Fear not, Mary, for thou hast found favor in the sight of God. . . . The Lord is with thee, and thou shalt conceive. . . . the Holy Ghost shall come upon thee, and the power of the Most High shall overshadow thee; wherefore that which shall be born of thee shall be holy, and shall be called the Son of the Living God, and thou shalt call his name Jesus." . . . And Mary said, "Behold the handmaid of the Lord; let it be unto me according to thy word. . . ."[48]

We may never know whether this story is true or merely fabricated by the church to establish Mary's virginity, but it does match the visitation stories in the canonical gospels of Matthew and Luke. And if the Celtic legends are true, then Joseph of Arimathea is either Mary's older brother from Anna's previous marriage, or her younger brother, conceived by Anna and her new Essene husband after Mary was given to the temple. In either case, this makes Joseph of Arimathea Jesus' uncle. Stuart Wilson and Joanna Prentis maintain that Joseph was indeed Mary's older brother (by some four years), and that Anna remarried only shortly after arriving in Palestine.[49] This explains the puzzling mystery of how Joseph of Arimathea could have lived until 76 or 82 c.e., when British records report he died. The relationship is significant because, under both Roman and Hebrew law, the next male kin becomes the legal guardian of the family on the death of the father, explaining why Joseph of Arimathea should have been the one to step forward at the time of Jesus' death, and request his body for burial from Pontius Pilate.

The Protevangelion did not surface until nearly 200 years after Jesus' death. Given the church's reputation for destroying, altering, and manufacturing records, we must take its content with the proverbial grain of salt. This very "Christianized" account portrays Anna as an obedient Hebrew wife, willing to sacrifice her long-awaited little girl to the patriarchs of the Jewish temple. Yet older Celtic accounts of Anna describe her as an independent, headstrong woman with powerful mystical gifts—a woman with the courage to choose her own path. Understandably, the church would not want to portray the grandmother of their god as an independent Celtic woman, instead of as an obedient, compliant Hebrew wife. In fact, in the decades following the Crucifixion, with both the Sanhedrin and the Romans in pursuit of any followers of Jesus, even his disciples might have wanted to conceal this connection with Britain to protect the Holy Family when they fled to their ancestral home.

CHAPTER 15

The Mysterious Druids

Ancient man contained in his mightly limbs all things in heaven and earth.[1]

—William Blake, Chosen Chief of the Druids Order from 1799–1827

Today, little is known of the daily life of the Druids, but we know enough about their beliefs to know that there were many similarities between this ancient philosophy and modern Christian teachings.

The term *druid* has many different meanings, including "to enclose within a circle."[2] This term honored the unity of Creation, and referred to one who is admitted into the innermost circle of wisdom. The symbol of the circle was thus holy to the Druids, representing the entryway into the innermost Mysteries. The circle symbolized the essence of life and was often displayed as an evergreen wreath like those we use at Christmas to express the eternal renewal of life.

The name Druid may come from *dero*, or *derry*, the Irish word for oak. Barry Dunford, however, thinks it "far more probable that the oak tree was named after the Druids," adding that the word *druid* itself derives from "the Persian *duru*, meaning a good holy man; [and] the Arabic *deri*, meaning a wise man."[3] Harold Bayley notes that the word for "[t]ree is the same word as true, and *dru*, the Sanskrit word for tree." Trees in general, and oaks in particular, were central to the Druids' teachings about the Tree of Life—a symbol found in many Mystery traditions around the world. In fact, the Welsh word *derwyd* and the Irish word

FIGURE 38. Celtic wreath with the two pillars of wisdom.

drui are both derived from the Sanskrit root word *Veda*, which means "to see" or "to know."[4] Thus the word *druid* draws on multiple meanings.

"The Druid beliefs were as sophisticated as any spiritual teaching in the world today," write John and Caitlin Matthews. "[They] have been likened to the profound Eleusinian Mysteries of ancient Greece, the Egyptian Mysteries of Isis and Osiris, the Hindu Brahmins of India, and the Christian Mystery of being 'born again.'"[5] Like their Essene counterparts, the Druids believed in reincarnation, the immortality of the soul, and the purity of nature as the handiwork of God. Unlike the Essenes, however, who were forced to hide their esoteric wisdom from the local religious authorities, the Druids were able to teach openly and without fear of retribution.

They believed in one eternal God expressed in a trinity, representing the totality of being as three concentric circles. The one God behind it all they called *Duw* or *HU*, the great creator of light, the One without whom darkness would pervade the entire universe. In the beginning, there was nothing but God and *Annwn*, or the spirit world. Life began when the Word-God pronounced his ineffable name, and the primal substance of the universe was formed. The universe was "conceived of as a multitude of tiny, invisible atoms, each being a microcosm, for God is complete in each of them, just as each is part of God, the Whole. In the innermost circle of the three concentric rings lay *Abred*, the place from which life itself sprang. The next circle was *Gwynedd*, or purity, in which life is manifested as a pure rejoicing force, having attained its triumph over evil. And the last and outermost circle was *Ceugant or infinity*."[6] This circle was inhabited by God alone, and its image was represented by the luminous rays of the Sun.

FIGURE 39. The three-fold Celtic leaf expresses the concepts of the trinity, the three circles of initiation, and the multi-dimensional levels of reality.

This trinity can also be seen in the classic emblem of Druidism, three golden rays of light. It is also revealed in the ancient symbols of the three-fold oak leaf, and three rotating spirals. The first symbol contains the Vesica Pisces, formed by the merger of two interlocking circles, the perfect balance of male and female, and also forming the shape of an Eye, a symbol sacred to many traditions and honored by the Egyptians, the Buddhists, the Celts, the Greeks, and the Hindus under a variety of names. In the 1525 Renaissance painting the Supper of Emmau, it appears above Jesus' head enclosed within a triangle. It has been painted within the walls of the Vatican, and above the altar of Saint Aloysius Church in London, which was built by French Catholics in 1808.[7] The symbol represents the spiritual Sight, or Third Eye, that each initiate must awaken, a sight Jesus referred to in the Gospel of Thomas when he said: "When you make [the two] eyes into an eye . . . then you will see the Kingdom of Heaven."[8]

The Druids' belief in a trinity, which can be found throughout their celebrations and teachings, also related to the past, present, and future—represented by *Beli*, meaning "light, *Taran*, whom many equate with the Greek, Roman, and Sumerian gods of thunder, and *Yesu*, whom they predicted as the ruler of the coming age."[9] And this three-fold symbolism appears under many other guises as well. The Welsh Triads, a collection of medieval manuscripts preserving Welsh history and folklore, reveal three objects of remembrance essential to a soul's enlightenment: the properties of all being, the knowledge of all things, and the power to conquer evil. The Druids acknowledged three masculine qualities—courage, honor, and manliness—and three feminine qualities—decency, chastity, and decorum.[10] They defined three kinds of knowledge: the knowledge to name each thing, the knowledge to learn its cause, and the knowledge to understand its influence. They sought the decrease of three things in the world—

darkness, falsehood, and death—and the increase of three others—light, life, and truth.

The Druids were physicians, poets, and prophets, and their educational system was superior to that of their colleagues on the Continent. Like others who honored nature as their finest teacher, the Druids strove to live in harmony with the Earth. They believed in a fairyland of nature spirits that manifested in the mortal world. "All happenings were motivated by an interplay of unseen rays from the Source. Therefore the running of a hare, flight of birds, fall of leaves, patterns in sand, and the sound of waters, were all meaningful."[11] *The Kolbrin Bible*, a collection of ancient writings preserved at Glastonbury Abbey, says that the Druids "believed in the One Supreme Being, but also held that there was a body of lesser Beings."[12]

Similarities between the Druid tradition and Christianity run deep. Manly P. Hall writes:

> The Druids had a Madonna, a Virgin Mother, with a Child in her arms, who was sacred to their Mysteries; and their Sun God was resurrected at the time of year corresponding to that at which modern Christians celebrate Easter. Both the cross and the serpent were sacred to the Druids, who made the former by cutting off all the branches of an oak tree and fastening one of them to the main truck in the form of the letter T. This oaken cross became symbolic of their superior Deity. . . . They also had great veneration for the Nature spirits, little creatures of the forests and rivers to whom many offerings were made.[13]

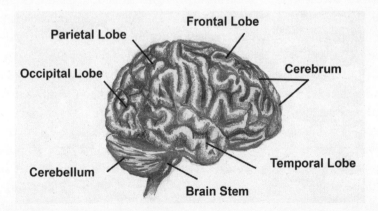

FIGURE 40. Seven areas of the brain, reflecting the seven paths of the Celtic spiral.

The Druids also had great knowledge of the stars and the seasons, the magnetic fields of the Earth, and the seen and unseen relationships between dimensions. They knew of the golden-mean spiral upon which all life is based, and they inscribed this symbol on the stones and landscapes of their open-air temples—in the giant earthworks at Glastonbury Tor, with its huge seven-circuit spiral, and in the stone engravings at Newgrange in Ireland.[14]

The seven-layered labyrinths used across the world can all be traced back to the Druids. This labyrinth pattern was used as a means of balancing the left and right sides of the brain, and providing an interactive, third-dimensional metaphor for the soul's journey through the seven multi-dimensional planes of the universe. These seven sacred circuits also represented the seven parts of the brain, and the seven types of serotonin receptors found within it.[15] Today, we see this labyrinth pattern inlaid in the nave of Chartres Cathedral in France. Yet centuries before this glyph was laid down by the Freemasons who built Chartres, it was etched on the rock walls of forests in ancient England and used in Druidic ceremonies of initiation at Glastonbury Tor. The Celts called it the Never-ending Circle.[16]

The Druid Path

Because Druidry was primarily an oral tradition, there is still much that we do not know about its teachings. We do know, however, that, like their Essene counterparts, the Druids had three orders of initiates and two orders of teachers. Like most Mystery Schools, they taught a simple moral code to the lower aspirants and a deeper esoteric science to the higher initiates. And like the Essenes and Therapeutae, they used color to denote the rank of their students—green for healers, blue for historian/teachers, and white for masters—the students wearing sashes of these colors like Therapeutae and Mithraic priests.

The Ovates, or healers, dressed in green; the Bards were robed in sky blue; and the masters wore white for purity, the color closest to that of the Sun.[17] Aspiring students wore robes of green, blue, and white stripes. The healers were trained in medicine, astronomy, poetry, and music. The Bards were expected to memorize some 20,000 verses of Druidic history, transmitted through poetry, legend, and song, and were often depicted holding Celtic harps. In fact, one of the chief ways we know about the Druids today is through the poetry of the Celtic Bard Taliesin, a sixth-century mystic poet and teacher who predated Merlin.[18] The Druids, the last and highest order, ministered to the religious needs of the entire community, provided leadership and counsel, and oversaw the ceremonial rites of the order.

There were two classes of Druidic teachers: the *dryones*, who were masters of medicine and divination, and the *druthin*, who were gifted with twin-sight.[19] The *dryones* had their seat at Abri, now modern Avebury; the *druthin* presided at Avalon, "the Isle of indestructible apples"—the island where Jesus is believed to have lived.[20]

At the head of the Druid order were two Archdruids, third-level initiates who had passed through six additional degrees.[21] Understandably, very few candidates made it through all three grades, let alone these last six degrees, to become one of the two Archdruids, acknowledged as the wisest sages of the land. Candidates were chosen for their integrity, spirituality, and heart. And just as Jesus had twelve disciples, the Archdruids had twelve chief Druids who served them, placing them, like Jesus, in the center like the Sun.[22]

Over the course of the full twenty-year training program, each initiate was instructed in the creation of the universe, the personalities of the divinities, the laws of nature, the secrets of medicine, the science of celestial mechanics, and the rudiments of Magic.[23] As with most Mystery Schools, students were bound by secrecy and only the best advanced through the ranks. Like the Therapeutae and Essenes, the Druids lived close to nature in communities of small houses similar to monasteries, giving them time for both solitude and social gatherings. And many Druids retired from the world altogether, living in caves or hermitages deep in the forest.

Diogenes Laertius writes that the Druids taught through symbols and allegories, not unlike Jesus. Aspirants died a symbolic death and were then

FIGURE 41. Celtic bards were often depicted with a harp. Druidic bards were required to learn over 10,000 songs that transmitted their histories and could be used as a teaching tool for spiritual and lay people alike.

regenerated from the womb of Ceridwen, the Earth Mother. In one initiation, newly born initiates were set adrift in a small boat without oars, symbolic of the ark.[24] To return to shore, they had to master the ability to direct both the wind and the waters, abilities that Jesus demonstrated during his ministry in Galilee.

The Druids' greatest initiations took place at Caer Gaur, better known as Stonehenge. The word *Caer* means "castle" or "gate," a reference to the inter-dimensional doorways associated with the Druids' rites. Jesus once made his home among the Druids at Caer Sidi, the "revolving castle of light."

Stonehenge consists of two great circles of stones, one inside the other. When Jesus studied in Britain, this open-air temple was intact and in use as one of the Druids' main ceremonial sites.[25] Its dimensions were based on the Egyptian royal cubit (20.610 inches or 523.5 millimeters), clearly indicating that the Druids had access to the advanced architectural and astronomical knowledge of the Egyptians.[26] The outer circle—which is comprised of sixty giant stones, one for each of the sixty minutes in an hour—is thirty-three Egyptian royal cubits in diameter, a number reflected in the initiation steps used in Masonic lodges. Leadbeater writes:

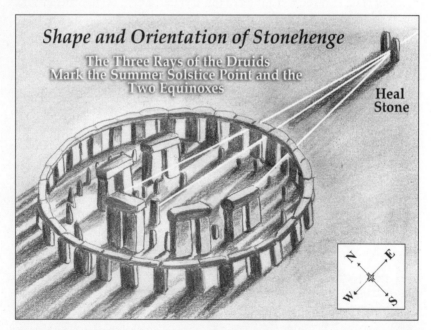

FIGURE 42. At Stonehenge, three rays of light were created by the movement of the Sun each year through the four key solar points: the summer and winter solstices, and the vernal and autumnal equinoxes.

The origins of the Mysteries of the Druids may be traced to the great
World Teacher [Thoth] . . . though they were also influenced somewhat
by the still older Mysteries of Ireland which date from Atlantean times.
The lyre of Apollo become the harp of Angus; and the old worship of
God, as the divine beauty manifesting through music, thus passed down
into Britain.[27]

Other indications of Egyptian influence in the British Isles include a number of pyramids and obelisks scattered throughout the countryside.[28]

Modern researchers believe that Stonehenge was dedicated to the larger
solar cycles of the year, and was also used to predict eclipses and the Moon's
cycles, and the 26,000-year cycle of precession, which encompasses all twelve
signs of the zodiac and systematically aligns our solar system, like a great celestial clock, with the center of the galaxy.[29] In Britain, this wheel of stars was
known as Arianrhod's Silver Wheel, named after the Goddess of Fate.[30] This
described the slow turning movement of the luminous stars around the world
axis of the pole star. During the course of its revolution, the north pole aligns
with the center of the galaxy and the constellation Lyra, and then slowly rotates
toward the North Star, Polaris, bringing levels of greater or lesser awareness to
mankind. Knowledge of these great cosmic cycles was taught by the Druids, as
well as by the Egyptian and Persian Mystery Schools. Much of the encoding of
hermetic symbols transmitted by the Mystery Schools was intended to preserve
this knowledge during cycles of spiritual slumber.

At the heart of this cosmic science was an awareness that the Sun stood at
the center of the zodiacal wheel, encircled by the twelve signs. Thus, the number twelve was central to Druidic symbology: twelve hides of land were granted
to Joseph of Arimathea in Avalon after the Crucifixion; twelve disciples formed
the first church; twelve monks under Saint Patrick continued this tradition;
twelve knights graced the Round Table; the Glastonbury Zodiac was twelve
miles wide.[31] Yet, even when Jesus lived, much of this sacred science had already
gone underground. Only the keepers of the Mysteries would have known of it.
The fact that Jesus chose twelve apostles informs us that he was a student of
these star Mysteries and had trained in this wisdom.

DRUIDRY AND CHRISTIANITY

Like modern Christians, the Druids celebrated the birth of the Lord of Light on
December 25 and the resurrection of the solar lord at the time of year we now
celebrate Easter. Their teachings also included a Virgin Mother with a child in

her arms, most likely based on Isis and her savior son, Horus, who were the early progenitors of the mother and son known in Christianity today. Similar to modern Christians, the Druids believed that the world had three divisions, roughly equating to the celestial and terrestrial realms, and the underworld—although their versions of heaven and hell were far less punishing than Christian conceptions. And, like the Roman Catholic Church, the Druids taught that there were seven deadly sins: hypocrisy, theft, cowardice, fornication, gluttony, indolence, and extortion.[32]

As we discovered earlier, the Druids used the symbolic language of hermetics to teach their highest concepts, and many of their symbols are still used in Christianity today—the trinity, the lion, the dove, the savior god on the cross of life, and the circle mirrored in evergreen wreaths. Like other Mystery Schools, they also used the Great Cosmic Egg as a symbol of the unity from which the universe sprang—a symbol seen in Easter eggs each spring to celebrate new life. But perhaps their most powerful symbols were the One World Tree, the One World Mountain, and the Holy Spring. We'll explore these in the next three chapters.

CHAPTER 16

The Tree of Life and the World Tree

Grant, O God, Thy protection; and in protection, strength;

And in strength, understanding; and in understanding, knowledge;

And in knowledge, the knowledge of justice; and in the knowledge of
     justice, the love of it;

And in that love, the love of all existences;

and in the love of all existences, the love of God—God and all goodness.[1]

—The Universal Druid Prayer, Ross Nichols

To the Celts, the study of trees was a sacred science, for they believed that trees possessed memory and held the power of witness.[2] Thus tribal meetings and spiritual ceremonies often took place beneath a particularly holy tree. In the most practical terms, without trees, life would have been extraordinarily difficult, for they provided food, shelter, and firewood. The forest itself was a sanctuary connected to the divine Source of all that is, and the Druids categorized the various trees according to their physical, spiritual, and vibrational qualities. To this end, they developed a language called *Ogham*. This was a Magical alphabet of twenty-five runic ciphers known only to the Druid priests and used by the initiated to communicate with one another. In this alphabet, each rune was associated with a specific tree, and these stick-like tree figures were inscribed on markers to indicate both land boundaries and holy places.[3]

The Druids also believed that trees had a deeper spiritual purpose, serving as portals into the Otherworld and opening up a way into the world of spirits, gods, and ancestors. The English word "door," in fact, derives from the Celtic word for oak, *daur*. So, symbolically, the roots of the oak tree were considered doorways to the Otherworld. This is why the Druids chose a tree to represent their spiritual path—the Tree of Life, an ancient mystical icon of the connection of the human with the heavenly realms. The Druids believed that a tree sits at the center of the heavenly Garden of Eden—a tree symbolized by the strong and noble oak. At the top of this tree was the Pole Star, around which the entire heavens turned. This tree was the World Axis, around which moved Arianrhod's Silver Wheel, the wheel of the galaxy. At the bottom of the tree ran the holy spring, the place of the waters of Nun, the Ocean of Love and Mercy that had first given birth to the Universe. All of these are powerful hermetic symbols honored by mystics throughout the ages in many religions.

These symbols are also common in Christian lore, and were well known to mystics across the world, including Jews, Mayans, Sumerians, Native Americans, and Buddhists. Both Jewish and Christian theologies refer to the Tree of Life and the Tree of the Knowledge of Good and Evil. John speaks of a similar vision of heaven in Revelation: "And he showed me a pure river of the waters of life, clear as crystal, proceeding from the throne of God and of the Lamb. In the middle of the street, and on either side of the river, was the Tree of Life, which bore twelve fruits, each tree yielding its fruit every month. And the leaves of the tree were for the healing of the nations" (the Revelation of Jesus Christ 22:1-2). In Psalms, we read: "He shall be like a tree planted by the rivers of water that brings forth its fruit in its season, whose leaf also shall not wither; and whatever he does shall prosper" (Psalms 1:3). Jesus tells us: "To him who overcomes I will give to eat from the Tree of Life, which is in the midst of the Paradise of God" (The Revelation of Jesus Christ 2:7). And again: "Whoever drinks of this water will thirst again, but whoever drinks of the water that I shall give him will never thirst. But the water that I shall give him will become in him a fountain of water springing up into everlasting life" (John 4:13–14). So, in the language of the Mysteries, the Tree of Life and the holy waters represent the nourishment, wisdom, and immortality to be gained through connection with the inner worlds.

In the apocryphal Book of Enoch, studied by the Essenes and Gnostics, Enoch is taken by an angel to a high mountain where he is shown a grove of fragrant trees encircling the throne of the Most High. "Among them was a tree like no other. Its fragrance was beyond all fragrance, and its leaves and blooms and wood never withered. Its fruit was beautiful, resembling the dates of the palm." The archangel Michael then tells Enoch about the tree:

> As for this fragrant tree, no mortal is permitted to touch it till the great judgment when God's justice redresses all and brings everything to its

ultimate consummation. The tree shall then be given to the good and holy. Its food shall be food for the elect. It shall be transplanted to the holy temple of the Lord, the eternal king.[4]

What are we to make of this statement? Manly P. Hall offers this:

> The Tree of Life represents the spiritual point of balance—the secret of immortality. The Tree of the Knowledge of Good and Evil, as its name implies, represents polarity, or unbalance, the secret of mortality. . . . Though humanity is still wandering in a world of good and evil, it will ultimately attain completion and eat of the fruit of the Tree of Life growing in the midst of the illusionary garden of worldly things. Thus the Tree of Life is also the appointed symbol of the Mysteries, and by partaking of its fruit man attains immortality.[5]

Certainly we find that, throughout history, many saviors and sages carried rods, wands, or staffs hewn from the wood of sacred trees, including Moses, Aaron, Thoth/Hermes, and Aesculapius. Celtic Druids carried staffs on which their most sacred beliefs were inscribed in the runes of Ogham. This custom was continued by early Christians and is recorded by one of the writers of the

FIGURE 43. Perhaps the earliest depiction of the Tree of Life comes from Sumeria, believed to have been the home of the Garden of Eden. The vine-like nature of this Tree is connected to the quest for immortality, for its fruits were said to grant eternal life.

Acts of Saint Patrick, preserved in the *Book of Armagh*. These staffs were still in use in Ireland in the fifth century among Christian monks. The fathers of the early Christian church sometimes used the tree to symbolize Christ, hoping that, like the mighty oak, the church would overshadow all other faiths. Because of the tree's annual cycle of life, death, and renewal, it was also seen as a symbol of resurrection and rebirth.[6]

THE KABBALISTIC TREE OF LIFE

To the Jews, the sacred tree was epitomized in the sacred Kabbala, a roadmap back to the heart of God. The root of the word *Kabbala* (also spelled Qabbala, Cabbala, and Cabala) means "to receive," "to reveal," or "to accept." The Kabbalistic Tree of Life reveals eleven basic cosmic principles that initiates must master as they ascend to merge with the Supreme Creator. These principles are depicted as spheres called *sephiroth*. They can also be seen as divinities or god/goddesses that exist within us, archetypes that must be embraced or embodied to come to mastery. The lowest sphere, Malkuth, represents the earthly world of form. In order to access the spheres above it, initiates had to move into the intuitive world of the emotions, Yesod, the lunar sphere of the Divine Feminine. Above the Moon lies Tipareth, the sphere of the Sun, long identified with Jesus or the Christ, the radiant energies of the heart. Directly above that, leading to the highest pinnacle, is Daath, the hidden sphere of Pluto, the great lord of life, death, and resurrection.

Jesus is associated with both the radiance of the Sun and the Lord of the Dead, representing hidden knowledge. This is made clear in the apocryphal Gospel of Bartholomew, where Jesus tells us: "The souls of the righteous, when they leave the body, go to Paradise, and unless I am present there they cannot enter."[7] This is, of course, the role ascribed to Osiris in ancient Egypt, who was seen as the Lord of Light who waits for us in the Halls of the Dead. Thus the sphere of Daath represents the most hidden realms of wisdom, available only to those who have integrated their shadow selves, died to their ego, and been reborn in spirit (born again), as taught by the Mysteries. Without this alchemical process, it is impossible to reach Kether, the crown sphere, which represents the unity of the All.

In the ancient world, each of these eleven spheres was dedicated to a planetary body or a god who represented the archetypal energies of Venus, Mercury, the Moon, Mars, the Earth, Jupiter, Saturn, Uranus, Neptune, and Pluto. In their most perfected form, these aspects of the Divine symbolize the qualities of splendorous love, victory of thought, intuition and feeling, physicality in action, our grounded kingdom, expansion, light and mercy, the structural laws of karma, awakening wisdom, mystic illumination, and the doorway to the unseen realms beyond our solar system. As gods and goddesses, these archetypes exist as a living potential within us all, and were well known to Mystery initiates of the ancient world. The Mysteries taught that each of us has God within and that, by embracing these aspects of our own nature, we can fully awaken to our own divinity and unite with God. Jesus reminds us of this when he says: "Is it not written in your law, I said, 'Ye are gods'? If he [Moses] called them gods, to whom the word of God came, do you say of Him whom the Father sanctified and sent into the world, 'You are blaspheming,' because I said, 'I am the Son of God'" (John 10:34–36).

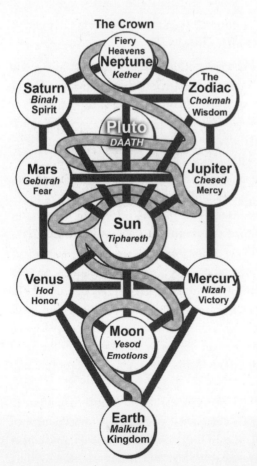

FIGURE 44. A refined and complex Hebrew Tree of Life depicts the many steps to self-mastery through Sephiroth (spheres) linked to the archetypal energies of the planets and the gods and goddesses that live within us all. These qualities range from love to wisdom, courage to intuition. Ascension can only take place in the world of Malkuth, the earthly world of form, accessed through the realm of the emotions, Yesod.

As an archetypal vision of Jesus on the cross, the Tree represents the worlds of time and space. Jesus' head and body are in exact alignment with the Moon, the Sun, and Pluto. Thus, the image of Jesus hanging on the cross becomes a hermetic emblem for his mastery of both the male and female energies, his identification with the solar matrix as the Sun/Son of God, and his assumption of the role once held by Osiris, who greets souls in the heavenly worlds when they die. The icon of the Christian cross also links Jesus back to Osiris, who was perennially connected to the ankh, a symbol of eternal life, and to the vine of life. Like Osiris, Jesus is often depicted as the "green man," a human version of the Tree of Life from whom all life flows. Jesus, as you may recall, even referred to himself as the "true vine," which was one of the most potent symbols for Osiris. This again confirms that Jesus was initiated into the most profound secrets of the Mystery Schools.

THE WORLD TREE

The symbolic Tree of Life was a blueprint of the soul's journey back to God in many ancient cultures—Hebrew, Egyptian, Greek, Celtic, Essene, and Druid. Philo Judaeus, a contemporary of Jesus, taught that an understanding of the Tree of Life was the "Way of the Great Return," drawn from the very foundations of Egyptian wisdom. And many other traditions taught that the Tree revealed the underlying structural principles behind the entire universe.[8]

The great Buddha received enlightenment beneath a Bodhi tree, revealing that he, too, had discovered the portal linking him to the Otherworld. In the Hindu path, this same symbolism is found in the Tree of Jiva and Atman—the freedom (Jivan) of the soul (Atman) to move into the higher worlds. To the Norse, the Tree was connected to the cosmic Ash, the great Mother Tree, which they called Yggdrasil. Below it, legend says, lay a vast pool of water in which the three Norns spun out the fate of the world—past, present, and future. The Druidic name for this tree was Nuin, revealing its Egyptian roots—Nun as the great Cosmic Water from which the visible Universe arose.[9] Some Jewish and Christian traditions even represented the Tree as having its roots in the heavenly worlds and its branches spread out to the three visible worlds of time and space.

The Mayans believed that the Tree of Life was the cord between our human world and the celestial realms. They described it as an umbilicus that nourished us from the great central Sun. This cord they called the *Kuax Sum,* yet another name for the Tree of Life, portrayed as the 400-foot Yaxche tree, whose trunk

FIGURE 45. Like many savior gods, Jesus was often depicted as, or on, the Tree of Life. This was not only a literal translation of his Crucifixion on the cross, but his willingness to offer his life as the unblemished sacrifice upon the cross of time and space.

reached into the sky and whose branches, the Mayans believed, supported heaven.[10]

Native Americans use the Cottonwood tree to symbolize this same principle, placing it at the center of their Sundance ceremonies.[11] Traditionally held at the height of midsummer, this rite is seen as one of "rebirth, renewal, procreation, and thanksgiving."[12] In this circular ritual, eagle dancers tie themselves to the Sun Pole, dancing without food, water, or rest for four days and nights to renew their world. They aim to transcend the suffering of their bodies and experience a union with the Divine. Like the eagle dancers, Jesus was pierced in the flesh and offered up to suffer on the Tree of Life.

In Egyptian culture, the Tree of Life was epitomized by three trees: the persea, the sycamore, and the tamarisk, which was sacred to Osiris, the world savior whose life, death, and resurrection lay at the heart of Egyptian theology. It was from a tamarisk tree, also called the acacia, that the crown of thorns that Jesus wore at the Crucifixion was formed. This tree has the ability to sprout new leaves, even after it has been cut down and planted as a doorpost.[13] It was the tree that enfolded Osiris' coffin as a form of protective benediction, again strengthening the link between Jesus and Osiris. The persea tree was often inscribed with the names of the god-kings of Egypt, as seen at the temple of Heliopolis, the city of the Sun. All of these trees were symbols of the *axis mundi*, or World Axis, in Egypt. By following the tree to the top, one was led back to the center of the galaxy, the place of greatest light. At the top of the Egyptian Tree of Life sat the glorious phoenix, a symbol of resurrection long associated with both Jesus and Osiris—a symbol that appears again at Avalon.

All of these symbols are merely different ways of revealing the same cosmic story. They all honor the great solar lords who return to our planet to regenerate the world. Osiris was but an earlier incarnation of Jesus, and of other savior gods who came to help mankind move toward enlightenment. Through the love, wisdom, and sacrifice of these two great avatars, Jesus and Osiris, we are shown a way, a path, a road back into heaven. This knowledge lay at the very heart of what Jesus learned among the Druids.

Who's HU?

The Celtic god HU came periodically into the world to sacrifice himself upon the Tree of Life. Known as a Sun god, HU was linked to legends of the invisible god Celi, the Celtic bard Taliesin, and, centuries later, to the legends of the famous Sun king, Arthur. He was also most certainly linked to Jesus himself through the biblical concept of the Word.[14]

Historically, HU is connected to a heroic savior figure named Hu Gadarn. He was said to be the common ancestor and father god of the Welsh people who led his people to safety from the summer country of Atlantia (Atlantis?) after the flood.[15] He is also known as HU-Hesus, a name remarkably similar to Jesus. "Hesus is the spirit of growth in the tree [the seed that becomes the All]."[16] Like

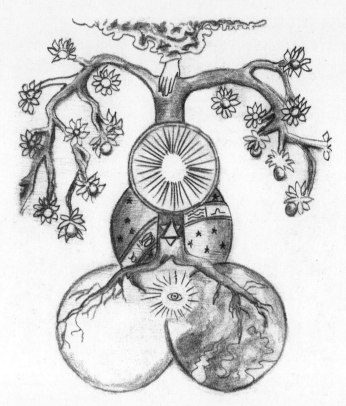

FIGURE 46. IMagined as a celestial Tree rooted in the realms of God, the hermetic Tree of Life extends its branches down into the world's matter, providing a ladder upon which each of us may climb back to mastery on our way to God.

FIGURE 47. The Mayan Tree of Life bears a striking resemblance to the Tau cross we have already seen. This Mayan glyph depicts the Great Eagle, or divine Father, at the top of the Tree.

FIGURE 48. The Egyptian Tree of Life, surmounted by the Sun.

FIGURE 49. Hu Gadarn, the Celtic archetype of the solar lord who sacrificed himself upon the Tree of Space and Time.

Osiris and later Jesus, HU arrived from the east.[17] Like Osiris and later Horus, he brought the arts of music, dance, and agriculture to the Druid people.

Migrating Hebrews in the Celtic lands also associated HU with Jesus and the biblical Joshua—Jesus is the Greek rendering of the Hebrew name Joshua.[18] Common derivatives of Hu Gadarn are Hesus and Esus, both close approximations of Jesus or Issa.[19] But the name HU stems from a far earlier age and perhaps an earlier incarnation of this same Christed being. Some scholars even claim that the word "God" can be plausibly derived from the Sanskrit word *HU*. Eleanor Merry observes that "HU was the all-ruling Divinity of Western Celtic mythology [that] represented the power and the glory of the spiritual world."

> The Mysteries of HU revealed the other pole [or tree] of human life: the ascent out of the body into the "glorified" state of expansion of the consciousness in the spiritual world; that HU could bring music to the consciousness of waking man and teach it to him, because he himself could hear in sleep the harmonies of the spheres, and his passage from waking

to sleeping to waking was unbroken by any obliteration of consciousness. This was always the summit of initiation experience.[20]

Merry appears to be referring here to a knowledge of the Sound Current, the Audible Life Stream, or the Word—a concept mystics have spoken of throughout the ages that refers to the underlying vibrational Song of God. By linking to the Tree of Life and attuning to these inner worlds, mystics opened their inner hearing to an awareness of this sacred sound. Thus it is not surprising that HU is also linked to the issuing sound of creation itself—called "the Lost Word" in Freemasonry.

"In the Beginning was Braham, with whom is the Word. And the Word is Braham," we read in the *Vedas,* just as the Gospel of John tells us that the universe was created by means of a vibratory emanation: "The same [Word] was in the beginning with God. All things were made by Him; and without him was not anything made that was made" (John 1:1–3). Ross Nichols, Chief of the Druids (1964-1975), identifies HU with this first breath of Spirit, also called Hu Hesus:

> Now . . . the sound of breath, [the] Greek E is not only that of the later Welsh Hu or Heuc'h, but is known to have the same essential meaning . . . E was over the tall gateway entrance to Apollo's temple at Delphi, signifying divine breath or prophecy. So it is a fair inference that here the HU sound from between the two Ts or trees [the Birch and the Elder trees representing the Alpha and the Omega] descends from the high level of the first Manifestor and unites with Aesus or Hu Hesus or simply Hesus, in the same manner that the [Jewish] letter Shin descending from the four letters of the mystic Tetragrammaton [the Jewish name for God] changes YHVH into YEHESHUA.[21]

Likewise, we know that the Egyptians required that every incoming pharaoh or higher initiate find the Shu Stone—the true Philosopher's Stone—a metaphor for this same vibrational Word. In the Egyptian language, Shu was the god of the air or the Holy breath, and the name Ye-shu-a contains this sound.

The Druids linked HU to the Tree of Life through the birch, a tree that stood for the creation of the world. Thus the white birch was the feminine tree identified with the winter solstice—she who gave birth to the world. Four days after the solstice, the "rebirth" of the Sun occurs, on December 25, a date associated with the birth of all great solar lords: Jesus, Mithra, Horus, and Osiris. Thus the Virgin gives birth to the Holy Son or Sun of God. The animal form

Figure 50. To the Druids, the birch and the elder represented the principles of the beginning and ending of time. Thus these trees took the role of the two pillars through which each initiate must pass to enter the worlds beyond time and space. The birch was said to have the power to heal the elder.

of the birch tree, and the god HU, was the pure, unblemished stag or unicorn, symbolized by the higher initiatic emblem of Capricorn. The unicorn is the splendid king of the forest who has awakened his inner sight or Third Eye.

As the youngest and oldest of all the trees, the birch and elder represent the female and the male, the alpha and omega. The Celts believed that the birch had the power to heal the wounds of the masculine elder tree. These two trees were said to stand on either side of the One Nameless Day, the day beyond the worlds of time and space when the soul stands before the throne of the Divine. They represented the two pillars between which each initiate must pass, like the columns on the Temple of King Solomon, the link between life and death.[22]

The name *HU* is also linked to two Aryan roots that mean, respectively, "to invoke" and "to offer sacrifice." Thus, this deity's name reflects not only Braham's first breath at creation, but the eternal luminous dying god who sacrifices himself upon the Tree of Life, a reflection clearly resonant of Jesus and of other incarnations of the four great Kumaras or sons of God. In the most ancient sacred texts, these four beings are known as serpent lords, aspects of

FIGURE 51. The serpent has both positive and negative connotations in spiritual lore. In its highest meaning, the serpent is symbolic of the "Wise Ones," or Teachers of wisdom who sacrifice themselves upon the cross of time and space to raise the kundalini or frequency of humanity. Jesus was considered just such a Serpent King. At its lowest expression, the serpent is the reptilian nature inside of each of us that must be raised up (the kundalini) and harnessed in order to master one's power.

the great serpent Sesha, who, along with the divine Mother and Father, existed before space and time. This is the true meaning of the serpent wrapped around the Cosmic Egg, as well as of the serpent draped over the cross of time and space that is frequently misinterpreted by most Christians as Satan, because of the "deceiving serpent" story told in Genesis. Yet in the ancient world, the term serpent meant "wise one." Jesus says: "May you be gentle as doves and wise as serpents" (Matthew 10:16).

These four great serpent lords incarnate in human form to raise the kundalini of the planet—a life force that resides in the spine, a serpentine structure that shelters the nervous system. As an incarnation of one of these divine beings, HU was the archetype of the eternal, yet dying, god who comes into the world of form, is born anew, and leads humanity back to its divine origins. This same divinity is also found in Egypt in the symbol of the Sphinx, long identified with Osiris, the sacrificial god. One of the Sphinx's most ancient names was, in fact, *Huwana*.

CHAPTER 17

The One World Mountain and the World Axis

The nature of infinity is this: That everything has its own vortex,
and when once a traveler through Eternity has pass'd that Vortex,
he perceives it roll backward behind his path,
into a globe itself unfolding like a sun. . . .[1]

—William Blake, *Milton*

When Jesus first arrived in Britain at the age of fifteen, his voyage took him around the tip of the English coast to Land's End, then northward along the Bristol Channel and into the Severn Sea. From there, the ships entered the estuaries of the Rivers Parrot and Brue, sailing inland toward the area now known as Glastonbury, then known as Avalon, a sacred island of grassy slopes and forests surrounded by the sea. Here, a chain of seven great islands rose from the sea in a series of hills that looked like the back of a huge undulating dragon. Today, the waters have receded leaving fertile pastures, and the British coast now lies some seventeen miles northwest in the Bristol Channel.[2] But in the days when Jesus first arrived, Glastonbury was known as the holy Isle of Avalon.

Avalon was called by a variety of Celtic names: Ynnis-witryn, the Isle of Glass; Avilion, the Isle of the Departed; and Avalon, the Isle of Apples, from its association with the Greek legends of the Hesperides, the "garden of the gods," a holy spring and a Magical tree with golden apples that bestowed immortality and guaranteed the ascent of the soul into Paradise.[34] Avalon was also known as the Enchanted Isle, the Crystal City, and the Isle of the Dead, an earthly paradise where the souls of the deceased awaited rebirth. Legends claimed it as the gateway to the Otherworld and the abode of the gods—a place where the three worlds of the Above, the Below, and Middle Earth merged through the Tree of Life, the One World Mountain, and the Holy Spring.

Avalon had three sacred hills: the enormous Tor, the shorter fish-shaped Wearyall Hill, and the gentle feminine mound of Chalice Hill where the healing waters emerged—two mystical springs, one white, one red, representing the reconciliation of opposites. In the centuries after Jesus, this was called Chalice Well and was associated with legends of the Holy Grail. The island also boasted a grove of apple trees where the White Hind of Wisdom lived, an animal long associated with the sign of Capricorn and the purity of the unicorn, a creature linked to the birth of the solar lords and, later, the Christ child.[5] All these hermetic features

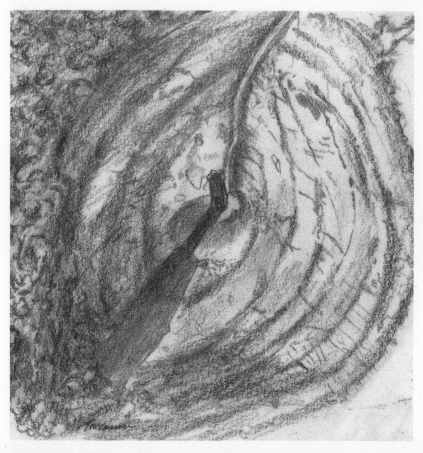

FIGURE 52. An aerial view of the Tor with its seven spiral paths. Saint Michael's tower, representing the Tree of Life, sits at the top.

held great significance in the ancient Mystery traditions, symbolically representing ancient aspects of creation itself. Thus, from the first, Avalon reflected the unity, the duality, and the trinity found in nearly all world religions.

AVALON AND THE ONE WORLD MOUNTAIN

At the center of the island sat the enormous Tor, a huge hill whose history goes back to at least 3000 B.C.E. Like so many other things about the island, however, the provenance of the Tor remains a mystery, even to the British people.[6] When viewed from the air, the Tor, the largest feature on the island, looks like a huge, elliptical egg with seven concentric terraces that form a spiral path up to the top of the green grassy mound.

Legends of such holy mountains permeate Celtic, Buddhist, Hindu, Jainist, and Egyptian culture—the Hindu Mount Meru, the Hebrew Mount Sinai, and the Greek Mount Olympus. These ancient cultures spoke of a One World Mountain that lay at the center of the Earth and connected our world with the abode of the gods.[7] These symbolic mountains, which were often surrounded by water, were seen as a reflection of the Cosmic Egg that arose from the primordial waters of Nun at the beginning of time. The Egg was the womb of creation.[8] This same hermetic symbol now appears atop Jewish synagogues, Moslem temples, and Christian churches as enormous acorn-shaped domes—among them the Dome of Saint Peter's at the Vatican—representing the *omphalos*, or seed energy of life.[9] Like the "oval office" in Washington, D.C., these domes are symbolic of the lotus pod, the "navel of creation," from which arose the visible light of the Sun. In Christian faith, this light is represented by Jesus; in more ancient times, it was symbolized by solar lords like Beli, Lugh, Horus/Apollo, and Ra.

To enter the World Mountain was to enter the mysteries of God. The mountain was a center that linked the underworld, the middle world, and the heavenly worlds. The path between these worlds lay in the World Tree, which created a road upon which initiates could journey. The Mountain and the Tree were also generally associated with a water source—a well, a spring, a lake, or a river—that the shaman's soul had to cross as the frontier between the worlds, usually by means of a perilous bridge.[10] Thus the World Mountain was often situated on an island, and initiates had to cross water to reach it—a perfect description of the Isle of Avalon.

When Jesus first arrived on the Isle of the Blessed, the Tor was still covered with forest. An avenue of stately oaks, "the ancient ones that guard the doorway,"

FIGURE 53. The One World Mountain reveals the opening to the three worlds—the Upper, the Lower and the Earthly planes of existence. The Tree of Life is the pathway that connects them. Above the Mountain spins the wheel of the galaxy, known to the Celts as Arianrhod's Silver Wheel. At the forefront sits the prize of the Holy Grail, found only when one has awakened and mastered one's inner dragons. Illustration by Sylvia Laurens.

led up to a succulent grove of apple trees near the top.[11] Frances Howard Gordon notes: "Apples were associated with the Goddess . . . and with a western paradise where the sacred apple tree is guarded by the serpent or dragon."[12] Only a few miles from Glastonbury, we find a number of place-names that include the word "paradise": a farm by the village of Burnham; a beautiful spot on the northeast side of the Tor; and an ancient road that leads away from the high, rounded hill. This road may mark the exit point for initiates completing their life, death, and rebirth experiences beneath the hollow of the sacred hill.[13]

All these mystical elements—water, mountain, and sacred tree—marked Avalon as a place of true spiritual power. Such a convergence of mystical signs indicates a cosmic doorway linking our Earth with the celestial realms above and the subterranean worlds below, confirming that the ancient rites of the Mystery traditions were practiced there—rites that allowed initiates to pull back the veils to other worlds and realize their own immortality as advanced souls.

HOME OF THE GODS

The county of Somerset, where the community of Glastonbury now stands, was called the Summerland in Jesus' time. The name Glastonbury derives from three words: *glas*, meaning "grassy"; *ton*, meaning "hill"; and *bury*, meaning "borough." Thus Glastonbury was a small borough marked by a large grassy hill—the Tor.[14] From the beginning, Avalon was seen as a place of Magic—a place where communication with the gods was not only possible, but encouraged.[15] At the heart of its mysteries lay the Tor, a hill rising some 518 feet that can be seen from as far as twenty-five miles away.[16] The Tor, which has been called a perfect natural pyramid, is composed of distinct layers of rock: marlstone, clay, Jurassic Blue Limestone, and the sandstone that forms its peak.[17] Many believe it to be hollow, making it the source of the ancient legends of hollow hills and crystal caves that permeate the area. Geological excavations in the 20th century support this belief.[18]

In the late 12th century, the Christians built an Abbey on the summit of the Tor called Saint Michael's Abbey. It was destroyed in an earthquake in 1275. Today, all that remains is a 14th-century tower dedicated to the Archangel Michael.[19] Carved into the sides of this tower are hermetic images that long predate the Christian era: the balance scales of judgment associated with the Egyptian Weighing of the Heart ceremony, and an image of Saint Brigit, a Catholic saint who was folded into a far earlier aspect of the Celtic goddess

FIGURE 54. The Glastonbury Tor photographed from the rear, revealing the earth mound spirals of the serpentine labyrinth around it, and the road leading away. Photo: Daniel Boulet, copyright 2000.

Brighde, or Bride,[20] a likely incarnation of Isis, or Hathor, the divine Mother.[21] As we shall shortly learn, many of the most important Egyptian gods seem to have been involved in the spiritual, cultural, and physical development of the Celtic lands.

In truth, Avalon, the Isle of Golden Apples, had long been sacred to Isis, the original Virgin Mother, and her husband Osiris, the White Lord of the Dead whose Celtic name was Gwynn ap Nudd, Lord of Annwfn, King of the Underworld.[22] Aspects of these primordial figures were later turned into the Celtic Brigit/Ceridwen and the famous King Arthur, the "once and future king" who would return one day to set the world aright.

The Tor itself was sacred to both Thoth and Horus, Egyptian wisdom gods who played a serious part in shaping the spiritual landscape of Britain in earlier ages.[23] Julius Caesar writes that Thoth was one of the chief deities of the Druids.[24] He was known as Theutates in Britain, a name strikingly similar to Therapeutae. In fact, Theutates, Tehuti, Thoth, Hermes, and Mercury are all names for the same being—the universal father "from whence emanates the things of wisdom such as speech, specific wisdom or writing methods," including the runic tree script known as Ogham.[25] British historian John Michell writes: "Thoth, the Egyptian Mercury, whom the Druids called Theutates and Baal the sun god, can still be found at many spots where no church has been placed to obliterate their memory. . . . The former dedication of each place to a god . . . was often continued by the substitution of the Christian saint or angel whose attributes corresponded to those of the displaced deity."[26] In later centuries, the roles of these deities would be adopted by the Archangel Michael, who is often depicted, like Horus and Thoth, with the balance scales of life, a torch of knowledge, or a sword of truth.

The Tor itself was dedicated to Horus, honored in Avalon as Apollo, the Greek god of music, dance, and healing.[27] Long before the Archangel Michael took his place, Horus was the original dragon slayer who vanquished the evil reptile Set, Satu or Typhon, who is often equated with the Christian Satan. Set was "the evil serpent" that plunged Egypt into darkness, a reference to his inability to subdue his instinctual animal nature. Conversely, Horus was the bringer of truth, the rising Sun, "Horus of the Horizon," just as Osiris, his father, was known as the Lord of Light in the mysterious Land of the Dead.

In Greece, Horus was called Apollo, who, like his grandfather, Thoth, brought the arts of music, mathematics, and healing, and the geomantic sciences to cultures around the globe. The 110-foot Colossus of Rhodes on the Greek Isle of Lindos, with a torch of knowledge in his hand, his lute slung over his back, and his bow in hand clearly marks Apollo as an incarnation of a solar lord and one of the four great kumaras. Thus we should not be surprised to learn that, in Britain, the annual festivals of the Tor were designed around the eight high holy days of the Sun: the two solstices, the two equinoxes, and the four midpoints. Diodorus, a first-century B.C.E. Greek historian, tells us that, in Britain, Horus/Apollo was honored above all other gods, noting that " . . . there is also on the island both a magnificent precinct of Apollo and a notable temple which is adorned with many votive offerings and spherical in shape . . . [where] its inhabitants are players on the cithara [a form of ancient lute]; and they continually . . . sing hymns of praise to the god, glorifying his deeds."[28][29] Thus we see that Avalon had long been dedicated to bringing light to humanity from ages long before the Christian era.

THE COSMIC EGG AND THE HOLY SPIRIT

Around the spherical shape of the Tor are seven great rings that encircle the hill in a great, coiled labyrinth that is clearly visible from both the air and ground. This is reminiscent of the serpent coiled around the Orphic Egg, a mystical symbol long known in the Mystery Schools to represent the movement of the Holy Spirit around the Egg of Brahma. The Hindus called this serpent Sesha, representing the Breath of God.[30] Like the Holy Spirit or the Hebrew concept of the Shekinah, the snake encircles the One World Mountain, symbolic of the Great Cosmic Egg. "From this axis, like the hub of the wheel, everything extends, radiates and rotates spirally," writes Jill Purce, author of *The Mystic Spiral*. "The entire universe, with all its spatial and temporal states, is but the spiral manifestation of the still centre; as it rotates it expands, and while still rotating it contracts and disappears to the source whence it came."[31]

From the 17th-century writings of the Indian saint, Śrila Visvanatha Chakravarti Thakura, we read: "Eternally present within that Yoga-pitha is a youthful Divine Couple. Illuminating all horizons . . . [they] are seated in the whorl of Their extremely brilliant jeweled lotus flower throne."[32] This is the great Abba/Amma, or Father/Mother God to whom Jesus referred in his teachings. In the Gnostic book *The Sophia of Jesus the Christ*, Jesus teaches his disciples: "Primordial Archetypal Man is creative, Self-perfected wisdom. He meditated with his bride Sophia and his first offspring was born, an androgyne. His male part is named the Son of God. His female part, the Sophia, Mother of the Universe. Her name is Love. . . ."[33]

FIGURE 55. Hermes, the god of wisdom, with winged sandals carrying a caduceus staff.

FIGURE 56. Apollo as the Sun god Helios.

FIGURE 57. The Celtic labyrinth with its seven spirals inward and outward, and the cruciform shepherd's staff found at the center.

These primordial beings of infinite grace have long been conceived by the Mysteries as floating on an eternal ocean of love and mercy, existing beyond the worlds of time and space. Significantly, the image of the universal lotus blossom, or Cosmic Egg, around which is wound the spiral serpent, was held in great veneration by the cultures of Egypt, India, and Britain, and Avalon's topography reflected these primordial beginnings.

In fact, the ancients, who were far more deeply attuned to the soul's path toward enlightenment than we are today, took the time to design landscapes that reflected these great cosmic principles, expressing in their surroundings the hermetic axiom: "As above, so below; as below, so above." They designed " . . . places of initiation and worship [that] were generally circular or spiral, because the circle was a significant emblem of the universe, governed and pre-served by an omnipresent deity, who is described in the writings of Hermes Trimegistus [Thrice-Great Hermes or Thoth] as a circle whose centre is every-where, and whose circumference is nowhere . . . a doctrine distinctly asserted by the Druids."[34]

Thus the spiral of the Tor was a kind of walking meditation for the initi-ate, a journey of reflection encircling the Great Cosmic Egg. It was a meta-phor for the seven-fold circuitry of the brain, the seven days of the week, and the seven major chakras of the human body known to students of yoga. These same seven circuits, which move up the spine in meditation, were depicted as the caduceus staff of Thoth/Hermes. They represent the connecting links be-tween our spirits and our bodies whose activation brings us to the pinnacle of enlightenment. These serpent staffs, which also reflect the entwining ladder

Figure 58. The Great Cosmic Egg floats on the cosmic sea inside a lotus blossom, with the divine Mother and Father inside. The serpent Ananta-Sesha floats with them, symbolizing the energies of the great serpent kings who come periodically into the physical worlds to uplift mankind. Illustrated by Sylvia Laurens.

of DNA, were associated with Aesculapius, the Greek father of medicine, and with Moses, the Jewish patriarch, and are emblematic of healing in the medical world even today.

In classical times, the labyrinthine spiral was also essential to the building of a city, for it was seen as reenacting the original creation of the cosmos. Thus, when a labyrinth was constructed, the landscape became sanctified—order was carved out of chaos.[35] Episcopalian Minister, Lauren Artress writes:

> The labyrinth captures the mystical union between heaven and earth, an understanding of death and rebirth. It is a path of faith and doubt, the complexity of the brain, the turns of the intestines, and the birth canal, and the Celestial city. . . . The walk, and all that happens on it, can be grasped through the intuitive, pattern-discerning faculty of the person walking it. The genius of this tool is that it reflects back to the seeker whatever he or she needs to discover from a new level of awareness. . . . This is the gift of being able to see the infinite in the context of the finite.[36]

Labyrinths were often inscribed on tombs, implying that the journey into death was but a reentry into the womb of the Earth Mother—a journey that had to be made if the soul was to be reborn in the Land of the Dead. Peter James and Nick Thorpe, authors of *Ancient Mysteries*, tell us: "Clues from a number of different cultures suggest that the labyrinth shape was widely used in ancient times as an icon of the Underworld with its paths spiraling in and out to represent death and rebirth."[37] Jill Purce agrees:

FIGURE 59A. The Tor, the Vesica Piscis, and the Eye of God, each reflecting a depiction of the Great Cosmic Egg. This deliberate shaping of the land created a portal through which the initiate could pass into the higher worlds.

FIGURE 59B. The caduceus with the infinity sign over it, representing the pinnacle of enlightenment.

The spiral . . . is the key which opens the door into the next world. It is
the spiral clue, the . . . ball of thread that guides him through the labyrinth. . . . Entry is thus initiation, a step on the path of knowledge. But
before knowledge is revealed, the old preconceptions must be dissolved
by re-entry in the pre-formal state of the womb. The [labyrinth] is a symbol of the . . . womb of the Mother, and in Neolithic Europe it was often
marked with the windings of the underworld.[38]

Thus the hidden inner cave that lay beneath the Tor was seen as the Cauldron of Ceridwen, the Great Mother, a name that translates to "fortress of wisdom."[39] In later centuries, this hidden spring was associated with the vessel of
the Holy Grail, both becoming synonymous with the womb from which the
healing waters flow—a place where initiates could return to the still point of
centeredness within themselves.

THE PATH TO ENLIGHTENMENT

The seven-coiled pattern of the labyrinth is also described in the stories of the
Greek hero Theseus, who was said to have fought the Minotaur in the king's
underground palace at Knossos, whose catacombs were once part of the Mystery dramas of the ancient world. In the Greek story, Theseus, the hero, must
enter the maze, slay the Minotaur, and then find his way back out. He is aided
by Ariadne, the daughter of the king and the spinner of the thread of fate.

This story has endured for over 2500 years because it encodes a set of hermetic symbols that are a parable for the Mysteries. It reveals elements of the
initiation process inside the labyrinth, or beneath the Tor, and addresses the
fundamental process of facing the Shadow—the negative, selfish part of the
ego, or "evil dragon," that resides within each of us. The hero, Theseus, battles
with his own animalistic nature, represented by the half-man, half-beast Minotaur. He is aided by the goddess, the Divine Feminine—Ariadne, the princess
who connects him with his higher self via the thread of destiny. The Minotaur
recalls images of solar lords standing on top of a crocodile or reptile, symbolizing the subduing of this inner enemy, and of Archangel Michael and Mother
Mary standing on the dragon of their own lower natures, represented in Christian mythos by Lucifer. The task of facing the Shadow and integrating its powerful energies into our lives in a productive and illuminated way lies at the heart
of the Mysteries. The labyrinth was the symbolic arena where this initiatory
battle between the Soul and the ego took place.

Spiraling, underground labyrinths have been found in places as diverse as Java, Syria, India, Italy, Greece, Egypt, Australia, North and South America, and Ireland.[40] The Hopi Indians called the labyrinth the Mother Earth symbol, and likened it to their own underground kivas used in sacred ritual.[41] Herodotus describes an enormous underground labyrinth in Egypt that was used in the Mystery initiations there. Sometimes above ground, sometimes below, these intricate paths were built of every type of material—from stonework to hedges—and were used to awaken initiates within the Mystery Schools in virtually every culture of the world. Labyrinths have even been found carved into rocks in the mystical forests of Tintagel, a Magical, wind-swept village on the Cornish coast said to be the birthplace of Merlin and Arthur, revealing that the seven-circuit path had long been sacred to the Celts.

The details of what candidates experienced within these underground chambers were always a closely guarded secret. We know, however, that initiates spent three days and three nights in the underground vaults of the sacred mountain, undergoing the initiations of air, earth, fire, and water. Like their Eleusinian and Egyptian counterparts, Celtic aspirants went through a "near-death" experience, crossed to the other side, and then returned. Candidates were then "born again" on the morning of the fourth day, breaking free of the mortal body to glimpse the spiritual realities beyond this world and reemerging in Paradise into the light of a brave, new Sun.

Could the three days and nights that Jesus spent in the tomb correlate to this simulated three-day death and resurrection? The concept of life, death, and rebirth (being "born again") lay at the heart of all the Mystery religions and was certainly central to the drama Jesus enacted on the world stage—not merely in symbolic form, but in a literal sense. Thus the journey through the labyrinth can be seen as a metaphor for the circuitous journey we all take as we descend into the seven lower worlds of time and space, awaken to the truth of who we really are, and then return to the heavenly worlds.

Jesus speaks of this in the Gospel of Thomas, where he says: "Let him who seeks not cease from seeking until he finds; and when he finds, he will be turned around; and when he is turned around, he will marvel, and he shall reign over the All." This is an apt description of one who has traveled the spiral path of the labyrinth. At the center of the labyrinth, we connect with the Spirit of our souls. "The Kingdom is in your centre and is about you."[42] Then we make our way back to the world of form and into the realm of Paradise.

In later centuries, Christianity adopted this same seven-circuit pattern, laying it into the floors of Chartres Cathedral in France and in the exquisite

Cathedral of Siena in Tuscany. Throughout the Middle Ages, artists took it up, constructing over 500 non-ecclesiastical labyrinths in Scandinavia alone![43] In the Greek and Roman world, square and circular floor mosaics were often framed in a meandering border pattern, frequently with a minotaur or centaur at the center to symbolize our own half-human, half-animal natures. By gaining victory over the minotaur, we are reborn into a state of wholeness.[44] The center represents a place of perfect repose within the zero-point mind of God that can only be achieved when we slay our inner demons. These designs were all linked with the resurrection of the spirit in a triumphant return to light. One Roman family even had a mosaic labyrinth laid into the floor of their family tomb. Before the entrance were inscribed the words: "Enclosed here, he loses life"—a message that only an initiate of the Mysteries could understand.[45]

British historian Sir Geoffrey Ashe, best known for his well-researched Arthurian studies, has discovered that Glastonbury Tor is laid out according to this same seven-circuit pattern, and has charted the upwelling of magnetic energies that make it a genuine temple of the Sun. Similar designs can found in pyramids in Europe, China, Mexico, and the Americas, particularly in the city of Tlaxcala, Mexico. Later, the spiral was painted onto the domes of Islamic mosques and used in the famous whirling dances of the Sufis.[46] This same seven-layered spiral is described in the *Meccan Revelations* written by the great Sufi master Muhyiddin Ibn al-Arabi in 1202. He speaks of it as the gradual ascent through the seven spheres of the self, accompanied by an angel of God. The angel who travels with him says: "I am the seventh degree in my capacity to embrace the mysteries of becoming. . . . I am knowledge, the Known and the Knower; I am Wisdom, the Wise man and his Wiseness."[47]

CHAPTER 18

The Dragon, the Unicorn, and the Phoenix

Sirs! We are soldiers of the rock and ring; Our Table Round is earth's
  most honored stone;
Thereon two worlds of life and glory blend, the boss upon the shield of
  many a land,
The midway link with light beyond the stars! This is our fount of fame!
  Let us arise,
And cleave the earth like rivers; like the streams that win from Paradise
  their immortal name.[1]

—Robert Stephen Hawker, *The Quest of the San Graal*

Geomantic practitioners called the naturally occurring electromagnetic lines
that move throughout our planet "dragon lines." British authors Paul Broadhurst and Hamish Miller have spent over two decades charting these powerful
serpentine energies, which act as natural magnetic conductors for this upwelling of energy. In China, these currents were also known as tiger lines, perhaps
because of their undulating and aggressive movements. Today, modern dowsers
call them ley lines. These magnetic circuits, which mirror the meridian lines of
the human body, are energetic markers for the currents of life force that reside
within the Earth. These electromagnetic currents have been found to follow
underground springs, mountain ranges, and flowing rivers, and they are particularly strong at holy sites.

Today, we are no longer attuned to these energies. But our ancestors, who
did not live surrounded by electricity, cell phones, and satellites, were particu-

larly sensitive to them. They learned how to detect and harness these ley lines, deliberately placing temples, stone circles, and, later, Christian cathedrals over these very spots to benefit from the flow of nature's rhythms. British geomantic expert John Michell writes:

> As late as the Middle Ages those who understood the Magic science of invoking the spirit of revelation and ecstasy set up the naves, passages and cloisters to their great cathedrals. . . . In this way the churches oriented upon the course of a ley preserved not only its line but also its character and atmosphere. Placed at an angle which allowed the heavenly rays to shine at a certain season down the nave through the windows east and west, the church transmitted the beneficial influences of the line on which it stood. It became a powerful instrument in the hands of those who knew its secret.[2]

Over the last few decades researchers have begun to appreciate how vast territories like Britain, Egypt, Greece, and France were once organized into huge "ritual landscapes."[3] Temples were actually designed to harness the energies of the heavens and reflect it back to Earth. In the Celtic lands, these centers were marked by megalithic circles, large stone dolmans, sacred springs, legendary burrows, and sculptured hills. In China, dragon lines were marked by pagodas, stupas, and towers; in Egypt, they became the sites of temples, pyramids, and obelisks. All of these structures harnessed the electromagnetic currents of the Earth, allowing individuals to come into resonance with the healing power of the universe. The conical shape of the Tor, like the pyramids of Egypt, actually generates a perpetual spiral known to scientists as a field, *torison*, a powerful spinning energy field that mirrors the spin of the galaxy.[4]

Our ancestors understood these subtle energy levels, harnessed these regenerative forces, and aligned them with the cycles of the Sun and Moon to stimulate growth in the animal, vegetable, and human kingdoms. Then, through music, dance, and prayer, they energized the surrounding landscape for the benefit of the community, as we do in our churches today when we sing, dance, or pray, and as Tibetan monks do in their chanting ceremonies. In these sacred places, the life force of the Earth is so concentrated that people experience healings and visions. Thus, these sites became focal points where human beings interacted with the Earth to enhance the prosperity of the world. In many ancient cultures, these highly energized sacred sites were deliberately harnessed to awaken the higher consciousness of the human race and remind us of our own divine origins.

Harnessing the Sacred Mountain

Today, the keys to this sacred science have, unfortunately, been lost. While the Christian church certainly used geomancy for their own strategic purposes, the common people were fed myths about the dragon slayers Saint Patrick and Saint George, who rid the world of serpents—stories meant to mask the higher truth. John Michell writes, "The policy of the Christian Church was to destroy all documents relating to the former science and to suppress the practice of astronomy [or geomancy]. As a result of their rejection of the mysteries and of traditional scholarship, Christian philosophers lost the ability to fully appreciate the system of names, numbers and symbols they had inherited."[5]

Later, the Catholic Church built churches over these same sites to conscript their power. The newly forming church sought to control these centers for, with them, they could control the world. "The first requirement of a ruling priesthood," John Michell observes, "is to locate and occupy the natural powerful centres of spiritual energy in the landscape. . . . This principle is now recognized by archaeologists who have discovered in recent years that temples and old stone monuments in all countries are related to their surroundings in two ways, astronomically and geologically."[6]

Thus we should not be surprised to find that there are ley lines flowing through the heart of Avalon and running right through the Tor. The orientation of the oval hill lies along a southwest-to-northeast axis, pointing exactly toward the rising and setting Sun at the midpoint between the two equinoxes and solstices—May 1st and August 1st for the rising Sun; November 1st and February 2nd for the setting Sun.[7] These are high holy days in the calendar. These electromagnetic ley lines also extend through Salisbury Cathedral, Stonehenge, and Avebury, running all the way down to Saint Michael's Mount off the Cornish coast—all places of power that Jesus visited.[8] In later centuries, these dragon lines were overseen by Saint Michael and Saint George, warrior saints said to have been capable of harnessing their energies. In truth, these saintly figures were only the Christianized heirs to a much earlier tradition.

A growing number of researchers, armed with the tools of both ancient and modern science, are beginning to reconstruct this sacred lore, which can help us understand why Jesus and, later, Joseph of Arimathea chose to settle in Avalon, a place that geomancers call "the Dragon's Heart."[9] Historian Nicolas Mann, author of *The Isle of Avalon*, *The Cauldron and the Grail*, and *Glastonbury Tor*, suggests an answer:

We may conclude from the literary, topographical and physical evidence that the British Celts and their Druids—quite likely the equivalent of shamans—held the Isle of Avalon to be the place of the World Axis, with its attendant caves, pathways, openings, World Mountain, and World Tree. . . . The Tor—whether or not its terraces were carved during prehistory—is the prototypical sacred and spiral mountain. It provides the steps to the above. The springs provide the means of egress from, and the means of access to, the Magical realm of the spirit beings below.

In truth, Avalon, with its elements of air, earth, fire, and water, contained virtually all of the ingredients associated with the dragon's heart. "The dragon's heart is to be found at a lonely knoll standing in a small plain or valley among the hills. . . . From the central spot, the veins of the dragon current run over the surrounding ridges. Near the heart, its force, pent in by the hills, is strong and active. At this center, the dragon and the tiger, the male and female currents, meet harmoniously."[10] Such a convergence of elemental powers created a doorway for "subtle energies so refined that it can only be described as spiritual alchemy."[11]

This brings us to the fascinating subject of the Glastonbury Zodiac, a series of thirteen enormous figures laid onto the land surrounding Avalon whose origins are now lost in prehistory. This large zodiacal circle, sometimes called the Temple of the Stars, is roughly thirty miles in circumference and twelve miles wide, and can only be seen from the air. The subtle patterns of the animal shapes are formed by the contours of ancient boundaries, hills, and earthworks, and by natural and artificial waterways. Similar earthworks are found in the Nazcal Plains of Peru, the Serpent Mounds of Ohio, and the serpentine configurations at Avebury. John Michell insists they were created for a reason:

> The hidden patterns of the sacred geometry in and around Glastonbury Abbey illustrate the ancient practice by which the whole world was laid out according to a cosmic scheme. . . . In the eyes of the philosophers of that time the earth was a living creator and its body, like all living creatures, had a nervous system within and relating to its magnetic field. The nerve centres of the earth, corresponding on the human body to the acupuncture points of Chinese medicine, were guarded and sanctified by sacred buildings, themselves laid out as microcosms of the cosmic order, the universal body of God.[12]

FIGURE 60. This powerful Freemason image shows the turning of the astrological ages in the heavens, the various archetypes of the gods and goddesses from the Tree of Life, the seven stages of initiation, and the quest for the perfected man or woman within the hidden chambers of the hill. Notice the seven steps of enlightenment that lead to a hidden underground chamber revealing a sun and a moon, and crowned by the celestial phoenix. Engraving by Raphael Custodis from *Cabal Spiegel der Kunst und Natur* by Steffan Michelspacher, 1616.

FIGURE 61. The Glastonbury Zodiac reveals the twelve signs of the zodiac inscribed upon the landscape of the county of Somerset, England. This was the place where the legendary Holy Grail was sought by King Arthur and his knights. Notice the signs of Pisces, Aquarius, and Capricorn at the top, and the four Watcher stars Regulus, Aldebaran, Formalhaut and Antares at each of the four corners.

The Somerset Zodiac, as it is also called, was rediscovered by Catherine Maltwood, who speculated that it had been designed by the Sumerians over 5000 years ago.[13] While most of the creatures found in the Glastonbury Zodiac conform to the classical figures known to Western astrologers today, there are a few exceptions. Aries, Taurus, Gemini, Leo, Virgo, Sagittarius, and Pisces are all represented by familiar shapes, but Cancer is depicted as a ship thought to represent the ark upon which the soul travels to the other worlds.[14] The air signs of Aquarius and Libra are depicted as the phoenix and the dove respectively, images well known within the Christian mythos to symbolize both Jesus and the more feminine aspects of the Holy Spirit.

THE UNICORN, THE FISH, AND THE PHOENIX

At the northernmost point of the zodiacal circle at Glastonbury sits the Magical Isle of Avalon, crowned by the signs of Pisces, Aquarius, and Capricorn.[15] Each of these three signs holds great significance within the Christian Mysteries, since they mark the age that is just now ending (Pisces), the birthday of the Christed King (Capricorn), and the age we are now entering (Aquarius). In this zodiac, Capricorn is represented by the unicorn, the pure unblemished one who has awakened his inner sight. This Magical creature can only be tamed by the Lady (a Virgin), and it is its blood that grants man eternal life—the Eucharist rites—an apt metaphor for the wisdom of Jesus' teachings. The sign of Pisces encompasses the peninsula of Wearyall Hill, with its fan-like tail extending into the waters. The center of this fish is the exact site where Joseph of Arimathea planted his famous staff when he arrived with eleven other disciples, a staff that later blossomed into the Holy Thorn Tree, thus marking Avalon as central to Jesus' teachings.

Although Aquarius is traditionally known as the water bearer who brings the wisdom from the stars, it is also represented by the more esoteric symbol of the phoenix, acknowledged as the Aquarian eagle. Since the eagle has long been used as a hermetic emblem for the Father God, the phoenix represents God's son, or the perfected man, the Adam Cadmon who has died and been reborn.[16] This Magical bird, or Son of God, was said to arrive periodically from the higher worlds, alight upon the Tree of Life, sing its song of beauty, and then perish in its own flames, laying the seeds of wisdom for the coming age before it died.

The phoenix had long been associated with Osiris, another of the four great Kumaras and the first god-man to be resurrected from the dead. Later, it was adopted by the early Christian church as a symbol for Jesus. As a place of rebirth marked by the Aquarian phoenix, Avalon was the perfect place for Jesus to settle.

When seen from the sky, the head of the Glastonbury phoenix encompasses the entire Tor. Its beak points directly to the springs at Chalice Well, as

FIGURE 62. The phoenix was adopted by Christianity as a symbol for Jesus, but it was first attributed to Osiris, the resurrected lord of Egypt.

if revealing that, from this place, the waters of Christ's message will flow to humanity once again in the Age of Aquarius. As Mary Caine, author of *The Glastonbury Zodiac*, states:

> The resurrection is portrayed by the Aquarius Phoenix, rising from its own ashes. For death, say the stars, is not the end: it is only the end of a day, a cycle, the beginning of a new life, for better or worse, according to our efforts. Aquarius, too, is the Man with the Water pot who led the disciples to the Upper Room in Luke's gospel. It is the place of Pentecost, where new vision and understanding enlightened the mourners, flooding them with courage so that many begin to tread the path that only one could tread before.

Knowledge of this zodiac was long held secret among the monks of Glastonbury Abbey. The 12th-century monk-historian William of Malmesbury calls it "a heavenly sanctuary on earth," words that seem to allude to a celestial alignment. Some believe that Merlin was referring to this zodiac when he spoke of the "Thirteen Treasures of Britain," which he then hid so well that their very nature has been forgotten. The twelve signs of the Glastonbury Zodiac are protected by the figure of a dog, thought by many to embody Anubis, an Egyptian deity kown as "the opener of the ways." The Welsh Triads also speak of the "Chief Master-Works of the Island of Britain," but fail to say what they were. And, in the mysterious medieval manuscript known as the *High History of the Holy Grail* that purports to have been written at Glastonbury Abbey, the Grail is sought among a variety of strange zodiacal animals like lions, giants, and dragons, and a Virgin with a holy chalice—images that can all be found within the Glastonbury Zodiac.[17] These stories, along with the "round table" of the heavenly wheel, seem to suggest that the quest for the Holy Grail was actually centered on Avalon.

The pre-Christian poem "The Spoils of Annwn," attributed to the sixth-century bard Taliesin, reveals that the quest for the cauldron of wisdom (the Holy Grail) would pass through the Glass Castle, the Corbenic Castle (Grail Castle), another name for the hidden caverns beneath the Glastonbury Tor. In Arthurian legend, Wearyall Hill becomes the Fisher King's Castle, which can only be reached by crossing a perilous bridge over the river of Death.[18] The Fisher King, as guardian of the Grail, lay ill and waiting beneath the Tor for the pure-hearted hero to ask the right question: "Who serveth the Grail?" All of these references confirm the site of Avalon/Glastonbury as a place of flowering wisdom for the coming age.

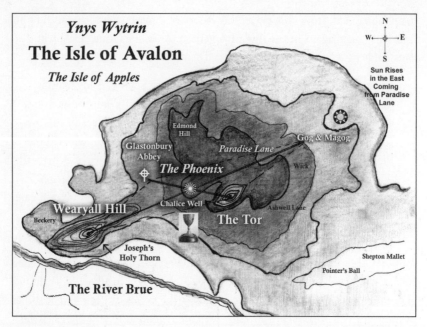

FIGURE 63. The shape of the phoenix laid over the Tor, the fish shaped peninsula of Wearyall Hill, the location of Joseph's Holy Hawthorne Tree, Chalice Well, Paradise Lane, the avenue of oaks, and Glastonbury Abbey, once the home of Jesus.

That Jesus chose Avalon as the site to pass on the heart of his teachings cannot have been accidental. It is certain that, as initiates of the Mysteries, both Jesus and Joseph of Arimathea would have been familiar with the concept of sanctified land. That they both understood the crucial placement of the Isle of Avalon within the Mystery traditions is clear, since this is where Joseph returned after the Crucifixion to set up his first community. It is also clear that Jesus aligned himself with this geomantic wisdom, for it was at this place that he chose to live during his time in Britain.

Hidden within the Mysteries of this island are hermetic keys to the coming age. The beak of the phoenix, after all, points to the holy springs of Chalice Well, where the Grail was said to have been hidden. The Grail itself, a receptive chalice long identified with the search for the divine feminine (entrusted to a virgin in the courts of King Arthur), is the quest for the Divine Feminie needed to bring balance to the Earth and to the healing of the Fisher King, the illuminated human or god-man, the Christ, the "Once and Future King," who awaits those heroes strong enough to follow his example and lead their people in love.

CHAPTER 19

Jesus and Joseph among the Druids

Westward Lord Jesus looked His latest love,
His yearning cross along the peopled sea,
The innumerable nations in His soul.
Thus came that type and token of our kind,
The realm and region of the set of sun,
The wide, wide West; the imaged zone of man.[1]

—Robert Stephen Hawker, *The Quest of the San Graal*

When Jesus first arrived on Avalon as a student, he was ferried by long canoe through the misty waters of the Severn Sea from one of the surrounding islands. There, on the northeast side of the Tor, beneath an avenue of huge oak trees, the Druids who protected the island came to meet him and slowly led him up the hill to the sacred springs. Reverend Smithett Lewis writes: "The sea must have come up to just below the oaks, and it would have been a very possible landing place."[2] Around him rose the wide boulevard of noble oak and yew trees that flanked the two lower terraces of Chalice Hill. These trees, most sacred to the Druids, were a testament in wood—the oak tree a symbol of the Ancient of Days; the yew, one of the Seven Chieftain trees, "the guardian of the mysteries that brooded over the sacred waters . . . and [also over] academies of metaphysical learning."[3] Today, only two of these ancient giants remain. Tragically, the rest were cut down by a farmer in the early 1900s to clear a pasture. When the rings of the trees were examined, they revealed that the trees had been alive for over 2000 years![4]

While various parts of Avalon were doubtlessly reserved for sacred ceremony, there was a village where the priests and priestess who guarded the island lived. These instructors of the Mysteries, both male and female, lived in quarters that were close to one another, but separate. Qualified candidates and graduates who still had duties on the island lived close by—close enough to attend the college, yet with a certain independent austerity.

It was here that Jesus built a little wattle hut beneath a large oak tree not far from the springs. Today, this is the exact site of Glastonbury Abbey. His hut was made with sturdy wooden frameposts fastened into the ground, a platform floor of layered wood and clay, and walls woven from tall, pliable water reeds daubed with clay. The circular roof was thatched with woven reeds and the entire house washed with lime.[5] These sturdy wattle houses could withstand even the most severe weather and examples of this kind of construction can be found in England even today.[6]

This mud-and-wattle hut became Jesus' sanctuary when he returned to Britain at thirty before embarking on the events that would ultimately lead to his Crucifixion.[7] No doubt Avalon's beauty, grace, and power offered a place of sanctuary to him—in sharp contrast to the turmoil of Judean politics. Conversely, the deep, contemplative energies of Jesus and his community became embedded in the land.

When Joseph of Arimathea returned to Avalon in 37 C.E., shortly after the Crucifixion, he used this little wattle hut as the center of his early Gnostic community. William of Malmesbury, historian of Glastonbury, writes in 1126 about the building of this first Christian settlement, citing that the followers of Jesus' teachings called themselves Culdees. "These [twelve] holy men built a chapel of the form that had been shown them. The walls were of osiers wattled together, rude and misshapen."[8] Later, these circular homes were called anchorite huts, and this wattle hut construction became a part of the building traditions of the early monastic Christians.[9]

Twelve round huts were built in a circle around Jesus' house, placing it at the center like the Sun. The disciples agreed that, whenever one of them died, another would take his place, thus preserving the symmetry of the twelve signs of the zodiac around a central light. British historian John Michell documents how this twelve-rayed motif was encoded again and again into almost every major oracle site in the ancient world, including the city of Jerusalem and the oracle temples of Delphi.[10]

Today this holy site near the village of Glastonbury is part of the ruins of the much larger Glastonbury Abbey, destroyed by Henry VIII in the 16th

FIGURE 64. The hut that Jesus built was similar to the wattle and reed huts built by the Celts, later called anchorite huts. Illustrated by Sylvia Laurens.

century. It is called the Chapel of Mary. During excavations of the Abbey's original mosaic floor in the early part of the 20th century, archaeologists discovered a geometric design with twelve spheres around a central orb, inscribed into the floor of the chapel.

THE FIRST CHRISTIAN CHURCH

Sabellus, an early Christian theologian, tells us that "Christianity was privately confessed" in many places and that Britain was "the first nation to proclaim it their religion." The learned Italian historian Polydore Vergil wrote: "Britain . . . was of all kingdoms, first, that received the Gospel." In the 15th century, four separate Church Councils formally recognized this fact, including Pisa (1409), Constance (1417), Sienna (1424), and Basle (1434). All these councils declared that "[t]he churches of France and Spain, must yield in point of antiquity and precedence to that of Britain, as the latter Church was founded by Joseph of Arimathea immediately after the Passion of Christ."[11]

Catholic sources compiled in the 16th century by the curator of the Vatican library record the voyage of Joseph of Arimathea to Britain. Cardinal Baronius shares how Joseph left Palestine by ship with a number of disciples.[12] His

FIGURE 65. Joseph of Arimathea's community in Avalon was the first above-ground Christian community in the world. Its design reflects the deeper teachings of the Precession of the Equinoxes taught by the Mystery Schools. Each of the twelve huts measured 21.6 feet in diameter, while the center hut was almost 26 feet wide, reflecting the 25,920-year cycle of one entire Great Year and the 2160-year cycle of each zodiacal age. Illustrated by Sylvia Laurens.

passengers included Mary Magdalene, Martha, and Lazarus; Mary Jacobi, the wife of Cleopas, thought to be the younger brother of Jesus' father; Eutropius, Cleon, Saturninus, Martial, Trophimus, and Sidonius (Restitutus); Sarah, the black woman; Marcella, the Bethany sisters' maid; the disciple Maximin, whose sight Jesus had restored; and the famous Mary Salome, who was at the foot of the cross with Mary the Mother and Mary Magdalene during the Crucifixion.

> In that year the party mentioned was exposed to the sea in a vessel without sails or oars. The vessel drifted finally to Marseilles and they were saved. From Marseilles Joseph and his company passed into Britain and after preaching the Gospel there, died.[13]

Vatican reports claim that Joseph's ship was set adrift without oars by members of the Sanhedrin. Wilson and Prentis claim, however, that this was a deliberate rumor put about by Joseph of Arimathea through his Roman friends to discourage the Jewish authorities from pursuing them.[14]

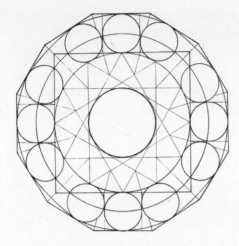

FIGURE 66. The zodiacal design inscribed into the floor of Mary's Chapel at Glastonbury Abbey reveals the original symmetry of the twelve circles around a central one, representing the Sun or Son of God.

The fleeing outcasts first landed in the south of France, at a place now called Saint Marie de la Mer, a small fishing village with a most unusual spring that had once been sacred to the Egyptian Sun god Ra. The town was originally called Oppidum Priscum Ra, which means the "town of the Sun god Ra." It had also been the home of a fourth-century B.C.E. Roman temple dedicated to Mithra, the great solar lord of Persia.[15]

According to church records, the apostle Philip was waiting for them when they landed. In France, Philip consecrated Joseph and prepared him as the chief apostle to Britain.[16] William of Malmesbury tells us that Philip sent Joseph to Britain to set up the church at Glastonbury, and that Philip was Joseph's "dearest friend."

> In the year of our Lord, 63, twelve holy missionaries, with Joseph of Arimathea (who had buried the Lord) at their head, came over to Britain, preaching the Incarnation of Jesus Christ.[17] The king of the country and his subjects refused to become proselytes to their teachings, but in consideration that they had come a long journey, and being somewhat pleased with their soberness of life and unexceptional behavior, the king, at their petition, gave them for their habitation a certain island bordering on his region, covered with trees and bramble bushes and surrounded by marshes, called Ynis-Wytren.[18]

Gildas the Wise, writing only four centuries after the birth of Jesus, tells us that "Christ, the True Sun, afforded His light, the knowledge of His precepts to our island in the last year, as we know, of Tiberius Caesar."[19] Tiberius Caesar died in 37 C.E., the year that other records tell us Joseph arrived. This may mean that Jesus himself appeared in Britain in 37 C.E., or merely that Joseph and his disciples, carrying the teachings of Jesus, arrived in that year.

From the shores of southern France, the pilgrims traveled north to Marseilles, following the ancient path of the tin traders, then to Narbonne and west by horseback to the coastal peninsula, following the old Phoenician trade routes that Joseph knew so well. Finally, they sailed across the English Channel and into the port of Ictis, making their way to the small Celtic town of Marazion.[20] Some accounts say that, from there, they traveled on small hide-covered skiffs around Land's End at the west of Cornwall and up the western coast to what was called the Severn Sea, coming finally to the northern inlet of Cornwall. At that time, the sea flowed inland along the River Brue toward the seven sacred hills of the dragon's back, taking the travelers to the chain of islands of which Avalon was a part. In the distance, they would have seen the mound of the Tor and six other islands rising from the mists.

"Joseph landed not far from the town," writes Reverend Smithett Lewis. "[T]hen he and his companions marched these to a Hill, near a mile on the south side of the town, and there being weary, rested themselves, which gave the hill the name of Wearyall Hill."[21] An oak was planted at the site of this landing that came to be known as the Oak of Avalon. R. W. Morgan, gives an account of Joseph's arrival:

> Joseph and his company, including Lazarus, Mary, Martha, Marcella and Maximin came at the invitation of certain Druids of high rank from Marseilles into Britain, around 38--39 C.E.; [They] were located at Ynys Avalon, the seat of a Druidic cor, which was subsequently made over to them in free gift by [King] Arviragus. Here they built the first church, which became the centre and mother of Christianity in Britain. Here, they also terminated their mortal career, the gentle and conciliatory character of Joseph securing the protection of the reigning family, and the conversion of many of its members. Joseph died and was interred in 76 A.D.[22]

Some believe that Joseph sent word before they arrived to the royal house of Siluria in Britain, asking for asylum. Noble Arviragus was ruler of the Silurian tribe of Cornwall, and accounts from the *Bronze Book of Britain* report that it was well known that "Joseph was related to Avaleck, whose kingdom bordered that of Arviragus, through Anna the Unfaithful."[23][24] This seems to be a reference to Anna, the mother of Mary and Joseph of Arimathea. Perhaps Anna was called "the Unfaithful" because she left her husband behind, fleeing to Judea, where she remarried and gave birth to Mary.

This ancient book also states that Joseph and his company arrived "seaborne in a ship of Tarsis from across the sea of Wicta . . . sailing thence towards the rising sun, they came to the place beyond Sabrin called [the] Summerland." There, it continues, "in the Kingdom of Arviragus they came under the mantle of the High Druid of the south whose ear was inclined towards them, for he understood full-well the nature of the three-face god"—perhaps a reference to the trinity.[25]

In Avalon, the travelers were met by a second delegation: King Guiderius of Siluria and his entourage of nobles. The first official act by Prince Arviragus was to present Joseph with a charter for twelve hides of land, one for each of the twelve disciples who came with him. A hide was the equivalent of 120 acres, making this a handsome gift of 1440 acres.[26] This present was recorded in the *Doomesday Book of England*, a national survey of taxes and lands compiled around1086 for William the Conqueror. Thus, Avalon became the first mission of the Nazoreans established in the Celtic Isles.[27]

THE KOLBRIN BIBLE AND THE BRONZE BOOK OF BRITAIN

The Bronze Book of Britain, also known as the *Britain Book*, was unearthed from the grounds of Glastonbury Abbey after the great fire of 1184 destroyed the Abbey library. The book, written on thin sheets of bronze, had been sealed inside a copper-lined box that had preserved it for centuries. This fascinating artifact contains the story of Joseph of Arimathea's arrival in Britain and his first meetings with the Druids.

> Joseph Idewin [another name for Joseph of Arimathea] and his brave
> band came to flowering Britain three years after the death of Jesus. . . .
> After landing, he and his band passed through an avenue of oaks and
> standing stones. They first built huts over against the holy vineyard where
> the fruits were bitter.[28]

Even the selection of the vineyard as their place of shelter reveals Jesus' associations with the Mysteries, for both Jesus and Osiris were associated with the "true vine."

The Britain Book is a rich source of teachings by Jesus that are not found in the traditional Bible. Hidden beneath the Abbey, it was one of the monks' most precious possessions. While the antiquity of these writings is obviously great, the actual dates of origin can only be inferred from other records. After the fire that destroyed the Abbey's famous library, and much of early Christian history with it, the monks divided what remained of these sacred texts into four groups and took them to four separate locations for safekeeping, so that if something happened to one group, all would not be lost. In recent years, a quarter of these texts have resurfaced and are now being published as *The Kolbrin Bible*.[29]

The Kolbrin Bible gives an extremely detailed account of Joseph's first meetings with the Druids almost 2000 years ago.

> Joseph, our father in faith, came across the storm-tossed seas to the place called Balgweith and from thence to Taishan where he met the envoy of the king who was sorely troubled. . . . Now, the king called together a great conclave of the people, and the Druthin were there. The king said to our father [Joseph], "Speak now before the people. Tell us of your ways and we will judge whether they be worthy."
>
> Joseph spoke a tongue understandable to these people, but he spoke slowly and not after their fashion. Our father said, "As the light came first and called the eye into being to see it, so it is with God who is the already existing light. The heart does not create the thought, but the thought produced the heart. This, so it could manifest, for the heart is created to serve in the world of effects. The world of causes lies in another kingdom."[30]

The Druthin agrees, confirming that they know of the light and that "these things are not strange to us." The light, he explains, comes from "the original crystal which is always virgin," a possible reference to both the Virgin of the World, a more universal form of the Divine Mother, and to the light as an aspect of mankind itself. Joseph, in a spirit of ecumenism sadly lacking in the early church, replies:

> I have not come to batter down your house of hope, for it has many pleasing features, even as ours. So let us not disagree, but take the best from both and, discarding what is less good, fashion something of value to all. Let us weigh one thing against the other, rejecting that which less clearly shows the way.

Joseph goes on to describe a shipboard vision in which God "opened the eyes of his spirit," revealing to him that there was "no difference between the nature of His Spirit and the spirits of men, only that His was of an infinitely greater purity." The Druthin again agrees, saying: "Often have I thought on this. All men are alike in nature and all aspire to the same goal. All seek to make the same journey's end, only the route differs. Therefore, let us not argue whether men should follow your road or mine, but find between us a path better than either."

One of the priests then asks about "the worlds within the ever moving circles," to which Joseph replies: "The hidden worlds are numbered as sands on the seashore. If a man concerns himself with many things, he benefits none and derives no benefit himself. Let us concern ourselves with this world first."[31]"What know you of the Eye of God in men?" another asks. Joseph replies: "What is written in the heart is the Eye of God in men, this sees everything. Knowing right from wrong it puts things in instant perspective. Men in whom this eye is closed are little better than the beasts of the field and forest. I come as one who opens the eyes of such as these."[32]

This is a most interesting exchange, for, as we can see, the Druids are testing Joseph to discern the extent of his knowledge. They speak of the light within every human being, the multi-dimensional planes nested inside of one another in "ever moving circles," and the third eye, or inner sight that allows each one of us to perceive beyond this world. Joseph very clearly tells them that he is a man who values the heart above all things—a true expression of Jesus' message—and that, through the heart, one can open the inner eye. He also says that he is open to the Druids' ways, and willing to combine the best of the two paths. Clearly, Joseph passes the test, for the Druids graciously bestow upon the pilgrims the large tract of land described above.

> Then were the ship borne wanderers given land over from the Isle of Departure [Avalon], saying that if they could they live where no one else could because of the spirits, then their holiness would be established before all the people. The strangers were sorely tried by the Druids, but the spirits troubled them not. Nor did the sickness of the place come upon them and the people wondered.[33] They were troubled because of where the strangers were, and were stirred up by the Druthin, but the shield of Arviragus protected them.[34]

Prince Arviragus was later baptized in the Christian faith.

FIGURE 67. The Eye of God has had associations with the opening of the Third Eye in many spiritual traditions. It is through the opening of this eye that we gain our inner sight, the goal of all initiates.

The Staff and the Holy Hawthorne Tree

The hawthorne has long been a symbol of Jesus' power. The tree itself is indigenous to Syria, the seat of the Damascus Great White Brotherhood.[35] The particular tree known as the Holy Hawthorne has a gnarled and twisted trunk, like the caduceus staff of Thoth and the double helix of DNA; it bears snow-white flowers and bright-red fruit. It blooms twice a year, once at Christmas and again at Easter. The Celtic kings took cuttings from it each year as a symbol of renewal and hope. Shoots of the original Hawthorne still grow on Wearyall Hill and within the Abbey gardens of Chalice Well.

The story of the Holy Hawthorne begins with a dream that changed the course of history. *The Kolbrin Bible* tells the tale:

> Islass was the daughter of the queen's youngest sister and a holder of the king's favor, and when she attended him, she divulged her dreams. It happened that she dreamed the same dream thrice, and this was the manner as she told it to the king:
>
> "Behold I saw a moon which had three changing faces and as I watched the changes the moon itself changed and became a sun, and within this sun, another sun appeared, inferior in brightness. Then the two became one and its brilliance filled the sky. In the midst of this I saw the king and many Druthin and priests of the strangers. Then I saw a great battle sword and the brilliance faded as did the figures, and only the sword remained, from which blood dripped drop by drop. Then too, it faded."

When the king gave the strangers a large parcel of land, the Druid priests questioned his generosity, demanding a divine sign from Ilyid, the leader of the newcomers (Joseph of Arimathea), who agreed to deliver such a sign within six months.

> Ilyid struck his staff into the soil to mark the covenant. The following Eve of Summer there was a gathering and it was found that a small green shoot was coming up from the ground beside the staff, which was an offshoot of the staff. The king decreed that this was a sign that the land accepted the strangers, and these took it as a sign that what they taught fell on fertile ground and would take root. . . . Here, on twelve portions of land, the wise strangers dwelt in peace and they built a church which was a full sixty feet long, by a full twenty-six feet wide.

Joseph of Arimathea is buried beside the forked path before the church, in a tomb inscribed: "I brought Christ to the Britons and taught them. I buried Christ and now here my body is at rest." Islass became Joseph's first convert and she alone knew the secret of the Holy Hawthorne, around which many legends grew.

> "[F]rom here shall come that which will be the salvation of mankind in the years to come," it was prophesied. Here was the resting place for the souls of the dead, where they received their last sustenance before passing through the glass wall. From here, ran the old road to the place of light where the bright winged spirits flew freely in the place called Dainsart in the old tongue.[36]

FIGURE 68. The Holy Hawthorne was planted on Wearyall Hill some 2000 years ago by Joseph of Arimathea. Today it has produced several offspring. The Tor can be seen in the distance. Illustrated by Angel Terrazas

These hauntingly beautiful passages reveal the depth of a culture that listens to the world of dreams and honors the Great Spirit that moves through the universe, speaking to each of us if we will only listen.

In the centuries that followed Joseph's death, this holy place became the site of the Chapel of Mary, a structure perfectly aligned with the ley lines of both Stonehenge and Glastonbury Tor.[37] The chapel was originally laid out using the same geomantic principles as Stonehenge. "Stonehenge and Glastonbury were both founded on the same pattern," John Michell writes, "It is impossible to say whether that model was transmitted by the Freemason temple builders over the two thousand years which separate Stonehenge from Glastonbury, or whether it was renewed by revelation at the beginning of the Christian era. However one explains it, the evident fact is that both Stonehenge and Glastonbury share a common ground plan."[38]

This church became known as the Vetusta Ecclesia, or old church, and was said to have been dedicated to Mary by Jesus himself. While most assume the church honors Mary the Mother, it is possible that it was dedicated to Mary Magdalene, whom many believe to have been Jesus' wife. William of Malmesbury supports the former: "The said twelve saints residing in this desert, were

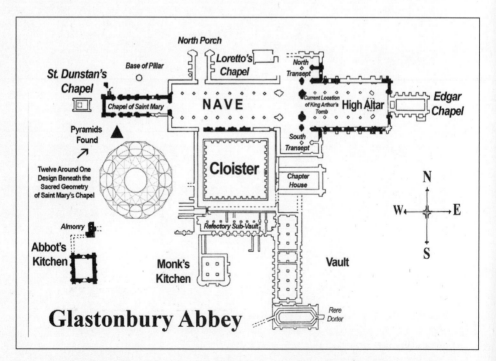

Figure 69. Glastonbury Abbey and the location of Mary's Chapel, built over Joseph's original community.

in a very short time warned by a vision of the Angel Gabriel to build a church in honor of the Holy Mother of God and Virgin Mary in a place shown to them from heaven ... and it was the first in the kingdom. God's Son distinguished it with greater dignity by dedicating it in honor to his Mother."[39]

Over the centuries, this humble center of meditation and prayer developed into a great place of worship, becoming the heart of the much larger Glastonbury Abbey that was constructed in stages beside it. Welsh historian Geoffrey of Monmouth (1100–1154), quotes from an early Celtic manuscript:

> Thereupon the twelve Saints, so often mentioned, paying devout homage in that same spot to God and the blessed Virgin, spending the time in vigils, fasts and prayers, were constantly sustained ... the said Saints continued to live in the same hermitage for many years, and were at last liberated from the prison of the flesh. The place then began to be a covert for wild beasts, the spot which had before been the habitation of Saints—until the Blessed Virgin was pleased to recall her House of Prayer to the memory of the faithful.[40]

THE FIRST 1000 YEARS

Joseph's original community was renewed in 166 by two Celtic missionaries named Faganus and Duvanus, who came from Rome to baptize the family of the British King Lucius. When the papal emissaries arrived, they found a well-established tradition:

> ... the whole story in ancient writings of the coming of Saint Joseph and his companions and the giving of twelve hides of land; that they loved this spot above all others and they also, [and] in memory of the first twelve chose twelve of their own, and made them live on the said island with the approval of King Lucius. These twelve thereafter abode there in divers spots as anchorites—in the same spots, indeed, which the first twelve inhabited ... and thus many succeeding these—but always twelve in number, abode in the island many years up to the coming of Saint Patrick the Apostle of the Irish.[41]

When the Irish monk Saint Patrick discovered these same twelve huts almost 300 years later, in 433 C.E., he appointed himself Abbot—a position that he held until his death in 472 at the ripe old age of 111. In the sixth century, Saint David added a chapel to the community's east end, which was later enlarged to become the Abbey Church of Saint Peter and Saint Paul. In the 7th

century, Saint Paulinus (625–644), Archbishop of York, encased the original
wattle house of Jesus in boards and covered it with lead to preserve it. In the
eighth century, King Ina, one of the earliest rulers of the Anglo-Saxon kingdom of Wessex, built a larger church at Glastonbury, claiming that a far older
wooden temple, long known as a gathering place for Christians, had been there
first. Finally, Saint Dunstan, the noted Abbot of the tenth century (940-957),
having procured sizeable funds for expansion, established the famous library at
Glastonbury and enabled the Abbey to become the wealthiest monastery in all
of Britain, second only to Westminster in London.[42] John Michell reports:

> In the days of their greatest glory, when the Abbey with its famous
> library and other treasures was the largest and richest in Britain, the
> Glastonbury monks preserved and venerated the site of the original
> Church of Saint Mary, built of wattles by Saint Joseph and his followers .
> .. after it [the Abbey] was destroyed by fire in 1184, its dimensions were
> preserved in the new chapel, dedicated to Saint Mary and Saint Joseph,
> built on the same site."[43]

This site did, indeed, become one of the most powerful places in all England, and the home of the famous Glastonbury Abbey, with its many dormito-
ries, exquisite chapels, nave, towers, reliquary, kitchens, and barns.

After the accidental fire of 1184 that destroyed most of the Abbey, the cathedral was rebuilt by Henry II. It took 120 years to complete, but when finished, it was magnificent. Henry II wrote about the Abbey's great significance
in his charter, calling it the "source and origin of all religion in England."[44] In
1190 C.E., as if in response to Henry's request for a divine sign that his financial investment in the Abbey was justified, one of the Glastonbury monks had
a dream in which he was shown the graves of the legendary King Arthur and
Queen Guinevere somewhere on the Abbey grounds. Knowing that many famous saints and heroes had been buried there, the Abbey brothers began exca-
vating the location indicated in the monk's dream. The grave was found in the
section of the Abbey grounds called the Churchyard of Saint Dunstan, marked
by two vertical pyramid-shaped stones.[45] It lay exactly on the major ley line that
runs through the altar of Mary's Chapel, aligned with the ley line of the Tor
and with Stonehenge itself. There, some sixteen feet below the surface, they discovered a stone slab and a lead cross.[46] Beneath these was a large hollowed-out
coffin made from an oak tree, the sign of burial for an ancient king.[47]

Later, in 1662, the tomb of Joseph of Arimathea was found amid the ru-
ined shrine at Mary's Chapel. Joseph's sarcophagus bore an Egyptian caduceus

inscribed between the letters J & A. Reverend Lewis observes: "There could be no badge more suitable for the Messenger of Christ to this country than the caduceus, the badge of Mercury, the messenger of the gods."[48] The inscription clearly indicates that the Great White Brotherhood's teachings were known by the Druids and the Essenes alike, a fact that will become increasingly apparent as we follow Jesus through his many years of study in India and Egypt.

The Destruction of the Abbey

The power of Glastonbury Abbey did not survive the Reformation. Furious over the Roman Church's interference, Henry VIII ordered the dissolution of all the great monasteries in Britain. He was convinced that a secret treasure existed within the grounds of Glastonbury Abbey—something like the Holy Grail—that would bestow upon him special powers. He took the Abbey's treasures, destroyed its library, and co-opted its power.

When Richard Whiting, the 80-year-old Abbot, refused to divulge the location of the Abbey's "sacred treasures," even under torture, Henry hanged him from a gallows erected on the Tor. He placed the Abbot's severed head over the the Abbey's entrance, then cut his body into quarters and sent its parts to various churches as a warning to all those who resisted him.[49]

In their subsequent search of the Abbey's cellars, Henry's men discovered some 500 precious items, including one golden chalice, but no evidence of the Grail. Afterward, Henry burned the library and dismantled the Abbey piece by piece, selling off what remained of its valuables for a pittance. Despite Henry's rampage, however, some documents did survive. Two vital manuscripts—*The Kolbrin Bible* and the *Bronze Book of Britain* (now published in one volume as *The Kolbrin Bible*)—were retrieved, ensuring that the legends of Glastonbury itself, which had existed even before Jesus arrived, would survive.

Thus Britain is part of the heritage of both Jesus and Joseph of Arimathea. It was here that Jesus studied, built his home, and learned the foundational precepts of Christianity—the belief in a singular God with both male and female aspects, and a trinity. From the Druids, he learned about life after death, the immortality of the human soul, and the soul's ascent into heaven or hell between lifetimes. In Britain, these principles were not repressed or hidden, as they were in Jerusalem. The Druids taught openly about the Tree of Life, the One World Mountain, the Divine Mother, and the "Way" that leads back to Paradise. They believed in the existence of a divine god-man who died upon a cross—a tradition that foretold the story of Jesus' own life and Crucifixion.

The Avalonian tradition was thus Christian all along. Nicholas Mann writes,

> The nature worshipping shamans or Druids were the early monks. . . .
> The death and rebirth of the initiates [with the goddess Ceridwen] was
> the "Virgin Birth" of Christ and its crucifixion and resurrection. The
> spiral or revolving castle on the Tor was a mount that traced the footsteps
> of Christ at Calvary. The celestial patterns in the surrounding landscape
> were the twelve hides of land granted to the Abbey. The Magical Caul-
> dron of Rebirth was . . . the Holy Grail. The Great Goddess was the Virgin
> Mary. The World Tree was the cross.[50]

The beauty and mythos of this sacred land has survived for over 2000
years, a testament to its strength and power. Jesus loved this land and blessed it,
as it blessed him. And Avalon was the perfect way station for Jesus as he began
to synthesize the foundational teachings of the mystical Essenes who had raised
him and the vast wisdom of India, where he would later travel.

Part V

Jesus
in the East

CHAPTER 20

Jesus in the Land of Buddha

He sees all sides and knows His own Self, from and by Himself, boundless, unknowable, deathless, beyond comparison. He is immutable goodness, perfect, without flaw, immortal.[1]

—The Sophia of Jesus Christ

For centuries, there have been rumors, reports, and even published accounts of Jesus' years of study in the Far East. While these are usually swept under the rug by the established church, there are many written and eyewitness testimonies that support the theory. Manly P. Hall describes "persistent rumors that Jesus visited and studied in both Greece and India, and that a coin struck in His honor in India during the first century has been discovered. Early Christian records are known to exist in Tibet, and the monks of a Buddhist monastery in Ceylon still preserve a record which indicates that Jesus sojourned with them and became conversant with their philosophy."[2] Other scholars draw on historical accounts and stories from the Great White Brotherhood to corroborate this claim. In this chapter, we'll explore what Jesus learned in India and how those lessons affected his teachings.

THE AQUARIAN GOSPEL OF JESUS THE CHRIST

The Aquarian Gospel of Jesus the Christ was written by a Civil War chaplain in 1908. In this account, Levi Dowling claims to have transcribed the life of Jesus of Nazareth directly from the Akashic Records, laying out his journeys through the Far East and then his many years of study in Egypt. The Akashic Records purport to be an "etheric library" that contains every event that has ever happened on on Earth. Today, we would call Dowling's book channeled material, because it lies outside knowledge we can validate. Thus we must take his accounts of Jesus' life as apocryphal and try to discover what parts of them can be backed up by substantiating historical data.

Dowling's book is grounded in the belief that humanity, having fallen into ignorance, is working its way back to remembering its own divinity. Its key points are that, through discipline, consciousness, heart, and prayer, Jesus made himself the perfect vessel for the spirit of the Christ, and thus became the fulfillment of the god-man for his age. He was "the anointed one," awaited for centuries. The book reveals that Jesus taught that no soul is ever abandoned by God, and that all souls will eventually become perfected through experience. It also speaks about reincarnation, a theology that Jesus supported, but that was later suppressed by the Council of Nicea in Rome.

Dowling tells us that Jesus traveled to the East around the age of fourteen, accepting the invitation of an Indian prince named Ravanna, who visited Jerusalem at the time of the Passover and heard Jesus speak at the temple. Intrigued by the depth of the young man's wisdom, the prince offered to become his patron and invited him to travel to India. Mary and Joseph eventually gave their consent, and Jesus left with the royal caravan for Jagannath, where he was accepted as a student of the *Vedas*, thought by many to be the oldest spiritual literature extant, having been compiled over 5000 years ago by seven sacred Rishis (holy men).[3] Dowling writes that Jesus spent a total of six years in India, studying in the cities of Benares, Rajagriha, Puri, and Cuttack.[4]

While there is much to ponder in Dowling's account, our Celtic research suggests that his timeline is slightly off. We simply can't ignore the many accounts of Jesus in Britain at age fifteen, or the extensive documentation from those lands. While Jesus may not have left Britain until his sixteenth or seventeenth year, however, he still had plenty of time, before returning to Judea, to make the voyage to India, stay for several years, and then return to Palestine through the passes of Central Asia.

We know that Jesus traveled to Britain a third time around the age of thirty, and there are several reports of him studying in Egypt as a mature adult. Furthermore, the apocryphal *Acts of Pilate* report that he was back in Judea when he was twenty-eight or twenty-nine, perhaps to see his family and reestablish contacts with his childhood friends.[5] Presumably, he would have kept a low

profile during this visit to avoid any notice from the Sanhedrin priests until he
was ready to begin his ministry.

The Great White Brotherhood appears to confirm Dowling's account, describing how Jesus left Britain for India as a companion of the serene healing
master Ramanchana. According to Eugene Whitworth, author of *The Nine Faces
of Christ*, they sailed aboard a ship called the River Hindus, with Jesus acting
as the ship officer's and aide to Captain Ramanchana, who was a learned adept
within the Fellowship of Light. Ramanchana taught Jesus about the philosophies of the East, the disciplines of yoga, and the thirty-three steps to mastery
that would allow him to "yoke himself, body and soul" to the Divine.

It is not surprising, then, that Jesus' training focused strongly on breath-
ing exercises that opened the pathways for the *siddhis*, the paranormal spiritual
gifts, to awaken. The term *siddhi* means "perfection of the Spirit" or "the at-
tainment of flawless identity with Reality (also called Brahman, the Creator)."[6]
Through these spiritual powers, one can heal, cast out demons, walk on water,
raise the dead, levitate, pass through walls, and move objects by paranormal
means.[7] Many of these gifts are attributed to Jesus.

In Whitworth's account, Jesus describes the ship's arrival in India some five
months after their departure from Britain:

> One day, almost five months later we sailed into the harbor near a city
> on the west coast of Hindu's land and after we had tied to a wharf, my
> beloved Guru sent me to gather my bundle and follow after him. This I
> did without hesitation or question, although my heart was heavy at leav-
> ing so many sweet comrades, as were the sailors on the River Hindus. We
> made our way by boat and on foot for several hours and rested overnight.
> Then we continued on until at last we stood at the entrance to the cavern
> of Elphanta, ancient and sacred cave of initiation.

According to this record, Jesus lived for two years in a small stone house
beside this ancient cave—one of the oldest known sanctuaries in the world,
where adepts had trained for centuries. The cave was carved from solid rock, its
entrance guarded by two gargantuan statues. Its eighteen-foot ceiling was supported by four massive pillars. Here, Jesus became a vegetarian and acted as a
holy man and healer for the local village. He listened to their problems, healed
their bodies, and ministered to their needs. He also worked to perfect the spiritual disciplines he had learned onboard ship. At the end of two years of training, he was eligible to take his four initiations in the Hindu path—initiations
known as Char Asherum.[8]

Whitworth's account is corroborated by famed humanists and artists, Nicholas and Helena Roerich, who, in 1923, traveled across Central Asia in search of evidence that would help explain and document the lost years of Jesus' life. Specifically, they sought to verify the writings of Nicolas Notovitch, a Russian journalist who, in 1894, published a book called *The Unknown Life of Jesus Christ* that told of Jesus' life in the Himis monastery in the Himalayas of Tibet. While traveling in the province of Ladakh in late 1887, Notovitch fell from a horse, fractured his leg, and was taken to the remote Buddhist monastery of Himis to recover. Himis is one of the most celebrated spiritual centers in Ladakh, both because of its high elevation (11,000 feet above sea level) and its collection of ancient treasures.

During Notovitch's many months of recovery, he slowly gained the trust of the monastery's head lama and was eventually shown an ancient Buddhist manuscript that told of Jesus' missing years in India. These ancient texts were originally written in Pali, the sacred language of the Buddhists, and later translated into Tibetan. They had traveled from India to Nepal, and then to Tibet.[9] According to Notovitch, the text was composed of isolated verses scattered out of sequence. Notovitch copied down the translations and then reordered them chronologically, calling them *The Life of Saint Issa: Best of the Sons of Men*. Later, he published them in a slender volume entitled *The Unknown Life of Jesus Christ*, which gained immediate attention around the world.

Notovitch was not the only person to see these ancient texts. In 1922, a highly regarded Indian holy man named Swami Abhedananda undertook his own journey to the Himis monastery to confirm Notovitch's account. Swami Abhedananda's credentials were impeccable: he had studied at the Oriental Seminary in Calcutta, lived abroad in England, and was familiar with Western methods of scholarship. He was also a dedicated swami, a holy man committed to God. Abhedananda's discoveries were later published in his own book, *Journey into Kashmir and Tibet*:

> The lama who was acting as our guide took a manuscript from the shelf and showed it to the Swami. He said that it was an exact translation of the original manuscript which was lying in the monastery of Marbour near Lhasa. The original manuscript is in Pali, while the manuscript preserved in Himis is in Tibetan. It consists of fourteen chapters and two hundred twenty-four couplets (slokas).[10]

Similar reports have been made by an impressive list of witnesses, lending credence to the authenticity of Notovitch's discovery at Himis.[11]

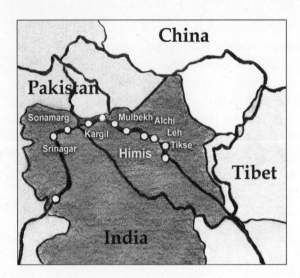

FIGURE 70. Map of the Himis monastery region.

THE UNKNOWN LIFE OF JESUS CHRIST

Notovitch relates how Jesus came to India to study with the Brahmins, and how they taught him to heal the sick, perform exorcisms, and read the Vedas.[12] Jesus, Saint Issa, spent six years studying and teaching at the temples of Jagannath, Rajagriha, and Benares, and, during that time, was held in the highest esteem by the sages of India and Tibet. When the masters of India later heard of Jesus' death, they were appalled:

> The Earth trembled and the heavens have wept, because of the great crime just committed in the land of Israel. For they have put to torture and executed the great and just Issa, in whom dwelt the spirit of the world; which was incarnated in a simple mortal, that men might be benefited and evil thoughts exterminated thereby. And that it might bring back to life of peace, of love and happiness, man degraded by sin, and recall to him the only and indivisible Creator whose mercy is boundless and infinite. This is what is related on this subject by the merchants who have come from Israel.[13]

When Notovitch returned from India in the late 1870s, he visited several well-respected ecclesiastical leaders, thinking his discovery would be of the greatest importance to them, anticipating that the Catholic Church would be thrilled to learn of his amazing find. He first met with a cardinal in Rome, then an archbishop in Kiev, and finally another Cardinal in Paris, each of whom warned him that he would make great enemies if he published these documents. In fact,

Cardinal Rotelli (in Paris) claimed that the documents would "only furnish new food to the calumniators and detractors of the evangelical doctrine." In Rome, he was told: "nobody will attach much importance to it," and was offered money to "defray any costs for his efforts and research."[14] Notovitch turned down the cash and decided to publish anyway.

In the course of his inquiries, Notovitch learned that the Vatican Library contained some sixty-three manuscripts in various Oriental languages that refer to the legends of Saint Issa in the East. Over the centuries, Christian missionaries had brought these records back to Rome from India, China, Egypt and Arabia.[15] Notovitch even suggests that the original writer of these Indian histories may have been the apostle Thomas, whom Biblical accounts tell us was sent to India in the years following the Crucifixion.[16] Indeed, Jesus is believed to have sent Thomas to evangelize India and the territory between the Persian Gulf and the Caspian Sea, enjoining him to learn the language in order to preach to men who spoke only Pali or Sanskrit. So it is possible that the narratives Notovitch discovered are based on stories that Thomas himself wrote some 2000 years ago."[17] Other traditions suggest that Bartholomew and Matthias also preached in India, Tibet, and China, so the manuscript may also have been authored by them.[18]

We do know that Jesus mastered the Pali language, because it was the tongue of Buddha. In *The Unknown Life of Jesus Christ*, we read: "Having perfectly learned the Pali tongue, the just Issa applied himself to the study of the sacred rolls of the Sutras. Six years later, Issa, whom the Buddha had chosen to spread his holy word, could perfectly explain the sacred scrolls."[19]

Today, historians believe that Christianity reached the south of India right after the Crucifixion. Jesus' "twin" brother, Thomas, is said to have brought the gospel to Muziris in India, in 52 C.E., only fifteen years after Jesus' death. In the apocryphal Acts of Thomas, we learn that the apostles drew lots to decide which countries they would visit to spread Jesus' teachings.[20] Thomas drew India, but refused to go. Then, one night, Jesus appeared to him and said: "Fear not, Thomas, go to India and preach the word there, for my grace is with you." When Thomas asked that he be spared the journey, Jesus appeared to a nearby Indian caravan merchant named Abban and offered to sell Thomas to him as a servant. When the merchant agreed to buy Thomas, he finally relented, and agreed to travel to India under the king's protection.[21]

Thomas Didymus founded seven churches in India before moving further east, baptizing both Brahmins and Jews. Anglo-German scholar Edward Conze (1904–1979) writes in his seminal book *Buddhism: Its Essence and Development*

FIGURE 71. Judas Thomas
Didymus, the apostle sent to
India by Jesus.

that "Buddhists were in constant contact with the Thomas Christians in southern India. Trade routes between Greco-Roman and [the] Far East were opening
up at the time that Gnosticism flourished for generations." History reports that
some twenty years after his arrival, Thomas was martyred.

WHAT JESUS LEARNED IN INDIA

Whitworth relates that, during his time in India, Jesus went through four major
initiations with the Brahmin, under whose tutelage he was trained in the spiritual laws of karma, dharma, and reincarnation. These initiations are called the
Char Asherum—the initiations of air, earth, fire, and water. Issa learned about
the Zennar and the Gerishth, the sacred cords that bind the human body to
the elements. He learned about the tyrants of the mind and eventually fought
through the Seven Caverns of Illusion that correspond to each of the seven
chakras.[22]

Like other chapters of the Great White Brotherhood, the Brahmins taught
a knowledge of the great spiritual Sun that lies behind our own physical Sun—a
teaching that lay at the core of the Mystery Schools. Jesus would also have been
taught that, behind the faces of the male gods Brahma, Vishnu, and Shiva, lies
the presence of the Divine Mother, the eternal divinity of unconditional love.[23]
In the East, this exquisite goddess has been known by many different names—

among them, Devi, Parvati, Durga, Sita, Radha, and Lakshmi. In Judaism, she is Sophia, the goddess of wisdom; in Christianity, she is the Shekinah, or Holy Spirit. We know that Jesus honored the Divine Mother, for he speaks of her in the apocraphal gospel The Sophia of Jesus Christ:

> His [God's] Bride is the Magnificent Sophia who first, through immortal man, appeared as Divinity, the Kingdom and the Father, the Self-originated, who revealed all. . . . And the male triumvirate—Brahma, Vishnu, and Shiva—that was in Sophia, brought forth God, Divinity and the Kingdom.

Jesus goes on to say that the planes of the universe were created "by the will of the Divine Universal Mother."[24] Notovitch also conveys the master's words on the nature of women:

> Listen, then, to what I say unto you: Respect woman, for she is the Mother of the Universe, and all the truth of divine creation lies in her. She is the basis of all good and beautiful, as she is also the germ of life and death. On her depends the whole existence of man, for she is his natural and moral support. She gives birth to you in the midst of suffering. By the sweat of her brow she rears you, and until her death you cause her the gravest anxieties. Bless her and worship her, for she is your one friend, your one support on earth. Respect her, uphold her. In acting thus you will win her love and her heart. You will find favor in the sight of God and many sins shall be forgiven you.[25]

Eventually, Jesus synthesized these Brahmin teachings with his training in the other Mystery traditions and began to teach his own profound wisdom in India. He preached the importance of coming into human form in order for each soul to obtain perfection:

> Life cannot be improved from the spiritual plane alone. Human life is improved by human qualification of divine energy. . . . The spiritual energy must be qualified by the human mind, agitated by great emotion to bring about the curing of disease, or the raising of dead nature.[26]

Jesus is saying here that it is not enough for us simply to float around in heavenly bliss. To evolve, we must experience life and death, suffering and joy, so we can choose of our own free will to be one with the Creator. It is only through the emotional and physical passion of such deep life-altering experiences that we gain the power to truly love, understand, and nurture others.

Enter into your temple, into your heart, illuminate it with good thoughts and the patience and immovable confidence which you should have in your Father. And your sacred vessels, they are your hands and your eyes. See and do that which is agreeable to God, for in doing good to your neighbor you accomplish a rite which embellishes the temple wherein dwells He who gave you life. For God has created you in His own likeness—innocent, with pure souls and hearts filled with goodness, destined not for the conception of evil schemes but made to be sanctuaries of love and justice. Wherefore I say unto to you, sully not your hearts, for the Supreme Being dwells therein eternally.[27]

Jesus taught that all people have a right to life, knowledge, and happiness. Clearly, this did not sit well with the Hindu upper classes, particularly the priestly and warrior castes who saw his message as a catalyst for social reform.

All loved him because Issa dwelt in peace with [the] Vaishas and Shudras [merchants and peasants] whom he instructed and helped. But the Brahmins [priests and scholars] and Kshatriyas [nobility and military classes] told him that Brahma forbade those to approach who were created out of his womb and feet. The Vaishas [merchants and artisans] were allowed to listen to the Vedas only on holidays and the Shudras [peasants and farmers] were forbidden not only to be present at the reading of the Vedas, but could not even look at them.[28]

The Hindu caste system forbade the lower classes to hear the holy scriptures except at festivals, if at all, yet Jesus empowered all people to awaken, including the servants and untouchables, threatening to upset the entire social balance of their world.[29] Thousands of people flocked to hear Jesus speak, just as later, in Judea, he would feed 5000 by the river. The authorities saw him as a maverick, a wild card, and a threat.

In defiance of God, he has taught that all men are equal. In defiance of Reason, he has taught that Untouchables are as divine as the Brahmins. In defiance of Truth, he has taught that karma is not ever enduring. In defiance of Love, he has taught that Brahmins are not pure and perfect. In defiance of Training, he has taught that all men have a right to life, liberty from caste and such happiness as the flesh may know. In defiance of Teaching, he has taught that a Guru is not essential to help man reach to the Supreme. In defiance of the Vedas, he has taught that there is not one single law which is sacred and divine. In defiance of the Law of the Land, he has taught resistance to authority and breaking of caste. In defiance of Justice, he has taught the taking of food from the lands of Brahmans to save lives of common people at times of famine.[30]

The depth of Jesus' wisdom and compassion led him beyond the laws of the secular world to the heart of the matter. He was a champion of all people, not just the special classes. Thus, "the white priests and the warriors becoming cognizant of the discourse addressed by Issa to the Soudras [Shudras, peasants], resolved upon his death and sent their servants for this purpose in search of the young prophet. But Issa, warned of this danger by the Soudras, fled in the night from Juggernaut, and took refuge in the mountainous Gothamide Country, the birthplace of the great Buddha."[31]

The Great White Brotherhood tells us Jesus was rescued by the Magi—the same masters that had overseen his life from the beginning. Balthazar, Gaspar, and Melchior joined Jesus in India and stole him away by night.[32] They took him to southern Nepal, the birthplace of the great Buddha five centuries earlier.[33] There, Jesus was accepted as the successor to the Buddha, who had prophesied Jesus' arrival some 500 years before.

CHAPTER 21

The Divine Purusha and the Christed Spirit

> There will come into the world a master, a fully illuminated Buddha, complete in wisdom and action, illuminated and blessed as myself. He will instruct in the Dharma and institute the holy life in completeness and in simplicity.[1]
>
> —From the Teachings of the Buddha, Digha Nikaya 26:25

Legend tells us that Jesus studied at the Buddhist temples of Jagannath, Rajag-riha, and Benares. Rosicrucian records claim he attended a monastery school at Jagannath for nearly a year and that one of his principal teachers was a master named Lamaas. Then he traveled to Benares to learn that monastery's extraordinary methods of healing under the powerful Hindu sage Udraka.[2] There, the sages welcomed him with open arms, because they saw in him the fulfillment of their own teacher's prophecy of an avatar to come—one referred to in the Digha Nikaya, or "Collection of Long Discourses," as "the second Buddha," who would appear 500 years after the Gautama Buddha was gone.[3] "There will arise in the world a lord, a fully-enlightened Buddha, endowed with wisdom and conduct, enlightened and blessed, just as I am now. He will teach the dharma and proclaim the holy life in its fullness and purity."[4] Jesus remained in Juggernaut for six years, learning the Pali language and studying the teachings of Buddha.

Scholars have long commented on the similarities between the teachings of Jesus and Buddha since the end of the 19th century. Both came from princely bloodlines; both began renewal movements within their inherited religious traditions; both were given exalted, divine status by their followers; and both were born to virtuous women called "virgins."

These are all attributes of the divine Purusha, a transcendent male being said to have been born of the first female creative principle of the universe, called Prakriti, yet another name for the Divine Mother.[5] She is the Virgin of the World, the birth-giver of life. Both Purusha and Prakriti are described as different aspects of the principle of Brahma, the Creator, also known as Iswara, a name remarkably similar to Issa, that marks Jesus as an incarnation of God, or one of the four great Kumaras.

The name Prakriti means "that which gives shape," a reference to the intelligent feminine consciousness behind the expression of nature, the Divine Mother herself. Prakriti is the field in which we live, the body of the universe with all its constituent parts. Her son's name, Purusha, means "eastern dawn," a phrase often found in Egyptian and Freemasonry rites to describe the masters Horus and Jesus. Both of these Kumaras were identified with the Morning Star. Likewise, Jesus says: "I am the Root and the Offspring of David, the Bright and Morning Star" (Rev. 22:16). Thus, the divine Purusha signifies a being who sets in motion the entire creative process of the world, the first creative principle at the dawn of time—Brahma. Therefore, the classic Christian imagery of the divine Mother and Son born from the Cosmic Egg was known in India as Prakriti and her son, Purusha, both of whom "participate, regulate and implement the universal creative process."[6]

A second-century carving of Siddhartha's mother, Gandhara, shows Siddhartha Gautama Buddha being born from his mother's side, just as, in Egypt, Ra, the god of light, and Thoth, the god of wisdom, were born at the opening of the Great Cosmic Egg. Like Aion, the solar lord who inaugurates the incoming age, and Jesus, the savior god who was born of Mary, the divine Purusha was born of a Virgin Mother (called Kore by the Greeks). And, in Persia, we find that Mithra, another "Son of God," struck a rock in heaven (the Cosmic Egg), thus causing the waters to flow out and form the universe. Each of these stories is but a metaphor for the Christ, the "first son of God," who was perennially seen as the savior of mankind in many cultures around the world.

THE CREATOR GODS

Buddha was also called the Maha Purusha, meaning the "Great Purusha." The idea of the Buddha as an avatar (meaning "one who descends from heaven") of Vishnu, the all-sustaining Creator God, is hinted at in various Buddhist books, including the Pali Cannon, the Digha Nikaya, and a discourse entitled "Sutra of the Marks" from the Pali texts Lakkhana Sutra. In Buddhism, the divine Purusha is an incarnation of the Creator himself, the same theology that later Christians adopted in the Father who is born as the Son in the world of form. This is in keeping with the stories of the four great Kumaras, who are direct emanations of the cosmic Father. The Purusha is the incarnation of this divinity, who lives a life of complete sacrifice that leads to *anatman*, or complete selflessness. He is epitomized by the Bodhisattvas of compassion, spiritual masters who have come down voluntarily from the higher realms to serve the world. The Buddha was "The Awakened One" who awoke from the slumber of forgetfulness to uplift mankind. This state of cosmic ignorance was believed by the Gnostics to be man's state of original sin.[7] The Brahmins, who were considered experts in reading these signs, described Siddhartha as having the thirty-two physical signs of the Maha-Purusha, known in Buddhism as the Mahapurisa Lakkhana.[8]

While the Purusha has long been known as the sacrificial lord who comes to Earth so that the cycles of life can be renewed, he can also be defined as the "divine self" that pervades the universe. He is not only the first expression of God, but the indwelling "Witness" of pure, egoless consciousness that exists beyond the senses and the mind.[9] He is the small still voice of Spirit that lies within each of us—the Christ, or "true inner master." Indeed, all the various expressions of the gods and goddesses are just different interpretations of the many facets of the supreme Purusha, the Divine One behind it all.[10] Thus, the Purusha can be considered pure consciousness itself.

At another level, the Purusha is the Adam Cadman, the Cosmic Man who has become God realized—the one whose death regenerates the world.[11] His story is ultimately the story of each of us in our quest for mastery—we are the divine sons (and daughters) who descend into the world of illusion. There we are dis-membered like the great god Osiris, cut into many pieces by the emotional, mental, and spiritual fragmentation of the physical realm. To return to our place of celestial origin, we must "re-member" to be made whole. And at some point we must also sacrifice our egos so that our true Self, our eternal Self, can shine through. The awakened Purusha knows that life and death are but a circle. All is consciousness. His willing sacrifice, like that of Jesus or Buddha, is the path that shows others the way to eternal life. And it is this act of love that regenerates the universe.

The concept of the ever-renewing savior god, whose life, death, and sacrifice regenerate the world, was also woven deeply into all the major Mystery

FIGURE 72. Buddha in
Meditation. Illustrated by
Sylvia Laurens

religions. The Egyptian Serapis, the Sumerian Tammuz, the Persian Mithra, the
Scandinavian Yimir, the Greek Adonis, the Celtic HU, and the Hebrew Lion of
Judah all save the world through their voluntary sacrifice. And, of course, this
also describes Jesus.

Sanskrit scholar Ralph Thomas Hotchkin Griffith (1826–1906), translator
of the Rigveda, one of the four holy books of Hinduism, quotes a passage that
is considered one of the most important Vedic hymns in all of Hindu worship,
one found in all four Vedic books:

> A thousand heads hath the Purusha, a thousand eyes, a thousand feet. On
> every side pervading earth he fills a space ten fingers wide. This Purusha
> is all that yet hath been and all that is to be . . . the Moon was gendered
> from his mind, and from his eye the Sun had birth.

Elsewhere, he notes, that "the Purusha is tied to a stake and symbolically
killed."[12] This description certainly fits both Jesus and Buddha, as well as other
noble avatars like Krishna, Osiris, and Adonis. Both Jesus and Buddha were
princes who surrendered their worldly thrones to a higher power on the altar
of unconditional love; both were attended by sages who had foreknowledge
of their births; both births were signaled by "celestial signs in the heavens";

both teachers forsook their positions of wealth in the secular world to follow a higher spiritual calling; and both were revolutionaries who acted outside their respective religions. Siddhartha Gautama Buddha taught outside the caste system of traditional Hinduism, while Jesus renounced the repressive dogma of the Brahmins first, and then that of the Pharisees and Sadducees. During the course of their respective ministries, both masters were accused of consorting with thieves, murderers, and prostitutes, and both avatars became defining points for our Eastern and Western paths of spirituality.

It is also significant that both Jesus and Buddha called their spiritual paths "the Way." In fact, the biblical book of Acts tells us that the earliest name for the Jesus movement was "the Way," a term that invokes the imagery of a road less traveled. Both masters strove to light a lantern on the path of self-realization, using their wisdom to transform men's hearts and minds and connect us with our own divinity. Like Jesus, Buddha was also identified with the light. Like Jesus, who says "I am the light that is above them all," Buddha is known as "the Enlightened One."[13] Thus, both are the Purusha—the all-pervasive consciousness that encompasses the universe.

Buddha taught the process of detachment, or letting go, to alleviate suffering; Jesus taught that those who empty themselves will be exalted, and those who exalt themselves will be emptied, emphasizing the importance of the ego death and the liberating process of being "born again." Both recognized compassion as the highest human virtue. Buddha said: "The last shall be the greatest"; Jesus said: "Many who are first will be last, and many who are last will be first" (Matthew 19:30). Buddha was called "the Lion of the Law, the Lord of Mercy"; Jesus was called "the Lion of Judah" (Hosea 5:15). Neither master saw himself as the founder of a new religion, but rather as setting straight the path of a far more ancient tradition that had become corrupted over time. In the same way that Jesus later became known as the Son of God, Buddha was said to have been the incarnation of the Cosmic Buddha, the "God of gods."[14] Jack Kornfield points out, however, that neither of these enlightened men would have recognized themselves in the exalted language we use to speak of them today.

Even the respective deaths of Jesus and Buddha are marked by similarities. When Jesus breathed his last, "the curtain of the temple was torn in two, from top to bottom. The earth shook, and the rocks were split" (Matthew 27:51). The Digha Nikaya says that, at the Buddha's passing, "[t]here was a great earthquake, terrible and hair-raising, accompanied by thunder" (Digha Nikaya 16:6–10).

FIGURE 73. Jesus in Meditation. Illustrated by Sylvia Laurens.

Pontius Pilate reports that a great storm swept Jerusalem on the afternoon of the Crucifixion:

> A loud clamor was heard proceeding from Golgotha, which, borne on the winds, seemed to announce an agony such as was never heard by mortal ears. . . . So dreadful were the signs that men saw both in the heavens and on the earth that Dionysus the Areopagite is reported to have exclaimed, "Either the author of nature is suffering or the universe is falling apart."[15]

In 1997, scholar Marcus Borg published *Jesus and Buddha: The Parallel Sayings*, in which he demonstrates the similarities between the philosophies of the world's two most famous teachers—Buddha and Jesus. In it, he points out parallel sayings from their teachings on nonviolence and virtue, the path of forgiveness, and the heart to which they were both committed. You can find a sampling of these parallels in the Appendix.

RETURN TO HIMIS

We find evidence of Jesus' kinship with Buddha at the Tibetan monastery of Himis as well. During Notovitch's sojourn there, the lamas told him that "[t]he spirit of Buddha was indeed incarnate in the sacred person of Issa, who without aid from fire or sword, has spread knowledge of our great and true religion throughout the world."[16] The monks thus saw Jesus as "a son of Buddha."

Issa is a great prophet, one of the first after the twenty-two Buddhas. He is greater than any one of all the Dalai Lamas, for he constitutes part of the spirituality of our Lord. It is he who has enlightened you, who has brought back within the pale of religion the souls of the frivolous, and who has allowed each human being to distinguish between good and evil.

FIGURE 74. Carved into the rock walls of Afghanistan are two glorious stone statues of Jesus and Buddha, towering some 170 meters above the sheer rock cliffs. Pilgrims come to pay homage.

His name and his acts are recorded in our sacred writings. And in reading of his wondrous existence, passed in the midst of an erring and wayward people, we weep at the horrible sin of the pagans who, after having tortured him, put him to death.[17]

Certainly Buddhism had already made its way to Egypt, Greece, Britain, and Rome by the time of Jesus' birth. There were Buddhist missionaries in Alexandria and, as we have already seen, the Essenes were open to Buddhist philosophy. Roman accounts also underscore the widespread presence of this philosophy, telling us of Buddhist monks who traveled to these regions and influenced the philosophical currents of the time. Clement of Alexandria relates that "[a]mong the Indians are those philosophers who also follow the precepts of Boutta [Buddha], whom they honor as a god on account of his extraordinary sanctity."[18] Origen tells us that the Buddhists had long coexisted with Druids in pre-Christian Britain: "The Island [of Britain] has long been predisposed to it [Christianity] through the doctrines of the Druids and Buddhists, who had already inculcated the doctrine of the unity of the Godhead."[19]

Thus, it is clear that there are many parallels between these two masters. History tells us that the passage from Israel to India had been open for at least 300 years prior to Jesus' birth. Alexander the Great cut a swath through Central Asia with his army, invading India in 326 B.C.E., and caravans of spices, silks, and other trade items moved regularly between India and the Middle East. While it is possible that Jesus picked up Buddhist philosophy during his travels to Egypt and Britain, and among his own beloved Essenes, the discovery of the documents in the Himis monastery speaks to a far greater connection. The evidence for Jesus' years of study in India is strong, and the similarities between Jesus' and Buddha's teachings, miracles, and philosophies strongly suggests that Jesus not only studied among the Buddhists in India, but was the fulfillment of the prophesy that a "fully enlightened being" would come to India 500 years after the Buddha left this world.

CHAPTER 22

Mithra and the Solar Lords

There is a light that shines beyond all things on Earth,
Beyond us all, beyond the heavens,
Beyond the highest, the very highest heavens,
This is the Light that shines in our heart.[1]

—The Upanishads

After Jesus left the caves of the Far East and traveled with his beloved Magi teachers into Persia, he encountered yet another incarnation of the illuminated, sacrificial Purusha: Mithra. The Great White Brotherhood tells us that Jesus' teachers took him from India into Persia, and then to the sacred caves of Bokhara, a city that lay along the merchant trading routes of the famous Silk Road. These caves had once been the initiation chambers of Mithra. Crossing the high Torugart Pass, Jesus would have spent time in Samarkand, a city not far from these caves. While today, only four historical records tell us of his journey into Persia, a great deal of circumstantial evidence argues that it is not only plausible, but virtually certain, that Jesus spent time there.

The Himis documents tell us: "[Jesus] arrived in Persia where the doctrines of Zarathustra were followed" and then "returned to his homeland at the age of twenty-nine."[2] This supports our earlier contention that Jesus may have traveled to Galilee for a year or so before returning to Britain. The Humane Gospel of Jesus the Christ and The Gospel of the Holy Twelve confirm this, while the Great White Brotherhood provides what purports to be a first-person account by Jesus of the journey:

We took the rugged pathways to Lahore and bore northward across the mountains into the Indus River Valley west of Kashmir. . . . We then turned down the Indus and followed southward. . . . When at last we left the caravan, taking to foot, I knew that we were headed for the Sacred Cave of Bokhara.[3]

Bokhara and Samarkand were once municipalities of the ancient Persian Empire that became havens to thousands of Jewish refugees during the Assyrian invasion of Samaria in 722 B.C.E. In 597 B.C.E., when King Solomon's temple in Judea fell to the Babylonians, there was a second influx of Jews into this area.[4] Finally, following the Crucifixion and the subsequent escalation of conflict between the Jews and the Roman Empire, a third wave of Jews—this time Nestorian Christians—sought safety in Bokhara and Samarkand.[5]

The Nestorians were led by Nestorius, an early church father who held views different from the Catholic orthodoxy regarding the divinity of Jesus. He believed that Jesus was human as well as divine—both aspects coexisting in one being who had attained the mantle of the Christ. The Catholic Church emphasizes that Jesus was divine from the moment of his birth, perhaps implying that he had no need for teachers—a convenient way to discourage others from following in his footsteps and threatening their stranglehold on truth. Nestorius was excommunicated from the established Roman Church at the Council of Ephesus in 431 C.E., and fled with a number of followers to the Sassanid Persian Empire. The dominant religions throughout this Empire were Zoroastrianism

FIGURE 75. Map of the Silk Road through China, Tibet, India, Pakistan, and Afghanistan, showing the location of the sacred cave of Bokhara where Jesus was initiated into the Persian Mysteries.

and Mithrism, but there were also many Jews and Christians. Nestorius was welcomed with open arms by the Assyrian Church of the East. Today, thousands of Jews live in this predominantly Muslim area who consider themselves descendants of one of the ten lost tribes of Israel.[6] They also claim that the biblical city of Habor mentioned in the Old Testament is really Bokhara.

Bokhara was founded by the Persian sage Zoroaster, otherwise known as Zarathustra, whom many scholars believe lived between 500 and 600 B.C.E., although some claim his history goes back as far as 1000 B.C.E.[7] Today, archaeologists know that the oasis villages from which Bokhara sprang were inhabited by an advanced Bronze Age culture at least as far back as 3000 B.C.E. By 330 B.C.E., when Alexander the Great swept through with his mighty army and conquered Persia, these cities were already thriving and were certainly flourishing by the era of Jesus. Since Samarkand and Bokhara were the two most important trading posts in all of Central Asia, if Jesus went through Persia, it is likely that he traveled through this region.

MITHRA, LORD OF THE COSMIC AXIS

The mysterious caves of Bokhara were used as initiation chambers by the followers of Mithra, a Persian savior lord whose religious rites have many astonishing correspondences with modern Christianity, as well as with the ancient Essenes, who were compared by Philo to the Persian Magi and the India yogis.[8] Mithra was linked with the spiritual power of fire and was known as a solar lord. Traditionally, he, like Jesus, is said to have been born on December 25—a date chosen as the birthday for many solar lords, including Horus, Osiris, and Adonis. Mithra was also linked with the Roman Sun god Apollo, the Greek hero Perseus, and the semi-divine champion Hercules. He was the Sol Invictus, or Victorious Sun, who brought light to mankind. To Mithrans, fire was the most sacred of all the four elements because of its obvious link to the Sun and to light.[9] Thus Mithra was often invoked by the Persians and Romans to witness ordeals by fire. As in other chapters of the Great White Brotherhood, Mithran priests wore white, practiced Sun-gazing, and built most of their temples in the open air.

Like their Druid and Egyptian counterparts, Mithran priests used large, roughly shaped standing stones to mark their astronomical temples, and believed that the all-pervasive creator of the universe could not be confined to any one building, church, or temple. The deepest levels of their Mysteries were usually conducted in caves, representing the primordial womb of the Great Mother.

The arched ceilings of their shrines and sanctuaries, representing the heavens, were built into the ancient catacombs and grottos beneath many Christian cathedrals, honoring the sacredness of Mother Earth and Father Sky.[10]

Although we do not know the exact year that Mithra was born, we do know that Mithraism predates Zoroastrianism by many centuries. In fact, Zoroaster honored Mithra as a central figure in his teachings. Moreover, the hermetic symbols linked to Mithra give us clues to the age in which he came. In the most famous stone carvings of Mithra, he is portrayed holding the head of a bull (signifying the Age of Taurus), while at his feet lies the scorpion of Scorpio and the snake of Ophiuchus, the serpent bearer, a constellation that sits between Scorpio and Sagittarius. Scorpio and Sagittarius are exactly 180 degrees across the zodiacal wheel from Taurus. As if to emphasize this, Mithra and the bull are flanked by the twins of Gemini, one of whom holds a torch while the other stands beside a tree. This hermetic symbolism shows us that Mithra was born between the Ages of Gemini and Taurus, and across from Scorpio and Ophiuchus—in other words, sometime around 4400 B.C.E.

In the stone carving described above, there are symbols that represent the seven visible planets of the ancient world (the Sun, the Moon, Mercury, Venus,

FIGURE 76. This hermetic carving of Mithra slaying the bull reveals the emblems of the twins of Gemini, the bull of Taurus, the scorpion (Scorpio) 180 degrees away, and finally the seven lanterns of enlightenment, which must be lit to become enlightened.

FIGURE 77. The seven branches of the Menorah: The Hermetic symbology of the Hebrew Menorah has many levels of meaning. Among the most important, but less well known, is the lighting of the seven chakras within mankind that then allow the initiate to climb the Tree of Life to become enlightened.

Mars, Jupiter, and Saturn) above Mithra's head. As we know from the Tree of Life, these planets are symbolic gateways through which souls pass to achieve freedom in the ancient Mystery Schools. They represent the rungs of the ladder we must climb to reach enlightenment and correspond to the seven major chakras, or energy centers, of our bodies. This symbol of the seven lights was later used by the Jews in their sacred menorah.[11] These seven "celestial lights" also represent the seven archetypes of personality that must be met and mastered to attain enlightenment and can also be linked to the "Sevenfold blessings" spoken of in the Manual of Discipline found among the Dead Sea Scrolls of the Essenes.[12]

> I saw seven golden candles; and in the midst of their blazing light
> I saw one like unto the Son of Man, clothed in white, white as the snow.
> And his voice filled the air with the sound of rushing waters;
> And in his hands were seven stars, full of the flaming light of the heavens
>   from when they came.
> And when he spoke, his face was streaming light, blazing and golden like
>   a thousand suns.
> And he said, "Fear not, I am the first and the last; I am the beginning and
>   the end.
> Write the things which thou hast seen, and the things which are,
> And the things which shall be hereafter;
> The mystery of the seven stars which fill my hands,
> And the seven golden candles, blazing with eternal light.
> The seven stars are the Angels of the Heavenly Father,
> And the seven candles are the Angels of the Earthly Mother . . . .

In stone steles dedicated to Mithra, these lanterns (or five planets) of knowledge are flanked by the Sun and the Moon, thus representing the balance between the divine male and female energies. Mithraic wisdom, like that of the modern Kabbala, taught that souls either ascended into the higher realms from Earth or descended into the earthly plane via these circles or spheres.[13]

The Egyptian and Tibetan Books of the Dead both speak of how the soul enters the Higher Worlds after death, providing roadmaps into the higher planes based in the movement of the stars and planets. Throughout the ancient world, these enormous time cycles were keenly studied by the priests, Magi, and sages. Even early Gnostic and orthodox Christian scholars honored the knowledge of these Star Mysteries, as evidenced by the Sun wheels, obelisks, and paintings of the zodiac that still grace the walls and gardens of the Vatican. While it is clear that Jesus had knowledge of these astronomical Mysteries from his earliest years of training with the Therapeutae and Essenes, however, there is little evidence left of it in traditional Christian gospels. Paul acknowledges that: "Our homeland is in the heavens, from where we also expect a savior . . . . Who will transform our humble bodies so as to remember his glorious body, by means of the power which he has to subdue the entire universe" (Philippians 3:20–21). And this was, in fact, the very power attributed to the god-man Mithra, two of whose names were Lord of Celestial Time, and Lord of the Cosmic Axis. We know from the Gnostic book The Sophia of Jesus the Christ that Jesus also knew of these astronomical Mysteries, and some believe this knowledge may have been incorporated into The Secret Book of John, which has been called "a primary Gnostic cosmological treatise giving an account of the earliest, purely spiritual phases of world evolution."[14]

SOL INVICTUS

Mithra, like Jesus, was said to have existed beyond the realms of time and space and was known as the kosmokrator, or Cosmic Ruler and Lord of Genesis.[15] Mithra and Jesus are often depicted holding a rod with a small globe at the top, a symbol of the celestial pole around which the heavens turn.

Mithra, like the god of light, Ra, emerged from the Great Cosmic Egg at the beginning of time. Like Jesus, he had the power to insert himself into the worlds of matter whenever he chose, usually arriving on Earth between the change of the ages. Indeed, one of Mithra's most potent titles was "He who stands beyond the Ages." Mithra, like Jesus, had twelve disciples, symbolic of the twelve signs of the zodiac that revolve around a central Sun. Like the later depictions of Jesus within the Christian mandorla, or sacred oval, Mithra stands in the doorway of the Vesica Piscis, a shape reminiscent of the Great Cosmic Egg. This

FIGURE 78. Jesus inside the mandorla, the Christian Vesica Piscis, holding the cross.

oval shape, created by the overlapping of two circles (the male and female in balance), also represents the same Eye of God used to depict the presence of the Divine throughout Egypt, as well as the fish shape chosen by Jesus as his own initiatic symbol. This hermetic symbology thus demonstrates Jesus' legacy as a solar lord and links him to the higher realms from which he came.

Depictions of Mithra, like those of Thoth, Horus, and Archangel Michael, show him holding the staff of wisdom in one hand (the cosmic pole) and the torch of illumination in the other, portraying him, like other solar lords before him, as a "way shower." Mithra is often shown wearing a crown of light and with wings that mark him as a celestial messenger. Coiled around his body are the seven coils of the caduceus, linking him to other incarnations of the four great Kumaras sent to raise the kundalini of the planet.

The legends of Mithra's birth are shrouded in hermetic symbolism, much like the stories of Jesus' birth. Born of a virgin mother in a grotto, stable, or a cave on December 25, Mithra was attended by three shepherds, thus linking him to the legends of the shepherd kings—those who "shepherd" their people. Mithra's Mysteries include a baptism, a Eucharist, and even a resurrection drama.[16] And the sign of the cross was inscribed on the forehead of every person admitted to the Mysteries of Mithra, just as, in the Eleusinian Mysteries of Greece and the Egyptian Mysteries, the Tau cross was inscribed on the foreheads of its initiates.[17] Mithra, like Jesus, was called the Light of the World, a name linking him directly to the solar lords of the past.[18] John Lundy also contends that Mithra died on a cross:

> Mithras was put to death by crucifixion, and rose again on the 25th of March. In the Persian Mysteries the body of a young man, apparently dead, was exhibited, which was feigned to be restored to life. By his sufferings, he was believed to have worked their salvation, and on this account he was called their savior. His priests watched his tomb until midnight on the vigil of the 25th of March, with loud cries, and in darkness; when all at once the light burst forth from all parts, the priest cried, "Rejoice, O sacred initiate, your God is risen. His death, his pains and sufferings, have worked your salvation."[19]

Some legends claim that Mithra was born from a rock, at the foot of a tree, beside a sacred stream. This encoded symbolism is clear. The stream is the Milky Way; the tree is the Tree of Life; the rock is the Great Cosmic Egg from which the universe was born—Vishnu, the all-sustaining principle of the Creator. This enormous egg, the One World Mountain of Avalon, drifts upon the waters of the eternal ocean; within it dwell the everlasting Divine Father and Mother. In India, these divinities are called Vishnu and Lakshmi, other names for the immortal, celestial aspects of Isis and Horus, the Egyptian Mother and Father of the All.[20] I know them as Rigel and Auriel whose symbols are the eagle and the dove.

Just as Moses struck a rock to bring forth water, Mithra shot his arrows into this primordial rock to release the "waters of life," which gushed forth and filled the world with substance.[21] In modern astronomy, this rock is "the singularity" of creation before the Big Bang.

> The base of the universe seethes with creativity, so much so that physicists refer to the Universe's ground state as "space-time foam" . . . [and] "universal possibility waves . . . " The density of the original matter is a billion times greater than rock. . . . That Great Power that had, there, at the birth place of the universe, gushed forth in all the energies and galaxies. . . .[22]

These words echo the ancient myths, leading us to realize that, in some unknown manner, our ancestors knew about these scientific mysteries. Mathematical cosmologist Brian Swimme continues:

> The universe began as an eruption of space, time, matter and energy out of the all-nourishing abyss, the hidden source of all creativity. . . . That which blossomed forth as the Cosmic Egg fifteen billion years ago, now blossoms forth as oneself, as one's family, as one's community of living beings, as our blue planet, as our ocean of galaxy clusters; the same fecund source—then and now; the same numinous energy—then and now.[23]

MITHRA AND THE SOLAR LORDS

In Persia, as in other areas where the rites of Mithra were practiced, a perfect white bull was sacrificed once a year in the solar lord's name. This sacrifice was related to the cultic stories of a young Mithra seizing an enormous bull by the horns and riding it. Eventually the bull unseated him, but the young god did not release his grip. He was dragged behind the bull until finally it collapsed from exhaustion. Then, hoisting the animal to his shoulders, he dragged it back to his cave and sacrificed it. The story says that, when Mithra "plunged the knife into its flank . . . wheat sprang from the bull's spinal cord, and from its blood [sprang] the vine; the bread and wine of the sacramental meal. Its seed, gathered and purified by the moon . . . produced the useful animals by which man is served."[24]

This story is a metaphor for the soul who conquers his animal nature through courage, heroism, persistence, and strength, and, in doing so, brings forth bounty for all of mankind. These ancient rites of bread and wine link Mithra with the Christian Eucharist, a sacrament long sacred to Osiris in Egypt as well. Osiris, in fact, was also linked with the white bull. In Memphis, a perfect white bull was kept in the Temple of Osiris and treated like a king. Toward the end of its life, it was sacrificed to the Nile, the sacred waters from which it came. The Nile represents the Milky Way; the white bull is the pure, unblemished solar lord. This entire rite was an externalized symbol of the return of the divine Purusha, who sacrifices himself for the sake of the world.

Many of the rites of Mithra harken back to the earlier rituals of Osiris, perhaps the first globally acknowledged lord of light. These traditions include the use of underground grottos found within all the Mystery Schools; the Eucharist meal of wine and bread, also celebrated by the mystical Essenes and the

FIGURE 79. Mithra slaying the bull.

Therapeutae; and the esoteric symbols of the eagle, the dove, the lion, the snake, the cross, the Sun, the Eye of God, the labyrinth, and the Tree of Life. Echoes of these symbols are found in the religious iconography of cultures as diverse as Norway, China, India, Australia, England, Egypt, Mesopotamia, and North, South, and Central America.

In one remarkably beautiful Norwegian wood-carving of a solar lord standing before the Tree of Life, we can identify many aspects of Christian, Mithraic, and Egyptian symbology. At the solar lord's back rises the Tree of Life, which is aligned with his spine. Atop the tree perches a majestic eagle (Rigel or Horus), representing the Divine Father principle. At its base lies the mortal world of life, death, and dissolution. In the middle stands the "cosmic mediator," Jesus, Osiris, HU, or Mithra. The figure is encircled by the Cosmic Egg and, from the egg's base, flow the waters of life, just as they do in the ancient stone carvings of Mithra, whose waters were depicted as bringing life to all the kingdoms of the world.

In this remarkable carving, the solar lord, who is one with the Light of God, willingly places himself upon the Tree of Life—in other words, he enters the world of time and space, taking the path that all of us take through the difficult task of being fully human. Yet he has a connection to the Source of All; he knows the way back to the Source; he holds the keys to eternal life. His birth from the Cosmic Egg is the action that causes the waters of life to flow. Below await the wise ones (the Magi), hoping to catch the water and pour it out to humanity. The sage is flanked by a woman and a man, reminding us of the need to balance the male and female energies within ourselves in order to transcend the world of death and ascend the Tree of Life.

Within the Egg with Jesus are two doves—incarnations of the Divine Mother (or Holy Spirit) that accompany each solar lord on his journey into the mortal realms. In the worlds of matter, this energy will often be the lord's mother, or his wife or mate. In the life of Jesus, these feminine roles are played by Mary, his mother, and Mary the Magdala (Mary Magdalene), his mate. In Krishna's life, they are represented by Yashoda, his mother, and Radha, his mate, both feminine incarnations of unconditional love. In ancient Egypt, two ex-

Figure 80. A Norse depiction of HU Hesus or Jesus inside the Cosmic Egg aligned with the Tree of Life. At the top of the tree is the eagle, a symbol for the Divine Father. Inside the Egg with Jesus are doves, representing the two aspects of the Divine Mother who accompany the great solar lord to Earth. At the bottom of the Tree is the mortal world of dissolution.

pressions of the divine feminine are symbolized by the two winged goddesses
Isis and Nephthys, often shown flanking the *djed*, or backbone of Osiris, upon
which is perched the great solar disc. Later, these same winged figures were
transformed in the Hebrew culture into the two golden angels atop the Arc
of the Covenant. On the Arc's side, we see the symbol of the Sun and, lying in
front of it, a stalk of wheat that symbolizes the Tree of Life, and the anointing
jar of "the Christed One." These two winged female angels are also used in the
rites of Freemasonry, and are associated with the deepest initiatory secrets of
life, death, and rebirth.

Mithra has also been described as another Adam, a "first son" of God who
issues forth from the Divine Father principle. Like Jesus, Mithra is marked as
the "first born son of God." Although his legends say that he eats of the Tree of
Wisdom, there is no sin attached to this act, only bounty. One worn rock image
of the god shows him residing within the Cosmic Egg above several figures: a
bird, a snake, a dog, and a fish—each representing one of the four elemental
kingdoms of air, earth, fire, and water. These elements also represent the four
major levels of initiation in the Mithraic Mysteries. Each stage has three successive degrees, making a total of twelve degrees, one for each of the twelve
astrological signs humans must pass through on their way to enlightenment.

FIGURE 81A. The Egyptian goddesses Isis and Nephthys flank the *djed* with their wings. The *djed* is
the regeneration symbol for Osiris, who, like Jesus, is aligned with the cosmic principle of the Sun.

Like the hermetically encoded story of the twelve labors of Hercules, each stage represents the mastery of an archetype.[25]

Manly P. Hall describes these initiatory rites:

> In the first degree the candidate was given a crown upon the point of a sword and instructed in the Mysteries of Mithras' hidden power . . . [He] was taught that the golden crown represented his own spiritual nature, which must be objectified and unfolded before he could truly glorify Mithras; for Mithras was his own soul, standing as mediator between Ormuzd, his [God-like] spirit, and Ahriman, his animal nature [represented in Christian beliefs by Satan].
>
> In the second degree he [the initiate] was given the armor of intelligence and purity and sent into the darkness of the subterranean pits to fight the beasts of lust, passion, and degeneracy. In the third degree he was given a cape, upon which were drawn or woven the signs of the zodiac and other astronomical symbols. After his initiations were over, he was hailed as one who had risen from the dead, was instructed in the secret teachings of the Persian mystics, and became a full fledged member of the Order.

FIGURE 81B. The Ark of the Covenant reveals similar hermetic symbols: the Sun, the Tree of Life represented by the shaft of wheat, the two winged guardians, and the anointing vial for the Lion of Judah or "Christed One."

Candidates who successfully passed through the Mithraic initiations were called lions and were marked on their foreheads with the Egyptian cross. Mithra himself is often pictured with the head of a lion and two pairs of wings. Throughout the entire ritual, there are repeated references to the birth of Mithra as the Sun God, his sacrifice for man, his death that men might have eternal life, and his resurrection that ensured salvation by his intercession before the throne of Ormuzd [God].[26]

The initiatic symbols associated with this tradition have remained in the rites of Freemasons, whose master's degree is called the "Grip of the Lion's Paw," a reference to the power of the Lion, or Christed One. There are even links between Mithra's iconography and Jewish symbolism, since Mithra is called the great "Lion of God," just as the Jews later called Jesus the "Lion of Judah" (Hosea 5:14). Mithraic initiates passed through seven degrees to become a master, reflecting the seven aspects of the Jewish Tree of Life and corresponding to the seven planetary spheres discussed earlier.[27] For example, the Initiation of Mars mastered the emotions of anger and courage; the Initiation of Mercury corresponded to the "hidden master" of thought within; and the Initiation of the Moon revealed the world of dreams. These planets were used as archetypal symbols of the microcosm hidden within each of us as we have seen in the Kabbala or Tree of Life.

In *Masks of the Gods*, Joseph Campbell writes:

> The individual had derived from each planetary sphere a specific temporal-spatial quality, which on the one hand contributed to his character, but on the other was a limitation. Hence, the seven states of initiation were to facilitate passage of the spirit, one by one, beyond the seven limitations, culminating in a realization of the unqualified state.[28]

These seven major initiations also match seven of the eleven levels of the mystical Kabbala, corresponding to the planetary realms of Mercury, Venus, Mars, Saturn, Jupiter, and the Sun and the Moon—in short, initiations of the mind, heart, courage, form, spirit, conscious, and subconscious realms within ourselves. The mastery of these realms led to self and God awareness.

MITHRA AND THE CHRIST

Some have argued that the similarities between Mithraism and Christianity derive from the fact that Constantine was head of the Mithraic Order when Rome sanctioned Christianity as the official religion of the Roman Empire (312 C.E.).[29]

The site of the Vatican itself sits on top of a destroyed Mithraic temple.[30] And, since Emperor Constantine did once hold the rank of Sol Invictus, he probably did seek to graft some of the ancient Mithraic rites onto the newly formed Catholic Church. We can see this influence most clearly in the designation of December 25 as Jesus' birthday. But the similarities between the lives and beliefs of Mithra and Jesus go deeper than that.

As we have seen, Jesus and Mithra both chose twelve disciples and were themselves portrayed as the central Sun. Jesus used the rite of baptism by water, a custom practiced by the Essenes, the Therapeutae, the Egyptians, and the Mithrans. The sacrament of bread and wine as archtypes of the body and blood of the sacrificial savior was also practiced by the Mithrans. In fact, hermetic scholar Joscelyn Godwin quotes from an ancient Persian text that sounds astoundingly like the words of Jesus: "He who will not eat of my body and drink of my blood, so that he will be made one with me and I with him, the same shall not know salvation."[31] Jesus is known by the initiatic symbols of the dove, the fish, the serpent, and the lion, all symbols used in the Mysteries of Persia and Egypt. And he sacrificed himself on a cross, a spiritual emblem well known only to initiates of the ancient paths and linked to Krishna, Mithra, Osiris, Adonis, and Quetzalcoatl—all incarnations of earlier savior gods.

As if enacting a great cosmic play, these transcendental beings incarnate again and again as the archetypal Aion, a divinity known to the Greeks as the Lord of Eternity. In Persia, this god was known as Zervan, or Boundless Time, from which the negative and positive forces of life are born.[32] His head is that of a lion and he holds the torch of enlightenment in his hand. Around his body coils a serpent, telling us that he has awakened all seven chakras. Zervan wears four wings, designating him as a celestial being and, like Moses, Jesus, and Apollo, he carries the staff of wisdom in his hands. Zervan stands upon a sphere that represents the world; and the sphere bears a large X that represents the *chi rho*, or the turning of the world ages. Thus, writes Professor David Ulanskey, "The lion-headed god is clearly a being who embodies the cosmos: he stands upon the cosmic sphere, and the signs of the zodiac are seen between the coils of the snake that wrap around him."[33]

While many scholars have puzzled over the meanings of Aion/Zervan's hermetic symbology, it is clear that he is the same eternal "lion of God," or divine Purusha, who returns from the celestial realms to uplift mankind in each successive age. Like Jesus, Apollo, Mithra, and Osiris, all of whom used the same icons, Aion inserts himself in space and time to inspire, inform, and enlighten us with the nobility of his example. Like Jesus, he is beyond the reach of the ages and yet stands at the center of them all.[34] Like the divine Purusha, both Mithra and Aion/Zervan exist eternally in all ages. As Lords of the Cycles of Time, they transcend the mortal wheel. These are the four great Kumaras.

Mithraic Mysteries centered on the effect that the great world ages have upon human consciousness. These hermetic symbols were part of a greater stellar calendar that accurately predicts the beginning and end of each world age, as well as the return of the great solar lord. Victoria LaPage tells us that "[t] he tauroctony . . . turns out to be more than a mythological record of the trails and blessings of a Mithraic initiate. It is a map of certain constellations in the zodiac that act as timekeepers of the cosmos."[35] Certainly, at the time of Jesus, exciting predictions swept the Middle East, causing astronomers, rabbis, priests, and initiates to expect the birth of such a person. Professor Ulansey writes:

> Mithraic iconography was a cosmological code created by a circle of
> religious-minded philosophers and scientists to symbolize their possession
> of a secret knowledge: namely, the knowledge of a newly-discovered god
> so powerful that the entire cosmos was completely under his control. . . .
> For the possession of such a carefully guarded secret knowledge concern-
> ing such a mighty divinity would naturally have been experienced as
> assuring privileged access to the favors which this god could grant, such
> as deliverance from the forces of fate residing in the stars and protection
> for the soul after death during its journey through the planetary spheres.
> If we understand salvation to be a divinely bestowed promise of safety in
> the deepest sense, both during life and after death, then the god whose
> presence we have discerned beneath the veils of Mithraic iconography
> was well suited to perform the role of savior.[36]

In fact, during the first four centuries of our common era, early church fa-thers considered Mithraism to be the major rival to Catholic Christianity. And since followers of Mithra believed that he, too, was a son of God who had come to bring enlightenment, the church ensured that the symbols of Mithra were either incorporated into Christianity or forced underground.

Mithra played out his role in the great cosmic dramas of his age, just as Jesus acted out this same drama in ours. Mithraism and Christianity thus share similarities precisely because both of these great solar lords tried to express certain fundamental principles. Jesus can, in fact, be seen as the fulfillment of the Mithraic promise, incarnated in human form.

CHAPTER 23

Zoroaster and the Mysterious Magi

Myth is a whole; it transcribes a fundamental knowledge of the laws
of genesis, which applies to everything. Myth is a deliberately chosen
means of communicating knowledge. While it is possible, even probable,
that the ancients could not have expressed that knowledge in modern
philosophical language, this is no shortcoming. It is we who are at the
disadvantage. To make sense of the myth, we must first convert it to a
form the intellect will accept; thereafter, it may or may not work upon
our emotional center and allow us to arrive at understanding.[1]

—John Anthony West, *The Serpent in the Sky: the High
Wisdom of Ancient Egypt*

Philo Judaeus, the Jewish historian of Alexandria, tells us that the famous Magi
of the Bible were the Magicians or "wise men" of his day: "By their careful scru-
tiny of nature's works for purpose of the gnosis of truth, in quiet silence, and
by means of [mystic] images of piercing clarity [i.e., hermetics], are made initiates into the mysteries of godlike virtue, and in their turn initiate [those who
come after them]."[2] Certainly, the mysterious Magi, who entered Jesus' life at
birth and then simply vanished from it, have long been the subject of myths
and legends.

The synoptic gospels of Mark, Luke, and John do not even mention the
Magi, but in Matthew 2:1 we read: "Now when Jesus was born in Bethlehem of
Judea . . . there came Wise Men from the east to Jerusalem saying, 'Where is He
who has been born King of the Jews, for we have seen His star in the East and

have come to worship Him.'" We know from Herod's report that at least one of the three came from Egypt, but we can only guess the origins of the other two. Christian literature tells us only that their names were Balthazar, Melchior, and Gasper.[3]

While some speculate that these three men were really incarnations of three Great White Brotherhood masters named El Morya, Kuthumi, and DK, who reportedly taught theosophist Madame Blavatsky in the 1800s, there is little proof to substantiate this theory.[4] In *The Acts of Pilate*, we find a letter from Pontius Pilate that tells of a "dreadful earthquake in lower Egypt" that occurred on the day of the Crucifixion, in which "Balthazar, the aged and learned Jew of Antioch" apparently died.[5, 6] This is the first contemporary historical document that may validate the existence of one of the three Wise Men who attended Jesus' birth.

For centuries, many have believed that one of the three Magi came from Persia, or Mesopotamia, a region long respected for its sages and astronomical acumen. We know from the reports of the Essenes recorded by Wilson and Prentis that there was a chapter of the Great White Brotherhood in Damascus.[7] Persia, Syria, and Ur also had strong communities of astrologer-mages who had

FIGURE 82. The three Magi Balthazar, Melchior, and Gaspar arrived from three of the four directions of the compass, countries that are believed to be Persia, Egypt, and possibly India.

inherited Sumeria's wide-ranging and sophisticated astronomical and astrological science—a tradition that has resurfaced through archaeological excavations over the past 150 years. Others speculate that the third Wise Man came
from Nubia, yet it is equally possible that he traveled from India, China, or even
the Celtic Isles.

THE SARMOUNG SOCIETY

In his research into Persia's links to the mysterious Magi, author Adrian Gilbert
uncovered a clandestine, mystical society called the Sarmoung Society (also
known as the Sarmang Brotherhood), that had long awaited the birth of Jesus. His research led him to investigate the turbulent regions of Commagene,
Armenia, Osrhoene, and Pontus, a territory long contested by the Greeks, Romans, and Parthians, and finally brought him back to the cities of Bokhara and
Samarkand.[8]

Bokhara had reached the glittering, but brief, zenith of its civilization, art,
and learning by the tenth century C.E. under the Samanid dynasty. These noble
achievements were demolished, however, when Genghis Khan's Golden Horde
made its way across these lands in 1219, burning, pillaging, and destroying both
the people and the written records of the ancient mystic societies that had long
nurtured the Mystery traditions. Thus the Sarmoung Society, a branch of the
Great White Brotherhood that had extensive knowledge of the ancient traditions of Egypt, Chaldea, and Sumeria, as well as the Persian Mysteries of Mithra
and Zoroaster, was driven underground.

The word Sarmoung means "those who have become enlightened." In Persian, *sar* means "the head" or "chief," and refers to a quality transmitted from
a distinguished race or family through heredity, as well as the repository of an
heirloom or tradition. Thus, the word *sarman* can be translated as "the chief
repository of a tradition."[9] Like the pharaohs of ancient Egypt, members of
this society took the bee as their symbol.[10] Armenian and Syrian legends also
confirm that the bee was associated with a mysterious power transmitted from
the time of Zoroaster and finally made manifest at the time of Jesus.[11] Ancient
Armenian texts refer to the "Sarmang Society" as a famous esoteric school that,
according to tradition, was founded in Babylon as far back as 2500 B.C.E. and
that was known to have existed in Mesopotamia up to the sixth or seventh
century of the Christian era. The school was said to possess great knowledge
and hold the keys to many secret mysteries. In later times, the philosopher and
mystic George Gurdjieff (1877–1949) claimed to have had direct contact with

the Sarmoung Society, relating his cosmological and theological theory of the Enneagram, a diagram of "perpetual motion," to their tradition of Chaldean, Zoroastrian, and Atlantean wisdom.[12]

Certainly, this society would have known of Zoroaster's prophecies of the three incarnations of the Saoshyant, or the Christ, to come. Jesus was recognized as one of these three incarnations. Presumably, the last two incarnations have not occurred. The Sarmoung Society would also have understood the astrology of the changing cycles of time and known that Jesus arrived between the fading glory (and oppression) of the Age of Aries (2260 B.C.E. to 100 B.C.E.) and the spiritual promise of the Age of Pisces (100 B.C.E. to 2060 C.E.). Researcher Jonnie Hill acknowledges the existence of this secret society and comments on the similarities between it and other orders of the Great White Brotherhood:

> There is solid evidence that . . . there were secret organizations, and religions known as the Ancient Mysteries . . . The most important of these Mysteries were the Osiric in Egypt, the Mithraic in Persia, the Cabiric in Thrace, the Andonisian in Syria, the Dionysiac and Eleusinian in Greece, the Scandinavian among the Gothic, and the Druids among the Celts. Others were the Sarmoung Society, Manicheism, Zarathustra, Crata Repoa, Magism, Brahman, and many others. In all the Mysteries, we find certain basic similarities: qualifications for admission; ceremonies of initiation that celebrated the death of an admired figure and their resurrection; doctrines of a system of secret knowledge; and an oath of secrecy, which, if violated, was considered a sacrilegious crime, and carried a serious penalty.[13]

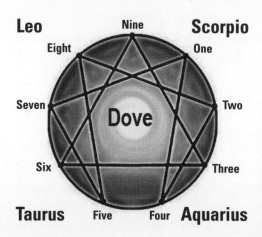

FIGURE 83. The Enneagram and the Four Fixed Ages reflects the mystical number nine, the number of Perfected Man, representing the nine stages that the soul passes on its way to enlightenment. This glyph shows the hermetic symbols of the lion, the bull, the man, and the scorpion, and the dove which sits at its center.

The Sarmoung Society was also known as the "Keepers of the Flame of Knowledge" and had strong links with both Mithra and Zoroaster. Some believe its members may have joined with the elusive Sufi mystics, a sect known for their deep devotions to both the Divine Mother and Father. The hermetic symbol of the Sufi order, the winged heart, is linked to the worship of the Divine Feminine, as well as to the path of Jesus. This honoring of the Divine Feminine may, in fact, account for the merciless persecution the Sufi have suffered at the hands of their less enlightened, patriarchal Islamic brothers.

If one of the three Magi that attended Jesus at his birth was indeed a Persian sage, he was most likely a member of the Sarmoung Society, who would have understood the intricate astrological alignments in the heavens and known the hermetic signs that predicted Jesus' birth. He would also have had the purity of heart and dedication of purpose to trust these signs enough to make the long and arduous journey to Bethlehem. Only members of the Great White Brotherhood would have known the vast cycles of time that pass between the return of each solar lord and gone to such great lengths to welcome him into the world and honor him on behalf of those who knew the greater Mysteries.

The three gifts brought by the Wise Men also hold clues to the Magis' purpose. The New Testament tells us that they brought gold, frankincense, and myrrh—all objects of hermetic significance. Gold is a sign of kingship, long associated with the gods. Frankincense represents wisdom. Myrrh represents both longevity and healing. Frankincense was a very expensive oil used only in spiritual and religious rituals; myrrh was a healing herb used in Egypt in the embalming of pharaohs. Joseph of Arimathea and Nicodemus brought myrrh and aloe with them to Jesus' tomb after the Crucifixion (John 19:38–40). Diodorus Siculus reports that both frankincense and myrrh originated in the Arabian Peninsula, while the Old Testament's Song of Solomon refers to both herbs, linking these special plants to Jewish, Egyptian, and Arabian royalty and associating the Sarmoung Society of Persia with the three Magi of the New Testament.[14]

ZOROASTER AND THE STAR MYSTERIES

Zoroaster was a great leader and a prophet of wisdom. Yet, although he carried the implements of the solar lords, he did not claim to be "a son of God." Like the Biblical Jeremiah, Zoroaster considered himself a forerunner of the "Christ to come," whom he called the Saoshyant.[15] His teachings were studied by the Essenes and had doubtless exerted great influence on the Jews during their years of captivity in Babylon. Despite the morality inherent in Zoroaster's teachings, however, his conception of the universe was basically dualistic. He taught the ultimate confrontation between the forces of good and evil, similar to our modern-day conception of Armageddon.

Many scholars think that Zoroaster was born around 640 B.C.E., although there is still much debate over this. Some have placed his birth as late as 300 B.C.E. and others as far back as 1800 B.C.E. It may be that there was an original prophet called Zoroaster (Zarathustra) as far back as 4000 B.C.E., and that the lineage of eponymous priests that sprang from this line each took the name Zoroaster. Zoroaster is mentioned in the Rig Vedas, which are believed to date back to 5000 B.C.E. In the Rig Veda, Zoroaster is described as a renegade teacher (like Jesus) who broke with the Hindu caste system and sought to transcend the rigidity of that regime with a more egalitarian way. Aristotle tells us that the Persians of his time dated Zoroaster's birth as far back as 6000 B.C.E., suggesting that this tradition is even more ancient than we know.[16] In fact, Zoroastrianism may represent a very ancient chapter of the Great White Brotherhood.

According to legend, Zoroaster was born in either eastern Iran or Central Asia, although the exact location is still under debate. Unfortunately, many of the original writings of this mystical sect were destroyed at the time of Alexander the Great, and even more of their oral traditions were lost when the Macedonians plundered Mithran temples and shrines and murdered their priests. The sect did eventually recover, however, and became the state religion of the Sassanian Empire, which ruled from the third to the seventh centuries C.E. This Empire was the last major pre-Islamic power in the areas we now know as Iraq, Iran, Armenia, western Afghanistan, the southern Caucasus, parts of Turkey, Syria, Pakistan, the Persian Gulf, and some coastal parts of the Arabian Peninsula.[17]

The name Zarathustra, or Zoroaster, may have come from the Greek words *astra*, meaning "star," and *zorós*, meaning "undiluted."[18] What we know today about Zoroaster's life derives from two main sources—the Avesta and the Gathas—both scriptures attributed to Zoroaster himself. The Gathas contain allusions to personal events like his vision at the age of thirty, in which he first meets Ahura Mazda, the higher god of the Iranian pantheon. The Gathas also relate the difficulty the master experienced spreading his teachings, and how he was treated badly in his mother's hometown—a negative reception strangely reminiscent of Jesus' reception in Nazareth. They also describe specific family events like the marriage of his daughter, at which he presided.

Eventually, Zoroaster triumphed over the competing priests of his day by converting a neighboring king to his teachings. The Magi at the court of

FIGURE 84. Zoroaster, as the forerunner to the next solar lord, holds the staff of wisdom, the torch of enlightenment, and wears the solar crown radiating from his head. Illustrated by Sylvia Laurens

King Vishtaspa, the Bactrian king of Khorasmia, accepted Zoroaster's teachings when the king's priests tested his spiritual credentials and found that his initiations went beyond what they knew. The king was converted on their advice.[19] Although Zoroaster's death is not told in either the Avesta or the Gathas, it was written about in an epic poem called the The Epic of Kings, in which he is said to have been murdered at the altar of fire by the Turanians in the storming of the Persian city of Balkh.[20]

In his teachings, Zoroaster encouraged others to align with the god of light and be judged according to their deeds. He believed in right action, something he called *Asha*—a concept similar to the Law of Dhamma taught by the Buddha, the Law of Ma'at taught in Egypt, and the Ten Commandments taught by Moses. *Asha* was based on the principle that right thoughts and right intentions produce a responsible, happy life. Like our Christian saints, Zoroaster is often shown with a radiant light around his head and is sometimes shown standing between two pillars of knowledge, reminding us of the columns of King Solomon's temple and the two obelisks of Luxor and Heliopolis. Zoroaster's turban looks strangely like a beehive, linking him to the earlier Sarmoung Society and ultimately to modern Catholicism. At the center of his hat is a cross, confirming that this symbol had been used for at least five or six centuries before Jesus was born. Sometimes Zoraster is seen carrying a torch of knowledge or a staff from which flames emerge, recalling that, in Mithraic teachings, fire was considered the closest element to God. Zoroaster often holds a trinity of sunflowers, revealing the three-fold stages of initiation connected to the Sun, and the three-fold mastery of man's physical, emotional, and mental natures. And like the Essenes, the Druids, and the Egyptian Therapeutae, the Zoroastrian priests always wore white.

Zoroaster is also linked with the shamanic symbols of the winged lion, the noble eagle, and the serpent of wisdom—like Moses, King David, Zeus, Mithra, and Jesus. He sometimes appears with a bear at his side, a reference to the constellation of Ursa Major, the Great Bear, long associated with hero myths—including legends of King Arthur, whose name, Arturo, was identified with that constellation. These hermetic animal symbols represent the mastery of fire, air, and earth (lion, eagle, and snake), symbols that were associated with the various stages of Zoroastrian initiation. Other images show the sacred bull atop Zoroaster's pillars, linking him to both Mithra and Osiris. And, like the statues of Serapis in Egypt, Archangel Michael in England and France, and the Virgin Mary around the world, Zoroaster is often depicted standing on a dragon, revealing that he has conquered his ego and perhaps even that he knows how to use and master the magnetic gridlines (ley lines) of the Earth.

Zoroaster taught the importance of accountability established in the Great Avesta, a moral code of precepts to help people distinguish right from wrong—like the Hebrew Ten Commandments, Mesopotamia's Code of Hammurabi, and Egypt's Law of Ma'at. These books clearly spelled out rules against lying, cheating, murdering, and stealing, and provided guidelines that the masses could understand and use in their everyday lives.

Zoroaster also taught philosophy, reincarnation, the immortality of the soul, and the law of karma. Like the Essenes, he honored cleanliness, fidelity, truth, and responsibility, and believed in no killing. As in the Egyptian and Sumerian cultures, Zoroastrians used the sign of the cross and the dove as occult initiatic symbols.[21] They also honored Mithra as the "Son of God," whom they associated not only with the victorious Sun, but with fertility, just as Osiris was called "the god of the grains." Unlike the Jews, they did not practice animal sacrifice.[22] In this, they were far closer to the Egyptian priests of Osiris who, like their Essene brothers and sisters, were strict vegetarians.[23] In fact, in Egypt, as in the Hindu culture of India, there were many animals that the people were

Figure 85. Zoroaster stands triumphant on a crocodile, revealing that he has conquered his own reptilian nature. In his hand, he holds the hermetic images of the sunflowers in a trinity, and he wears the beehive hat with the ancient symbol of the cross emblazoned on it.

forbidden to kill or to eat, including cats and dogs, hawks and ibises, and even cows and pigs.[24]

Zoroastrians believed in a great Queen of Heaven, whose "crown sparkles in supra-earthly radiance." Like Isis and the Mother Mary, "her countenance is the most sublime that one can behold." They called her the Queen of Purity and Love, and her flower was the red rose. This is the same great Goddess of Heaven that is still honored throughout the world, and whose appearances as the Lady of Guadeloupe, the Lady of Lourdes, and the Immaculate Mother have created miracles of healing for millions.

Dualism: Gods of Light and Darkness

Zoroastrianism was deeply dualistic, teaching that there is a supreme god, Ahura Mazda, who fights against a negative force called Ahriman.[25] Ahriman is the prototype of the materialistic Lucifer, the spiritual tempter of mankind. Zoroaster's central theme was that the entire cosmos is locked in a constant struggle between these two forces: the god of light and the god of darkness. Unlike the Christian version of this battle, however, in which the outcome is already decided, in Zoroastrianism, the two players are more or less evenly matched and their conflict will eventually lead to Armageddon—the ultimate confrontation of good and evil.[26]

This dualistic worldview had a major influence on biblical Judaism that was carried over into Christianity by Saint Paul, the most zealous of the early apostles. Paul was trained as a Pharisee and had some genuine experience in the Mysteries, but he did not actually study with Jesus while he was alive. Like Zoroaster, Paul and many traditional Jews of Jesus' time believed in a cataclysmic confrontation between the forces of good and evil, perhaps as an archetype of the brutal Roman and Jewish conflicts of their day. In this dualistic battle, the evil forces would finally be defeated, the Earth renewed, and the righteous resurrected. This belief later influenced fanatical Christians at the time of the Inquisition, and eventually made its way into the Muslim world as the holy *jihad*, the call to eradicate the unfaithful, or "infidels."

Yet Jesus never spoke about an Armageddon.[27] Our Christian concept of it today derives entirely from the writings of Paul, further reinforced by the aprocryphal visions of the apostle John, who, in his later years, gave us the confusing New Testament Book of Revelation. This clash of opposites was also mirrored in the Jewish teachings of Jesus' times, as evidenced by the War Scroll of the Essene Zealots discovered among the Dead Sea Scrolls. This military strategy manual contained an apocalyptic prophecy of a war between the sons of light and the sons of darkness—a way that some believe had already taken place in mankind's distant past.[28] The Jews of Israel, suffering as they were under the oppression of both Rome and the Sanhedrin, found it easy to believe in a life-or-death struggle against a mighty empire. The same was true of the early Christians. In eras of frustration and persecution like these, the idea of an Armageddon makes sense. This may be why the apocalyptic belief in a war between God and Satan has remained embedded in our theology even today, underwriting a persistent conflict and polarity that is externalized as endless strife among nations.

In Zoroastrianism, however, Ahriman and Ahura Mazda were not really enemies. They were twin brothers who had created the world together, fathered by an even greater power—Zervan, represented by Mithra, the god who stood outside the ages, the god of boundless time. When Ahura Mazda created life,

Ahriman created death. When Ahura Mazda created a celestial host, Ahriman created an infernal host (the fallen angels and the devils). For every act of truth and beauty, Ahriman created its opposite. So, just as Christians believe that the Archangel Michael is locked in eternal warfare with Lucifer, Zoroastrians believe that Ahura Mazda and Ahriman are trapped in endless battle. Yet beyond this conflict, all is reconciled in Zervan, the all-pervasive, sustaining principle that transcends polarity.

Jesus speaks to exactly this condition in the Gospel of Philip:

> Light and darkness, life and death, right and left, are inseparable twins.
> For the good are not wholly good, nor the wicked wholly wicked, nor
> is life merely life, nor death merely death; each will return to its primal
> source. But those who transcend these apparent opposites are eternal;
> worldly names are full of deceit and delude our minds. They muddy the
> distinction between right and wrong with words like father, spirit, son,
> life, light, resurrection and church. In the eternal world there are no such
> deceptions.[29]

In the Himis manuscripts, Jesus seems to reconcile the two in the power of "the Eternal Spirit . . . the soul of all that is animated":

> You commit a grievous sin in dividing it into the spirit of Evil and the
> spirit of Good, for there is no God save that of good, who, like the father
> of a family, does only good to his children, forgiving all their faults if they
> repent of them. The spirit of Evil dwells on this earth, in the hearts of
> men who turn the children of God from the right path. . . . Your doctrine
> is therefore the fruit of your errors, for in desiring to approach the God of
> Truth, you have created false gods.[30]

Salvation thus lay at the end of another path—the "middle way" taught by Jesus, Buddha, Lao Tzu, and other solar lords. This is the path of balance fundamental to the ancient Mysteries.

PART VI

Jesus in Egypt

CHAPTER 24

The Motherland of Mysteries

> Moreover, every aspect of Egyptian knowledge seems to have been complete at the very beginning. The sciences, artistic and architectural techniques and the hieroglyphic system show virtually no signs of development; indeed many of the achievements of the earliest dynasties were never surpassed or even equaled later on.[1]
>
> —John Anthony West, *The Serpent in the Sky: the High Wisdom of Ancient Egypt*

The Gospel of Matthew tells us that Jesus spent his early years in Egypt (Matthew 2:13–15). For centuries, legends have persisted that he also studied there as an adult and took his final initiations in the Mysteries inside the Great Pyramid. Given Egypt's proximity to Jerusalem and its legacy as the motherland of Mysteries, this is easy to believe.

Hebrew history had long been tied to that of Egypt. Abraham, the acclaimed Jewish patriarch, had traveled from his home city of Ur to Egypt with his wife, Sarah, and been treated as a visiting noble in the courts of the pharaoh. Sarah was wooed by the Egyptian king after Abraham told the pharaoh that Sarah was just his sister instead of his wife and, by lying to the pharaoh, Abraham broke eithical laws that nearly brought the wrath of "the Lord" down upon everyone. Joseph, Abraham's great-grandson—the Joseph of the coat of many colors— was sold by his brothers to a traveling caravan and taken to Egypt as a slave. His great ability to interpret the dreams of the pharaoh helped him rise to a position of great power. He became the wise "shepherd," not only controlling the granaries and well-being of Egypt itself, but influencing many other countries throughout the Mediterranean that depended on Egypt for food. And Moses, a true prince of Egypt, was trained in the highest Egyptian Schools and imparted many of Egypt's greatest Mysteries to the people of the Exodus, thus bringing ancient wisdom into Hebrew philosophy.

In truth, Egypt was the source of huge chunks of Jewish and Christian theology. The Ten Commandments, for example, are derived from the Egyptian Law of Ma'at and are actually a shortened version of the forty-two statements recited by souls as they stood before the throne of Osiris in the Halls of Amente, the Egyptian name for heaven. During this recitation, supplicants declared before God that they had not lied, cheated, stolen, killed, or dishonored their parents—the very same precepts given in the Ten Commandments. Yet the Law of Ma'at predates the Ten Commandments by several thousand years.

Timothy Wallace-Murphy and Marilyn Hopkins, authors of *Custodians of Truth*, describe the deep Egyptian roots of both Christianity and Judaism, citing countless parallels between Judaeo-Christian mysticism and the teachings of ancient Egypt. These similarities range from the rites of circumcision to the great Kabbala and the mystical Tree of Life. In fact, the ten archetypal qualities attributed to God in the Kabbala's sephiroth were once listed as the very attributes of the pharaoh himself.[2] And the Hebrew nation's Ark of the Covenant ("ark" is a word borrowed from the Egyptian language) was originally located in Egypt, where it was a means to communicate with the Egyptian Sun god. The custom of placing sacred texts above the doorways of Jewish temples also came from Egypt, and Antoine Fabreeven claims that "the idiom of Hebrew sensed in the Sepher [the scriptural scrolls of the Torah] is a transplanted branch of the Egyptian language."[3]

All this indicates that there was a transfer of ancient theological knowledge that went back much farther than that which took place between the Egyptians and the loosely organized group of slaves and refugees that became known as the Hebrew people. In fact, even the Levitical priesthood appears to have been derived from the Egyptian tradition of heretical descent among its sages. The Egyptian priests who oversaw the Mysteries of the Heliopolan temple complex originally descended from an ancient line of mystics known as the Shemsu-Hor, which means "those who follow the path of Horus."[4] The history of these mysterious, illuminated sages goes back to a time that, in Egypt, is called the *Zep Tepi*, or the "First Time."[5]

The history of the Exodus and the Diaspora was not recorded until at least 700 years after the event, making it highly probable that the true story of Moses leaving Egypt was subject to a great deal of literary license, not unlike the story of Jesus' life.[6] Certainly at the time of Jesus' birth, some 1400 years after Moses had trained as a high priest in Heliopolis and long after the destruction of King Solomon's temple and the beginning of the Babylonian captivity, much of this history had been lost, altered, or entirely suppressed.

For years, Egyptian scholars have recognized that early Judaism owed its ethnic and spiritual origins to Egypt, but this has had little impact on historians of the Jewish, Christian, or Islamic faiths. Furthermore, the history of the Jews from the time of Moses until Jesus' era reveals that the beliefs of the "chosen people" were constantly evolving, influenced on one hand by Persian and Babylonian dualism, and on the other by Hellenistic and Roman customs. In truth, the Judaeo-Christian and Muslim traditions owe many more of their beliefs to polytheism, paganism, and the transmission of sacred wisdom than most modern theologians care to admit.[7]

The Road to Egypt

We know that Jesus traveled to Alexandria with his family and spent time among the Zadokite and Therapeutae brotherhoods. We also know that the temple at Bubastis, established in 170 B.C.E. by the Zadokite priesthood, awaited the birth of an "anointed one"—a Messiah that devout Hebrews hoped would deliver them from the Sanhedrin and the military might of Rome. And we know that Jesus was later to study at Heliopolis, one of the two major settlements of the Great White Brotherhood, where the apostle Mark also spent years training as a scribe.[8]

The writers of the Gospel of Matthew claimed that the prophecy of the Old Testament prophet Hosea, who claimed that the "chosen one" would come out of Egypt, was fulfilled by Jesus' sojourn in Egypt as an infant (Hosea 11:1). But this claim obscures a deeper truth. Jesus was a full-blown adept of the Egyptian Mystery Schools and a fully initiated yogi who had doubtless attained profound levels of consciousness. He was accepted as the second Buddha and hailed as an avatar throughout Persia for his healing skills. And, while it is clear that Jesus was deeply committed to freeing his own people from the social and religious tyranny of the Sanhedrin, he was hardly a traditional Jewish teacher. If he had been, he would never have been crucified.

As we have seen, Jesus did not bow to the religious politics of his day, nor was he aligned with any single race, creed, culture, or dogma. His teachings transcended all national and racial boundaries, for he was aligned with the masters of perennial light whose chapters were scattered around the globe, but centered in Egypt.[9] And it was to Egypt that the Magi returned after Jesus' birth, after leaving instructions for his education with their Essene brothers at Mount Carmel.[10]

"The presence of this secret centre belonging to the White Brotherhood had much to do with Egypt's greatness throughout the ages," writes C. W. Leadbeater, claiming that Egypt was, in fact, "the prototype of the Mysteries of all the nations around. Egypt was thus the centre of spiritual illumination for the entire western world, and all those who sought the Great Initiations were attracted to it."[11] This explains the reverence paid to the Egyptian Mysteries by learned Greeks in later times, and the fact that Jesus was sent there by the Essene masters to perfect his wisdom.

Several documented accounts show that Jesus was trained by the Great Mystic Lodge in Egypt, but let us first consider a more accurate timeline of Jesus' life before we examine those historical sources. Traditional church teachings tell us that Jesus began his ministry around the age of thirty and died at age thirty-three. Even Jesus' return to Galilee around the ages of twenty-eight or twenty-nine, and his visit to Britain at age thirty in 23 or 24 C.E. still place him within the acceptable time frames taught to us by the church. But now we must consider the evidence for the seven years that Jesus studied in Egypt. Let us start with an excerpt from the Gospel of Luke (3:1–4):

> Now in the fifteenth year of the reign of Tiberius Caesar, Pontius Pilate being governor of Judea, Herod being tetrarch of Galilee . . . Anna and Caiaphas being high priests [of the Sanhedrin High Council in Judea], the word of God came to John the son of Zacharias in the wilderness [John the Baptist]. And he went into all the region around the Jordan, preaching a baptism of repentance for the remission of sins . . . saying, "The voice of one crying the wilderness prepares the way of the Lord. . . ."

This account says that John the Baptist began preaching fifteen years after Tiberius Caesar took the throne or in 29 C.E. Sometime afterwards, perhaps a year or two, we know that Jesus came to John for baptism. Jesus had to have been at least thirty years old at this time. We arrive at this figure merely by adding fifteen years to 14 C.E. (the starting date of Tiberius Caesar's reign), which brings us to 29 C.E. Then, when we add the year of Jesus' birth, which we are conservatively calculating at 6, 7, or 8 B.C.E., we realize that Jesus had to have been at least thirty-seven or thirty-eight years old when he came to John for baptism. And if Jesus was born as far back as 10 B.C.E., he would have been at least forty when John began preaching.

Jesus' Age at His Crucifixion

However, the Gospel of Luke tells us that Jesus seemed to be a man around thirty (Luke 23), but in order for this to be true, Jesus would have had to have been born four years after Herod the Great died or in 0 B.C.E. This was the original supposition by the Scythian monk, Dionysius Egnacius, who pieced together our Christian calendar backward from the year 533 C.E.[12] But this calendar is clearly off by at least some seven or eight years since we know that Herod the Great's death took place in April of 4 B.C.E.—a fact now acknowledged by secular and religious authorities. If Jesus was born in 6, 7, or 8 B.C.E., and if his ministry in Palestine lasted three years, then he would have been somewhere between forty and forty-three at the time of the Crucifixion.

Even Irenaeus, the early church father, who was highly critical of the early Gnostics, upbraids the misperception of Jesus' age in his book *Against Heresies*. He says that in making the legends of Jesus conform to the archetypal myths of the young hero savior gods, those who wrote the Gospels are "robbing Him of that age which is both more necessary and more honorable than any other, that more advanced age, I mean, during which also as a teacher He excelled all others."

> For how could He have had His disciples, if He did not teach? And how could He have taught, unless He had reached the age of a Master? Now, that the first stage of early life embraces thirty years, and that this extends onward to the fortieth year, everyone will admit; but from the fortieth and fiftieth year a man begins to decline towards old age, which Our Lord possessed while He still fulfilled the office of a Teacher, even as the Gospel and all the elders testify; those who were conversant in Asia with John, the disciple of the Lord [affirm] that John conveyed to them that information.[13]

Irenaeus goes on to imply that whoever changed Jesus' age within the scriptures did so to conform to the archetypal myths already current in that age; i.e., the young virile prince or Shepherd-King who is cut down in his prime. Yet in the traditional cycles of life, a man became a husband, a householder, and then, finally, a rabbi or a holy man in the wise later years of his life.

We must also remember that Luke did not actually know Jesus. Like Paul, Luke only became an apostle after Jesus died, thus his information was, at best, second hand. Establishing reliable dates for both Jesus' birth, ministry, and even Crucifixion, has long been a problem for even the most arduous biblical scholars, and as Irenaeus seems to imply, those who compiled and translated the New Testament gospels may have chosen to alter small, but important details for a multitude of reasons.

We know from Roman records that Pontius Pilate ruled Judea as governor from 26 to 36 C.E., establishing a ten-year period in which Jesus' public ministry, death, and resurrection took place. Moreover, we know that John the Baptist was executed a year before Jesus was crucified. Ananias, an officer in the Roman guard during the reign of Emperor Theodosius (379 to 395 C.E.), claims to have found references to the Crucifixion among the Roman and Jewish records of Pontius Pilate's time that establish that the event took place in "the nineteenth year of the reign of the Roman Emperor Tiberius," or 33 C.E.[14] If 33 C.E. was the year of the Crucifixion, Jesus would have been thirty-nine or forty years old at the time of his death. Yet researchers like Michael Baigent have put forth the argument that Jesus may have died as late as 36 C.E., since "[s]o far as can be ascertained, the marriage of Herod Antipas and Herodias took place in 35 C.E."[15] If this is correct, then the Crucifixion took place in 36 C.E., the year following John the Baptist's death—a beheading instigated by Herodias and

FIGURE 86. Jesus with a crown of thorns.

her daughter Salome. All these dates dovetail with the arrival of Joseph of Arimathea in Britain in 37 C.E. Thus Jesus may have been as old as forty-three or even forty-five at the time of the Crucifixion. And, in fact, the Gospel of John seems to indicate that Jesus was older than allowed by conventional accounts (John 8:56–59).

Interestingly enough, the Gospel of John seems to indicate that Jesus was, in fact, quite a bit older. In John 8:56–59, Jesus speaks about having existed before Abraham, and the Jews who are listening think that he is crazy. They respond by saying to Jesus that he is not yet fifty—not the kind of comment you would make to a thirty year old: "'Your father Abraham rejoiced to see my day, and he saw it and was glad.' Then the Jews said to Him [Jesus], 'You are not yet fifty years old, and you have seen Abraham?' Jesus said to them, 'Most assuredly I say to you, before Abraham was, I am.' Then they took stones to throw at Him; but Jesus hid Himself and went out of the temple, going through the midst of them, and so passed by."[16]

By fostering the myth that Jesus died at the age of thirty-three, the church has unfortunately dismissed, for nearly two millennia, all public speculation about Jesus' missing years. But if Jesus did not begin teaching in Judea until he was in his late thirties, it becomes far more likely that he married, had children, and spent years traveling the world. And some of this time, he spent in Egypt.

HISTORICAL RECORDS OF JESUS' EGYPTIAN STUDIES

Six separate accounts refer to Jesus' training in Egypt, including a letter from Caiaphas, high priest of the Sanhedrin Council at the time of the Crucifixion, who wrote about Jesus' years in Egypt in his official documents, and Herod Antipas, Herod the Great's son. As we shall soon see there are also other accounts of Jesus in Egypt as a man that come from *The Humane Gospel of Jesus Christ* and *The Gospel of the Holy Twelve*, plus two manuscripts from the histories of the Great White Brotherhood.[17]

In an attempt to gain the quorum he needs in the Sanhedrin to ensure Jesus' death, Caiaphas, cites the differences between Jesus' teachings and those of the powerful Levitical priests, specifically mentioning Jesus' training in Egypt. Jesus, he claimed, did not teach "as the Jews taught," but rather "resorted to the allegorical method of the Egyptian Hebrews."

> Jesus of Nazareth spent two years in Egypt under the instruction of Rabbi Joshua, and learned the art of thaumaturgy to perfection, as has never been taught in any of the schools of necromancy among the heathen.

If the healing miracles of Jesus are true, as they must be (for they are so acknowledged by his foes as well as his friends), he must have learned it from Horus and Serapis, as practiced by those heathen priests.[18]

Likewise Herod Antipas, in a letter to the Roman Senate, recounts why he chose to have Jesus put to death. Herod's comments lend weight to the thesis that Jesus studied extensively abroad. Jesus, he claims, "wandered about from place to place having no home."

He had learned soothsaying, while in Egypt, to perfection. I tried to get him to perform some miracle while in my court, but he was too sharp to be caught in a trap; like all necromancers, he was afraid to show off before the intelligent.[19]

The Talmud corroborates the accounts of both Caiaphas and Herod Antipas, saying that Jesus was killed by the Jews because he was accused of "practicing Magic in Egypt . . . and [thus] led astray and deceived Israel" (Sanh 107). Ahmed Osman, author of *Jesus in the House of the Pharaohs*, writes: "What the Bible calls signs and wonders, the rabbis of his day called Egyptian Magic, not miracles worked by the power of God."[20]

What is clear from both of these contemporary accounts is that the Pharisees and the Sadducees feared Jesus' growing power. Like the Brahmins and the military castes of India, who feared Jesus for his democratic approach to spirituality, the Jerusalem priests saw him as a threat precisely because of his popularity. They feared the power of his miracles, with which they could not compete, based as they were in a higher wisdom.[21] So they sought ways to discredit his growing influence. Whether Jesus was able to perform his miracles because of his innate divinity, or because he had spent a lifetime of study perfecting the spiritual gifts of a true master in the schools of the Great White Brotherhood does not matter. The net effect of his mastery was to bring him into direct conflict with powerful factions in Jerusalem and with the political power structure of Rome. Valleus Paterculus, a Roman historian, writes that the Jews were divided in their opinions of Jesus; the poor saw him as the deliverer from Roman authority, while the rich "called him an Egyptian necromancer," and "were as afraid of him as death."[22] A necromancer is a person who speaks with the dead.

Two "lost gospels" written around the first century c.e. corroborate accounts of Jesus' many years of study in India, Persia, and Egypt. *The Humane Gospel of the Christ*, part of a group of Gnostic and Essene writings discovered among the Nag Hammadi texts in 1945, was originally written in ancient

Aramaic and Hebrew, then translated by John Marc Allegro, prolific author and renowned biblical scholar.[23] Allegro came into contention with traditional scholars when he began to challenge orthodox views of these Gnostic texts. Fearing that the self-serving agendas of the academic and theological establishment would impune the integrity of these controversial scrolls, Allegro smuggled them out of the research library and entrusted their translation to a friend, who ultimately published a limited edition of what has become known as *The Humane Gospel of Christ*, in which we find a fascinating account of Jesus' travels and secret teachings.[24] Unfortunately, since we don't know the whereabouts of the original scrolls, the legitimacy of the account remains in doubt.

What we do know is that the story presented in *The Humane Gospel* fits well with information we have from other sources.

> And it came to pass, that Jesus went into many nations to teach the holy law of God, into Assyria and India and into Persia and into the land of the Chaldeans. And Jesus did travel into many different nations and spake unto many peoples of the holy way of life."[25]

The document also speaks about Jesus' return to Egypt as a man:

> And it came to pass that Jesus returned into Egypt to the holy brotherhood, and was further instructed in truth and wisdom, even as Moses was before him.[26] And there did Jesus meditate and fast in the desert sanctuary, praying and obtaining the miraculous power of the Holy Name, by which NAME he worked many wonders and taught much wisdom of holy things.[27]

There, the Gospel claims, he remained "for seven years," until "there remained no thing hidden unto him, whether it be times and seasons of the sun and the moon and the stars in their appointed times and places or the powers of the sacred letters and mysteries of the square and the circle and the transmutation of things, and of forms, and of numbers and of signs."[28]

Thus this manuscript confirms that Jesus was trained in astronomy, astrology, mathematics, sacred geometry, herbology, aromatherapy, crystal therapy, vibrational sound therapy, and spiritual healing, and that he knew hermetics, the symbol language of the soul—the cornerstone of the Brotherhood's Mysteries. It goes on to tell us what he learned in these Schools:

> Yea, Jesus did understand every law of nature both visible and invisible to man, even the very secrets of the Aeons [dimensional planes and ages]

did he discern and know. So it was that there remained nothing hidden to his mind, for all the natural decrees of God were manifested in him and through him, making the silence to be heard and the darkness, light.

When Jesus ended his stay "with his brothers and sisters of the holy way in Egypt," he returned to Nazareth where he was "approved as a Rabbi in Jerusalem, instructing many in the holy things of God."[29]

The Gospel of the Holy Twelve, which also dates from the first century C.E., was first discovered in 1892 in a Buddhist monastery in Tibet. The document somehow managed to escape the orgy of destruction that swept the world in the third and fourth centuries, when Roman fanatics destroyed nearly all evidence of Christianity's ancient legacies. Scholars agree that evidence strongly suggests the Gospel was indeed written in ancient times.[30]

The Gospel of the Holy Twelve corroborates the account given in *The Humane Gospel of Christ*:

And after a time [Jesus] went into Assyria and India and into Persia and into the land of the Chaldeans. And he visited their temples and conversed with their priests, and their wise men for many years, doing many wonderful works, healing the sick as he passed through their countries.[31]

Then it speaks of his time in Egypt, again claiming that he spent seven years there in study and contemplation:

And Yeshua, after that he had finished his study of the law, went down again into Egypt that he might learn of the wisdom of the Egyptians, even as Moses did. And going into the desert, he meditated and fasted and prayed, and obtained the power of the Holy Name, by which he wrought many miracles. And for seven years he conversed with God face to face . . . and he learned the motions of the Sun and the Moon and the stars, and the powers of the letters, and mysteries of the Square and the Circle and the Transmutation of things, and of forms, and of numbers, and of signs.[32]

The close congruence of these accounts, right down to the details of the course of study Jesus pursued, strongly suggests that they are authentic records of this crucial time in Jesus' life.

Two documents that come to us through the annals of the Great White Brotherhood itself also place Jesus in Egypt at this time and lend weight to the already substantial records we have from India, England, and Egypt. They are *The Aquarian Gospel of Jesus the Christ* and *The Nine Faces of Christ*. They relate that, after Jesus returned from the East, he made his way to Egypt to meet with the priests at Heliopolis.

> Jesus stayed in Zoan [a town in Egypt] many days; and then went forth unto the city of the sun that men call Heliopolis, and sought admission to the temple of the sacred brotherhood. The Council of the Brotherhood convened, and Jesus stood before the hierophant [the high initiate]; he answered all the questions that were asked with clearness and with power. The hierophant exclaimed, "Rabboni of the rabbinate, why come you here? Your wisdom is the wisdom of the gods; why seek for wisdom in the halls of men?"

Jesus answers that he seeks to sit "in every hall of learning" and to know "the heights that any man has gained." He entreats the hierophant: "Let me go into your dismal crypts; and I would pass the hardest of your tests."

> The master said, "Take then the vow of secret brotherhood." And Jesus took the vow of secret brotherhood. Again the master spoke; he said, "The greatest heights are gained by those who reach the greatest depths; and you shall reach the greatest depths."[33]

These powerful words clearly confirm Jesus' choice to embrace, move through, and master the great Mysteries of every land, and foreshadow the fact that he would reach the greatest heights and also know the greatest pain.

CHAPTER 25

Temples of the Eternal

Never have I not existed, nor you, nor these kings;
and never in the future shall we cease to exist.[1]

—Bhagavad-Gita

Aside from fulfilling the scriptural prophecies, what deeper purpose did Jesus
have in traveling to Egypt and studying there? He was, after all, already an adept
in the Essene, Druidic, Buddhist, and Mithraic teachings, and legends of his
remarkable healing abilities had already spread across Mesopotamia. To answer
this question, we must journey into the Egyptian Mysteries themselves and decipher the profound, multi-layered wisdom hidden there for over 3000 years.

As we have already seen, the Mysteries were deliberately concealed in symbols, parables, and allegories, and could only be penetrated by those who were
pure of heart, resolute in purpose, and dedicated to uplifting mankind. Egypt's
vast and complex spiritual legacy helps explain what may have led Jesus to the
same temples where Pythagoras, Socrates, and Plato studied centuries before.

Egyptian culture, like Christianity, was, at its heart, monotheistic. Egyptologist E. A. Wallis Budge writes: "It is not difficult to show that the idea of
monotheism which existed in Egypt at a very early period is [of] at least the
same character as that which grew up among both the Hebrews and Arabs
many centuries later."[2] Like the Jewish Kabbala, Egyptian lore used zoomorphic
and anthropomorphic forms to express the multi-dimensional nature of a singular God. While the historical origins of the "gods" may originally have been
based on living beings, they ultimately came to represent the cosmic principles

that penetrate the universe. Ma'at, for example, represented cosmic law. Thoth stood for wisdom and knowledge. Shu was the cosmic breath, expelled at the beginning of time. Ra was the god of the Sun.

The Egyptians believed that the entire universe was alive and that each living thing was an expression of the Divine, having the power to influence the whole. The highest vibrational principles behind the cosmos were called *neters*; the gods and goddesses were called *neteru*.[3] Egyptologist John Anthony West explains:

> The Egyptians regarded the universe as a conscious act of creation by the one great and supreme God. But that single act of creation immediately results in the fabulously complex world that we experience. This world is alive in its entirety and infused with divine spirit. The functions and principles that operate in the universe, that govern it, and that are responsible for its order and maintenance are all aspects or functions of the one supreme God. These aspects, each of which has a name, are the neteru, the "gods" of Egypt. They are the divine principles, and once this is understood, the question of polytheism versus monotheism largely disappears.[4]

Unlike the "rational" explanations we find in the Greek traditions, the Egyptians expressed their cosmology in symbolism—through carefully chosen hermetic glyphs that reveal how the one Supreme Intelligence, God, expresses itself throughout the universe. The early church father, Origen, tells us: "The Egyptian philosophers have sublime notions with regard to the Divine nature, which they keep secret, and never discover to the people but under a veil of fables and allegories. . . ." Likewise, Iamblichus describes the sacerdotal theurgy Egyptian priests used to ascend from a material state of consciousness to realization in the universal essences. Manly P. Hall writes: "To the initiated of the sanctuary, no doubt, was reserved the knowledge of the god in the abstract, the god concealed in the unfathomable depths of his own essence. But for the less refined adoration of the people were presented the endless images of deities sculptured on the walls of the temples."[5] He adds:

> It was not possible to contemplate the State Mysteries of Egypt, Greece, India and Persia and not be profoundly impressed by the nobility of their teachings, the beauty and solemnity of their rites and ceremonies, and the profound meanings of their symbols, emblems and initiatory rituals. It became evident . . . that these sacred institutions and colleges were the custodians of a universal wisdom, and conferred upon their initiates the

keys to a sublime science or art dedicated to the regeneration of man and the reformation of human society.

English historian James Bonwick summarizes the powers possessed by these adepts: "Egyptian mystics could levitate, walk on air, handle fire, live under water, sustain great pressure, harmlessly suffer mutilation, read the past, foretell the future, make themselves invisible, and cure disease."[6] Hall confirms the respect in which their knowledge and skills were held:

> It is now generally acknowledged that the Egyptians, of all the ancient peoples, were the most learned in the Occult sciences of Nature. The wisest of philosophers from other nations visited Egypt to be initiated in the sacred Mysteries by the priests of Thebes, Memphis and Hermopolis. Thales, Solon, Pythagoras and Plato journeyed from Greece to the delta of the Nile in quest of knowledge. Upon returning to their own country, these illumined men acknowedged the Egyptians to be the wisest of mortals and the Egyptian temples to be the repositories of the most sublime doctrines concerning the history of the Gods and the regeneration of men.[7]

A Template for Awakening

Egyptians believed in the immortality of the soul. And while some have interpreted this as a preoccupation with death, this is only because our own culture has lost sight of the multi-dimensional nature of the unseen realms. Egyptian culture was based on two major themes: the creation of the universe and man's role in it. Egyptian masters sought to align themselves with the highest energy of the cosmos in order to open gateways into these higher realms while still living. Thus, Egyptian spirituality had one specific purpose: the spiritual enlightenment of the human being.

Not surprisingly, these principles are reflected in Egyptian art. Egyptian sculptures, paintings, temples, and religious rites were used symbolically to invoke cosmic order here on Earth. Ceremonial jewelry, clothing, language, and customs all served this ideology. "The art and architecture of ancient Egypt was sacred art," Egyptologist John Anthony West observes. "It had a different purpose and a different motivation from virtually all art and architecture produced today. It was an art dedicated wholly to religion." Even the Egyptian language existed on three distinct levels, mirroring the trinity: the phonetic, the conceptual, and the spiritual. Their temples were also designed on hermetic principles, as if seen from the viewpoint of the *neter* (or principle) to which they were consecrated. "The temples of Egypt . . . are meant to evoke a consciousness of divinity: to illuminate."[8]

Egyptian mystics knew that the microcosm reflects the macrocosm, just as today our own scientists have come to see the blueprint of the solar system in the geometry of the atom. The Nile was a mirror of the Milky Way, and each human being carried a similar river of energy within himself—the kundalini life force that moves along the spine. This metaphysical knowledge dwelt at the heart of all Egyptian Mysteries, and the mastery of the inner Tree of Life was intrinsic to spiritual development. Like the masters of the Far East, the Egyptian sages knew that the chakras were connected to enlightenment, as West confirms: "Advances in modern neurology prove that the Egyptians understood in detail the workings of the nervous system, and the relationship between the areas of the brain and the manner in which these controlled the bodily functions."[9]

Through the principles of correspondence, the Egyptian sages sought to imprint a roadmap of the heavens onto the contours of the land with the aim of reaching the "outer limits of inner space." They knew that the key to enlightenment lay in the activation of the kundalini (the fiery life force of the human body lodged within the perineum)—that by opening these channels within ourselves, we attain the wisdom that leads us back to the sea of infinite light. Knowledge of these human spiritual centers is reflected in seven great temple centers built along the Nile: Abu Simbel, Philae, Edfu, Thebes/Luxor, Dendera, Memphis (the Great Pyramid of Giza complex), and finally Heliopolis, the famous city of the Sun. These temples symbolized the fiery energy of the life force itself and addressed the spiritual lessons associated with each chakra: awakening the life force (first chakra), incubating creativity (second chakra), overcoming fear with courage (third chakra), surrendering to service through love (fourth chakra), using the power of creative expression to heal our world (fifth chakra), awakening our inner sight (sixth chakra), and freeing ourselves from the physical world through our connection with the divine (seventh chakra).[10]

The three major teaching temples were Thebes, Memphis, and Heliopolis, each of which embodied a trinity: the divine male, the divine female, and the divine offspring. Thebes was the place of the new Horus-king's coronation ceremony (the Opet Festival); Memphis was the place of the Horus-king's renewal ceremony (the Jubilee or Sed Festival); Heliopolis was the place where Jesus once lived and studied. "Heliopolis revealed the primordial creative act . . . Memphis revealed the work of Ptah, producer and animator of form. . . . Thebes revealed the reunion of that which had been separated," West explains.[11]

The Teaching Temples of Egypt

The apex of the seven-chakra temple system was the Great Pyramid complex at Memphis, which lay at the heart of the great initiation ceremonies for both Memphis and Heliopolis. This complex, protected by the Sphinx, represents the awakening of the spiritual sight that allows access to the inner worlds. Here initiates pulled back the veils to discover the immortality of the spirit.

The great city of Memphis was established long before either Thebes or Alexandria.[12] Its Egyptian name was Ineb Hedj, meaning "white walls," although it was also known in ancient Egypt as Ankh Tawy, meaning "that which binds the Two Lands," a name stressing the city's strategic position between Upper and Lower Egypt.[13] Herodotus described it as a beautiful city with four enormous gates, each built by various rulers in different centuries. Memphis was the secular capital of Egypt from pre-dynastic times until 2200 B.C.E., or throughout the entire Old Kingdom era.

Memphis was also a major spiritual center, located only seventeen miles southeast of the Great Pyramid. It represented the sixth chakra, or the third eye, the enlightened center of consciousness. And just as the sixth chakra is the gateway to the crown or seventh chakra, so was Memphis the gateway to the Giza temple complex, overseen by the priests of Heliopolis. Memphis housed several

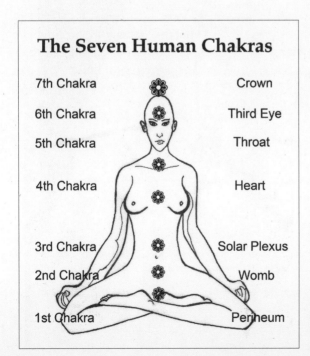

The Seven Human Chakras

7th Chakra	Crown
6th Chakra	Third Eye
5th Chakra	Throat
4th Chakra	Heart
3rd Chakra	Solar Plexus
2nd Chakra	Womb
1st Chakra	Perineum

FIGURE 87A. Within every person are seven complex chakra centers or wheels that govern and store information. These centers are aligned with the endocrine system along the axis of the spine, and are numbered from the base of the spine to the top of the head.

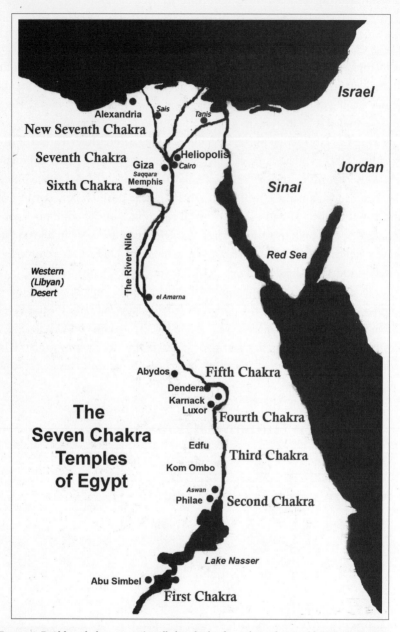

FIGURE 87B. Although there were virtually hundreds of temples and pyramids in Egypt, many still undiscovered today, these seven major centers correspond to the functions of the seven major chakras.

major temples, including sanctuaries to Ptah, Sekmet, Imhoptep, and Osiris. Its trinity of Ptah, Sekmet, and Imhoptep represented three kinds of fire. Manetho, the famous Egyptian chronicler and high priest of Heliopolis, referred to Memphis as Hi-Ku-P'tah, meaning the "place of the ka of Ptah."[14]

Ptah, the founding father of Egypt, had long been considered the father of the gods and the architect of the heavens. Through his brilliant knowledge of hydraulics, Ptah raised the lands from the waters of the Nile after the Flood. He was a master craftsman, engineer, and architect.[15] In Egypt and Greece, his generous gifts of knowledge served as a torch for all mankind, bringing civilization to the world. His city of Memphis was dedicated to the principles of life-giving fire, particularly through the philosophies of illumination, healing, governance, architecture, and mathematics. Dubbed Hephaestus by the Greeks, Ptah was the ancient bearer of light, and thus the lighthouse of Alexandria was dedicated to him, as well as to all other world saviors who have come to uplift humanity. His half-sister and companion, Hathor/Sekmet, represented the twin aspects of

Figure 88A. Ptah, usually portrayed with the traditional crook and flail, was the Father of all of Egypt, the great god who brought the arts of civilization to mankind. As the father to Ra, brother to Hathor, grandfather of Osiris and Isis, Ptah represented the master craftsman that raised the lands of Egypt from the Nile.

FIGURE 88B. The lion-headed goddess Sekmet wears the solar crown of Ra/Re. As the goddess of healing and war, Sekmet's main temples were at Memphis, but she was revered across Egypt.

creative and destructive fire. Their symbolic child was Imhoptep, the half-mortal, half-divine architect credited with building the step pyramid of Saqqara during the early days of the Old Kingdom.

Memphis was also the home of the Apis bull, an animal that symbolized Osiris, the lord of regeneration, and ultimately came to be synonymous with the health of Egypt itself. The bulls, which were born only infrequently, were sacrificed in old age to the Nile as a tribute to the death of all world saviors who return to the great cosmic ocean from whence they came.

The Apis bull was linked, as was Osiris, to virility, and to the yearly cycles of vegetation that flower, die, and are reborn. As the eternal god of resurrection, Osiris, like Jesus, was the green man who regenerates the world. Thus he, and later Jesus, was said to contain the seeds of the next cycle of regeneration within himself. Knowledge of these profound cycles appears in the ancient Mystery Schools as the path from slumber to awakening that leads to spiritual consciousness. The apostle Paul refers to these Mysteries when he writes, "What you sow does not come to life unless it dies. And what you sow is not the body which is to be, but a bare kernel, perhaps of wheat or of some other grain . . . What is sown is perishable, what is raised is imperishable" (I Corinthians 15:36–37, 42).[16] Here Paul reveals that he, too, is an initiate of the Mysteries, whether through the schools of Greece or through the teachings of Jesus himself.[17]

The temple complex at Thebes, now called Luxor, is the largest in all of Egypt. The capital of both religious and secular power during the New Kingdom era, it lies north of the temples of Edfu and Kom Ombo, and south of the healing temples of Dendera. Here we find two amazing structures joined by a two-mile-long causeway—the Temple of Luxor, best known as the Temple of Man, and the Temple of Karnack. These temples, attributed to Amenhotep III and Ramses II, are dedicated to the awakening of the heart. The Luxor temple represents the human heart; Karnack represents the high heart, or Christed spirit.

The complex at Thebes was the second major teaching school at the time when Jesus studied. Here, we find the three aspects of time expressed in the divinities of Amon, Mut, and Khonsu. Amon, or Amun, meaning "the hidden one," represented the Holy Spirit that moves throughout the universe; Mut was the dark mother veiled behind the visible world, a symbol of the hidden Sun behind the visible center of every galaxy; Khonsu, their son, represented the world of mortal time and his symbol was the moon. Thus, the complex at Thebes was dedicated to both eternal and ephemeral time.

FIGURE 89. The apis bull of Memphis was sacred to Osiris. This rare bull was entirely black with a white eagle emblazoned on his back, a white star on his forehead, thickly plaited double tail hairs, and a scarab beetle on his tongue. When found, he was tended in the temples of Osiris in Memphis for 25 years, then sacrificed back into the Nile at the end of his life.

Pioneer archaeologist, mathematician, and philosopher Schwaller de Lubicz, who spent nearly two decades exploring the sacred geometry of Luxor, discovered that the Temple of Luxor (also called the Temple of Man), when seen from the air, reveals the exact proportions of a man who seems to be stepping forward. He concluded that the ancient Egyptians had created the temple to reflect key activation points associated with the chakras, making it a blueprint of the perfected human being—the Adam Cadman. Egyptologist John Anthony West agrees: "The proportions found were those . . . of the perfected Man who has regained his Cosmic consciousness . . . [The Temple] is a library containing the totality of knowledge pertaining to universal creative powers, embodied in the building itself."[18] As a student of the Mysteries, de Lubicz knew enough of the hermetic and mathematical keys to begin to decode the temple's architecture, which demonstrates clearly how the Egyptians used the disciplines of science, religion, philosophy, and art through the language of hermetics to achieve "an exact and complete understanding of the laws of creation, of the manner in which spirit becomes matter." This knowledge, West contends, is expressed in the Egyptian temples "in geometry, harmony, proportion, and formulated upon the walls of the temples in myth and in symbol."[19]

Why does this matter in a book about Jesus? Because Thebes was the place where Egyptians consecrated their kings—indicating that this kingmaking ceremony was as much about transforming a human being into a Christ as it was about transferring secular power. The Egyptian king-making rite was intended to reconcile the human aspect of the pharaoh with the higher principles of divine kingship. It was, in essence, about turning a human into a God-man or HU-man, a being that many believe Jesus to have been. And as we shall see, this rite profoundly echoes the nature of Jesus' Crucifixion.

THE MAKING OF A KING

The custom of king-making was a deep initiatory rite practiced among the Egyptian priest-initiates to render them representatives of Horus here on Earth. This transformation signified that the king would stand for truth, freedom, and spiritual awareness, and avoid oppressive rule. Jesus assumed this role in his very vocal chastisements of the Pharisees and Sadducees and in his democratic teaching of the common people. Moreover, the Egyptian rite required that incoming pharaohs surrender themselves to a near-death experience, during which they journeyed into the other worlds and received their kingly commission from Osiris himself, thus becoming the new Horus-king.

West writes: "The king of Egypt . . . in spiritual terms represented the divine in man, the living representative of the gods here on earth. When the king, the 'Royal Man,' [the pharaoh] died, his spiritual essence did not die with him, but traveled in 'the boat of millions of years' to a higher and more glorious realm."[20] The boat became a metaphor for this spiritual journey. On the other side, the deceased pharaoh joined with Osiris, the Lord of Light, to become one with the Christ. It was this divine light that allowed him to rule as the embodiment of wisdom—as a god-man in human form. "Resurrected to the astral world, he would intercede for his people as their heavenly benefactor and judge, rain blessings on their crops, and succor them in times of need," Victoria LaPage explains. "And so, prepared by initiation into the highest wisdom of his race, in death he was divinized, honored, and worshipped as a risen god, the supreme example of the spiritual adept."[21]

As Messiah, or "anointed one," Jesus was to become this Horus-king. He underwent a similar initiation before the entire world, allowing himself to die and be reborn, not just symbolically, but in actual fact. As the new Horus-king, come to restore the purer teachings of truth to humanity, Jesus claimed his Osirian identity, thus lighting a path for others to follow.

The Egyptian king-making ceremony was replete with hermetic symbolism:

> Wearing the blue khepersh helmet, the King is seated on a throne flanked by two lions and protected by two Ma'ats [a reference to Truth]. The Throne is carried on two litters by twelve princes, their heads are adorned with feathers . . . . During this ceremony, the statue of the Neter [the principle of Min which represents the first human Egyptian King] is carried on a shield. With two feathers on his head and with seals and mummy swaths around his neck, a white bull precedes the statue while the reader-priest declaims the danced hymn of Min . . . .[22]

These hermetic images all relate to Horus, the god of truth, or to Osiris, the Christed Light. The lions are linked to Jesus, Horus, and Osiris. The bull is the pure, unblemished spirit of Osiris. The pharaoh's dedication to Ma'at or cosmic truth links him to the Sun, as does the number twelve. These symbols make even more sense when their hidden aspects are revealed:

> Once the statue of Min is set down upon a temporary altar formed of steps, the King released four birds bearing the names of the four sons of Horus . . . [representing the four great Kumaras] . . . The name of the Pharaoh is then written on the fruits of the Persea tree [the Tree of Life] by Thoth, and lastly, four birds are released toward the four directions in order to announce the royal accession to the respective divinities of the four cardinal points . . . [thus forming the cross].[23]

Clearly, this event transcended considerations of bloodlines or victories in battle, and encompassed the initiate's spiritual mastery—his ability to move into a near-death state, cross into the other worlds, receive a blessing from the Christed realms, and return uninjured.[24] Christopher Knight and Robert Lomas write about this profound ritual in *The Hiram Key*:

> . . . the central and crucial process of king-making involved the candidate traveling to the stars to be admitted as a member of the society of gods and there to be made the Horus, possibly being spiritually crowned by the dead king—the new Osiris. At some point in the events of the night, the [spirit of the] old king and the new king journeyed to the constellation of Orion together, one to remain in his celestial home, and one to return and rule the land of men.[25]

After "death" by means of a potion—perhaps a hallucinogenic that slowly induced a catatonic state—the newly-made Horus returned "precisely as the morning star rose above the horizon":

> From that moment on, no mortal would ever think about usurping his power, divinely given in a council of the gods in the heavens above. Once the members of the king's elite, the holders of secrets, had decided whom to raise to the sublime and unique degree of Horus, the time for any possible competition had passed.[26]

During this process, the new pharaoh or "anointed one" was said to have gained the Shu stone—a tone, a stone, or a sound linked with the power of the Word. This hermetic phrase tells us that he traveled on the currents of sound, the Christian equivalent of the Word, or the Logos, the blueprint behind all matter.[27] The existence of this Word was known only to the highest of initiates and its existence was among the deepest Mysteries of the Essenes. *The Essene Gospel of Peace* describes it thus:

> And you shall bathe in the Stream of Sound, and the music of its water shall flow over you; for in the beginning of the times so did we all share in the Holy Stream of Sound that gave birth to all creation. And the mighty roaring of the Stream of Sound will fill your whole body, and you will tremble before its might. Then breathe deeply of the angel of air, and become the sound itself, that the Holy Stream of Sound may carry you to the endless kingdom of the Heavenly Father, there where the rhythm of the world rises and falls.[28]

In the New Testament John calls it the Word of Life (John 1:1). Jesus refers to it in the Gospel of Thomas when he says: "He who drinks from my mouth shall become as me; [a Christ] and I myself will become him, and the hidden things shall be manifested."[29]

De Lubicz tells us that this Shu stone is "the final union of the elements which were originally opposed." For the Egyptians, that meant the reconciliation of the divine and mortal natures, represented by the opposing gods Horus and Set.[30] In other words, the Holy Stream of Sound—the Word—resolves the seemingly irreconcilable aspects of our human and divine natures. Jesus reveals his knowledge of this concept when he says, in the apocryphal Gospel of Thomas, "When you make the two into One, and you make the inner as the outer . . . then shall you enter the Kingdom."[31] This tradition is also linked to the legendary Philosopher's Stone, the alchemical (s)tone sought by alche-

mists and philosophers throughout the Middle Ages that promised to bestow
eternal life. As such, it becomes a symbol of initiates' ability to travel to the
inner planes, return alive, and remember their own enlightened natures. Jesus
reminds us of this same inner divinity when he says: "Is it not written in your
law . . . 'Ye are gods'?", reminding us that, by serving the higher truth (Horus),
we too can become a Christ—an Osiris (John 10:34). This merger of the personal self with the resurrected Osiris, or inner Christ, was at the heart of the
Egyptian Mysteries.

FIGURE 90. On either side of the incoming pharaoh stand the gods Horus and Set, anointing
him with oil from the Tree of Life, represented by the ankh. In this image, Horus represents the
pharaoh's higher nature, while Set represents his ego. It is in the integration of these two natures,
that the true pharaoh was born. It is from this act of christening, KRST, that we get the word
Christ today.

The Temples and the Great White Brotherhood

The sacred Temple at Luxor was chosen as the location for this powerful king-making ceremony because it symbolized the heart, the vibration of the perfected man, the divine Purusha who has attained his eternal nature. West reminds us, "The very ancient Egyptian belief in the king as a Son of God dates back before the Temple of Luxor was built and continues throughout Egyptian history, taking on special prominence in the immediately pre-Christian era."[32] Thus, the procession from Karnack to Luxor symbolized the journey of the pharaoh's human heart into a perfected state of Christed consciousness.

For over 1500 years, these temples had acted as halls of activation for the evolution of humankind. "Behind the whole splendid scheme of the Egyptian Mysteries, the Lodge of the Great White Brotherhood in that country ever stood in silence and secrecy, guarding them and using them as a channel of the Hidden Light—its very existence being unknown to all who remained outside the inner circles," writes C. W. Leadbeater.[33] The Brotherhood created these experiential dramas, which were supported with the teachings of the liberal arts and sciences, for the primary purpose of helping mankind to ascend in goodness, spirituality, and morality. Joscelyn Godwin, author of *Mystery Religions in the Ancient World*, writes:

> The primary object of these initiations was to take the candidate through the gates of death. The hierophant told Apuleius before his initiation that it was like a voluntary death followed by a slow recovery . . . . [T]he candidate was placed in a trance, his consciousness taken out of his body, and in this state he experienced higher states of being and met some of the denizens of the invisible worlds. Proclus describes certain of them as forms of light that take on human shape. Through direct experience the candidate would learn that he could live freely without his physical body, and that the gods he worshipped were perfectly real. Then he would return to earth fully convinced of his immortality and prepared to meet death fearlessly, knowing it as the gate to freedom and his soul's true home. Plutarch said that when death comes it is like an initiation into the Greater Mysteries.[34]

Later, Gnostic Christians carried on some of these traditions in their three levels of initiation: purification, illumination, and perfection.[35] Clement of Alexandria calls the last stage "the scientific knowledge of God," referring to the experiential awe felt by those who had undergone these voyages.

The Egyptian king-making process has profound echoes in Jesus' life and death. The anointing ceremony enacted by Mary Magdalene just before the Crucifixion signified the anointing ritual of the Horus-kings. Jesus, like the pharaohs, died to the outer world, journeyed into other realms, and returned to life as the new Messiah. When we understand the theological concepts behind this role of sacred kingship, we begin to comprehend the choices of dedicated service that Jesus made in his life, death, and resurrection. To become the true Horus-king, the shepherd for the world, he had to transcend the concept of a merely social messiah and fulfill a spiritual role of theodotal kingship that stretched back thousands of years.

To do this in the fullest measure of the spirit, Jesus had to gain the ability to activate all nine of his subtle energy bodies and thus become the true "anointed one." And it was in Egypt, with the assistance of the Great White Brotherhood, that he learned this mastery. As an avatar who had already achieved tremendous levels of compassion and enlightenment, as evidenced by his astonishing powers of wisdom and healing, Jesus was well prepared to take this path—the path of the divine Purusha, the Bodhisattva or incarnated god-man who returns to Earth to uplift humankind. When seen in this light, his initiations in Egypt appear as a deliberate and rigorous dress rehearsal for his Crucifixion in Jerusalem, and his voluntary death and resurrection reveal the deepest secrets of the Mystery traditions, presented on the world stage.

CHAPTER 26

The Lion and the City of the Sun

I am the lord of eternity . . . I am the only One born of an only One,
I am within the eye of the Sun. I open the door of heaven. . . .
It is I who make you strong for millions of years, whether ye be in the
    heavens, or in the earth. . . .
I am the pure one who dwells within the sacred eye. I shall not die
    again.[1]

—The Papyrus of Ani, XLII

Of all the temples along the Nile, none was so grand as Heliopolis, the ancient City of the Sun, the center where Jesus lived and studied for almost a decade. The most ancient of Egyptian temples, Heliopolis, a nine-day journey up the Nile from Thebes, is located today in an area called Tell Hisn on the northwestern outskirts of Cairo. The temple complex of Heliopolis was built in the Thirteenth Lower Nome of northern Egypt—a number appropriate to its position as the center for the worship of the Sun. Like the Sun that sits at the center of the zodiac, Heliopolis was the central pillar around which the entire Egyptian world turned. So it is appropriate—and certainly not accidental—that Jesus studied there.

The ancient name for the city was On, or Anu, derived from *iwnw*, a word that means "pillar," linking it to the sacred Tree of Life, the central axis or pillar of the world.[2] In the Old Testament, we first hear of the city of On in Genesis 41:45, when Joseph, the pharaoh's overseer, marries Asenath, a daughter of the high priest of On. In biblical Hebrew, On was also called Awen, a name strangely reminiscent of Annwfm, the name for the shining lord of the dead at Glastonbury—a possible reference to Osiris, who acts as the lord of light in the judgment halls of heaven.[3] These symbolic connections all establish Heliopolis as a doorway into the celestial world of the gods and the Mysteries of the underworld.

Heliopolis was ancient even before the pyramids.[4] It was the first spiritual center ever built in Egypt and remained the single most important temple complex until only a few decades before the Christian era.[5, 6] This vast temple complex was the spiritual seed energy of Egypt, the *omphalos*, the "navel of the world," and stretched to include the twenty-two-acre Giza plateau that was the apex of the Heliopolan temple system. The city itself was built to align with both the heavens and the geomagnetic ley lines of the Earth to assist spiritual candidates in awakening to divinity. This ancient science of aligning buildings, temples, and megalithic sites with the stars is now called archeoastronomy. Graham Hancock and Santha Faiia, authors of the beautifully illustrated book *Heaven's Mirror* call it a "'science of immortality' designed to release mankind 'from the mouth of death.'"[7]

The Temple at Heliopolis was called the "house of the Sun." As large as both the Karnack and Luxor temples combined, it spanned a vast enclosure running 1200 meters east to west and 1000 meters north to south—the equivalent of ten football fields in length and twelve football fields in width. From the funerary stele (tombstones with carved hieroglyphs) of Djedatumiufankh, found not far from its ruins, we know that the walls were twelve meters (36 feet) high and 15.6 meters (45 feet) thick, making it a virtual fortress of stone.[8]

Heliopolis' schools of science, mathematics, philosophy, and astronomy became the repository for the highest wisdom in Western civilization, at the heart of which lay the knowledge that the universe was based on four interlocking disciplines: mathematics, the study of pure number; geometry, number expressed in space; harmonics, number expressed in time; and astronomy, number expressed in both space and time, as observed in the movement of the heavens.[9] These schools informed the minds of Orpheus, Homer, Pythagoras, Plato, Thales, Solon, and many other famous thinkers.[10] Plato, who studied in Egypt for thirteen years, wrote that the Egyptian canons of music and proportion had sustained the integrity of that civilization for thousands of years.[11]

The Egyptians claimed that they had acquired most of their knowledge from the writings of Thoth, who kept his sacred books at Heliopolis, several of which dealt with the secrets of the motions of the stars.[12] In its heyday, Heliopolis housed over 13,000 scholars—astronomers, priests, and scientists—who

Figure 91. The obelisks of Heliopolis marked it as the center point of connection between the Earth and the heavens, linking the temple complex to the knowledge of the great star cycles and their influence over the Earth via the Sun.

FIGURE 92. The seed energy of any holy site was consecrated with sacred stones shaped like eggs, called *omphalos*. These were used to mark such holy temples as Jerusalem, Delphi, Avalon, and Heliopolis. Illustrated by Sylvia Laurens.

studied the Sun, Moon, planets, and stars, and who focused on the changing cycles of the cosmos.[13] This focus was reflected in the title of its high priest, called the "chief of all observers" and "greatest of all seers." Timothy Wallace-Murphy and Marilyn Hopkins claim: "The Heliopolan priests were high initiates in the mysteries of the heavens and their dominant occupation was the observation and recording of the various motions of the sun and moon, the planets and the stars."[14]

OSIRIS AND THE CITY OF THE SUN

The Greek mathematician and philosopher Proclus Diodachus reveals that the Egyptians had full knowledge of the solar year many centuries before the Greeks, claiming "the Egyptians had already taught Plato about the movement of the fixed stars."[15] Aristotle confirms that the Greeks derived their knowledge from the Egyptians, "whose observations [of the stars] have been kept for many years past, and from whom much of our evidence about particular stars is derived."[16] This "science of the stars" was transmitted to Jesus at Heliopolis. There, he learned about the cycles of spiritual slumber and awakening that affect human consciousness, and that Earth was entering the Age of Pisces, an age of instinctual perception. He may also have learned of our eventual ascent out of this darkness into the Age of Aquarius, an age that promises enlightenment.

At the center of the studies pursued at Heliopolis lay the study of the Sun. The complex contained temples dedicated to Atum-Ra, Osiris, and Horus—all various aspects of the solar principle—as well as the Fountain of the Sun and the Egyptian Tree of Life, the famous Persea tree upon which the goddess Seshat and the god Thoth wrote the names and the years of the kings of Egypt at the time of their coronation.[17] In the language of the Mysteries, both the tree and the pool tell us that Heliopolis was connected with the highest heavens. The temple of Ra at Heliopolis boasted an enormous repository of the most ancient theological and historical records. It was from this library that high priest and historian Manetho produced the royal records for Ptolemy II (281–246 B.C.E.), proving that Moses, Akhenaton, and many other pharaohs had trained there and revealing an unbroken chain of rulers extending back some 36,000 years.[18]

Heliopolis, like Avalon, was situated on an island high above the Nile, a metaphor for the One World Mountain that arose from the waters of Nun, the great Cosmic Ocean, at the beginning of time—the "homeland of the primeval ones."[19] This sanctuary, like Avalon, was seen as a replica of creation itself, a doorway from the Mother's womb into the higher worlds.[20]

Atum, the one invisible Creator God who existed before the worlds of time and space, was the chief deity of Heliopolis. Thus, the largest temple in the complex was the "great house," or Per-Atum, dedicated to the boundless, eternal, all-knowing God. The Pyramid Texts, the oldest written literature of Egypt, explain that Atum arose as the god of light at the beginning of Earth's creation. In this form, as Atum-Re (Ra), he became an incarnation of the phoenix—a mystical symbol of the awakened Christ.

Heliopolis was also home to the Ennead, the nine *neteru* or gods who had first brought civilization to Egypt.[21] And at the center of the Ennead stood the most famous trinity in Egypt: Osiris, Isis, and Horus, analogous to Christianity's Father, Holy Spirit (Mother), and Holy Son. Their story became the foundation for much of Egyptian spirituality, with its central theme of love as the catalyst for redemption and eternal life—a theme that would become the foundation for Christian theology as well.

The story of Osiris goes back to what Egyptologists call the *Zep Tepi*, or "first time," when the gods walked among mortals and taught them the arts of civilization. Osiris was born on December 25. His mother, the goddess Nuit, lady of heaven, also mothered Isis, Set, Nephthys, and Harpocrates. Set and Nephthys were the "legitimate" children of Nuit's husband Geb (Seb), the Earth god. Isis was the daughter of Thoth (wisdom) and thus became the mistress of medicine, healing, and Magic. Osiris and Harpocrates were the sons of Ra (the Sun) and thus contained the luminous spirit of light. In the *Egyptian Book of the Dead*, Osiris is called the "king of kings, prince of gods and men, governor of the world, lord of multitudes of aspects and forms, the giver of life from the beginning, the king of eternity, whose existence is everlasting."[22] Many of these same profound titles later became ascribed to Jesus.

Ra divided Egypt into two parts, declaring that Set should rule one half of Egypt and Osiris should rule the other. Osiris married his half-sister, Isis, and, together, they ruled the land for many years. Osiris left Isis in charge of much

FIGURE 93. Osiris stands between the two Eyes of God, holding the crook and the flail. Osiris, whose name means "the Seat of the Eye," thus guards the threshold for the initiate, representing the Christed spirit or awakening of the inner sight. The crook points toward the left eye of Horus, representing the good shepherd; the flail represents the mastery of his three natures.

of Egypt while he traveled the world, bringing relief to the refugees of the Great Flood. She made laws, instituted learning, and taught the arts of civilization, bringing order out of chaos. Osiris taught the arts of agriculture, linking him with the cycles of fertility and vegetation and the regenerating cycles of life and death—a metaphor of the soul's regenerative evolution. Because of this, Osiris is often portrayed as the consummate regenerative force—the "green god" or "green man." Osiris was often depicted by the Egyptians with green or black skin, symbolic of the fertility cycles of the "black lands" for which Egypt is named.[23] Black and green were also the colors of the House of David, connecting Jesus to the same cycles of renewal as an Osirian king—another allusion to the secret teachings that lay at the root of Judaism.[24]

Osiris chose the symbol of the lion as one of his signs of kingship and passed it on to his son, Horus. In Egypt, the lion was originally called *Panthera Leo-pardus*, which later developed into the terms "panther" and "leopard." Thus, priests of Osiris wore a leopard skin over one shoulder. By choosing the lion, Osiris also associated himself with Leo, the astrological sign ruled by the Sun. When Leo (leo-pard) was pluralized, it became "leon," and finally "lion" in modern English.[25] This association appears in the lion-bodied Sphinx, a monument perennially linked to Osiris.

The highest priests of Osiris became a sacerdotal class known as the Panthers, who protected the Giza plateau and the gateway of the Sphinx, and developed a confidential teaching system around the Osirian rites. Their name became synonymous with secrecy and occult knowledge. Tony Bushby, author of *The Secret in the Bible*, tells us that "it was that group who were directly responsible for the advent of all later Mystery Schools."[26]

Israel also made the lion the emblem of its sacred king. Likewise, the lion-headed Zervan of Persia "embodied the organizing power of the entire cosmos," representing the kosmokrator, or Cosmic Ruler of the universe.[27] In the Talmud, Jesus is called Yeshu'a ben Panthera (the Latin equivalent of panther), powerful evidence that he had attained this sacerdotal order.[28] In the early centuries of Christianity, this symbolism carried over as the lion and the lamb, aspects of the courageous and sacrificial sons of God.

It was members of Egypt's sacred Panther order who opened Thoth's Secret Book to initiates.[29] We can only guess at the nature and contents of this occult book, but it may well have been the *Egyptian Book of the Dead*, which was said to show initiates the way through the Duat and the starry heavens. Years later, Christianity would adopt this same symbolism of the sacred book and the stars for the apostle Mark.[30]

FIGURE 94. A priest of Osiris, shown with a leopard skin, stands before the hawk-headed form of Ra.

FIGURE 95. The Lion of Saint Mark is a reflection of a far more ancient symbol within the Mystery Schools—the entrance into "the heart of the lion" through the doorway of the Sphinx's chest, in search of the lost Book of Thoth.

The symbol of the vine was also sacred to both Osiris and Jesus. As the pre-server of the grape, Osiris taught the people to make the "nectar of the gods." In Greece, the grapevine was associated with Dionysus, the Greek version of Osiris, and, centuries after that, with Jesus. Jesus clearly knew of the symbology of the vine and its connection to the Tree of Life, for he tells his disciples: "I am the true vine, and my father is the vinedresser. . . . I am the vine, you are the branches. He who abides in Me, and I in him, bears much fruit; for without Me you can do nothing" (John 15:1–5). These symbols were later adopted by the Catholic Church, who placed them on the Tau cross—the hermetic emblem of the balance scales that stood before Osiris in the Halls of Amente where he judged both "the quick and the dead." Moses had also taught this truth: "The vineyard . . . is the House of David" (Isaiah 5:57). Later, the Merovingian kings, said to be descendants of Jesus, reflected this symbology in their name. Like Jesus, Osiris celebrated the Eucharistic rite of wine and bread, and it is very possible that the rites of Mithra were based on those of Osiris. In the breaking of bread and the drinking of wine, celebrants expressed gratitude for the loving sacrifice of all virtuous beings who have come to Earth to help mankind.

All of these commonalities indicate strong ties between the Egyptian Osiris, the Jewish Messiah, and the Christian Jesus. And indeed, as the "anointed one," Osiris was also the Christ. One of his names was, in fact, Osiris-Kas. "[T]he

FIGURE 96A. The Tau cross with the grapes shows the familiar balance scales of heaven, decorated with entwining vines and hanging grapes, all symbols of Osiris, who, like Jesus, offered the hope of eternal life and resurrection in the world to come. This motif is from a Greek coin to Dionysus, the later Greek version of the Egyptian Osiris.

FIGURE 96B. The symbolism of the Tau cross, representing the balance scales of Heaven and the symbology of the grapes and the vine, were adopted by the Roman Catholic Church and used as symbols for Jesus, thus directly connecting him as an incarnation of Osiris, the Lord of Light in the Halls of Heaven.

name of Christ, Christos in Greek, Chrestus in Latin was derived . . . from the Egyptian word Krst," notes Egyptologist Gerald Massey. "The karast is literally the god or person who has been mummified, embalmed, anointed or christified." Massey goes on to explain: "Mes or mas in the hieroglyphics, signifies to anoint and to steep, as in making the mummy, and messu in Egyptian means the anointed; whence Iah the Mesu becomes Messiah in Hebrew."[31]

In Egypt, the pharaohs adopted the iconography of Osiris in the hope that, when they died, they would merge with the Lord of Light. On their sarcophagi, they carved the classic emblems of the crook and flail, symbols of the Lord of Resurrection, "to transform the outward appearance of the deceased into an image of the god Osiris, the single most important Egyptian deity, and the first in recorded history to have risen from the dead." Cassaro notes that these emblems recall the Christian Savior as well.[32] Enlightenment and spiritual mastery was the inner goal of the pharaohs, who believed that, if they managed to achieve oneness with the Christ within, they would be immortalized as a star in the heavens, the outward symbol of the inner light.[33]

Plutarch gives one of the most famous accounts of the murder and resurrection of Osiris—a perennial story that pits the forces of darkness against the forces of light. In the story, Set tricks his brother Osiris into a golden coffin, telling everyone that whosoever the coffin best fits shall have it. When Osiris agrees to lie down in it, he is sealed within and thrown into the Nile. When Isis hears this news, she goes in search of Osiris, but the Nile has already carried the golden coffin north toward Byblos, Lebanon, where it lodges in a tamarisk tree. The tree, perhaps knowing who lies within, grows around the coffin to conceal it. The king of Byblos, impressed with the enormous size and straightness of the tree, cuts it down and makes it into a temple column. By the time Isis arrives, the coffin is deep inside the palace, hidden within a column. Isis goes to the palace, reveals her identity, and convinces the king and queen to release the coffin from the pillar, returning with it to Egypt by boat. Isis, hoping to resurrect her love, leaves Osiris' body to find her father Thoth. But before leaving Osiris, she brings him back to life temporarily, and impregnates herself to conceive a child. Then, while Isis is gone, Set discovers the coffin with his brother's body still inside. Fearful that Thoth and Isis will be able to bring Osiris back to life permanently, Set cuts Osiris' body into fourteen pieces and scatters them along the Nile. When Isis returns, she retrieves the pieces and, with the help of Anubis, her nephew, puts Osiris' body back together thus instituting the first funerary rites. As he grows up, Horus, the rightful heir to the throne, is then

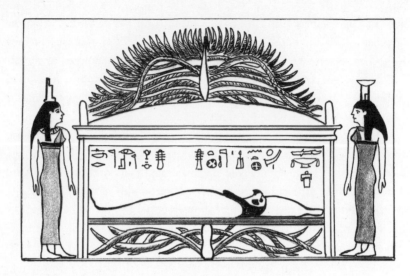

FIGURE 97. The coffin of Osiris covered with the tamarisk tree.

instructed by Osiris, his father, through visions.Eventually Horus vanquishes Set, restoring truth, order, and light to Egypt.

Plutarch was convinced that the Egyptians took this tale literally, as E. A. Wallis Budge points out:

> From what Plutarch says we are bound to conclude that the Egyptians did not believe that Osiris perished and came to an end with the dismemberment of his body. . . . The divine part of Osiris did not die, it was only the mortal body, which he put on when he came from the abode of the gods to reign upon earth, that suffered death. In the divinity and immortality of the god-man Osiris lay the strength of the power with which he appealed to the minds and hopes of the Egyptians for thousands of years.[34]

The significance of Osiris' story for us lies in how his life, death, and resurrection relate to Jesus and how they link Jesus to the ancient Mystery traditions. Isis, like the Mother Mary, and even Mary Magdalene, is clearly the agent of love and fidelity. She is mother, sister, wise woman, and queen. Osiris, like Jesus, is the great humanitarian, the illuminated soul. Horus is the young hero, the courageous god-man who contends with a legacy of darkness and vanquishes an enemy who is oppressing the people, bringing hope and healing back to the world. "Osiris is Light," Leadbeater observes. "He came forth from the Light; He dwells in the Light; He is the Light."

The Light is hidden everywhere; it is in every rock and in every stone. When a man becomes one with Osiris the light, then he becomes one with the whole of which he was part, and then he can see the Light in everyone, however thickly veiled, pressed down, and shut away. . . . Osiris is in the heavens, but Osiris is also in the very hearts of men. When Osiris in the heart knows Osiris in the heavens, then man becomes God, and Osiris, once rent into fragments, again becomes one.[35]

This description sounds very much like the words Jesus used to describe himself: "I came from that Primordial, self-originated, primal, boundless light that I may tell you all."[36] In the Gospel of Thomas, Jesus also tells his disciples: "I am the light that is above them all. I am the All. The all comes forth from me, and the all reaches towards me. Cleave the wood, I am there; lift up the stone, and you shall find me there."[37]

Over time, the trinity of Osiris, Isis, and Horus became the central focus of Egyptian worship, for these three beings together represented the victory of the qualities of truth, love, and fidelity over the unbridled, destructive ambition of Set. Osiris, as the Egyptian Christ, offered everyone the promise of immortality in return for a life of morality, service, and honor. His story also epitomized the struggle between the darkest aspects of the human psyche and the noblest aspects of the human soul. Osiris' son, Horus—Horus the light-giver, Horus the healer—is the one who pulls the world back from darkness and makes all things right. This theology lay at the core of all the Egyptian Mysteries.

CHAPTER 27

The Phoenix and the Promise of Resurrection

> May I, even I, arise . . . like unto a hawk of gold coming forth from his
> egg. . . .
> May I rise, may I gather myself together as the beautiful golden hawk
> (which hath) the head of a Bennu bird.[1]
>
> —The Papyrus of Ani, chapter LXXVII

Perhaps the most powerful hermetic symbol that was shared by Jesus and Osiris was the Bennu bird or celestial phoenix— that glorious messenger from the higher realms who, born from the Great Cosmic Egg, periodically descends to Earth to sing its song of beauty, die, and be reborn. "In ancient Egyptian iconography and hieroglyphs the Bennu bird 'was born before death existed' and symbolized the eternal return to all things and the triumph of spirit over matter."[2] The phoenix looks much like an eagle, icon of the divine Father, but with flaming red and gold feathers. In the Mysteries, this creature represented the returning Kumaras, or great sons of God whose spirits could never die. Its name recalls the Hebrew word *ben*, meaning "son," immediately associating the Bennu bird with the "son of God."

According to legend, the Bennu bird returned to Heliopolis to sing its song of beauty atop the Persea tree, or Tree of Life, and perish in its own flames—but not before laying an egg to ensure its rebirth and a new incarnation. Herodotus writes that the Bennu made its appearance only once every 500 to 600 years— the periodic cycle in which it was believed the sons of light, or Great Kumaras, reincarnated.[3] Others speculate that the phoenix only comes to Earth every

2160 years, at the cusp of each astrological age. Others have it as every 12,000 years. Whatever the actual cycle of rebirth, the phoenix only appears in the eastern sky at fixed points in history, points connected with the appearance of the Morning Star.[4]

Herodotus describes a pair of colossal obelisks at the Temple of Atum, symbols for the Tree of Life, upon which the Bennu bird dwelt. These obelisks were "twelve feet broad and a hundred and fifty feet high, each hewn from a single block of stone."[5] Their tops were crowned by a golden, pyramid-shaped capstone called a benben stone, meaning "seed" or "essence."

Egyptian legends tell us that the first benben stone fell from the heavens carrying the secrets of "the hiddenness of the Duat"— a roadmap of the starry skies.[6] This stone became one of the most sacred objects in Egypt, believed by some to have been the vehicle that carried the Sun god Ra to Earth. British researcher William Lethaby writes that the original benben stone was hollow and was used to house the lost books of Thoth.[7] Legend has it that the priests of Heliopolis constructed the first obelisk as a pedestal to receive the sacred stone, placing it at the center of the city. Beside this obelisk, they built the Mansion of the Phoenix and the Palace of the Ancient One, which was considered the dwelling place of Ra on Earth.[8] By the time Jesus came to Egypt, the original benben stone had already vanished.

Figure 98. Benben stone, which sat atop the massive obelisks at the Temple of Amun. Illustrated by Angel Terrazas.

The phoenix sprang from the heart of Osiris himself as a living symbol of the Christ, taking form in our world in order to share its wisdom and then die. Hermetically, it is a symbol of the bringer of light who perishes for his efforts. The Bennu bird was usually depicted as a heron, with a straight back and two long feathers adorning its head. These feathers belonged to the goddess Ma'at, signifying universal truth. Only Ma'at, Osiris, and Amon/Amun (Truth, Christ, and the Holy Spirit) were depicted with such feathers, signifying their alignment with the cosmic Word.[9] "The Egyptians set truth above all other virtues," Egyptologist E. A. Budge writes, "and in the Great Judgment Halls of Heaven, the man who had spoken the truth on earth triumphed. Osiris himself was declared by Thoth and by the jury of the gods as the 'Truth speaker,' or Maa Kheru."[10] Osiris took on that role for earlier ages; Jesus accepted it in ours. Both are truth-speakers—manifestations of the ever-renewing divinity from whose heart arises the living Christ. The early Christian church adopted the phoenix as a symbol of Christ's nature, recognizing the link between the two.

Ancient Egyptian theology, like Christianity, believed in the hope of resurrection and eternal life, and taught that this could be accomplished once souls joined with their eternal, radiant, and Christed self. "The chief fundamentals of [Osiris'] cult were the belief in his divinity, death, resurrection, and absolute control of the destinies of the bodies and souls of men," writes Budge. "The central point of each Osirian's religion was his hope of resurrection in a transformed body of immortality, which could only be realized by him through the death and resurrection of Osiris." This theology clearly pre-figures the Chris-

FIGURE 99. The Bennu bird perched before the pharaoh, clearly showing that the Pharaoh serves the light of the phoenix, who rests on a symbol for the Trinity.

tian belief that, through Jesus Christ, we can attain eternal life. Jesus, like Osiris, meets us on the other side of death, since he is the Lord of Eternity and the King of Everlastingness. Jesus, like Osiris, determines whether we shall go into heaven or return to Earth for another round of incarnation. Jesus is called "the Soul that Liveth again," "the Being who Becometh a child again," "the Firstborn Son of Unformed Matter," and the "Giver of Life from the Beginning"—all names originally ascribed to Osiris.[11]

Jesus, like Osiris, is seen as pre-existent, a being who is "one" with the heavenly Father. Osiris was "the divine Ancestor . . . the Father of the souls of the Egyptians, and the symbol of their hope of resurrection and immortality." Osiris "springs up to us from his destruction, and the germ that proceeds from him engenders life in both the dead and the living."[12] Jesus echoes this, saying: "Most assuredly, I say to you, unless a grain of wheat falls into the ground and dies, it remains alone; but if it dies, it produces much grain. He who loves his life will lose it, and he who hates his life in this world will keep it for eternal life" (John 12:23–24). Jesus later affirms that it is only through his embodiment as the Christed spirit that we can return to the Creator: "No one comes to the Father but through me" (John 14:6).

Figure 100. The Bennu bird with the staff of wisdom, sitting serenely on the Boat of a Million Years with the Sun above his head. The staff of the shepherds and the nine flags of the Ennead gods are close by. The Eye of God, or Eye of Horus, guides him as he journeys to the other world.

Dutch Egyptologist Henri Frankfort notes: "It may be well to emphasize that the identification of the dead with Osiris was a means to an end, that is, to reach resurrection in the Hereafter."[13] Budge agrees. Osiris "became the type and symbol and hope of every dead man, and the older gods in heaven seem to have thought it right to set apart for him a place in the Other World where he could live with all those who died believing in him, and rule over them."[14] This fundamental congruence in belief may be one of the reasons that Christianity was accepted so readily in Egypt and why, in later centuries, the phoenix was co-opted as a symbol of Christ's power.

In legend, the Bennu bird came from Arabia, carrying in its beak an egg of myrrh that contained its father's body. Myrrh was one of the three gifts of the Magi, and one of the two healing herbs taken by Joseph of Arimathea to Jesus' crypt to revive him after the Crucifixion.[15] The pharaohs also used it to prepare their bodies for burial and spiritual rebirth. The presence of this herb in the two legends can hardly be accidental, and it links Jesus again to the Mysteries. Likewise, the Bennu bird is often shown sitting beside a shepherd's staff, reminding us that Jesus was "the good shepherd . . . [who] gives his life for the sheep" (John 10:11). Hardly coincidence then that one of the epithets for Osiris was Asar-sa, or "Osiris the Shepherd"—"an appropriate title for a beloved spiritual leader whose religion of resurrection promised life after death for the wayward soul."[16] The shepherd of souls is a role that has always been ascribed to the evolved priest-king.

In a passage from an Egyptian funerary text, we read: "I am the great Phoenix which is in On . . . I am Hu and I never die in my name of Soul. . . . My soul is god; my soul is eternity. I am lord of millions of years. I have made my nest in the uttermost parts of heaven."[17] Isis echoes these words as she reveals to Horus that he, like his father Osiris, is an incarnation of the Light: "Thou art the Great Bennu who was born on the Incense Trees in the House of the Great Prince in Heliopoli. As the 'soul of Ra,' the sun rose in the form of the Bennu to shine out across the world renewed each morning." The *Egyptian Book of the Dead* contains formulae for transforming a deceased person into a phoenix, revealing how the soul of the dead longed to be identified with the Christed.[18] Egyptian theology taught that the phoenix rises from its own ashes, just as the soul rises from its dead physical form—a rebirth into eternal life that can only be accomplished when a soul embraces the lessons of forgiveness, truth, and love—the lessons of Osiris and of Jesus. Thus, we know that Horus, Ra, Osiris, Jesus, and the Sun are all one and the same.

ECHOES OF FORGOTTEN GREATNESS

At the time that Jesus studied in Egypt, Heliopolis was still a major seat of learning, although its greatness was in decline. Strabo writes that the town around the temple complex had fallen into ruin by 24 B.C.E., but that the priests still taught their students there. Many sphinxes and obelisks had been pilfered to use in Alexandria's monuments, and the official "house of wisdom" had been transplanted to the Royal Library in Alexandria.[19]

FIGURE 101. The pillars of the temple at Heliopolis. Illustrated by Sylvia Laurens.

Heliopolis had been a city of obelisks that reached to the sky, a city dedicated to the concept that we must climb the Tree of Life to embrace our eternal selves. Nearly half of these obelisks were pillaged by Roman popes and emperors—pillars that once marked the sacred lines of energy used by the priests in the science of geomagnetic harmony.[20] In 37 c.e., Caligula stole one of the largest obelisks for the Roman Coliseum; the Vatican moved it to Saint Peter's Square in 1585.[21] This 330-ton pillar, carved from a single block of granite, required 900 men, seventy-two horses, and five months to move one mile. Today it sits at the center of an enormous rayed Sun, affirming for all who care to see that Jesus, Christ of the Roman Church, was a spiritual descendant of the Mysteries of his Egyptian predecessors.

Yet the temple was still functioning when Jesus arrived at around the age of thirty-one and was still tended by the Great White Brotherhood, the keepers of the eternal flame.[22] The annals of the Brotherhood tell us: "When Jesus was ready for his entrance into the supreme college and monastery of the Brotherhood at Heliopolis . . . the records show that he was surrounded . . . with every comfort and convenience, and that for his study he was given many of the rarest manuscripts containing the texts of ancient doctrines and creeds."[23] Despite the best efforts of the Christian and Islamic worlds to co-opt or suppress all the Magic that was once Egypt, the legacy of Heliopolis has not vanished. Its wealth is scattered across the world, yet its legacy of wisdom is still embedded in the land itself. It is this wisdom that ultimately makes it a place of power even today.

CHAPTER 28

Osiris and the Alchemy of Enlightenment

Whether I live or I die, I am Osiris,
I enter in and reappear through you,
I decay in you, I grow in you. . . .
I cover the earth. Whether I live or die I am barley,
I am not destroyed.[1]

—The Egyptian Coffin Texts

When Jesus arrived in the motherland of Mysteries accompanied by Gasper, one of the Magi who had attended his birth, the magnificent white walls and statuary of Heliopolis rose on the sandstone cliffs above them, and they saw the smaller golden Temple of Isis in the distance.

Gasper came to the rail beside me. His hand swept out towards the golden temple. "Hore Kehru. We call it 'Virgin of the World'. . . . It is dedicated to the Eternal Virgin [Isis]. It is run as a training school for the Priestesses of all goddesses under the direction of Isis. . . . She is not named as a goddess. She is the Source of the gods."[2]

This first-hand account, from the annals of the Great White Brotherhood, describes how Jesus arrived at the temple of Thoth-Hermes to undergo a seven-day oral exam before a conclave of the world's greatest sages, who had all assembled for the event.

We . . . climbed granite stairs which were polished by thousands of feet, and entered the gate of the awe-inspiring Temple of Hermes. It was a sprawling complex of buildings and activities. . . . In the distance, at the end of this impressive corridor was the entrance to a mammoth temple, the Temple of Osiris. On each façade of this giant building were statues and fantastic symbols in pure gold encrusted with priceless gems. . . . We were stopped by a Hierophant at the lowest of thirty-three steps which led to the temple. Silently, to the sound of music, I was disrobed, bathed in ashes, manure, honey, milk, and then later clothed in a simple robe. . . . I was led on to a straw mat beneath the statue of Osiris. . . . No words were spoken, and no one paid attention to me. Slowly the music died, and the enormous golden doors to the temple were closed, cutting off the light from the setting sun. I was left alone, without instruction, to prepare myself for my forthcoming ordeal—seven days of examination by the greatest minds in the world.[3]

Thus we learn that Jesus was welcomed to Heliopolis by members of the Great White Brotherhood from around the globe. Present were masters from Britain, India, Syria, Greece, Persia, Israel, and the Caribes Islands.[4] Profoundly aware of the implications of Jesus' arrival in Egypt, these sages had gathered to greet him. Word of Jesus' wisdom had preceded him, and his spiritual gifts had already been amply demonstrated across India, Asia, and the Mediterranean.

The assembled Brothers put before Jesus a mission—a mission that had been hinted at, and even overtly stated, since the time of his birth. They wanted him to undertake the role of the Adam Cadmon, the human vessel of the savior-king, the Messiah, the anointed one.[5] Jesus' years of discipline and study had taught him profound truths. In the highest sense, he had become the evolved priest-king, the immortal human who could walk between the worlds. He had spent his whole life in preparation for this role, and his innate access to the higher worlds gave him the ability to see past the sectarian dogma and secular strife and enter the heart of the whirlwind.

The task set before him was, of course, the archetypal task of the Horus-king—the god-man [HU-man] who could alchemicalize his body with light and return to it after death. Cultural historian and anthropologist Jeremy Naydler writes that this role of kingship "was positioned at a pivotal point in the reciprocal relationships between the communities of the dead and the living, and the king's role was as chief mediator between the two realms."[6] This was, in fact, one of the roles ascribed to Osiris that Jesus inherited. Thus, when the Great White Brotherhood asked Jesus to become the new Horus-king, it meant that he must learn the mystical secrets of all nine of his subtle energy bodies so that he could fully unite with the spirit of Osiris. In this way, he would become the new Christ, the new lord of light in the awakening Age of Pisces.

Jesus describes his oral examination by the Brotherhood like this:

> I sat upon the straw mat, and began to review in my mind what I knew about the Egyptian Religion. After hours I began to iMagine that I was in the presence of a mighty host of priests, and that I was [being] asked questions. These questions I answered in my mind. It did indeed seem that these questions were asked by the whispers of wind in the giant temple. When I answered them it seemed that my thoughts were turned into words by the resounding statue of Osiris. I answered questions and more questions, and here is a summary of what I said . . . in this, the second most important trial of my life.[7]

In a lengthy discourse, Jesus reveals the depth of his understanding of Egyptian philosophy and his appreciation of how it melds with other traditions. His words as reported by the Brotherhood are eloquent and thought provoking. Of course, we cannot confirm the veracity of that report, but the answers it ascribes to Jesus reflect the teachings of Thoth and the ceremonies of Isis and Ra from which Christianity derives many of its tenets. We know that Jesus had trained extensively among the Essenes. And since he had also lived among the Great White Brotherhood as a child in Heliopolis and doubtlessly absorbed many of their prayers and teachings, it is likely that he was familiar with many of Egypt's religious texts. He spoke thus:

> The Egyptian religion is the Mother of Religion. It contains in its mystic depths all religions, both exoteric and esoteric. It is the source of all beliefs. Complicated as it seems, it is, in reality quite simple. In the outer sense and common practice it is nothing more than a screen for a sacred and secret inner training. For instance, it is said to have many gods, over a thousand gods, at least one for each day three times over! But in truth, it has only one God. As proof of this let me quote from writings over thirteen centuries old."[8]

Jesus goes on to explain Egypt's beautiful and mystical theology in depth, including the belief that there is an eternal part to each of us—the soul—a belief that lay at the heart of the Egyptian religion. Their sacred texts, indeed the entire Egyptian culture, were focused on teaching the individual that, through right action, right thoughts, and right heart, we can free ourselves from the density of matter and achieve the alchemy of enlightenment.

THE ALCHEMY OF ENLIGHTENMENT

This alchemical transformation occurs in successive initiations as the ego begins to diminish and the soul awakens. Modern day Freemasonry gives us insight into this process in their three major steps of initiation: the Apprentice, the Fellow, and the Master. Each level requires years of study and several initiatory journeys. At the first level, the Apprentice must undergo initiations involving the transcendence of all four elements: air, earth, fire, and water. At the second level, the Fellow undertakes five separate journeys, at the end of which he contemplates the Blazing Star, a reference to the same Morning Star associated with both Horus and Jesus.[9] At the last stage of initiation, candidates undergo a true near-death experience to become Masters.

This journey in the earthly realm corresponds to a journey into the celestial realms. The ceilings of the pharaoh's tombs, and of every Freemason's lodge, are decorated with stars, revealing how the temple acts as a mediator between human beings and the universe.[10] Eventually, the discipline produces an alchemy of enlightenment within the subtle energy bodies—a physical transmutation that is the highest level of mastery. To accomplish this process of internal al-

FIGURE 102. The soul, or ba, traveling to the stars as a human-headed hawk. Here, the ba is connecting, via the Third Eye, with the Sun, the source of light from whence it came.

chemy, initiates must master all nine separate aspects of the self—aspects that are described in esoteric texts as subtle bodies. While most theologies name only seven subtle energy bodies, the Egyptian teachers had mastered nine. This practice essentially turned a human being into a fully activated god-man. The ultimate test lay in the adept's ability to resurrect the body after death—an initiation to which few have ever voluntarily submitted, and that even fewer have survived.

Jesus discourses at length about these nine inner bodies, for they are integral to his reasons for going to Egypt in the first place. Even with all his yogic mastery, Jesus realized that it was essential for him to perfect these last subtle energy bodies if he was to transmute his body alchemically into light and resurrect it after death. This mastery would give him the ability to appear anywhere, at anytime, to anyone, in any manner—for instance, when he appeared to Saul (Paul) on the road to Damascus, blinding him with his radiance and prompting his conversion to Jesus' path. We also have the testimony of the apostles that Jesus appeared to them after the Crucifixion, and taught them for many weeks. The Gnostic Acts of John and The Sophia of Jesus Christ also include several accounts by disciples to whom Jesus appeared as a young boy, an older man, and, finally, as a pilgrim who walked with them along the road before vanishing before their eyes.[11]

The nine bodies are organized in groups of three, corresponding roughly to the emotional, mental, and spiritual selves, each of which has its own etheric, astral, and spiritual components.

> There seem to be within each individual the ability to develop several non-physical bodies. The Ka or Double seems to be a temple for the Heart Soul when absent from its seat in the physical heart. These two, in combination, seem still to be called the Ka. This Ka has an independent existence and freedom of movement. The Khaibit or Shadow seems to reside in the Heart Soul after it has been created out of the physical group of bodies. This seems to indicate a trinity of physical-emotional souls that are one, and yet three. We also have another trinity, the Sahu or Spiritual Body which is developed out of the physical group of bodies through the emotional-mental group. This becomes in turn the temple of the Khu or spiritual Soul. Thus man in his day by day progression develops independent and powerful non-physical bodies that move about under some sort of mysterious control.[12]

The great Indian sage Paramahansa Yogananda also wrote about this process of enlightenment, touching briefly on the soul's three natures (physical, emotional, and mental) and the seven subtle energy bodies that control them:

The physical body, with which man so affectionately and tenaciously identifies himself, is little more than inert matter, a clod of earthly minerals and chemicals made up of gross atoms. The physical body receives all enlightening energy and powers from an inner radiant astral body of lifetrons. The astral body, in turn, is empowered by a causal body of pure consciousness, consisting of all of the ideational principles that structure and maintain the astral and physical bodily instruments employed by the soul to interact with God's creation. The three bodies are tied together and work as one by knotting of life force and consciousness in seen spiritual cerebrospinal centers. . . . In its residency the triune body, the soul, takes on the limitations of confinement and becomes the pseudo-soul, or ego.[13]

Yogananda's understanding reflects a sacred teaching from Thoth:

I am Yesterday and Tomorrow; I was forever and forever will be. I have the power to be born a second time. I am the radiant, hidden soul which creates the gods and gives vital essence to the divine beings hidden in the Underworld [the tomb of flesh], in Amente [the Room of the gods] and in heaven [the Place of Radiant Beings]; I am the Lord of those who are risen out of the flesh; the Master who comes forth out of the darkness of the tomb. I work for all the bodies, and we travel on joining hands, each to each.[14]

From this, we realize that, while each subtle body must be awakened individually, they also must be joined in order to journey into the higher worlds. Yogananda continues:

The flow of the life force and consciousness outward through the spine and nerves causes man to perceive and appreciate sensory phenomena only. As attention is the conductor of man's life currents, and consciousness, persons who indulge the sense of touch, smell, taste, sound, and sight find the searchlights of their life force and consciousness concentrated on matter. But when, by self-mastery in meditation, the attention is focused steadily on the center of divine perception at the point between the eyebrows, the searchlights of life force and consciousness are reversed. Withdrawing from the senses, they reveal the light of the spiritual eye.

Through this eye of omnipresence the devotee enters into the realms of divine consciousness.[15]

Only those who had gained knowledge through the tutelage of the masters knew how to awaken these subtle energy bodies. Once the schools that held this sacred wisdom were destroyed, the true methods of spiritual ascension, physical or ethereal, went underground. Today, we are just beginning to reconstruct this path. Fortunately, the Egyptian and Indian sages left clues as to how it can be done.

AWAKENING THE EYE OF RE

The *Egyptian Book of the Dead*, also known as the *Per Em Heru*, meaning the House of Horus, and *The Book of Coming Forth into the Light*, gives us many clues about the process of spiritual ascension.[16] We know that the mission of the deceased soul was to travel through the Duat, "the way of the stars," and to become a Sun—or, more accurately, to become a fully enlightened being.[17] The Sun was a symbol of the great light of God. In a painting from the tomb of Queen Nefertiri, the wife of Ramses II, we see Osiris disguised as Khnum, the ram-headed creator god, who spins out our destiny on the potter's wheel of life. Above Osiris's crown chakra sits a Sun, telling us that he has now joined with Ra, the solar emanation of God.[18] Yet Osiris retains his individuality even though he has become one with the inner light. On the reverse of this painting are the mystical words: "It is Re [Ra] who rests in Osiris; it is Osiris who rests in Re [Ra] . . . [this is a' Secret, [a] Mystery, it is Re, it is Osiris."

These mysterious words refer to the personal self that is able to merge with the cosmic self by dying and being reborn into the light. This explains how the soul can come to identify with the gods who are the "very limbs of God;" and how Jesus could make seemingly outrageous statements like: "I was before Abraham."[19] He was speaking, not from his mortal self, but from the unbroken consciousness of God awareness.

The Sun and the Moon are the primary icons for this inner alchemy, symbolizing our conscious and subconscious natures. The Sun was called the Right Eye of Horus, the conscious mind. "[R]ecovery of this Eye represents, for man, the victory over all negative powers and the enrichment of his own consciousness, the ultimate goal of existence."[20] The Moon, or the Left Eye of Horus, represents the intuitive, the feminine, the more spiritually attuned aspects of a person. In kundalini yoga, the two meridians that run up the spine, the *ida* and *pingala*, represent the male and female polarities. By merging these two at

FIGURE 103. Khnum, the god who spun out destiny on the potter's wheel of life, flanked by Isis and Nephthys. In this image, we know it is really the Osirian or Christed nature that is being discussed, for on the other side of the wall is a duplicate image of Osiris. From the Valley of the Queens, Thebes, Eighteenth Dynasty, 1550 B.C.E.

the Third Eye, located at the center of the forehead, we can fully activate their higher subtle energy bodies.

Yogananda sheds further light on this:

> By the right method of meditation and devotion, with the eyes closed and concentrated on the spiritual eye, the devotee knocks at the gates of heaven. When the eyes are focused and still, and the breath and mind are calm, a light begins to form in the forehead . . . and the tri-colored light of the spiritual eye becomes visible.

Just seeing the single eye is not enough, however. The consciousness must be led inside the spiritual eye, into another world of vaster dimension.

> In the golden halo of the spiritual eye, all creation is perceived as the vibratory light of the Holy Ghost. The blue light of Christ Consciousness is where the angels and deity agents of God's individualized powers of

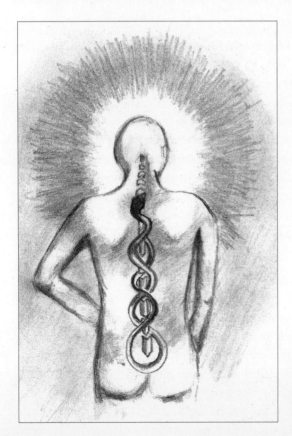

FIGURE 104. The double serpents moving up the spine, known to yoga practitioners as the *Ida* and *Pingala*.

creation, preservation, and dissolution abide, as well as the most highly evolved saints. Through the white light of the spiritual eye, the devotee enters Cosmic Consciousness; he ascends unto God the Father.[21]

The merger of these polarities reminds us of Jesus' words in the Gospel of Thomas: "When you make the two into One, and you make the inner as the outer, and the outer as the inner, and the above as the below, so that you will make the male and the female into a single one, in order that the male is not made male, nor the female made female; when you make eyes into an eye . . . then you shall enter the Kingdom."[22]

In Egypt, there were many funerary texts that addressed various aspects of this inner journey, each providing clues to a roadmap of the cosmos.[23] By far, the best known of these is the *Egyptian Book of the Dead*, which has been called the Bible of ancient Egypt. Conservative estimates date parts of this book to 4000 B.C.[24] This book is also known as the *Book of the Master of the Hidden Places*, a reference to its importance as a guide to the Duat and a roadmap to consciousness. It is

> . . . a secret manual of initiation from the mysterious First Times [the Zep Tepi] and describes a series of procedures and passwords to be spoken that purposely have two distinct levels of meaning, one spiritual and the other physical. The "Hidden Places" mentioned in the original title are particular underground chambers at the Giza complex and are described allegorically as mystical places in the abode of heaven. Underlying descriptions given in the Book of the Dead are the outline of an original priestly ritual used in Egyptian temples aeons ago. . . . Therefore, the *Book of the Dead* records the earthly method used in discovering heavenly mysteries of the hereafter, concealed in words and symbols that themselves were hidden in tombs of the deceased.[25]

The *Egyptian Book of the Dead* describes a complicated system of chambers, halls, temples, passageways, and gates through which Jesus would have passed in an underground complex that also represented the heavenly journey through the twelve divisions of the Duat. It includes descriptions of Magical prayers, incantations, and the names of guardians who protect the various gates and pylons (columns) that mark the initiate's journey. With proper training, initiates gained the power to pass through these gates and arrive at the Halls of Amente, where they came face to face with Osiris. There are also references to "those who live among the stars," and to "reaching the vault of the sky," revealing that this journey occurred on the astral or spiritual levels as well.[26] Probably the best of these descriptions appears in the famous papyrus attributed to the esteemed Chancellor Ani, a dignitary at the temples of Abydos and Thebes. Although the *Papyrus of Ani* is less than half the length of the *Book of the Dead*, its texts and illustrations are among the best preserved and illuminated of all the papyri that date from the Eighteenth Dynasty (1500 –1400 B.C.E.).[27]

COMING FORTH INTO THE DAY

The Book of Coming Forth into the Day is a translation of the Book of the Dead that describes the journey each soul must take through the body of the sky goddess Nuit into the highest heavens after life on Earth. This voyage is made in a vessel called the Boat of a Million years, a metaphor for the soul's journey through the Great Cosmic Ocean, reminding us that life on Earth is transitory, while life in the other worlds is eternal.

The soul made this journey through the Duat, accompanied by five great *neteru*, each signifying a cosmic principle that could assist it in becoming liberated. The word *Duat* means "place of morning twilight," or the region between night and day through which the soul travels to move from the blindness of physical incarnation to the illumination of the higher worlds.[28] As with everything Egyptian, these "gods" really represent aspects of our own inner faculties. Re/Ra symbolizes the light that is hidden within the soul; Thoth signifies wisdom or the proper use of thought; Ma'at represents truth, karma, and cosmic

FIGURE 105. The passage through the Duat marks the twelve hours of the night as the soul fights off Apophis, the many-headed serpent.

law; Isis symbolizes the redemptive power of love; Set represents the ego or personality.

On the journey through the Duat, the soul passes through the various gates of the solar system and arrives before the masters of wisdom in the courts of Osiris (the constellation of Orion). This journey is a metaphor for the chakras, a map that could be followed by an advanced initiate like Jesus to master the ancient science of soul travel. In the process, Jesus would have learned how to control the subtle energy bodies necessary to accomplish his physical resurrection.

Anthropologist Jeremy Naydler reveals that the first stage of this journey—finding the paths that lead from the tomb to the region of the underworld—took place in the Restau, a secret name by which the pyramid and the underground chambers below it were known.[29] The name of these chambers—also rendered as Rostau, indicating the Rose and the Tau cross—is related to the Rosicrucian Order, which derived their name from it. The cross represents the axis of space-time; the rose is the immortal soul fastened on the cross. Thus Rostau immediately signals to initiates the deeper purpose behind the Great Pyramid's construction, revealing its use as a physical-spiritual gateway to the higher worlds—a concept that lay at the core of all the Mystery Schools.

"From a spiritual perspective, what he [the initiate] goes through is not simply a series of halls but a series of states of consciousness, each of which reflects, as with the gateways and the pylons, a condition of Osiris in the cycle of his death, putrefaction, and rebirth."[30] Just as the Sun descends into darkness of night (a metaphor for death), so the soul leaves the light of day and enters the

FIGURE 106. The Rosy Cross, represented beautifully in the symbol for the Lutheran Church.

underground chambers beneath the pyramid. Thus the journey into the Rostau can be seen as a dress rehearsal for the soul's journey in the afterlife.

While passing through the Duat, we know initiates confronted the dreaded serpent Apophis, or Apepi, with his many fearsome heads. Apophis was the great adversary, the personification of our own worst fears, doubts, and addictions, and of the habits we have to subdue before we can enter heaven. Externalized as a monstrous beast with many heads, Apophis represented all the qualities of lust, anger, greed, vanity, and desire that keep our souls bound to the wheel of matter. Here, initiates struggled with their inner demons, hoping to defeat these negative attributes and emerge as a new Horus, a conscious being of light.

As the boat travels through the Duat, Set battles with Apophis. In the sixth hour of the night, just when all hope seems lost, the battle shifts, as Osiris, lord of light, the Christed One, reveals that it can only be won when the ego finally surrenders to the higher self. In the Egyptian texts, it is at this point that initiates stand within the coils of the serpent, pulling the flow of their spiraling kundalini up through their spines, and begin the task of regeneration. Gerald Benedict explains that the kundalini, "is the vital force empowering all human growth and development . . . the great evolutionary force, making of each body and its occupant, a potentially powerful source of solar wisdom."[31] Thus, the twelve-hour journey becomes a roadmap for the soul's ascension into the regions of celestial space, and the journey of consciousness through the various chakras of the body. The process of awakening these currents (the serpents) and pulling the energy up the spine (the Tree of Life) is also represented by the *djed*, or spine of Osiris.

The *Book of the Dead* describes this journey as a metaphor for the stages of transformation in the awakening of a more advanced twelve-chakra system. While the early hours are spent in raising the kundalini energy through the lower chakras, in the fifth hour (the heart chakra), "the Great Neter Osiris arrives."[32] Then the tide of the battle turns and the soul begins the process of dying to its old life and withdrawing into a cocoon like a caterpillar. Eventually, through surrender of the heart to this higher power (the Christ), initiates transform into butterflies. Note that there is a great emphasis placed on the heart throughout this journey, including the final ceremony, called the Weighing of the Heart in the Halls of Amente.

When the soul finally arrives at the sixth pylon, it meets "He Who Has Been Joined Together"—a clear reference to Osiris, whose body was torn into fourteen pieces and scattered across Egypt. Since Isis reassembled, or re-membered,

Osiris through the love of the Divine Mother, it is she who appears at the next pylon, coming to meet her beloved.[33] (It is significant that, when the digits of the number fourteen are added together—rejoined—their sum is five, the number of love in numerology.) By the eighth hour, the deceased soul has been joined by four ram-headed beings—representing the four Sons of Horus, or four great Kumaras, and the four stages of the soul's metamorphosis.

Initiates then enter four successive stages of evolution: the caterpillar stage, a metaphor for our tedious lives as we crawl about from leaf to leaf, never knowing there is a larger universe; the larvae stage, in which we give up the old life and let go of what no longer works; the cocoon stage, the gestation deep within the cave where we are alchemically reshaped into a purer, higher state of being; and the butterfly stage, in which we spread our wings and soar, opening our inner senses to a brave new world. Only after this stage is the "godlike form" (the Christed self) raised up at the ninth pylon, where the feeble one (the new Osiris) is clothed. The doorkeeper of this pylon is called "He Who makes Himself," an allusion to the rebirth of the soul in the image of the divine.[34]

In the tenth stage, Lucie Lamy writes:

> . . . the scarab pushes his oval "cocoon" [the egg-shaped auric field], while the birth of the left and right eyes, the moon and the sun, are announced. This means that the two polarized currents within the human nervous system have finally merged in the forehead, birthing the inner sight. The Left Eye emerges from between entwined serpents and the Right Eye from the symbol for divinity. . . . The Eleventh Hour shows a small human figure seated on a serpent, taking off for the stars, but the two-headed figures alone seem to inform us that in this place the union of opposites is realized.[35]

This union of the two kundalini circuits traveling up the spine activates the inner sight. Jesus describes this when he speaks about "the two eyes" becoming one.[36] Finally, in the twelfth hour, the Great Neter—a being of immense light often described by those who have near-death experiences—arrives.[37] In this stage, the inner Christ that lies dormant within us all awakens.

The human spine is composed of five distinct sections: the coccyx, sacral, lumbar, thoracic, and cervical vertebrae. These sections are separated by four demarcations or "gateways," not unlike those spoken of in the *Egyptian Book of the Dead*.[38] There are thirty-two vertebrae in the human spine, corresponding to the ladder of thirty-three steps described in many ancient texts—the thirty-third step being the pineal gland connected to inner sight and the crown chakra.[39] The four spinal "gateways" are connected to alchemical processes, once taught to initiates the world over, that facilitate out-of-body states like the ones Jesus, or any accomplished adept, used to interact with the higher-dimensional levels at will.

While all this may appear to be some strange, far-fetched fable, in truth, it is the description of a powerful alchemical process that most of us know nothing about today, steeped as we are in the materialistic traditions of our age. It is a process described by the Christian expression "born again"—an enlightenment that can only occur when we allow our "little selves" to die and transform, merging with the light of our Higher Self to be reborn. When all nine subtle energy bodies are linked together, moving like an undulating serpent along the spine, initiates become the new Horus/Osiris, a transformation of "the densest matter into the most volatile and subtle energy."[40] Jesus describes this conscious return to an original state of perfection when he says: "Therefore My Father loves Me, because I lay down my life that I may take it again. No one takes it from Me, but I lay it down of Myself. I have power to lay it down and I have power to take it up again. This command I have received from My Father" (John 10:17–18).

In *The Nine Faces of Christ*, Jesus responds to the master of the Great White Brotherhood with the profound words of Thoth. Within them, we hear an echo of the path he chose to walk:

> Oh, Gods, you are in me, and I in you. Your attributes are my attributes. My bodies are the bodies of the god Khepri, the ever-recreating self. . . . I am the God made of flesh, and the workers of iniquity shall never destroy my radiant being. I am the first born God of Primeval Matter; that is to say, I am the Radiant Soul; I have become the Soul of God, everlasting. My physical self has been the seed-ground of eternity. My Being is now everlasting. I have become the Lord of Time and King of Eternity. I have become Master of my source of life, and I can easily pass through the abyss which separates earth from heaven."[41]

CHAPTER 29

Between the Paws
of the Sphinx

Someday what we thought was myth will be found to contain the true
history of the past, while what we have always regarded as history will be
relegated to a myth of our own making.[1]

—Gerald Massey, *The Egyptian Book of the Dead* and the
Ancient Mysteries of Amenta

Two enigmatic structures mark the Giza plateau as the geomantic center of the
world: the inscrutable Sphinx and the monumental temple known as the Great
Pyramid. The origins of both these monuments are shrouded in mystery even
5000 years after they entered the accounts of history. Many speculate that their
true origins lie in the forgotten prehistory of our misty past. We know, however,
that Jesus, as a high initiate of the Egyptian Mysteries, would have undergone
his major initiations here.

The Great Pyramid sits at the exact geographic center of the earth—30
degrees north by 31 degrees east. It also lies at the exact center of the geomagnetic ley lines that cover the globe.[2] Thus, it is, quite literally the *omphalos*, or
navel, of the Earth. This placement cannot have been arbitrary, as many astute
minds have pointed out. And the sophisticated mathematics needed to determine this placement could not have been calculated by primitive minds—a fact
that strongly suggests that the culture behind the Great Pyramid's design was
far more sophisticated than conservative academics care to admit.

The Great Pyramid encompasses 13 acres—an interesting number because
of its solar associations.[3] The word "pyramid" itself derives from the roots *pyro*

and *mid*, and thus means "fire at the middle." This etymology supports recent theories posed by engineers and physicists that the Great Pyramid was originally designed as some type of power plant. At an esoteric level, however, the "fire" may have been the inner light and the discovery of our eternal souls. What is clear is that, to the Egyptian sages, this vast manmade mountain represented the apex of enlightenment, since one of its most ancient names was Khut, meaning "the Light."[4]

Legend tells us that the pyramid was once covered in a smooth, white limestone casing that bore formulas and ciphers related to mathematics, astronomy, astrology, and physics.[5] Tony Bushby writes: "An Eighth Century record said that [on] the external lining [there was]. . . . a radiant segment of seven horizontal bands of spectrum colors [that] ran unbroken around the uppermost levels of the structure. Engraved vertically down the bands of color were seven curious inscriptions, positioned in the center of the top band and dropping down each face to the bottom or seventh band. . . ."[6] These seven horizontal lines represent the seven multi-dimensional planes discussed in earlier chapters. A tenth-century Arabian writer describes the images inscribed on its face like this:

> On the Eastern or Great Pyramid, built by the ancients, the celestial
> spheres were inscribed, likewise the positions of the stars and their circles,
> together with the history and chronicles of past times, of that which is to
> come, and of every future event. Also one may find there the fixed stars
> and what comes about in their progression from one epoch to another . . .
> and images made of their forefathers' creations.[7]

At even the most superficial level, the Great Pyramid represents core hermetic concepts. It is comprised of four visible three-sided surfaces, yielding the number twelve. Its apex brings the number to thirteen, the eternal number of the Sun. Its capstone, now missing, is believed to have been the famous benben stone[8] a huge pyramidion of electrum, an ancient metal said to have been composed of both silver and gold—an alloy that modern science has not been able to duplicate.[9] As we know, it was referred to as Rostau, a word formed from the rose and the Tau, reflecting the esoteric principles required to release the rose of the spirit-heart from the density of the material world.[10]

The pyramid itself is precisely oriented to the four directions, with its entrance on the north face of the monument. Its guardian, the Sphinx, faces east, gazing forever at the rising Sun, and is precisely aligned with the spring and autumn equinoxes, thus greeting the coming age. The Sphinx was known as the

Figure 107. The Sphinx, guardian of the Great Pyramid. Illustrated by Sylvia Laurens.

guardian of Rostau—the two-sided lion Aker or Akeru, the one who carried the Sun on his back.[11] Like Osiris, a god who was both living and dead, the Sphinx is also linked to the concepts of yesterday and the morning. It was the keeper of ancient secrets that would be reopened in the dawning light of consciousness, and the guardian who waited patiently for the flow of time to ripen a civilization's understanding of its secrets before it released the fount of knowledge that it protected. Thus the Sphinx has strong alignments to two critical astronomical ages: the Age of Leo and the Age of Aquarius, whose attributes can be seen in its design. And, as we know, the lion and the phoenix, another symbol for Aquarius, both have profound associations with Jesus.

One of the Sphinx's most ancient names was HU, or Huwana, a name we have already encountered in Britain to signify the god-man who sacrifices himself upon the Tree of Life.[12] This gives us an immediate clue to one of the Sphinx's most hidden mysteries. In Egypt, HU was said to be the "Creative Utterance" that allows Ma'at to exist—the Word that brings life into being, the Logos, of which both Osiris and Jesus were expressions.[13]

The Sphinx was also called Heru-Khuti, meaning "Horus of the light," as well as Ra Harmachis, which comes from the Roman historian Pliny, who wrote that the "tomb of a ruler named Harmachis that contains great treasure"

FIGURE 108A. The two lions of Aker, connected with the concepts of "yesterday" and "tomorrow," are associated with the Brotherhood of the Panthers, or the sages of enlightenment who have become one with Osiris.

FIGURE 108B. The lions of Aker, the *djed*, and the wheel of the zodiac. As if to underscore the theme of the return of certain astrological ages in order to reincarnate or return to this world, the lions face the spinning of the zodiacal wheel.

was concealed deep below the Sphinx."[14] We know that the Sphinx has been called "the Great Harmachis" since the time when the army of Horus retook the throne of Egypt more than 15,000 years before. Horus promised his followers that, if they won, he would make them the rulers of Egypt—a promise that he faithfully fulfilled.[15]

Egyptologist Wallis Budge identifies Ra/Re-Harmachis with Re-Horakhti, or Horus of the Two Horizons, revealing that the great "king" Harmachis (the Greek spelling of Hor-em-Akhet) was really Horus himself, one of the chief forms of the Sun god worshipped by the Greeks. His best-known monument, Budge claims, was the famous Sphinx of Giza.[16] West tells us that "all parties agree that [the Sphinx] is a solar symbol . . . the body of the lion symbolizes the power and might of the spiritual in its physical form; the head of the man symbolizing intelligence and consciousness, the ability to partake of divinity."[17]

The Sphinx is carved out of a single ridge of living rock 240 feet long and 66 feet high. A recent survey discovered three separate rock strata in the Sphinx: a harder rock composing the head, a softer rock composing much of the body, and a harder limestone forming the base and covering the underground hypostyle hall that is shown clearly on the stele that lies between its paws. This stele

FIGURE 109. Ra-Horakhti or Horus of the Horizon. As a candidate courageously stepped onto the path of knowledge, each initiate became a budding Horus, a symbol for the great seeker of Truth.

FIGURE 110. The stone stele of Thothmes IV between the paws of the Sphinx. On the stele is a drawing of the hypostyle hall below the monument.

was placed there by Tuthmosis IV (1401–1391 B.C.E.), a young prince from the 18th Dynasty who later became pharaoh over his favored elder brothers.[18]

The hieroglyphs on the Sphinx's chest tell how the adventurous young prince, while out hunting with his chariot, fell asleep at noon in the shadow of the Sphinx. The Sphinx, which was covered up to its neck with sand, approached him in a dream, saying:

> O my son Thothmes; I am thy father, HARMAKHIS-KHOPRI-RA-TUM;
> I bestow upon thee the sovereignty over my domain, the supremacy
> over the living; thou shalt wear its white crown and its red crown on the
> throne of Seb [Geb, the earth god], the hereditary chief. May the earth
> be thine in all its length and breadth; may the splendor of the universal
> master illumine (thee); may there come unto thee the abundance that is
> in the double land, the riches brought from every country and the long
> duration of years. Thine is my face, thine is my heart; thy heart is mine.
> Behold my actual condition that thou mayest protect all my perfect limbs.
> The sand of the desert whereon I am laid has covered me. Save me, caus-
> ing all that is in my heart to be executed. For I know that thou art my son,
> my avenger. . . approach, behold I am with thee. I am (thy father).[19]

Upon awakening, the young prince heeded the Sphinx's pleas and set men to clearing the sand away from its body. He even tried to protect the Sphinx against future sandstorms by building a brick wall around it as a barrier. Then he erected a temple to the Sphinx and set a stone stele between its paws that told of his own experiences and revealed the blueprint to an underground chamber whose existence has persisted in legend. It may be that this underground chamber was the primary means by which initiates entered the subterranean temples used by the Mystery Schools. If that is true, it is certain that Jesus passed through these halls as part of his own initiation.

Despite the barrier built by the young pharaoh, the Sphinx was soon covered by the sands again, and we know that is was reclaimed by the Sahara a total of seven times. When it was uncovered in 500 B.C.E., workmen discovered that it had pointed brass claws large enough to sit upon. Until the mid 1700s, it had worn carved images of stone wings folded along its back and sides, like the smaller lion sphinxes found at the pyramid of Saqqara.[20]

While some traditional Egyptologists speculate that both the Sphinx and the Great Pyramid were built by Chephren, this is clearly impossible. In the 19th century, French Egyptologist August Mariette discovered an inventory stele on the Giza plateau that revealed that Chepren's predecessor and older brother, Cheops (also known as Khufu), had ordered a temple built alongside the Sphinx; this means the Sphinx must have predated Chephren's reign.[21] Egyptologist Gerald Massey places the birth of the Sphinx some 13,000 years ago, based on his research into the Egyptians' use of astronomy and mathematics.[22] Whatever its date of origin, the cat-like monument has been regarded throughout its history as a symbol of guardianship and protection. Doubtless, our modern custom of placing lion statues before entryways was inspired by this symbolism. Iamblichus writes that the entrance to the Sphinx:

> . . . may still be traced between the forelegs of the crouching colossus.
> It was formerly closed by a bronze gate whose secret spring would be
> operated only by the Magi. It was guarded by public respect, and a sort
> of religious fear maintained its inviolability better than armed protection
> would have done.[23]

Hidden Chambers and Secret Passages

Herodotus writes, in his second volume of the Histories, about a visit to a vast subterranean complex hidden below the Giza plateau. He was told by the Egyptian priests that the underground chambers and passages "connected this pyramid with the pyramids at Memphis [Giza]."[24] The labyrinth had:

... twelve covered courts, six in a row facing north, six south, the gates of the one range exactly fronting the gates of the other, with a continuous wall around the outside of the whole. Inside, the building is of two stories and contains three thousand rooms of which half are underground, and the other half directly above them ... [T]he upper rooms, I did actually see, and it is hard to believe that they are the work of men; the baffling and intricate passages from room to room and from court to court were an endless wonder to me, as we passed from a courtyard into rooms, from rooms into galleries, from galleries into more rooms and thence into yet more courtyards.

The labyrinth, he tells us, had 3000 rooms and twelve separate palaces, echoing the same solar geometry known throughout all the Mystery Schools.

The roof of every chamber, courtyard, and gallery is, like the walls, of stone. The walls are covered with carved figures, and each court is exqui-sitely built of white marble and surrounded by a colonnade. Near the cor-ner where the labyrinth ends there is a pyramid, two hundred forty feet in height, with great carved figures of animals on it and an underground passage by which it can be entered.[25]

Iamblichus confirms this report:

In the belly of the Sphinx were cut out galleries leading to the subterra-nean part of the Great Pyramid. These galleries were so artfully criss-crossed along their course to the Pyramid that, in setting forth into the passage without a guide throughout this network, one inevitably returned to the starting point.[26]

Perhaps these galleries made up the first of the world's great labyrinths. West writes: "Scholars . . . have long maintained that the system of passages and chambers in the Great Pyramid served as centers for initiation ceremonies and the performance of the sacred mysteries."[27] Crantor, a third-century B.C.E. Greek philosopher and initiate also tells us about the underground pillars lin-ing the access ways beneath the Sphinx.

A seismic survey in 1993 confirmed the existence of chambers underneath the Sphinx and suggests that Herodotus' description may reveal only the tip of the iceberg. Egyptians validated that survey with another discovery in 1994: "Workers repairing the ailing Sphinx have discovered an ancient passage lead-

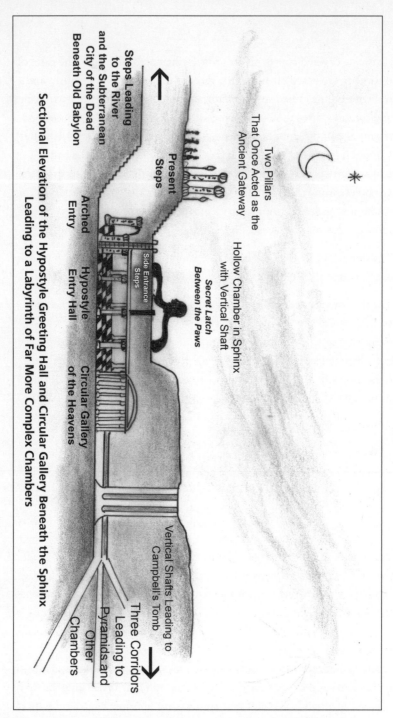

FIGURE 111. Below the Sphinx was the Hall of Greeting, from which, initiates tell us, branched countless halls and labyrinths. At the end of the long rectangular chamber was a circular Domed Hall, doubtless dedicated to the sacred movements of the zodiac.

ing deep into the body of the mysterious monument."[28] Tony Bushby tells us that this particular tunnel burrows into the northern side of the Sphinx, about halfway between the Sphinx's outstretched paws and its tail.[29] The Giza Antiquities Chief refused to remove the stones blocking the entrance, a strange decision in light of the amazing historical, spiritual, and archaeological treasures that might have been revealed.

The Rosicrucian and Masonic orders have long claimed to know of underground entrances to the Great Pyramid. In the 1400s, Rosicrucian founder, Christian Rosenkreuz, claimed to have penetrated "a secret chamber beneath the ground" and to have discovered a hidden library of books.[30] Subsequently, he constructed detailed maps of radiating underground corridors that connected the hall below the Sphinx to all the pyramids on the Giza plateau.[31]

Seismographic and ground-penetrating radar (GPR) have verified these claims, identifying twenty-seven unexcavated sites in geographical locations as diverse as Luxor's east bank, Saqqara, Dashur, Abu Rawash, and the Giza plateau.[32] Bushby writes: "The printouts of the Giza area show an almost incomprehensible mass of net-like tunnels and chambers crisscrossing the area, intersecting and entwining each other like latticework, extending out across the entire plateau."[33] West shares seismographic evidence produced by highly respected geophysicist Thomas L. Dobecki in his appendix to *The Traveler's Key to Ancient Egypt*:

> Dobecki's seismographs produced subsurface weathering profiles that corroborate our earlier dating for the Sphinx. More dramatically, the seismographs revealed several underground cavities or voids in the immediate Sphinx area. Their regular shapes and/or their strategic placing made it difficult to ascribe these [chambers] as naturally occurring geological voids. Most interesting was a large rectangular space some 12 x 15 meters in area, and 5 meters below the surface, between the paws of the Sphinx. That's roughly 36 x 45 feet in dimension, located some 15 feet beneath the sands of the Giza plateau.[34]

Certainly in the ancient world, initiates, Jesus among them, would have known of these underground chambers, whose secrets they were sworn to protect.

The City of the Ancients

Details about the subterranean city at Giza and the initiatic rites linked to the Giza plateau are buried deep in the Mystery tradition. According to that tradition, the true access to the temples beneath the Great Pyramid, once the entrance for all great initiations, lies between the paws of the Sphinx. In earlier centuries there were two upright columns at ground level approaching the Sphinx, through which initiates passed to begin the ritual. Entering through the secret gate between the Sphinx's paws, initiates descended a long set of stairs and entered a sizeable ante-chamber that contained two giant statues of Anubis, the *neter* known as the "Opener of the Ways." Behind this chamber was a large rectangular hypostyle hall with many columns, and behind this, another chamber, this one circular and surrounded with twelve large columns that reflected the same solar symbology we have seen before. This placed initiates in the middle as the Sun, appropriate for those who sought to become the "Son of God," the emerging Horus, or a follower of truth.

FIGURE 112. The hypostyle hall, flanked by twin statues of Anubis. Initiates dressed in white were taken by the priests between the pillars of knowledge into the secret chambers below. Illustrated by Sylvia Laurens.

From these two halls, many corridors branched off to a variety of temples, chambers, sanctuaries, and shrines, each used for specific initiatory rites. Three of these chambers were well known—the King and Queen's Chambers, and the pit. These symbolize the three levels of consciousness found in the celestial world, the physical world, and the Underworld. But in 1935, researchers discovered more extensive subterranean chambers below the plateau. The leader of this investigation, Dr. Selim Hassan, a Professor of Archaeology at the University of Cairo, later became the deputy of the Egyptian Archaeology Department, the first Egyptian to hold this post.[35] Dr. Hassan wrote extensively of his discoveries:

We have discovered a subway used by the ancient Egyptians of 5000 years ago. It passes beneath the causeway leading between the second Pyramid and the Sphinx. It provides a means of passing under the causeway from the Cheops Pyramid to the Pyramid of Chephen. From this subway, we have unearthed a series of shafts leading down more than 125 feet, with roomy courts and side chambers.[36]

The "subway" and its apartments were carved out of solid limestone bedrock, much as Herodotus reported some 2500 years before. Moreover, the archaeologists made another major discovery:

Halfway between the Sphinx and Khephren's Pyramid were four enormous vertical shafts, each about eight feet square, leading straight down through the bedrock into a passageway, and thus into a lower tomb. . . . Those four shafts ended in a large spacious room, at the center of which was another vertical shaft descending into a roomy court that was flanked with seven side chambers. Some of these chambers contained huge, sealed sarcophagi of basalt and granite—some as long as eighteen feet.[37]

The report goes on to describe other chambers below the plateau, all interconnected by secret, ornately decorated passageways. One of them, called the Chapel of Offering, was cut into a huge rock outcropping. "In the centre of the chapel are three ornate vertical pillars standing in a triangular shaped layout,"[38] Bushby reports. This three-pillar configuration, which has been used by the Freemasons in their initiation rites for over 2000 years, represents various aspects of the Trinity, a symbology that we know grew out of Egypt. The Jewish historian Josephus records something similar in Mesopotamia, speaking of a great underground temple constructed by the biblical patriarch Enoch, which consisted of nine such chambers, one of which also held three vertical columns.

Before these pillars, Enoch had placed a triangular tablet of gold bearing "the absolute name of the Deity."[39]

This three-column configuration represents the virtues of wisdom, strength, and beauty, as well as the Sun, the Moon, and the Blazing Star.[40] This is, of course, the classic trinity of the Divine Father, the Divine Mother, and the luminous child who brings light into the world. Bushby contends: "These pillars are highly significant points in this study, for their existence is recorded in the Bible. The conclusion is that the initiated Torah writer, Ezra, writing in 397 B.C.E., knew the subterranean layout of passages and chambers at Giza before he [ever] wrote the Torah."[41]

In addition to many other temples, chambers, and passageways, researchers also found an anteroom of initiation at the upper end of a sloping passage, cut deep within the rock on the northwest side of the Chamber of Offering, but higher up and closer to the Great Pyramid.[42] It held an enormous, twelve-foot-long white sarcophagus and its walls were sculpted with lotuses, a symbol of Creation and the opening of the Cosmic Egg.[43] Bushby tells us that, in 1904, Sir William Petrie discovered these same lotus-flower designs at the remains of an enormous temple atop Mount Sinai, or Mount Horeb, the very mountain where legend tells us the god Osiris was born and where, many centuries later, Moses received the Ten Commandments.[44]

Perhaps most significantly, these same researchers uncovered an enormous underground city built into the natural caverns east of the Giza plateau and the city of Cairo. This city was fed by a large underground river that ended in a one-kilometer-wide lake, described in the *Egyptian Book of the Dead* as the Lake of Fire. Nestled on the shores of this lake was an entire city, complete with streets, temples, statues, and palaces. Set into the cavern walls and ceilings were large crystalline balls that provided light with no known energy source. The city's main entrance once lay in the underground chambers of the Sphinx. But a second entrance was discovered in the underground passages of a Coptic church in old Cairo, an area once known as Old Babylon.[45] It was here, in this secret city of underground temples used by the priests of Heliopolis and Memphis, that Jesus underwent his initiations.

During this incredible expedition, researchers traveled down the river on inflatable rafts, carrying generators, supplies, and a movie camera, which recorded the journey in a documentary called *Chambers of the Deep*—a work seen only by selected private audiences. Why, you may ask, would such an incredible discovery be concealed? Because of the threat it posed to both religious and secular authorities. Yet such a discovery would be a great gift to the world,

FIGURE 113. The Chamber of Reflection, with its checker-board floor, representing the dark and the light aspects of life. The three columns in the middle represent the Divine Male and Female; above is the Star of Morning, or Horus Christed Self, approached by a stairway, or ladder to Heaven.

for it could illuminate mankind's vast cycles of evolution and inform us of the great achievements of our ancestors. This knowledge might help us remember who we are and where we came from, as well as helping us to discover where we are going by placing our civilization into a broader context.

THE CHAMBER OF REFLECTION

In the ancient traditions, the temple was the mediator between mankind and the universe, the guardian of the cycles of life, death, and rebirth. Its elaborate chambers harnessed the energy of the ley lines and opened gateways into the celestial realms. The ritual journeys from the physical world into the higher realms or the underworld that took place there meant that every aspect of the temple's construction had significance. The ceilings were often decorated with stars, and the floors and walls inlaid with complex geometric designs that represented what is seen with the eyes, as well as what lies beneath the visible world. As in the great Gothic cathedrals of the Middle Ages, some chambers were made up of three distinct courts or halls; in others, the number of the columns had purpose. Even the building materials—limestone and crystalline granite, stones that expressed the alchemical elements of fire and water—were meant to amplify the inner senses. Master Masons of the Middle Ages used similar materials for similar reasons.

The two enormous pillars that marked the temple entrance were decorated with lilies, pomegranates, and globes. Said to represent the great pillars that once stood before the temple of Hercules in Atlantis, they marked the passageway from the world of the familiar to the world of the unknown.[46] In Freemasony, these pillars are called Boaz and Joachim and signify our male and female (rational and intuitive) aspects that must be balanced.[47]

Leadbeater explains why so many Christian symbols appear to have grown out of Egyptian ritual:

> The disciple Jesus was an initiate of the Egyptian Lodge, and therefore much of the Egyptian symbolism was adopted by His followers, and was later woven into the Gospel story. . . . The ceremonies of Intitiaion used in the Great White Brotherhood of the present day [were in] the Egyptian rituals slightly different from these in form, although their essence was identically the same; for the Egyptian Lodge possessed the traditions handed down from the initiates of Atlantis, which was somewhat modified in later days, to suit the needs of the slowly evolving humanity of the Aryan race.[48]

He goes on to describe the three major initiations of the ancient Egyptians, the details of which come down to us from the *Crata Repoa*.[49] These were the Birth of Horus, Baptism, and Transfiguration at the Gate of Death, corresponding to the Christian Nativity, Baptism, and Passion (Resurrection) of Christ. While, in Egypt, these initiations focused on Horus or Osiris, similarities between them and Jesus are, as we have seen, striking: Horus, like Jesus, was born of a virgin mother, adored by wise men and shepherds at his birth, and heralded by angelic hosts. The Eastern Star shone forth at his nativity, thus we read in the *Egyptian Book of the Dead*: "Horus is the Solar Mount, the Star of Dawn."[50] Likewise, Horus had to flee the tyranny of his uncle, Set, just as Jesus fled from Herod.

In the Chamber of Reflection, a solitary cave lit by a single candle, beginning initiates usually underwent a preparatory phase that included circumcision, eating a balanced diet of fish and vegetables, and several months of meditation.[51] This time of reflection was deeply important in the process of transformation, for it represented the larvae phase, in which aspirants were encouraged to contemplate their lives and then write a philosophical will—a document in which they reviewed their lives to date and considered what they would leave behind as a legacy.[52] This deep self-reflection, which took place in a symbolic cave—an environment that had been used for centuries to foster spiritual enlightenment—was the beginning stage of the cocoon from which, many years later, aspirants emerged as butterflies. In this Chamber of Reflection, the Freemasons tell us, was a mural, painted white on a black background, with the Latin inscription: *vistita interiora terrae, rectificando invenies occultam lapidem*, which means: "Visit the center of the earth and by rectifying, you shall find the hidden stone."[53] This may well have been the lost Word or Shu stone/tone discussed earlier, the secret word of creation. At its most basic level, the chamber, or cave, represents the womb of the Mother, the place before birth, an image that appears in the legends of many world saviors, who are said to have emerged from the primoridal Egg. Both Mithra and Jesus were said to have been born in such a place.

Behold the Drama of Initiation

When Jesus came to the temple, priests knew he was already an advanced initiate. His reputation had preceded him, and the leading sages of the world had already gathered, in anticipation of his arrival. Jesus would have been examined as described in *The Nine Faces of Christ*, and then conducted to a gallery surrounded by the columns of Thoth.[54] A Pastophoris would then lead him to the Guardian of the Gate to the deeper chambers, at which he would knock and then pass through to begin his trials. The drama might have gone something like this.

Jesus is bathed, dressed in white, and then taken into the hypostyle hall below the Sphinx for the first initation, which focuses on the opening of the heart. Standing between the three columns that symbolize wisdom, knowledge, and beauty, and amid the symbols of the Sun, the Moon, and the Blazing Star, he kneels and takes an oath not to reveal to the uninitiated the secrets that he learns. A ladder is placed between the three columns to represent the seven planes of the universe and an allegorical figure with eight doors appears, representing the inner doorways or gates he must open to ascend the Tree of Life.[55] The teachings of reincarnation, metempsychosis, and the Tree of Life are revealed, illuminating how each lifetime builds upon another and how our actions in this life directly affect our advancement into heaven.[56]

Jesus then undergoes a series of tests presenting him with the temptations of lust, fear, and gluttony. He successfully resists these vices, is purified through baptism, and experiences a great expansion of his intellectual faculties. Then he is instructed in the sciences of geometry, architecture, mathematics, meteorology, anatomy, the healing arts, and compounding medicines.[57] He is also trained in the hermetic language of symbols and the common heiroglyphic writing, and taught the story of the fall of the human race. Ultimately, through this training, he wins the caduceus staff of Thoth, signifying his mastery of thought.

Jesus is then taken down into the most subterranean chambers, which are filled with an assortment of coffins and people preparing corpses. At the center of the vestibule is the white coffin of Osiris, appearing to bear traces of fresh blood. He is asked whether he took part in the murder of Osiris, which he denies, and is conducted to a hall by priests dressed in black. In the midst of these priests is a king who offers him a golden crown, signifying glory in the world of men. He rejects this crown, throws it down, and tramples it underfoot—an action that prefigures the biblical temptation in the desert, where Satan offers Jesus the kingship of the world, and he refuses.

After this, the worldly king ceremonially hits Jesus on the head, and he is overpowered by the other players in this cosmic drama. They envelop him in mummy wrappings and transport him through a door over which is written "Sanctuary of the Spirits." As the door opens, flashes of lightening are seen and claps of thunder heard, and Jesus finds himself surrounded by fire as he descends into the subterranean world of Pluto, the lord of the dead. There, he is instructed in the ways in which he has broken karmic law and is condemned to wander in the subterranean galleries until he can complete his next level of training. During the next eighteen months, he is trained in many of the seven liberal arts, giving him a solid foundation in the sciences of the universe. He is also trained in oration and taught a higher level of the hiero-grammatical alphabet.[58]

Jesus is now ready for the higher levels of initiation appropriate to advanced candidates. Because of his already advanced abilities, the focus for Jesus here is on the full activation of his nine subtle energy bodies, the culmination of which will allow him to raise a complete spiritual double that is known within esoteric teachings as a Radiant Self. Jesus himself tells us of these studies:

> The Three Wise Men, my beloved Father, Ramanchana, and the Jaguar Priest were assigned to the staff of my college of teachers in the Temple of Horus. But Skakus was the master teacher, and I was not altogether pleased. Skakus was like a hornet to my consciousness—he stung and prickled me.

Skakus lectures Jesus on the nature of God and then tells him:

> "You are here to learn to transmute your flesh into godly and radiant energy, and then back to perfect flesh again. My job is to see that you are brought to that point. You can hate me, you can despise me, but unless you leave this island and break your contract with the Brotherhood, you cannot escape me."[59]

Jesus tells us how Skakus kept him at the exercise.

> Control of the breath was his subject for almost all of the five years. During the first five months I was drilled endlessly upon the exercises which relaxed the cell-body. These were based upon control of the breath.

The training Skakus gives Jesus covers every aspect of raising the Radiant Self out of the flesh. Starting with breath and physical relaxation, it goes into mental and emotional development and control, and then into the spiritual exercises. Finally, he is questioned on what he has learned.

"Now tell me, Boy, how does God come to be in a man?"

The sudden question catches him off guard and he answers: "Why, by Divine Grace." To which Skakus replies:

> "True, partly, but if by Divine Grace only, what value all this work we are doing? Eh, Boy? It is true that man is born of both physical and divine essence. The Divine Central Atom of his being is given him at his birth

as the seed of his Godhood. But it is up to man to make that seed flourish and ripen. Divinity comes not by Grace alone, but by the development of the God-self within to reach, touch, and be absorbed in the Eternal Energy which is God. Your development of Divinity is not up to God, it is up to you. He gave you the seed. You must grow the fruit."[60]

Skakus teaches Jesus the mastery of his inner bodies, with the final goal of ac-tivating his Sahu, or spiritual body, and the two additional bodies associated with it. In the final degree of initiation, Jesus suffers the utmost loneliness and pain as he passes through the Valley of the Shadow of Death and then returns, learning to resurrect himself in the physical body.[61]

Jesus submits himself voluntarily to a near-death experience, laying him-self upon a cross with a hollowed-out trench that has been created specifically to support his body. His arms are lightly bound with cords, with the ends left loose to symbolize the voluntary nature of his sacrifice. He passes into trance, deliber-ately moving with full consciousness into the higher worlds. The priests carry this immense cross down into the subterranean vaults and place it in an enormous sarcophagus. There, Jesus remains for three days and three nights, until, on the morning of the fourth day, he is finally raised from the dead and carried out of the sepulcher at dawn on the eastern side of the Great Pyramid, where he, like the Sphinx, catches the first rays of the Sun. And thus, he becomes the HU-man, the solar man, half lion of God, half human.

The lessons Jesus learned through his initiation into the Egyptian Mysteries taught him how to die, go into the other worlds, and return to reanimate his physical body through the use of his Radiant Self. They taught him how to transform his physical appearance and to appear and disappear at will.

He learned to travel through the astral, causal, mental, and spiritual planes. He met many different spirits, including those who had died, but remained fettered to their worldly passions. Eventually, he arrived at the Nirvanic planes of Absolute Union, thus becoming one with the supreme Godhead.[62] When he returned to his body, his mission was clear: he had become one with the Father/Mother God, and he was pledged to uplift the world. Committed to the awakening of all beings everywhere, Jesus was now free to heal, teach, and lead both the living and the dead toward the highest light. And so the drama of initiation prepared Jesus for his Crucifixion and for the events that followed his resurrection.

In today's world of science, technology, and increasing cynicism, many have tried to rationalize the miracles of Jesus' life. Did he really walk on water?

Did he really control the winds and heal the sick? Was raising someone from the dead just a metaphor for bringing them back from excommunication, or was he really bringing Lazarus back to life? These are sincere questions, posed by honest researchers. But we will never find the answers to them until we regain contact with the knowledge of the nine inner bodies and the traditions of the Mystery Schools that taught their mastery. This is the way of the divine Purusha and the path that Jesus took.

The Path
of the Master

God is both Pure Being, the personal God to Whom we pray, Who
answers our prayers, and Who necessarily presents to us a personal face,
since we ourselves are persons—and the Impersonal Absolute, beyond
even Being itself, out of which the personal God eternally arises into Being, and into which He eternally returns, in a single motionless act.[1]

—Charles Upton, "He Is that He Is," *Parabola Magazine*

So what is the path of the master? In Jesus' case it was an expedition around
the world, mastering the highest Mysteries of his day—a journey that we have
shared over the course of this book. In the process we have visited far off lands,
uncovered the existence of a great spiritual Brotherhood that includes all races,
all creeds, and all sentient beings; we have learned the hidden language of hermetics taught to initiates around the world, the symbology of which conceals
some of the most profound wisdom of the ages. We have discovered ancient
ciphers whose deepest meanings can only be comprehended by those with the
courage to see past the surface illusions to the awe and splendor of the universe.
This journey through the language of the Mysteries reminds us of the words of
Jesus in the Gospel of Thomas: "The images are manifest to man, and the Light
that is amongst them is hidden. In the image of the light of the Father the Light
will reveal itself and His image is hidden by His light."[2] (Thomas 83:1–6).

We have discovered the deeper meanings behind such symbols as the rose,
the cross, the ankh, the trinity, the torch of illumination, and the staff of knowledge. We have encountered the enigmatic serpent entwined around the cross

of time and space, and discovered how the sacred vine and the human nervous system are connected with the Tree of Life, and the activation of our own enlightenment. We have also learned the difference between this "more enlightened" serpent and the instinctual reptilian nature, represented by the crocodile, which must be mastered on the path. We have discovered several symbols that speak of regenesis and rebirth: the snake, the phoenix, the butterfly, and the great solar lords Jesus and Osiris—all of which are linked, like the plants, to the regeneration of the world.

In our travels we have decoded the meaning of the numbers three, four, twelve, and thirteen—all connected to the celestial cycles of the zodiac and the sun, as well as to the Christ. And we have seen evidence that Jesus passed these secret teachings on to his uncle, Joseph of Arimathea, thus inspiring his early disciples to build the first Christian community in Avalon—a community based on this sacred science. We have also discovered some of the many reasons that Jesus identified himself with the sun, and why he was called "the light of the world."

Through the study of the ancient Mystery religions, we have identified keys to some of Jesus' more cryptic statements like: "Knock and the door shall be opened, seek and ye shall find" (Matthew 7:7), a reference to the keys and codes of the gates of inner knowledge; "I and my Father are one" (John 10:30), signifying the union of that personal self into the Greater Self; and "greater love hath no man than to lay down his life for his friends" (John 15:13), a role that Jesus clearly lived in full measure. And one of my own personal favorites, "So the last shall be first, and the first shall be last" (Matthew 20:6), telling us that he who is led by his ego does not advance his soul, yet he who is led by true service is honored by all the hosts of heaven.

Over the course of this journey, we have also discovered a version of history that has long been covered up by the leaders of mainstream religions who saw the sacred Mysteries as a threat to their control. While coveting the knowledge of the Mysteries for themselves, these religious leaders have largely kept it hidden from the people, much as the Pharisees of Jerusalem once did. We have discovered that for at least 5,000 years there existed a transmission of sacred knowledge far more profound than the "somatic Christianity" taught by many churches of the last 1,500 years during the Dark Ages of mankind's slumber; we have learned about a Christianity shaped more by political and social controls than the true desire to enlighten humanity. But we have also seen, over the course of this book, thousands of men and women behind the scenes who have been dedicated to awakening the human species from its sleep, and that these individuals went to great lengths to bestow wisdom on those who sought it. These were the scientists, sages, philosophers, and mystics whose arrows were pointed towards a higher truth. This ancient world of wonder, awe, and beauty knew the Divine by many different names, but behind them all was the eternal light of the Christ, epitomized in the phoenix bird.

Among our travels we have also discovered the footprints of the great solar lords Mithra, Horus, Osiris, Serapis, Thoth, and HU, each of whom belonged to an earlier age. What are we to make of such myths and legends? Are these beings real? Within the intricate matrix of their life stories, certain commonalities arise. Each, it is said, was born three days after the winter solstice, symbolically arising from the dark cave of the longest night of the year, on the fourth day, the very day when the sun begins to visibly return to our planet. Each identified himself with the sun and the light through various symbols: the lion, the leopard, the sign of Leo—all ancient ciphers for the kingly heart. All of them carried the staff of knowledge linked to the Tree of Life, marking them as the priest-kings who were the shepherds for their people. And each of them used the vine, the spiral, and the serpent as metaphors for the internal circuitry needed to ascend this Tree of Life; thus awakening the potential locked within our DNA.

THE FOUR GREAT KUMARAS

The pattern that lies behind these solar lords beings us full circle, back to the conversation of the four great Kumaras, the four sons of God mentioned in chapter one. The Vedas tell us these four Kumaras are the "deathless ones, the eternally young sons of God," and "the oldest of all living creatures . . . [who have] realized the truth of the Self."[3] Said to have been born from the Father principle Himself, Vishnu, known as Horus the Elder in ancient Egypt, they were known as the four sons of Horus, eternally young sons of the Father. Throughout this book we have seen ample evidence of their presence in the perennial wisdom of Thoth, an incarnation of Sanaka Kumara, whose role was to uplift mankind through the teachings of the Mystery Schools; Horus, or Sanandana Kumara, whose task it is to bring light to the world in times when the dark forces appear to be strongest on the planet; Sanat Kumara, the head of the Great White Brotherhood, whose role is the deployment of the forces of light through the great sages of the world; and finally Sananda Kumara, better known to us as Jesus Christ.

Sananda Kumara, or Jesus, is the expression of the *Issa ra animmana hetu*, (Issa) another name for Brahma, whose love for the world is so great that he

FIGURE 114. Jesus with the shepherd's staff is one of the most defining images of Jesus, depicting him as a shepherd king who, like Osiris, guides and protects his people.

comes into our world again and again at key moments in history. As the great solar lord Osiris, who has incarnated in human form, Sananda, or Jesus, melds both the male and the female aspects of the best of humanity. He is the rose laid upon the cross of time and space. He is HU, the god-man who saves his people. While it is not always necessary for him to be sacrificed on this cross, it seems many times that his fate is to be willing to give up his human life for the good of mankind, and in this sacrifice, he is eternally reborn.

THE JOURNEY TO AWAKENING

So what is the path of the master? It is the journey inward towards our highest selves, and the speed at which we travel is directly connected to the purity of our hearts. Kahil Gibran calls it "the cracking of the shell" that encases our old understanding, thus opening us up to a larger experience of the cosmos. Jesus, who was an enlightened being par excellence, had a pure heart from the first; he saw with clear eyes, a brilliant mind, and a sweet, discerning spirit. Yet still his mastery took a lifetime to achieve, even as he studied among the masters who had long awaited his arrival. It is clear that he chose to walk this path with full knowledge of the consequences of his sacrifice. As the returning phoenix of ancient legend, Jesus chose to publicly enact the great initiation rites of life, death, and resurrection before the entire world, laying out a template of unconditional love, service, and sacrifice that others might follow, and revealing that the eternal spirit that lives within each of us endures beyond the mortal body. Why, one might ask, would Jesus have enacted such a sacred, secret drama before the world? Jesus tells us bluntly in the Gospel of Thomas: "He who drinks from my mouth shall become as me; and I, myself will become him, and the hidden things shall be manifested"[4] (Thomas 108:1–5). In this statement Jesus reveals that within each one of us is the power to become a Christ, a divinely "anointed" HU-man being.

For each of us this journey into true humanity will take different forms. Some may find their role as a housewife or a parent, caring for a sick relative; another may be a minister, a doctor, a teacher, or a farmer. Yet another may be a philanthropist, a cook, an environmentalist, or a fireman. Some souls discover the wonder of God through sciences, mathematics, poetry, art, or music. Others commit to lives of service through writing, healing, or the deeper study of the mind. Yet each of these noble paths is but a shadow of the inner journey we are all traveling towards a higher truth. Where does this truth lead us? What is the landscape of its form?

FIGURE 115. This image from the *Egyptian Book of the Dead* (or *Book of Coming Forth into the Light*) depicts the Weighing of the Heart in the Halls of Amente—a ceremony in which the deceased's heart is weighed against the Feather of Truth. The hearts of those who have lived a good life are "light as a feather." The hearts of those who have not are "heavy or hard." Those who are "heavy of heart" must reincarnate and cannot ascend. Anubis leads the deceased forward; Thoth records the results in the *Book of Life*; Horus petitions his father, Osiris, who, like Jesus, sits on the throne of Heaven. The goddesses Isis and Nephthys stand behind Osiris. Illustrated by Sylvia Laurens.

The Egyptians tell us clearly: it is the place of the purified heart, the heart that is weighed in the Halls of Amente—the Halls of Heaven. Jesus, master that he was, brought his wisdom down to just a few simple rules: "Love your neighbor as yourself," "Do unto others as you would have them do unto you," "Judge not others, lest ye yourself be judged," and, of course, "The kingdom of heaven is within you."

Afterword

The writing of this book has been, for me, a profound experience. For several years I have lived with the presence of these masters, waking and sleeping, and behind them all has been the Master Jesus. His appearance in my life, after years of working with the illuminated Horus, the Divine Mother Isis, and the profound teacher Thoth, brought a sense of order to everything. Jesus' request that I put aside my own projects and write his story was one I could not refuse, as much as I squirmed and twisted at my fate. Yet what sustained me through this process, was the memory of his presence on that fateful day when he appeared in my office—the kindness of his face, the depth of his eyes, and the knowledge that whenever I surrendered to his presence there was no conflict, only the unfolding bliss of endless light. I am reminded of the words of one of his students long ago in Qumran, who tried to describe what it was like to be in his presence:

> It's like being transported to a different realm . . . quite remarkable. . . . It makes one want to get on one's knees and weep, the energy is so beautiful. It feels like going home . . . it was such a relief that he was there. We have known him right from the start, beyond time, beyond space. It goes so deep that we can only get a glimpse of the depth, the connection that we have with him, but he also reminds us of our pain and suffering and it's all right. It feels that in his presence one can release it.

> His eyes are like bottomless pools, deeper than space. . . . They have a million things in them. He has total empathy with each of us . . . I don't

want to leave him . . . I feel he has opened my heart . . . the love which he holds for each person is just beyond us. He accepts us as we are, whether we have done right or wrong . . . there are no boundaries and limits. We keep on having to remind ourselves of who we are . . . we are part of Jesus. He came to show humanity . . . a part of ourselves we had forgotten over time.[1]

"What has it been like writing this book?" one of my friends asked me as I was in the midst of it. My eyes filled with tears. A walk of faith, I thought, a surrender into the territory of the soul.

My friend responded, "Your book is an initiation, you know." It would be my hope that it has been an initiation for you, you who journeyed with me.

Like you, I live amidst the chaotic media-driven, violent cynicism of our times. Like you, I go to work and try to make a difference in the world. And like you, I look to love and be loved in spite of the inconsistencies of human nature. But now, beneath it all, I hear a song of beauty, a call to something greater, higher, and more powerful. I know that within each of us lies the courage to choose a higher path and, as a world, to remember our own divinity. The knowledge that such solar beings exist continues to touch my soul in a way that is impossible to put into words. Rather than dispelling my faith in Jesus, this journey has only affirmed it.

Jesus, Mithra, Osiris, Thoth, Horus, Krishna, and Buddha—all were beings who incarnated in eras quite different from our own. As divine Purushas who stand outside of time, these great lords can insert themselves into the worlds of matter, returning periodically to our earth. In their respective ages, each lord brought light into the world, dispelling ignorance with wisdom, dogma with love, and trying to redeem their people from the "sin" of guilt and blame and judgment—all erroneous ways of thinking. And they always taught the wisdom of the heart. They bucked the calcified religious systems of their day, shrugged off the antiquated limits of their castes, and endured the humbling experience of being human. And they had the incredible dedication and love to grace one small, somewhat insignificant planet among the billions in our galaxy.

It is my hope that in your journey you may come to know and love them as I have, and that the path before you be lit with the beacons of wisdom, truth, and beauty.

APPENDIX

Buddha and the Christ[1]

This small sampling illustrates the many profound parallels between Buddha and Jesus—both in the way they lived their lives, and in their teachings. This makes perfect sense when we realize that both Jesus and Buddha embodied the principle of the divine Purusha.

For those unfamiliar with the terminology of Buddhist texts, there are five basic volumes of the Buddha's teachings: the Digha Nikaya, comprising the thirty-four longer discourses; the Majjhima Nikaya, which includes 152 medium-length suttas (or teachings); the Samyutta Nikaya, a group of 7762 shorter, but connected, discourses; the Anguttara Nikaya, which is a list of 9557 numerically arranged shorter suttas; and the Khuddaka Nikaya, a heterogeneous mix of sermons, doctrines, and poetry attributed to the Buddha and his disciples.

Throughout all of these, the word *Nikaya* denotes a "discourse," *Sutta* means "teachings," and *Sutra* can be translated as "hymn." The abbreviations SN, DN, MN, AN, or KN are short-hand references to these texts, and indicate which compilation of discourses the author is citing. To make matters more complicated, these various hymns, teachings, and discourses sometimes appear in more than one collection of the Buddha's teachings, so they are often referenced merely by their individual names, followed by the words *Sutra* or *Sutta* and the numbers of the chapter and the verse included, just as today we reference Bible verses simply as John 3:16. In addition, there is also a collection of the Buddha's greatest teachings called the Dhammapada, which has been compared to Jesus' "greatest hits" from the Sermon on the Mount.

TABLE 1

Comparison of Jesus' and Buddha's Sayings

Jesus' Sayings	Buddha's Sayings
"Do unto others as you would have them do unto you." Matthew 7:12	"Consider others as yourself." Dhammapada 10:1
"That God gave us everlasting life." 1 John 5:11	"Nirvana is Deathless." Dhammapada 2:21–23
"And in Him is no sin." 1 John 3:5	"Stainless, you illuminate all the worlds." SN 2.[14] Dhammika Sutta
"If anyone strikes you on the cheek, offer the other also." Luke 6:29	"If anyone should give you a blow with his hand, with stick or with knife, you should abandon any desires and utter no evil words." Majjhima Nikaya 21:6
"Do not let your hearts be troubled, and do not let them be afraid." John 14:1	"May fear and dream not conquer me." Majjhima Nikaya 6:8
"Do not store up for yourselves treasure on earth, where moth and rust consume and where thieves break in and steal; but store up for yourselves treasures in heaven, where neither moth nor rust consumes and where thieves do not break in and steal." Luke 12:33–34	"Let the wise man do righteousness: A treasure that others cannot share, which no thief can steal; a treasure which does not pass away." Khuddakapatha 8:9
"There is nothing outside a person, that by going in (to the mouth) can defile, but the things that come out are what defile." Matthew 15:11	"Stealing, deceiving, adultery; this is defilement. Not the eating of meat." Sutta Nipata 242
"This is my commandment, that you love one another as I have loved you. No one has greater love than this, to lay down one's life for one's friends." John 15:12–13	"Just as a mother would protect her only child at the risk of her own life, even so, cultivate a boundless heart towards all beings. Let your thoughts of boundless love pervade the whole world." Sutta Nipata 149–150

Jesus' Sayings	Buddha's Sayings
"Truly I tell you, if you have faith the size of a mustard seed, you will say to this mountain, 'Move from here to there,' and it will move; and nothing will be impossible for you." Matthew 17:20	"A monk who is skilled in concentration can cut the Himalayas in two." Anguttara Nikaya 6:24
"Put your sword back into its place; for all those who take up the sword will perish by the sword." Matthew 26:52	"Abandoning the taking of life, the ascetic Gautama dwells refraining from taking life, without stick or sword." Digha Nikaya 1:1–8

Jesus' Miracles	Buddha's Miracles
"Jesus cured many people of diseases, plagues and evil spirits, and had given sight to many who were blind." Luke 7: 21	"As soon as the Bodhisattva was born, the sick were cured; the hungry and thirsty were no longer oppressed by hunger and thirst. Those maddened by drink lost their obsession. The mad recovered their senses, the blind regained their sight, and the deaf could once more hear." Lalitavistra Sutra 7
"Although the doors were shut, Jesus came and stood among them." John 10:26	"He goes unhindered through a wall." Anguttara Nikaya 3:60
"When he saw that they were straining at the oars against an adverse wind, he came towards them early in the morning, walking on the sea." Mark 6:48	"He walks upon the water without parting it, as if on solid ground." Anguttara Nikaya 3:60
"He woke up and rebuked the wind, and said to the sea, 'Peace! Be still!' Then the wind ceased, and there was a dead calm." Mark 4:39	"Now at that time a great rain fell and a great flood resulted. Then the Lord made the water recede all around; and he paced up and down in the middle on dust covered ground." Vinaya, Mahavagga 1:20:16

continued

Jesus' Miracles	Buddha's Miracles
"When he had said this, as they were watching, he was lifted up, and a cloud took him out of their sight." Act 1:9	"The venerable Dabba rose from his seat, saluted the Exalted One with his right side, rose in the air and sitting cross-legged in the sky, attained the sphere of heat, and rising from it passed finally away." Udana 8:9
"And he was transfigured before them, and his clothes became dazzling white, such as no one on Earth could bleach them." Mark 9:2-3	And he said, "It is wonderful, Lord, it is marvelous how clear and bright the Lord's skin appears! It looks even brighter than the golden robes in which it is clothed." Digha Nikaya 16:4-37

The next table compares the similarities between these two masters' actions, habits, and philosophies. You will also read Buddha's references to the concept of Dhamma. Some believe that all the teachings of the Buddha can be summed up in this one word—*Dhamma*, the rule of Cosmic Law, analogous to the Egyptian Law of Ma'at, which governs the universe. That Law is as unchangeable as the rising Sun, and, like all laws of the eternal, operates with its own precision. In Jesus' teachings, it is analogous to the famous statement: "For whatever a man sows, that he shall also reap" (Galatians 6:7)—a statement of the Law of Karma, or universal return.

Dhamma is the law of righteousness that exists, not only in a man's heart, but throughout the universe. All laws of nature are an embodiment of Dhamma. If the Moon rises or the Sun sets, it is because of Dhamma, which is what makes matter act in the ways studied in physics, chemistry, zoology, botany, and astronomy. Dhamma exists in the universe, just as it exists in the heart of man. Buddha taught that, by living in harmony with Dhamma, or perfect Universal Law, we can attain Nibbana (Nirvana), Buddha's word for the ultimate liberation for all beings.[2]

TABLE 2
Comparison of Jesus' and Buddha's Lives

Jesus' Life	Buddha's Life
"Jesus the new born prince is adored and predicted by seers "from the east" who celebrate his birth." Matthew 2	"Buddha, the new born prince is adored and predicted by the seer Asita, and the gods celebrate his birth." SN 3:11 Nalaka Sutta
"And in the fourth watch of the night Jesus went unto them, walking on the sea." Matthew 14:25 "Although the doors were shut, Jesus came and stood among them." John 20:26	"He goes unimpeded through walls, ramparts, and mountains as if through space. He walks on water without sinking as if it were dry land." DN 11: Kevatta Sutta
"Philip said to Him, "Lord, show us the Father, and it is sufficient for us." Jesus said to him, "Have I been with you so long, and yet you have not known Me, Philip. He who has seen Me has seen the Father; so how can you say, 'Show us the Father?'" John 14:8–11	"He who sees the Dhamma, he sees me; he who sees me, sees the Dhamma." Kindred Sayings - III, Khandhaa-vagga, Middle Fifty, Ch 4, 87, Vakkali Sutta
"Therefore go and make disciples of all nations, baptizing them in[a] the name of the Father and of the Son and of the Holy Spirit, and teaching them to obey everything I have commanded you." Matthew 28:19.	"Go forth, oh bhikkhus [monks], for the good of the many, for the happiness of the many, out of compassion for the world, for the benefit, for the good, for the happiness of gods and men. Let not two go by one way. Preach the doctrine that is beautiful in its beginning, beautiful in its middle, and beautiful in its ending. Declare the holy life in its purity, completely both in the spirit and the letter." Mahavagga Ch 5, Vinaya Pitaka

BIBLIOGRAPHY

BOOKS AND ARTICLES

Artress, Lauren. *Walking a Sacred Path: Rediscovering the Labyrinth as a Spiritual Tool*. New York: Riverhead Books, 1995.

Baigent, Michael. *The Jesus Papers*. San Francisco: Harper San Francisco, 2006.

Barnstone, Willis. *The Other Bible*. San Francisco: Harper San Francisco, 1984.

Bauval, Robert and Adrian Gilbert. *The Orion Mystery*. New York: Three Rivers Press, 2004.

Baynes, Norman H. *"Constantine The Great and the Christian Church" (Raleigh Lecture on History, March 12, 1930)*, quoted in *Christianism*, Blavatsky, H. P., *The Voice of Silence*. Pasadena, CA: Theosophical University Press, 1992.

Benedict, Gerald. *The Mayan Prophecies for 2012*. London: Watkins Publishing, 2008.

Bennett, John G. *Gurdjieff: Making of A New World*. New York: Harper and Row, 1973.

———. *The Masters of Wisdom*. Santa Fe: Bennett Books, 1995.

Beresniak, Daniel. *Symbols of Freemasonry*. New York: Barnes & Noble Books, 2003.

Bhagavad-Gita. Translated by Barbara Stoler Miller. New York: Quality Paperback Club, a division of Bantam Doubleday Dell Publishing Group, 1998.

Borg, Marcus. *Jesus and Buddha: The Parallel Sayings*. Berkeley, CA: Ulysses Press, 1997.

Bruce-Mitford, Miranda. *The Illustrated Book of Signs and Symbols*. New York: Barnes & Noble, 2004.

Brunton, Paul. *A Search in Secret Egypt*. York Beach, ME: Samuel Weiser, 1977.

Budge, E. A. Wallis. *Osiris and the Egyptian Resurrection*. New York: Dover, 1973.

———. *The Egyptian Book of the Dead*. New York: Dover Publications, 1967.

———. *The Gods of the Egyptians*. New York: Dover Publications, 1969.

Bushby, Tony. "The Lost History of the Pyramids," from *The Secret in the Bible*, Stanford Publishing Co., Queensland, Australia: Joshua Books, 2003.

———. *The Secret in the Bible*. Stanford Publishing Co., and Joshua Books, 2003.

Caine, Mary. *The Glastonbury Zodiac: Key to the Mysteries of Britain*. Surrey, England: Kingstone Press, 1978.

Campbell, Joseph. *Masks of the Gods III*, New York: Viking Penguin Books, 1964.

Cannon, Dolores. *Jesus and the Essenes*. Bath, U.K.: Gateway Books, 1992.

Capt, E. Raymond. *The Traditions of Glastonbury*. Thousand Oaks, CA: Artisan Sales, 1983.

Cartlidge, David R. and David L. Dungan, eds. and trans. *Documents for the Study of the Gospels*. Philadelphia: Fortress Press, 1980.

Cassaro, Richard Russell. "The Osiris Connection," *Atlantis Rising Magazine*, no. 27 (May-June 2001), 42–43.

Clarke, James Freeman. *Ten Great Religions*. n.p.: Eliot C. Clarke, Project Gugenberg, 1871.

Clement of Alexandria. *Stomata (or Miscellanies)*, Andover-Harvard University Library, Edinburgh, Scotland: T. and T. Clark Publishing, 1871.

Cornfield, Gaalyah and David Noel Freedman. *The Archaeology of the Bible: Book by Book*. New York: Harper and Row, 1976.

Diogenes Laertius. *The Lives and Opinions of Eminent Philosophers*, trans. C. D. Yonge. London: Henry G. Bohn Publishers, 1853.

Dobson, Cyril C. *Did Our Lord Visit Britain as they say in Cornwall and Somerset?* 8th ed. self-published, June, 1947.

Dowling, Levi. *The Aquarian Gospel of Jesus Christ*. Santa Monica, CA: DeVorss & Co., 1972.

Dunford, Barry. *The Holy Land of Scotland: Jesus in Scotland and the Gospel of the Grail*. Glenlyon, Perthshire, Scotland: Sacred Connections, 2002.

Edersheim, Alfred. *The Life and Times of the Messiah, Book I and II*. Massachusetts: Hendrickson Publishers, originally published in 1886, reissued in 1993.

Ellis, Ralph. *Jesus, Last of the Pharaohs*. Cheshire, UK: EDFU Books, 1998.

Evans, Joan. *Magical Jewels of the Middle Ages and the Renaissance*. New York: Dover Publications, 1976.

Fideler, David. *Jesus Christ, Sun of God: Ancient Cosmology and Early Christian Symbolism*. Wheaton, IL: Quest Books, 1993.

Flavius Josephus. *The Works of Flavius Josephus: Antiquities of the Jews*, trans. William Whiston. Grand Rapids, MI: Baker House, 1981.

Frankfort, Henri. *Kingship and the Gods*. Chicago: University of Chicago Press, 1948.

Freke, Timothy and Peter Gandy. *The Hermetica*. London: Piatkus Publishing, 1997.

Freke, Timothy and Peter Gandy. *The Jesus Mysteries*. New York: Three Rivers Press, 1999.

Gardiner, Philip. *Gnosis: The Secret of Solomon's Temple Revealed*. New Jersey: Career Press, 2006.

Geddes and Grosset. *Ancient Egypt: Myth and History*. Scotland: Gresham Publishing Company, 1997.

Gilbert, Adrian G. *Magi: The Quest for a Secret Mystical Tradition*. London: Bloomsbury, 1996.

Gilbert, Robert J. *Sacred Geometry Foundation Training: Essential Background Teachings and Practices*. Asheville, NC: Vesica: Spirit and Science Resources, 2005.

Ginsburg, Christian. *The Essenes and the Kabbala*. NY: Cosimo, Inc., originally published by Routledge & Kegan 1863–1864, republished in New York: Cosimo, Inc. 2005.

Godwin, Joscelyn. *Mystery Religions in the Ancient World*. New York: Harper & Row, 1981.

Godwin, Joscelyn. *The Golden Thread: The Ageless Wisdom of the Western Mystery Traditions*. Wheaton, IL: Quest Books, 2007.

Hagar, Stansbury. "The Zodiacal Temples of Uxmal," *Popular Astronomy Magazine*, vol. 79 (1921), p. 96.

Hall, Manly P. *The Adepts in the Esoteric Classical Tradition: Part Two: Mystics and Mysteries of Alexandria*. Los Angeles: The Philosophical Research Society, Inc., 1988.

———. *The Secret Teachings of All Ages*. New York: Jeremy P. Tarcher/Penguin, originally published in 1928 and reissued 2003.

———. *The Lost Keys to Freemasonry*, includes the classic works *Freemasonry of the Ancient Egyptians* and *Masonic Orders of Fraternity*. New York: Jeremy Tarcher/Penguin, 2006.

Hancock, Graham and Robert Bauval. *The Message of the Sphinx: A Quest for the Hidden Legacy of Mankind*. New York: Crown Publishers, 1996.

Hancock, Graham and Santha Faiia. *Heaven's Mirror: Quest for the Lost Civilization*. London: Michael Joseph, 1998.

Harwood, Jeremy. *The Freemasons*. London: Hermes House, 2006.

Hawkes, Jacquette. *Man and the Sun*. London: Cresset Press, 1962.

Henry, William. *The Healing Sun Code*. Nashville: Scali Dei, 2001.

Herodotus. *The Histories*, trans. Aubrey de Selincourt, rev. with Introduction and Notes by John Marincola. New York: Penguin, 2003.

Hoeh, Herman L. *Compendium of World History*, Vol. II. USA: A Dissertation Presented to the Faculty of Ambassador College Graduate School of Education in Partial Fulfillment of the Degree of Doctor of Theology, 1969.

Holweck, Fredrick. "Holy Innocents," in *The Catholic Encyclopedia*, vol. 7. New York: Robert Appleton Company, 1910.

Hopkins, E. Washburn. *The History of Religions*. New York: Macmillan & Company, 1918.

Howard-Gordon, Frances. *Glastonbury, Maker of Myths*. Glastonbury: Gothic Image Publications, 1982.

Humphreys, Colin. "The Star of Bethlehem," *Science and Christian Belief*, vol. 5 (October 1995), pp. 83–101.

Jacobs, Alan. *Sophia of Jesus Christ*. London: Watkins Publishing, 2006.

Jacobs, Alan, ed. *The Gnostic Gospels*. London: Watkins Publishing, 2006.

James, Peter and Nick Thorpe. *Ancient Mysteries*. New York: Ballantine Books, 1999.

Jowett, George F. *The Drama of the Lost Disciples*. London: Covenant Publishing, 1972.

Kereny, Karl. *Dionysus: Archetypal Image of Indestructible Life*. Princeton, NJ: Princeton University Press, 1976.

Kimball, Glen and David Stirland. *Hidden Politics of the Crucifixion*. Salt Lake City, UT: Ancient Manuscripts Publishing, 1998.

Kimball, Glenn Marshall Masters and Janice Manning, eds. *The Kolbrin Bible*. Carson City, NV: Your Own World Books, Inc., 2005.

Lamy, Lucie. *Egyptian Mysteries*. London: Thames & Hudson, 1981.

LaPage, Victoria. *Mysteries of the Bridechamber*. Rochester, VT: Inner Traditions, 2007.

Larson, Michael A. "Whatever Happened to the Dead Sea Scrolls?" *The Journal of Historical Review*, vol. 3, no. 2, 119–128.

Layton, Bentley. *The Gnostic Scriptures*. London: SCM Press, 1987.

Leadbeater, C. W. *Ancient Mystic Rites*. Wheaton, IL: Theosophical Heritage Classics, Quest Books, 1985.

Leloup, Jean-Yves. *The Gospel of Mary Magdalene*. Rochester, VT: Inner Traditions, 2002.

Lewis, David S. "East of Qumran: Searching for the Roots of Western Faith," *Atlantis Rising Magazine*, September/October 2005, 28, 30, 62–64.

Lewis, H. Spencer. *The Mystical Life of Jesus*. Los Angeles: Rosicrucian Press, 1929.

Lewis, James R. and Evelyn Dorothy Oliver. *Angels A to Z*. Canton, MI: Visible Ink Press, 1996.

Lewis, Lionel Smithett. *St. Joseph of Arimathea at Glastonbury or the Apostolic Church of Britain*, London: Mowbray, A.R. 1937; London: James Clarke, 1955; Cambridge, U.K.: Lutterworth Press, 2004.

Lundy, John P. *Monumental Christianity or The Art and Symbolism of the Primitive Church*, 1st ed. New York: J.W. Bouton, 1876; reprinted by Kessinger Publishing, LLC, 2003.

Mahan, W. D. *The Acts of Pilate*. Kirkfield, MO: Impact Christian Books, 1997.

Mails, Thomas E. *Secret Native American Pathways: A Guide to Inner Peace*. Tulsa, OK: Council Oak Books, 1988.

Maltwood, Catherine. *Glastonbury's Temple of the Stars*. London: Watkins Publishing, 1935.

Martin, Edward. *King of Travelers: Jesus' Lost Years in India*. Lampasas, TX: Jonah Publishing, 1999.

Massey, Gerald. *The Egyptian Book of the Dead and the Ancient Mysteries of Amenta*. New York: A&B Publishers Group, 1939.

Matthews, John and Caitlin. *The Encyclopedia of Celtic Wisdom*. Shaftsbury, Dorset, England: Element Press, 1994.

McCafferty, Patrick and Mike Baillie. *The Celtic Gods: Comets in Irish Mythology*. Gloucestershire, U.K.: The History Press, 2005.

McGaa, Ed Eagle Man. *Mother Earth Spirituality: Native American Paths to Healing Ourselves and Our World*. San Francisco: Harper San Francisco, 1990.

Mead, G. R. S. *Thrice Greatest Hermes*, vol. III. London, John M. Watkins, 1964.

Michell, John. *The Dimensions of Paradise*. London: Harper & Row, 1988.

———. *The New View Over Atlantis*. London: Thames and Hudson, 1983.

———. *Twelve Tribe Nations and the Science of Enchanting the Landscape*. Grand Rapids, MI: Phanes Press, 1991.

Miller, Hamish and Paul Broadhurst. *The Sun and the Serpent*. Cornwall, U.K.: Pendragon Press, 1989.

Morgan, R. W. *St. Paul in Britain*. Thousand Oaks, CA: Artisan Sales/Hoffman Printing, 1984.

Muller, W. Max. *Egyptian Mythology*. New York: Dover Publications, 2004.

Murray, Liz and Colin. *The Celtic Tree Oracle*. New York: St. Martin's Press, 1988.

Narby, Jeremy. *The Cosmic Serpent: DNA and the Origins of Knowledge*. New York: Jeremy P. Tarcher/Putnam, 1999.

Naydler, Jeremy. *Temple of the Cosmos: The Ancient Egyptian Experience of the Sacred*. Rochester, VT: Inner Traditions, 1996.

Nichols, Ross. *Book of Druidry*. London: Harper Collins, 1992.

Notovitch, Nicolas. *The Unknown Life of Jesus Christ*. Joshua Tree, CA: Tree of Life Publications, 1996.

Oliver, George. *History of Initiation*. n.p., Kessinger Publishers, 1997.

Origen. *Contra Celsum*, trans. H. Chadwick. Cambridge, U.K.: Cambridge University, 1965.

Pagels, Elaine. *The Gnostic Gospels*. New York: Vintage Books, Random House, 1979.

Paramahansa Yogananda. *The Yoga of Jesus*. Los Angeles: Self Realization Fellowship, 2007.

Phillips, Jonathan. "Gnosis: The Not So Secret History of Jesus," in *Towards 2012: Perspectives on the New Age*, ed. Daniel Pinehbeck and Ken Jordan. New York: Jeremy P. Tarcher/Penguin, 2008.

Potter, Charles Francis. *The Lost Years of Jesus Revealed*. New York: Ballentine Books, 1962.

Puech, Emile. "The Convictions of a Scholar," *Near Eastern Archaeology Magazine: Qumran and Dead Sea Scrolls*, vol. 63, no. 3 (September 2000), p. 160.

Purce, Jill. *The Mystic Spiral: Journey of the Soul*. London: Thames and Hudson, 1974.

Ransom, Victoria and Henrietta Bernstein. *The Crone Oracles: Initiates Guide to the Ancient Mysteries*. York Beach, ME: Weiser, 1994.

Robins, Andrew. *The Story of Writing: Alphabets, Hieroglyphs & Pictograms*. London: Thames and Hudson, 1995.

Roncalli, Francesco. *A View of the Vatican*, ed. Museu Vaticani. Rome: Tipografia Poliglotta Vaticana, 1989.

Rooke, Andrew. "The Sun: Powerhouse of the Mother/Father/Elder Brother," *Sunrise Magazine* (August/September 2002).

Ross, Hugh McGregor, ed. *The Gospel of Thomas*. London: Watkins Publishing, 1987.

Rudolph, Kurt, trans. R. McL. Wilson. *Gnosis*. Edinburgh: T&T Clark, 1976.

Rutherford, Ward. *Celtic Mythology*. New York: Sterling Publishing Co, Inc., 1990.

Sabbah, M. and R. *Les Secrets de L'Expode*. Paris: Godefroy, 2000.

Schwaller de Lubicz, R. A. *Sacred Science: The King of Pharonic Theocracy*. Rochester, VT: Inner Traditions, 1961.

Siblerud, Robert. *The Unknown Life of Jesus: Correcting the Church Myth*. Wellington, CO: New Science Publications, 2003.

Sitchin, Zecharia. *The End of Days*. New York: William Morrow, 2007.

———. *The Lost Book of Enki*. Rochester, VT: Bear & Company, 2002.

———. *The Wars of Gods and Men*. New York: Avon Books, 1985.

Smith, Morton. *The Secret Gospel*. London: Victor Gollancz, 1974.

Srila Visvanatha Chakravarti. *Rupa Chintamani: A Guided Meditation in 32 Sanskrit Verses*. Epworth, GA: Nectar Books, 2000.

Stough, Henry W. *Dedicated Disciples*. Muskogee, OK: Artisan Sales, Hoffman Printing, 1987.

Street, C. E. *Earthstar's Visionary Landscape: London, City of Revelation*. London: Hermitage Publishing, 2000.

Swami Abhedananda. *Journey into Kashmir and Tibet*. Bengali: Ramakrishna Vedanta Math Publications, Demy Octavo, 1922.

Swimme, Brian. *The Hidden Heart of the Cosmos*. New York: Orbis Books, 1996.

Szekely, Edmond Bordeaux. *The Essene Gospel of Peace, Books I and II: The Unknown Books of the Essenes*. Los Angeles: International Biogenic Society, 1981.

————. *The Essenes by Josephus and his Contemporaries*. Los Angeles: International Biogenic Society, 1981.

Taylor, John W. *The Coming of the Saints*. Muskogee, OK: Artisan Sales, Hoffman Printing, 1985.

Thiering, Barbara. *Jesus the Man*. New York: Atria Books, 1992.

Ulansey, David. *The Mithraic Mysteries: Cosmology and Salvation in the Ancient World*. New York: Oxford University Press, 1989.

VanderKam, James C. *Near Eastern Archaeology Magazine: Qumran and Dead Sea Scrolls*, vol. 63, no. 3 (American Schools of Oriental Research), "Calendars in the Dead Sea Scrolls" (September 2000): pp. 164–167.

Vermes, Geza. *The Nativity: History and Legend*. New York: Doubleday, 2006.

Walker, Barbara. *The Woman's Dictionary of Symbols and Sacred Objects*. San Francisco: Harper SanFrancisco, 1988.

————. *The Women's Encyclopedia of Myths and Secrets*. San Francisco: Harper San Francisco, 1983.

Wallace Murphy, Tim and Marilyn Hopkins. *Custodians of Truth*. Boston: Weiser Books, 2005.

Welburn, Andrew. *The Beginnings of Christianity*. Edinburgh, Scotland: Floris Books, 1995.

West, John Anthony. *The Serpent in the Sky: the High Wisdom of Ancient Egypt*. Wheaton, IL: Quest Books, 1993.

————. *The Traveler's Key to Ancient Egypt*. Wheaton, IL: Quest Books, 1995.

Whitworth, Eugene. *The Nine Faces of Christ*. Marina Del Rey, CA: DeVorss & Co, 1980.

Wilson, Stuart and Joanna Prentis. *The Essenes: Children of the Light*. Wheaton, IL: Ozark Publishing, 2005.

Web Resources

Middle East
http://www.middleeast.com/tyre.htm

Religion Facts: Just the Facts on the World's Religions
http://www.religionfacts.com/christianity/symbols/eye_of_god.htm

Cry Aloud: the Cybermagazine that Dares to Discuss Religion, Race, Sex and Politics
http://www.cryaloud.com/joshua_hu_gadarn_druids.htm

Order of Nazorean Essenes
www.essenes.net/index.php?option=com_content&task=view&id=764&Itemid= 179

Buried Mirror: Mesoamerica and Mayan World
http://www.buriedmirror.com/yaxche.htm

Absolute Astronomy: Exploring the World of Knowledge
www.absoluteastronomy.com/topics/Julian_the_Apostate

Nazarene Way of Essene Studies
www.thenazareneway.com/life_and_times_of_jesus_the_mess.htm

Early Christian Writings
www.earlychristianwritings.com/text/clement-stromata-book1.html

Pethiô's Web: Classic Rhetoric & Persuasion
www.classicpersuasion.org/pw/diogenes/dlpythagoras.htm

Nemeton, The Sacred Grove
http://www.celtnet.org.uk/gods_h/hu_gadarn.html

Geocities
www.geocities.com/Area51/Shire/3951/dryadart.html

Jewish Encyclopedia
www.jewishencyclopedia.com/view.jsp?artid=587&letter=M

New Advent
www.newadvent.org/cathen/07256b.htm

Greek Mythology
www.mlahanas.de/Greeks/Mythology/Labyrinth.html

Bible Searchers
biblesearchers.com/hebrewchurch/primitive/primitive6.shtml#Magdalene

Church of the Tree Saints
www.sacredsites.com/europe/france/church_of_three_saints.html

Encyclopedia Phoenician
phoenicia.org/britmines.html

Hindu
www.hinduwebsite.com/prakriti.asp

Early Christian Writings
www.earlychristianwritings.com/clement.html

Answers Online
www.answers.com/topic/bukhara

Jewish Encyclopedia
www.jewishencyclopedia.com/view.jsp?artid=1243&letter=B

Internet Medieval Sourcebook: The End of the Classical World
www.fordham.edu/halsall/sbook1b.html#Persecution%20of%20Christians

I Am the Beloved Mastery of the Self
www.iamthebeloved.com

Institute for Traditional Medicine
www.itmonline.org/arts/myrrh.htm

Masonic Light
www.masoniclight.com/papers/13Traveling%20Mason.txt

Search
www.search.com/reference/Zoroaster

The Official Website of John Marc Allegro
johnallegro.org/main/index.php?module=pagemaster&PAGE_user_op=view_
    printable&PAGE_id=1&lay_quiet=1

The Ancient Egypt Site: An Interactive Book of the History, Monuments, Lan-
    guage and Culture of Ancient Egypt
www.ancient-egypt.org/index.html

Tour Egypt
http://www.touregypt.net/featurestories/on.htm

New Kabbalah
www.newkabbalah.com/adam.html

The Stele of Thothmes IV
www.dabar.org/RecordsOfThePast/Vol2/SteleThothmes-4.html

Secrets of the Pyramid
www.galactic.to/rune/pyrmyst.html

Dhamma Web
www.dhammaweb.net/dhamma.html

Sacred Texts
www.sacred-texts.com/hin/rigveda/rv10090.htm

Renaissance Astrology
www.renaissanceastrology.com/hermesfixedstars.html

NOTES

THE INVITATION

1. The Bhagavad-Gita.
2. The Hebrew word Melchizedek is a combination of two other words: *Melchi*, meaning "king" and *Zedek*, meaning "righteousness." It can be translated as the right use of our mental and spiritual faculties, the qualities of any good leader or king. The New Testament also makes it clear that the Melchizedek Order was one of highly respected Kings of Peace who were known and honored throughout the ancient world (Hebrews 7:1-3).

CHAPTER 1

1. St. Augustine, *Retractions*.
2. Paul Brunton, *A Search in Secret Egypt* (York Beach, ME: Samuel Weiser, 1977), p. 186.
3. Timothy Freke and Peter Gandy, *The Hermetica* (London: Piatkus Publishing, 1997), p. 8.
4. Manly P. Hall, *The Secret Teachings of All Ages* (New York: Jeremy P. Tarcher/Penguin, originally published in 1928 and reissued 2003), p. 142.
5. Hall, *Secret Teachings*, p. 139.
6. Hall, *Secret Teachings*, p. 141.
7. Iamblichus' discussions with Porphyry, from his book *De Mysteriis Aegyptorum*, or *The Egyptian Mysteries*. on www.wisdomworld.org/setting/iamblichus.html (accessed: April 2, 2009).
8. C. W. Leadbeater, *Ancient Mystic Rites* (Wheaton, IL: Theosophical Heritage Classics, Quest Books, 1985), p. 98.
9. Brunton, *A Search in Secret Egypt*, p. 173.
10. Brunton, *A Search in Secret Egypt*, p. 173.

11. Leadbeater, *Ancient Mystic Rites*, pp. 89-90.
12. See Alan Jacobs, ed., *The Gnostic Gospels* for many of Jesus' teachings that were omitted from the Roman Catholic canon (London: Watkins Publishing, 2006), pp. 72-123, 162–186.
13. Jacobs, *Gnostic Gospels*, p. 110.
14. Brunton, *Search in Secret Egypt*, p. 172.
15. Plutarch, *Moralia*, "Isis and Osiris," (De Iside Et Osiride), trans. F. C. Babbitt (Cambridge, MA: Harvard University Press, first published 1936, reprinted 1993).
16. Brunton, *Search in Secret Egypt*, p. 177.
17. Elaine Pagels, *The Gnostic Gospels* (New York: Vintage Books, Random House, 1979), p. 14.
18. Willis Barnstone, *The Other Bible* (San Francisco: Harper San Francisco, 1984), pp. 304, 419.
19. Jacobs, *The Gnostic Gospels*, pp. 97, 121.
20. LaPage, *Mysteries of the Bridechamber*, p. 9.
21. W. D. Mahan, *The Acts of Pilate* (Kirkfield, MO: Impact Christian Books, 1997), p. 90.
22. David S. Lewis, "East of Qumran: Searching for the Roots of Western Faith," *Atlantis Rising Magazine*, September/October 2005, pp. 28, 30, 62–64. Smith later wrote an intriguing book called *The Secret Gospel*.
23. Kurt Rudolph, trans. R. McL. Wilson, *Gnosis* (Edinburgh: T&T Clark, 1976), p. 32.
24. Morton Smith, *The Secret Gospel* (London: Victor Gollancz, 1974), pp. 14–17.
25. Smith, *Secret Gospel*, p. 140.
26. LaPage, *Mysteries of the Bridechamber*, p. 9.
27. Pagels, *Gnostic Gospels*, p. 106.
28. Pagels, *Gnostic Gospels*, p. 104.

Chapter 2

1. John Greenleaf Whittier, "To Charles Sumner," *Barlett's Familiar Quotations* (Boston: Little Brown and Company, 1980), p. 513.
2. John Anthony West, *The Serpent in the Sky: the High Wisdom of Ancient Egypt* (Wheaton, IL: Quest Books, 1993), p. 129.
3. E. A. Wallis Budge, *The Gods of the Egyptians* (New York: Dover Publications, 1969), pp. 401, 414.
4. R. A. Schwaller de Lubicz, *Sacred Science: The King of Pharonic Theocracy* (Rochester, VT: Inner Traditions, 1961), p. 88.
5. Andrew Robins, *The Story of Writing: Alphabets, Hieroglyphs & Pictograms* (London: Thames and Hudson, 1995), p. 8.
6. Budge, *Gods of the Egyptians*, p. 414.

7. Although history says that Thoth wrote over 36,525 books, or a thousand for every day of the year, only five works remain to us today: *The Emerald Tablets*, *The Hermetica*, *The Kore Kosmu*, *The Kybalion*, and the *Papyrus of Ani* (or the *Egyptian Book of the Dead*, as it is better known). These five texts are believed to have been based on texts originally written by Thoth. They were then rewritten and added to by priests in both Heliopolis and Thebes for over 2000 years.

8. Alan Jacobs, ed., *Gnostic Gospels* (London: Watkins Publishing, 2006), pp. 96, 122–123.

9. Willis Barnstone, *The Other Bible* (San Francisco: Harper San Francisco, 1984), p. 420.

10. Manly P. Hall, *The Secret Teachings of All Ages* (New York: Jeremy P. Tarcher/ Penguin), originally published in 1928 and reissued 2003, pp. 600–604.

11. The Greeks called Osiris Dionysus and believed that, during the time of the Flood, he preserved the grape. In Dionysus' sacred rituals, wine symbolized the blood that was shed by the Lord of Light who sacrificed himself that all men might be reborn. The Romans created Bacchus, a god derived from Dionysus, or Osiris, but who engaged in far more drinking and revelry. Dionysis' rituals later became the Eucharist of the bread and wine, used in Christian rituals worldwide.

12. Hall, *Secret Teachings*, pp. 596–597.

13. Miranda Bruce-Mitford, *The Illustrated Book of Signs and Symbols* (New York: Barnes & Noble, 2004), p. 103.

14. Jacobs, *Gnostic Gospels*, p. 120.

15. Adrian G. Gilbert, *Magi: The Quest for a Secret Mystical Tradition* (London: Bloomsbury, 1996), p. 258.

16. Barbara Walker, *The Woman's Dictionary of Symbols and Sacred Objects* (Harper SanFrancisco, 1988), p. 488.

17. D. J. Conway, *Animal Magick* (St. Paul, MN: Llewellyn Publications, 1995), p. 229.

18. Conway, *Animal Magick*, p. 229.

19. Knowledge of the Merkaba field has resurfaced in the last twenty years thanks to the research of Drunvalo Melchizedek, author of the *Flower of Life* series (Flagstaff, AZ: Light Technology Publishing, 1990).

20. Elizabeth Van Buren, *The Sign of the Dove* (Suffolk, England: Neville Spearman, 1983), pp. 30–31.

21. Van Buren, *Sign of the Dove*, pp. 8–9.

22. Walker, *Woman's Dictionary*, pp. 414–415.

23. Bruce-Mitford, *Book of Signs and Symbols*, p. 56.

24. Walker, *Woman's Dictionary*, p. 488.

25. Gilbert, *Magi*, p. 258.

26. The coat of arms of Pope Urban VIII features the Barberini bees that became symbols of his family.

✓ 27. Charles Francis Potter, *The Lost Years of Jesus Revealed* (New York: Ballentyne Books, 1962), p. 51.

28. Timothy Wallace Murphy and Marilyn Hopkins, *Custodians of Truth* (San Francisco: Weiser Books, 2005), p. 15.

29. In his forward to Manly P. Hall's classic *The Secret Teachings of All Ages*, p. 5.

30. Paul Brunton, *A Search in Secret Egypt* (York Beach, ME: Samuel Weiser, 1977), p. 184–185.

31. Diodorus Siculus, *Bibliotheca Historica*, translated by G. Booth, 1814, (originally published by H. Valesius, I Rhodomannus, and F. Ursinus).

32. Quoted in "Great Theosophists, Iamblichus: The Egyptian Mysteries," *Theosophy* (Vol. 25, No. 4, February, 1937), pp. 149-157, from http://www.wisdomworld.org/setting/iamblichus.html (accessed May 20, 2009).

33. Michael Baigent, *The Jesus Papers* (San Francisco: Harper San Francisco, 2006), p. 170.

34. C. W. Leadbeater, *Ancient Mystic Rites* (Wheaton, IL: Theosophical Heritage Classics, Quest Books, 1985), pp. 113–114.

35. The viciousness of this destruction is described by Hall in *The Secret Teachings of All Ages*, pp. 650–651.

Chapter 3

1. Quoted in Michael Baigent, *The Jesus Papers* (San Francisco: Harper San Francisco, 2006), pp. 27–28. Josephus is also author of the books *Antiquities of the Jews* and *The War of the Jews*.

2. Adrian G. Gilbert, *Magi: The Quest for a Secret Mystical Tradition* (London: Bloomsbury, 1996), p. 218.

3. Michael A. Larson, "Whatever Happened to the Dead Sea Scrolls?" *The Journal of Historical Review*, vol. 3, no. 2, pp. 119–128. From www.vho.org/GB/Journals/JHR/3/2/Larson119-128.html (accessed: January 4, 2009). Larson is also author of *The Essene Heritage*.

4. Flavius Josephus, *The Works of Flavius Josephus: Antiquities of the Jews*, trans. William Whiston, vol. 3 (Grand Rapids, MI: Baker House, 1981), book 16, chap. 4, verse 4.

5. Gilbert, *Magi*, p. 218.

6. Baigent, *Jesus Papers*, pp. 27–28.

7. Gilbert, *Magi*, p. 220.

8. Fredrick Holweck, "Holy Innocents" in *The Catholic Encyclopedia*, vol. 7 (New York: Robert Appleton Company, 1910). Transcribed for *New Advent* website by Robert B. Olsonfrom 2008. www.newadvent.org/cathen/07419a.htm (accessed: May 1, 2009).

fraud?

✓ 9. W. D. Mahan, *The Acts of Pilate* (Kirkwood, MO: Impact Christian Books, 1997), pp. 126–130. This remarkable document is entitled "Herod Antipater's Defense to the Roman Senate in Regard to His Conduct in Bethlehem."

10. Baigent, *Jesus Papers*, p. 14.

✓ 11. Rev. W. D. Mahan, T*he Acts of Pilate*, Impact Christian Books (Kirkwood, MO: 1997), pp. 128–129.

12. Ibid, 130–131,

13. Colin Humphreys, "The Star of Bethlehem," *Science and Christian Belief*, vol 5. (October 1995), pp. 83–101. www.asa3.org/ASA/topics/Astronomy-Cosmology/S&CB%2010-93Humphreys.html (accessed: January 1, 2009). Humphreys is head of the Department of Materials Science and Metallurgy at the University of Cambridge.

14. Mahan, *Acts of Pilate*, pp. 50–62.

15. Mahan, *Acts of Pilate*, pp. 50–51.

16. Mahan, *Acts of Pilate*, pp. 50–53.

17. Geza Vermes, *The Nativity: History and Legend* (New York: Doubleday, 2006), p. 91.

18. Vermes, *The Nativity*, pp. 96-97. The Jewish *Book of the Upright*, or the Sefer ha-Yashar, composed in its present version in the eleventh or twelfth centuries, reports the appearance of a new star at the birth of Abraham.

19. Patrick McCafferty and Mike Baillie, *The Celtic Gods: Comets in Irish Mythology* (Gloucestershire, U.K.: The History Press, 2005).

20. Michio Kaku, "Parallel Worlds," *Evolve Magazine*, vol. 4, no. 1 (2005).

21. Dolores Cannon, *Jesus and the Essenes* (Bath, U.K.: Gateway Books, 1992), pp. 196–197.

22. More specifically, the Four Watchers are: Aldebaran in Taurus, the Watcher of the East; Regulus in Leo, the Watcher of the South; Antares in Scorpio, the Watcher of the West; and Fomalhaut in Aquarius, the Watcher of the North. Because of the slow progression of stars, Fomalhaut has now moved into the edge of the constellation Pisces. John P. Pratt, "The Lion and the Unicorn Testify to Christ," *Meridian Magazine* (November 8, 2001). http://www.johnpratt.com/items/docs/lds/meridian/2001/4corners.html (accessed: January 1, 2009).

23. Cannon, *Jesus and the Essenes*, pp. 196–200.

Chapter 4

1. Ancient Egyptian Pyramid Texts.

2. Sentius Saturninus, not Quirinius, was the governor of Syria from 9 to 6 B.C., but there are those who believe that Quirinius did have an appointment from the Roman Empire in Syria at that time. "Historical Evidence for Quirinius and the Census," *Bible History.net*, www.biblehistory.net/newsletter/quirinius.htm (accessed: January 13, 2009).

3. H. Spencer Lewis, *The Mystical Life of Jesus* (Los Angeles: Rosicrucian Press, 1929), p. 90.

4. Zecharia Sitchin, *The End of Days* (New York: William Morrow, 2007), p. 276.

5. Colin Humphreys, "The Star of Bethlehem," *Science and Christian Belief*, vol. 5 (October 1995), pp. 83–101. www.asa3.org/ASA/topics/Astronomy-Cosmology/S&CB%2010-93Humphreys.html (accessed: January 13, 2009).

6. R. M. Jenkins, "The Star of Bethlehem and the Comet of A.D. 66," *Journal of the British Astronomical Association*, vol. 114, no. 6 (2004), pp. 336–343. www.bristolastrosoc.org.uk/uploaded/BAAJournalJenkins.pdf (accessed: January 13, 2009).

7. J. F. Tipler, "The Star of Bethlehem: a type Ia/Ic Supernova in the Andromeda Galaxy" (March 2005) www.math.tulane.edu/~tipler/starofbethlehem.pdf (accessed: April 15, 2009).

8. Origen, *Contra Celsum*, trans. H. Chadwick (Cambridge, U.K.: Cambridge University, 1965).

9. R. M. Jenkins, "Star of Bethlehem," p. 336–342.

10. Dolores Cannon, *Jesus and the Essenes*, p. 195.

11. Passover of 5 B.C.E. was April 13 to April 27. Colin Humphreys, "The Star of Bethlehem," pp. 83–102.

12. Adrian G. Gilbert, *Magi: The Quest for a Secret Mystical Tradition* (London: Bloomsbury, 1996), pp. 221–227.

13. David Fideler, *Jesus Christ, Sun of God: Ancient Cosmology and Early Christian Symbolism* (Wheaton, IL: Quest Books, 1961), p. 166.

14. Gilbert, *Magi*, pp. 87, 143.

15. Vermes, *The Nativity*, pp. 96-97. The Jewish *Book of the Upright*, or the *Sefer ha-Yashar*, composed in its present version in the eleventh or twelfth centuries, reports the appearance of a new star at the birth of Abraham.

16. Gilbert, *Magi*, p. 41.

17. *Paganizing Faith of Yeshua* website, www:paganizingfaithofyeshua.netfirms.com (accessed: October 10, 2008).

18. Graham Hancock and Santha Faiia, *Heaven's Mirror: Quest for the Lost Civilization* (London: Michael Joseph, 1998), p. 36.

19. Henri Frankfort, *Kingship and the Gods* (Chicago: University of Chicago Press, 1948), p. 64.

20. Frankfort, *Kingship and the Gods*, p. 156.

21. This discovery of the alignment of Regulus and Sirius is based on the painstaking research of Adrian G. Gilbert, author of *Magi: The Quest for a Secret Tradition* (London: Bloomsbury, 1996). Along with the discovery of the Sarmang Society, the roots of the secret Magi themselves, Gilbert provides a

thorough examination of historical, astronomical, and spiritual documentation within the ancient world to support this date.

22. The fifteen Behenian stars are Algol, Pleiades, Aldebaran, Capella, Sirius, Procyon, Regulus, Polaris, Gienah, Spica, Arcturus, Alphecca, Antares, Vega, and Deneb. "Hermes on the 15 Fixed Stars and Their 15 Stones and Herbs," trans. by B. Thomas from BM Bodleian MS. 52, ff. 44–47. From Joan Evans, *Magical Jewels of the Middle Ages and the Renaissance* (New York: Dover Publications, 1976). Christopher Warnock, *Renaissance Astrology* website, www.renaissanceastrology.com/hermesfixedstars.html (accessed: January 13, 2009).

23. Gilbert, *Magi*, pp. 223–229.

24. Alan Jacobs, ed., *The Gnostic Gospels* (London: Watkins Publishing, 2006), p. 175.

25. Miranda Bruce-Mitford, *The Illustrated Book of Signs and Symbols* (New York: Barnes & Noble, 2004), p. 14.

26. Gilbert, *Magi*, pp. 223–224.

27. Elizabeth Van Buren, *The Sign of the Dove* (Suffolk, England: Neville Spearman, 1983), pp. 86–87.

CHAPTER 5

1. Stuart Wilson and Joanna Prentis, *The Essenes: Children of the Light* (Wheaton, IL: Ozark Publishing, 2005), p. 140.

2. H. Spencer Lewis, *The Mystical Life of Jesus* (Los Angeles: Rosicrucian Press, 1929), p. 94.

3. Jonathan Phillips, "Gnosis: The Not So Secret History of Jesus," in *Towards 2012: Perspectives on the New Age*, ed. Daniel Pinehbeck and Ken Jordan (New York: Jeremy P. Tarcher/Penguin, 2008), pp. 120–121.

4. The Epiphany has traditionally been a Christian feast to celebrate the revelation to humanity of God in human form. Today, in Eastern Orthodox churches, the emphasis is on the shining forth of Jesus as the Messiah and it is called the Feast of the Theophany, from the Greek for "God shining forth"). Pip Wilson, "Wilson's Almanac Book of Days: January 6." www.wilsonsalmanac.com/book/jan6.html (accessed: January 24, 2009).

5. Epiphanius, *Panarion*, sect. 4, chap. 31 (51), 24,1), "The Date of Christmas," *Thrice Holy* website. www.thriceholy.net/christmas.html (accessed: January 24, 2009).

6. "Ancient Egyptian Holidays," *Ancient Egyptian Lives* website. www.aelives.com/holidays.htm (accessed: April 15, 2009).

7. Adrian G. Gilbert, *Magi: The Quest for a Secret Mystical Tradition* (London: Bloomsbury, 1996), p. 229.

8. Wilson, "Almanac Book of Days."

9. Dolores Cannon, *Jesus and the Essenes* (Bath, U.K.: Gateway Books, 1992), p. 197.

CHAPTER 6

1. Paracelsus, quoted in Manly P. Hall, *The Secret Teachings of All Ages* (New York: Jeremy P. Tarcher/Penguin), originally published in 1928 and reissued 2003, p. 142.

2. "Theodosius I," unattributed article on *The Best Links* website. www.the-bestlinks.com/Theodosius_I.html (accessed: January1, 2009).

3. Manly P. Hall, *The Adepts in the Esoteric Classical Tradition: Part Two: Mystics and Mysteries of Alexandria* (Los Angeles: The Philosophical Research Society, Inc., 1988), pp. 25–26. Hall cites the *Vide Codex Theodosianus* as an indication of what constituted heresy to the early church. See also *New Advent* website, www.newadvent.org/cathen/07256b.htm (accessed: January 13, 2009).

4. Michael Baigent, *The Jesus Papers* (San Francisco: Harper San Francisco, 2006), p. 138.

5. *The Holy Family in Egypt*, text prepared and revised by a cathedral committee headed by His Holiness Pope Shenouda III, Pope of Alexandria and patriarch of the See of St. Mark, p. 9.

6. *The Holy Family in Egypt*, p. 9.

7. Joseph's older children are documented in the Protevangelion, one of the Lost Gospels, in Rosicrucian documents, and in other sources. One of Jesus' half-siblings was his stepbrother James, later known as James the Just, who was martyred by the Pharisees. A Salome appears several times in biblical writings as one of Jesus' disciples and as one of the three women present at the Crucifixion. If this is the same woman who married Zebedee and bore him two sons—James and John, the"Sons of Thunder"—then the apostles James and John would have been Jesus' step-nephews. "Feast of the Holy and Glorious Apostle and Evangelist John the Theologian," on *The Greek Orthodox Archdiocese* website. http://www.goarch.org/special/johntheapostle/ (accessed: January 28, 2009).

8. Dolores Cannon, *Jesus and the Essenes* (Bath, U.K.: Gateway Books, 1992), p. 201.

9. Alexander died in 323 B.C.E.

10. Baigent, *Jesus Papers*, pp. 140, 142.

11. Hall, *Secret Teachings*, pp. 60–61.

12. Hall, *Adepts in Esoteric Classical Tradition*, p. 43.

13. Hall, *Adepts in Esoteric Classical Tradition*, p. 59.

14. Hall, *Secret Teachings*, p. 61.

15. Hall, *Secret Teachings*, p. 60.

16. Michael was an amalgamation of Horus/Apollo, the victorious light bearer. Thoth was the master of the ley lines and sacred sites of the world.

17. In the ancient world these planetary spheres were the Sun, the Moon, Mercury, Venus, Mars, Jupiter, and Saturn. See Sir J.A. Hammerton, *Wonders of the Past* (New York: Wise and Company, 1953), p. 62.

18. Edmond Bordeaux Szekely, *The Gospel of Peace by the Apostle John* (London: C. H. Daniels, 1937). Reprinted as *The Essene Gospel of Peace* (Book I: San Diego: Academy of Creative Living, 1971; Book II: USA: International Biogenic Society, 1981), pp. 60–62.

19. Hall, *Secret Teachings*, pp. 63–64.

20. Hall, *Secret Teachings*, p. 63.

21. Jefferson Monet, "Serapis, the Composite God," article on the website *Tour Egypt*. www.touregypt.net/featurestories/serapis.htm (accessed: January 13, 2009).

22. William Henry, *The Healing Sun Code* (Nashville: Scali Dei, 2001), p. 154.

23. St. Augustine of Hippo, *Retractions*, quoted in "Christianity: Origins of Christianity and its Relation to Other Religions," *The Catholic Encyclopedia*, available on the website *New Advent*. www.newadvent.org/cathen/03712a.htm (accessed: January 13, 2009).

24. These temples were completed circa 246–222 B.C.E. by Ptolemy III, the last of Alexander the Great's generals.

25. Eratosthenes was born in Cyrene in 276 B.C.E. Upon the death of Callimachus he was offered the highly respected post of chief librarian of the Mouseion, the university complex at Alexandria.

26. The Kabbala is not only a profound system for understanding the many archetypal expressions of God as the One who descends from the world of the formless to the world of form, but also a roadmap for human consciousness to return to God.

27. Hall, *Adepts in Esoteric Classical Tradition*, p. 30.

28. For more on Pythagorus, see "Life of Pythagoras," part of Diogenes Laertius, *The Lives and Opinions of Eminent Philosophers*, trans. C. D. Yonge (London: Henry G. Bohn Publishers, 1853); "Life of Pythagoras" is included on the website *Pethiô's Web: Classic Rhetoric & Persuasion*. www.classicpersuasion.org/pw/diogenes/dlpythagoras.htm (accessed: January 13, 2009). See also "Pythagoreans," article on the website *The Order of Nazorean Essenes*. www.essenes.net/index.php?option=com_content&task=view&id=764&Itemid=179 (accessed: April 20, 2009) and Herodotus, *Persian War*, Book II (London: Penguin Books, 1954, revised 1972 and 1996), p. 81. Pythagoras was captive in Babylon at the same time that the Jews were captive there.

29. After the death of Socrates, Plato studied in Heliopolis, like Jesus, for some thirteen years before returning to Greece. Paul Brunton, *A Search in Secret*

Egypt (York Beach, ME: Samuel Weiser, 1977), p. 28. See also Porphyry in
Life of Pythagoras.

30. Pythagoras "… believed the motion of God to be circular, the body of God to
be composed of the substance of light, and the nature of God to be composed
of the substance of truth." See Hall, *Secret Teachings*, pp. 196–197.

CHAPTER 7

1. Isha Upanishad, XV (thought to be written by Issa, or Jesus).
2. "Jesus in Egypt," *Al-Ahram Weekly Online*, (December 2001, issue no. 565).
www.weekly.ahram.org.eg/2001/565/tr1.htm (accessed: January 1, 2009).
3. It was this act of desecration by Antiochus that prompted the insurrection
against the Syrians led by the Maccabees.
4. Some academics credit the formation of the temple at Bubastis to Onias IV
instead of Onias III, because of references in Josephus' *Antiquities of the Jews.*
Onias III, a high priest, had full authority to create such a temple, while his
son, Onias IV, a military commander, did not. Baigent tells us this temple
"was a fully functioning Temple, in which the Jewish priests carried out the
required daily sacrifices [and prayers] in just the same manner as was done
in Jerusalem." He also says, "This Temple survived… [until] the destruction
of the Temple of Jerusalem [in 68 C.E.]." Michael Baigent, *The Jesus Papers*
(San Francisco: Harper San Francisco, 2006), pp. 144, 157.
5. The Essene strongholds were near Jerusalem at Qumran, Hebron, Arad, and
En Gedi. In the north near Galilee were Jenin, Mount Carmel, and Rama.
Even further north there was a center in Damascus in Syria. To the south, in
Egypt, lay Alexandria, and the more hidden sanctuary of On in Heliopolis.
Lewis notes: "All these branches, however, used the same seals and symbols,
adhered to the same general rules and regulations, and paid allegiance to the
supreme body known as the Great White Brotherhood in Egypt." H. Spencer
Lewis, *The Mystical Life of Jesus* (Los Angeles: Rosicrucian Press, 1929), pp.
144–145.
6. Philo, "The Therapeutae of Ancient Egypt," article on the website *The Naza-rean Way of Essene Studies.* www.thenazareneway.com/therapeutae.html
(accessed: January 1, 2009).
7. Timothy Freke and Peter Gandy, *The Jesus Mysteries* (New York: Three Rivers
Press, 1999), p. 188.
8. Freke and Gandy, *Jesus Mysteries.* Philo writes of the Therapeutae in his trea-tise *De Vita Contemplativa* (The Contemplative Life).
9. John Michell, *The New View Over Atlantis* (New York: Thames and Hudson,
1983), p. 51.
10. Manly P. Hall, *The Adepts in the Esoteric Classical Tradition* (Los Angeles: The
Philosophical Research Society, Inc., 1988), p. 60.

11. Philo, "The Therapeutae of Ancient Egypt," (accessed: January 20, 2009).

12. The Nazarean Way of Essene Studies website (accessed: January 20, 2009). See also Hall, *Adepts in Esoteric Classical Tradition*, p. 62.

13. Strabo (63 B.C.E. to 23 C.E.) describes large buildings belonging to the priests and "men skilled in philosophy and astronomy," but says that the *o-uanjµa* and *iaicgats* (words used by Philo in speaking of the Therapeutae) had fallen into decay. The system was also described by Chaeremon the Stoic, a contemporary of Strabo's. Chaeremon's account resembles Philo's in many details. See also Hall, *Adepts in Esoteric Classical Tradition*, p. 61.

14. *Nazarean Way of Essene Studies* (accessed: January 20, 2009).

15. Edmund Bordeaux Szekely, *The Essene Gospel of Peace by the Apostle John* (London: C. H. Daniels, 1937). Reprinted as *The Essene Gospel of Peace* (Book I: San Diego: Academy of Creative Living, 1971; Book II: USA: International Biogenic Society, 1981), Book II, pp. 34-36, 89.

16. David Fideler, *Jesus Christ, Sun of God: Ancient Cosmology and Early Christian Symbolism* (Wheaton, IL: Quest Books, 1993), pp. 41, 325. Philo wrote three books about the Pentateuch, each divided into topics and describing each law and what it meant. These quotes are from *The Special Laws* and from Plato's *Laws*.

17. Quoted in Fideler, *Jesus Christ, Sun of God*, p. 325, from the *Enneads* 1.6.9.30, "On Beauty," Armstrong translation.

CHAPTER 8

1. Saint Francis of Assisi, *Hymn of the Sun*, New York: Broken Glass, Inc./Lancaster Productions, 1990.

2. Norman H. Baynes, *Constantine The Great and the Christian Church* (Raleigh Lecture on History, March 12, 1930), quoted in an article on Lino Sanchez, *Christianism ("Christianity"), Etc.* website. www:christianism.com/articles/13.html (accessed: January 13, 2009).

3. Quoted in David Fideler, *Jesus Christ, Sun of God: Ancient Cosmology and Early Christian Symbolism* (Wheaton, IL: Quest Books, 1993), p. 328. This quote comes from Clement of Alexandria, *Exhortation to the Greeks* 6 (Loeb Classical Library translation, 155).

4. This rite is called the Exultet. Jacquette Hawkes, *Man and the Sun* (London: Cresset Press, 1962), pp. 199, 202.

5. Hawkes, *Man and Sun*, p. 203.

6. Francesco Roncalli, *A View of the Vatican*, ed. Museu Vaticani (Rome: Tipografia Poliglotta Vaticana, 1989), pp. 20–23.

7. This plaza, designed by Michelangelo, clearly symbolizes the twelve divisions of the sky that are reflected in the twelve apostles. *Rome and Vatican: Vatican Museums-Borghese Gallery-Tivoli* (Rome: TPE Editore, 1981), p. 83.

8. Hawkes, *Man and Sun*, pp. 202–203.

9. "Religious Sungazing," unattributed page content on the website of the same name. www.sunlight.as.ro/history_of_sun_gazing.htm (accessed: January 2, 2009).

✓ 10. Fideler, *Jesus Christ, Sun of God*, p. 40.

11. Brian Swimme, *The Hidden Heart of the Cosmos* (New York: Orbis Books, 1996), pp. 41–42.

12. Graham Hancock and Santha Faiia, *Heaven's Mirror: Quest for the Lost Civilization* (London: Michael Joseph, 1998), p. 23.

13. Manly P. Hall, *The Secret Teachings of All Ages* (New York: Jeremy P. Tarcher/Penguin, originally published in 1928 and reissued 2003), p. 146.

✓ 14. H. Spencer Lewis, *The Mystical Life of Jesus* (Los Angeles: Rosicrucian Press, 1929), pp. 141–145. AMORC, or the *Antiquus Mystiqusque Ordo Rosae Crucis*, the Order of the Rosy Cross or Rosicrucians, trace their history to the Eighteenth Dynasty and the Pharaoh Thutmose III (1501 to 1447 B.C.E.).

15. Andrew Rooke, "The Sun: Powerhouse of the Mother/Father/Elder Brother," *Sunrise Magazine* (August/September 2002). Available online on *Theosophy Northwest*, the website of the Northwest Branch of the Theosophical Society. www.theosophy-nw.org/theosnw/science/sc-rook3.htm (accessed: January 1, 2009).

16. Geddes and Grosset, *Ancient Egypt Myth and History* (Scotland: Gresham Publishing Company, 1997), p. 265.

17. Hall, *Secret Teachings*, p. 136.

18. Lewis, *Mystical Life of Jesus*, pp. 193–194, 197.

19. Edmond Bordeaux Szekely, *The Gospel of Peace by the Apostle John* (London: C. H. Daniels, 1937). Reprinted as *The Essene Gospel of Peace* (Book I: San Diego: Academy of Creative Living, 1971; Book II: USA: International Biogenic Society, 1981), Book II, p. 66.

20. John Michell, *Twelve Tribe Nations and the Science of Enchanting the Landscape* (Grand Rapids, MI: Phanes Press, 1991), p. 85. The word *Aser* means "the Shining Ones."

21. The *Sefer Yetzirah,*, meaning "the Book of Formation," is an esoteric Hebrew holy book—a Kabalistic text related to the twenty-two letters of the Hebrew alphabet as creative forces and the speaking of the sacred power of numbers, specifically the numbers three, seven, and twelve. Robert J. Gilbert, *Sacred Geometry Foundation Training: Essential Background Teachings and Practices* (Asheville, NC: Vesica: Spirit and Science Resources, 2005), pp. 39–41.

22. Hall, *Secret Teachings*, p. 141.

23. *Hymn to Helios*, oration 4, verse 132. Quoted in the online article "Julian the Apostate," on the website *Absolute Astronomy: Exploring the World of Knowl-*

edge. www.absoluteastronomy.com/topics/Julian_the_Apostate (accessed: January 4, 2009).

24. John Michell, *The New View Over Atlantis* (London: Thames and Hudson, 1983), p. 176.

25. Edmond Bordeaux Szekely, *The Essenes by Josephus and his Contemporaries* (Los Angeles: International Biogenic Society, 1981), p. 40.

26. Clement of Alexandria, *The Stata, or Miscellanies: Book 1.* Reprinted on Peter Kirby, *Early Christian Writings* website. www.earlychristianwritings.com/text/clement-stromata-book1.html (accessed: October 1, 2008).

CHAPTER 9

1. Joseph, from Stuart Wilson and Joanna Prentis, *The Essenes: Children of the Light* (Wheaton, IL: Ozark Publishing, 2005), p. 133.

2. Wilson and Prentis, *Children of Light*, p. 38.

3. Willis Barnstone, *The Other Bible* (San Francisco: Harper San Francisco, 1984), pp. 383–392.

4. Barnstone, *The Other Bible*, p. 398.

5. Manly P. Hall, *The Secret Teachings of All Ages* (New York: Jeremy P. Tarcher/Penguin), originally published in 1928 and reissued 2003, p. 586.

6. Barnstone's translation of the Gospel of Pseudo-Matthew is taken from David R. Cartlidge and David L. Dungan, eds. and trans., *Documents for the Study of the Gospels* (Philadelphia: Fortress Press, 1980), pp. 98–103, 394, 407.

7. *The Lost Books of the Bible and the Forgotten Books of Eden: The Infancy Gospel of Jesus Christ* (Exton, PA: Alpha House, 1927), chapter 4, verses 15–20, 41–42.

8. *Infancy Gospel*, chapter 5, verses 3–5, 42.

9. *Infancy Gospel*, chapter 6, verses 5–15, 43; chapter 6, verses 17–19, 43–44.

10. *Infancy Gospel*, , chapter 6, verses 19–37, 44; chapter 15, verses 1–15, 53.

11. *Infancy Gospel*, chapter 19, verses 4–11, 55–56; chapter 28, verses 4–19, 55.

12. *Infancy Gospel*, chapter 24, verse 11–13, 53–54.

13. *Infancy Gospel*, chapter 6, verses 16–18, 45; chapter 7, verses 1–35.

14. *Infancy Gospel*, chapter 4, verse 13; chapter 4, verses 22–23, 42.

15. Szekely, *Essene Gospel of Peace*, books 2, 72. (Los Angeles: International Biogenic Society, 1981).

16. Willis Barnstone, *Infancy Gospel of Thomas*, (NY: Harper SanFrancisco,1984), p. 60.

17. Barnstone, *Infancy Gospel of Thomas*, p. 399.

18. Barnstone, *Infancy Gospel of Thomas*, 399–400.

19. Introduction to *The Lost Books of the Bible and the Forgotten Books of Eden* (Exton, PA: Alpha House, 1972), p. 8.

Chapter 10

1. Stuart Wilson and Joanna Prentis, *The Essenes: Children of the Light* (Wheaton, IL: Ozark Publishing, 2005), p. 133.

2. Robert Siblerud, *The Unknown Life of Jesus: Correcting the Church Myth* (Wellington, CO: New Science Publications, 2003), pp. 116–117. Quoted from *The Infancy Gospel of Jesus Christ*, chapter 21, verses 5–21.

3. Jenny Jobbins, "Jesus in Egypt," *Al-Ahram Weekly Online*. www.weekly. ahram.org.eg/2001/565/tr1.htm (accessed: January 2, 2009).

4. Josephus places Herod's death just after a lunar eclipse. Kepler dated it to April of 4 B.C.E., when a partial eclipse occurred. There were also two lunar eclipses in 5 B.C.E. Herod's death is thought by most scholars to be 4 B.C.E., however, because this is the year that all three of his sons, who inherited his kingdom, claimed rulership. *Ancient History* website. www.04bc.com (accessed: January 2, 2009).

5. Manly P. Hall, *The Adepts in the Esoteric Classical Tradition: Part Two: Mystics and Mysteries of Alexandria* (Los Angeles: The Philosophical Research Society, Inc., 1988), p. 87.

6. Alexandria passed into Roman jurisdiction in 80 B.C.E. It was destroyed in 115 C.E. by Greek-Jewish civil wars and then rebuilt.

7. Dolores Cannon, *Jesus and the Essenes* (Bath, U.K.: Gateway Books, 1992), p. 132.

8. Wilson and Prentis, *Children of the Light*, pp. 105–106.

9. Developmental-growth therapists tell us that, while we may absorb some 70 percent of our beliefs and attitudes before the age of seven, at six or seven, the strong cognitive reasoning mind kicks in. This is why students were enrolled in the Mystery Schools at ages seven and eight.

10. Victoria Ransom and Henrietta Bernstein, *The Crone Oracles: Initiates Guide to the Ancient Mysteries* (York Beach, ME: Weiser, 1994), pp. 1–3.

11. Cannon, *Jesus and the Essenes*, p. 48.

12. H. Spencer Lewis, *The Mystical Life of Jesus* (Los Angeles: Rosicrucian Press, 1929), pp. 92, 132-133.

13. Cannon, *Jesus and the Essenes*, pp. 211–219.

14. Cannon, *Jesus and the Essenes*, pp. 206–210.

16. Wilson and Prentis, *Children of the Light*, pp. 132–133.

17. Wilson and Prentis, *Children of the Light*, p. 134.

18. Wilson and Prentis, *Children of the Light*, p. 53.

19. Lewis, *Mystical Life of Jesus*, p. 38.

20. Lewis, *Mystical Life of Jesus*, pp. 38, 41.

21. Alfred Edersheim, *The Life and Times of the Messiah, Book I and II* (Massachusetts: Hendrickson Publishers, originally published in 1886, reissued in 1993). http://philologos.org/__eb-lat/ (accessed: December 30, 2008).

22. *The Catholic Encyclopedia*, "Geography and History of Mt. Carmel," from the website *The Nazarene Way of Essene Studies*. www.thenazareneway.com/life_and_times_of_jesus_the_mess.htm (accessed: January 6, 2009).

23. Edersheim, *Life and Times*, cited on the website *The Nazarene Way of Essenic Studies* (accessed: January 13, 2009).

24. Wilson and Prentis, *Children of the Light*, p. 106.

25. John Michell, *Twelve Tribe Nations and the Science of Enchanting the Landscape* (Grand Rapids, MI: Phanes Press, 1991), p. 120.

26. Michell, *Twelve Tribe Nations*, p. 120.

27. Jesus makes a reference to John as Elijah in Matthew 11:12–15.

28. In 1175 C.E., explorer Johannes Phokas visited the Grotto or Cave of Elijah, which he reported was close to the ruins of a large monastery. He was shown the remains of an even older monastic community located just below the summit and the remnants of the Essene school Jesus once attended.

29. *The Order of the Nazorean Essenes* website (accessed: January 13, 2009).

30. Szekely, *Essene Gospel of Peace*, book 2, 69.

31. Barbara Walker, *The Women's Encyclopedia of Myths and Secrets* (San Francisco: Harper San Francisco, 1983), p. 958.

CHAPTER 11

1. Tibetan Buddhist prayer.

2. There also were regional or district circuit courts scattered throughout the region.

3. "Sanhedrin," *Catholic Encyclopedia*, available on the website *New Advent*. www.newadvent.org/cathen/13444a.htm (accessed: January 1, 2009).

4. *The Reestablished Jewish Sanhedrin* website. www.thesanhedrin.org/en/ (accessed: January 1, 2009).

5. "Sanhedrin," Catholic Encyclopedia (accessed: January 13, 2009).

6. Tim Wallace Murphy and Marilyn Hopkins, *Custodians of Truth* (Boston: Weiser Books, 2005), p. 50.

7. The Midrash was a set of laws based on an interpretation of the Tanakh, or Hebrew Bible. *Midrash Halakha* dates from the captivity in Babylon; *Midrash Aggadah* was the interpretation of the nonlegal, or philosophical and historical, portions of the Hebrew Bible. See Isidore Singer and J. Theodor, "Midrash Haggadah," *The Jewish Encyclopedia* website. www.jewishencyclopedia.com/view.jsp?artid=587&letter=M (accessed: January 1, 2009).

8. Edwin Abbott, *Philochristos, Memoirs of a Disciple of the Lord Jesus* (Boston: Robert Brothers, 1878), p. 20.

9. Bryan T. Huie, "Who Were the Pharisees and the Sadducees?" (written March 1997, Revised September 2008), from the website *Here a Little, There a Little*. www.users.aristotle.net/~bhuie/pharsadd.htm (accessed: January 1, 2009).

10. From the Cairo Damascus Document 1:9–11, the only Qumran sectarian work that was known before the discovery of the Dead Sea Scrolls. Fragments of eight manuscripts of the Damascus Document were found in Qumran Cave 4 (4Q266-273), with scripts dating from the first century B.C.E. to the first century C.E. Evidence of these documents had been found many years earlier in the famous "Cairo Geniza," in a room adjoining a synagogue in Old Cairo. See J. R. Davila, "The Damascus Document and the Community Rule," *University of Saint Andrews School of Divinity*, February 2005. www.st-andrews.ac.uk/divinity/rt/dss/abstracts/ddcr (accessed: January 2, 2009).

11. *Habakkuk Pesher* 1QpHab 7:5. The Habakkuk Pesher is a Qumran document dating back to 120 B.C.E., found in 1947. The document gives us insight into the formation of the community at Qumran. See Michael D. Morrison,"QpHab—The Habakkuk Pesher: Relevance to New Testament Studies," article on the website *Life in Christ: Articles by Michael D. Morrison*. www.angelfire.com/md/mdmorrison/nt/1qphab.html (accessed: January 2, 2009).

12. Cairo Damascus Document 3:12–15.

13. *The Panarion of Epiphanius of Salamis: Book I (Sects 1-46)*, trans. Frank Williams (New York, E.J. Brill, 1987), Panarion 1:18.

CHAPTER 12

1. Flavius Josephus, *The Works of Flavius Josephus: The Wars of the Jews* (Grand Rapids, MI: Baker House, 1981), book 2, chap. 8, verse 6.

2. Dolores Cannon, *Jesus and the Essenes* (Bath, U.K.: Gateway Books, 1992), p. 303.

✓ 3. Michael Baigent, *The Jesus Papers* (Harper San Francisco, 2006), pp. 10-14, 266–273.

4. Flavius Josephus, *The Works of Flavius Josephus: Antiquities of the Jews* (Grand Rapids, MI: Baker House, 1981), vol. 4, book 18, chap. 1, verse 5.

5. Atum is the first motion of beginning made from the Great Cosmic Ocean. Ra is the light of the eternal Sun. E. A. Wallis Budge, *The Gods of the Egyptians* (New York: Dover Publications, 1969), pp. 69, 349–350.

6. Egypt was primarily a solar culture, but, at some point, Thoth instituted a lunar calendar at Thebes in the form of the male deity and lord of time, Khonsu, the symbolic child of Mut and Amon. Thus, Egypt came to honor

both solar and lunar calendars. See Budge, *Gods of the Egyptians*, pp. 413–415.

7. Zecharia Sitchin, *The Lost Book of Enki* (Rochester, VT: Bear & Company, 2002), pp. 157–161.

8. Ashtoreth or Ashera, considered the wife of Jehovah, appears forty times in nine books of the Old Testament. She had many forms, including a sacred tree bearing fruit in the desert, which was symbolic of her life-giving powers. See Philip Gardiner, *Gnosis: The Secret of Solomon's Temple Revealed* (New Jersey: Career Press, 2006), pp. 143–145. Ashera may have been derived from the goddess Hera (Ashera) of ancient Greece; the name Jehovah may well have been a derivative of Jove, another name for Jupiter or Zeus, the wargod, the "highest of the gods."

9. Baigent, *The Jesus Papers*, p. 165.

10. James C. VanderKam, *Near Eastern Archaeology Magazine: Qumran and Dead Sea Scrolls*, vol. 63, no. 3 (American Schools of Oriental Research), "Calendars in the Dead Sea Scrolls," (September 2000), pp. 164–167.

11. Tim Wallace-Murphy and Marilyn Hopkins, *Custodians of Truth* (Boston: Weiser, 2005), p. 23.

12. Flavius Josephus, *Flavius Josephus Against Apion*, book 1, verses 31–32, trans. William Whiston. (Grand Rapids, MI: Baker House, 1981), p. 791.

13. *Moü* is an Egyptian word meaning "water." Josephus, *Flavius Josephus Against Apion*, vol. 4, book 1, verse 31. See also Paul Brunton, *A Search in Secret Egypt* (York Beach, ME: Samuel Weiser, 1977), p. 179.

14. Ralph Ellis, *Jesus, Last of the Pharaohs* (Cheshire, UK: EDFU Books, 1998), p. 116.

15. Dolores Cannon, *Jesus and the Essenes* (Bath, U.K.: Gateway Books, 1992), pp. 156-168.

16. It was said that the hieroglyphs "speak, signify, and hide," indicating a three-fold meaning: the phonetic sounding of the words; a fuller symbolic expression of concepts and spoken words; and a deeper esoteric meaning relating to the process of initiation, enlightenment, and the sacred sciences. See Brunton, *Search in Secret Egypt*, p. 206.

17. Brunton, *Search in Secret Egypt*, p. 180.

18. Baigent, *The Jesus Papers*, pp. 28–29.

19. Josephus, *The Wars of the Jews*, vol. 1, book 2, chap. 8, verse 12.

20. Cannon, *Jesus and the Essenes*, p. 141.

21. http://essenes.net/index.php?option=com_content&task=view&id=290&It emid=633, "The Order of the Nazorean Essenes" website, article "Philo and the Essenes and the Therapeutae," excerpted from Philo of Alexandria's book *Quod Omris Probus Fiber Sit* preserved in Eusebius' *Praeparatio Evangilica*. (accessed: September 17, 2009).

22. Josephus, *Antiquities of the Jews*, Book 18, chap. 1, verse 5.

23. H. Spencer Lewis, *The Mystical Life of Jesus* (Los Angeles: Rosicrucian Press, 1929), pp. 14–15.

24. Emile Puech, "The Convictions of a Scholar," *Near Eastern Archaeology Magazine: Qumran and Dead Sea Scrolls*, vol. 63, no. 3 (September 2000), p. 160.

25. *The Order of the Nazorean Essenes* website. www.essenes.net/bnei1.htm (accessed: January 2, 2009).

26. "Teaching the Ancient Gnosis of Miryia, Jeshu and Mani," on the website *The Order of the Nazorean Essenes*, (accessed: January 2, 2009).

27. Discovered among the "lost gospels" was an astonishing text called *Poimandres*, attributed to the Egyptian divinity Thoth, which describes the mysteries of Creation, the destiny of man, and the importance of the soul. See Robert Silbelrud, *The Unknown Life of Jesus: Correcting the Church Myth* (Wellington, CO: New Science Publications, 2003), pp. 42–47.

28. Flavius Josephus was chosen as a delegate to Nero at the age of twenty-six, and then appointed governor of Galilee in the last fatal insurrection of the Jews against the Romans. While history is deeply indebted to Josephus for his works, much of what he says glorifies Hebrew history, as well as perspectives acceptable to his Roman patron. See Edmund Bordeaux Szekely, *The Essenes by Josephus and his Contemporaries* (Los Angeles: International Biogenic Society, 1981), pp. 11–13, 44–53.

29. Josephus, *The Wars of the Jews*, book 2, chap. 8, verse 11.

30. Herodotus, *The Histories*, Book II (London: Penguin Books, first published 1954, revised 1972, 1996, 2003), p. 144.

31. Josephus, *Antiquities of the Jews*, book 13, chap. 5, verse 9.

32. E. Washburn Hopkins, *The History of Religions* (New York: Macmillan & Company, 1918), pp. 552–556.

33. The *Essene Gospels*, books 1 through 4, make this very clear.

34. Szekely, *The Essenes by Josephus and his Contemporaries*, p. 37.

35. *The Essene Gospel of Peace*, Book II.

36. Edmond Bordeau Szekely, *The Essene Gospel of Peace, Book Two: The Unknown Books of the Essenes* (Los Angeles: International Biogenic Society, 1981), p. 7.

37. Szekely, *The Essenes by Josephus and his Contemporaries*, pp. 36–38.

38. Siblerud, *Unknown Life of Jesus*, p. 231.

39. The Atharva Veda, one of the four sacred Vedas of Hindu literature, tells us, "Whoever is not purified after birth with water from the Ganges, blessed by the holy invocation, will be subject to as many wanderings as years he has spent in impurity."

40. Michael A. Larson, "Whatever Happened to the Dead Sea Scrolls?" *The Journal of Historical Review*, vol. 3, no. 2, pp. 119–128. www.vho.org/GB/Journals/JHR/3/2/Larson119-128.html (accessed: January 4, 2009).

41. Josephus, *The Wars of the Jews*, vol. 1, book 2, chap. 8, verse 13.

42. Szekely, *The Essenes by Josephus and his Contemporaries*, p. 38.

43. "Oracle of Delphi," article on the website *Greece Taxi*. www.greecetaxi.gr/index/delphi_oracle.html (accessed: January 2, 2009).

44. Josephus, *The Wars of the Jews*, vol. 1, book 2, chap. 8, verse 7.

45. Cannon, *Jesus and the Essenes*, pp. 48–49.

CHAPTER 13

1. Flavius Josephus, *The Works of Flavius Josephus: The Wars of the Jews* trans. William Whiston (Grand Rapids, MI: Baker House, 1981), book 2, chapter 8.

2. Josephus describes four main designations of the Essene order: "…and so far are the juniors inferior to the seniors, that if the seniors should be touched by the juniors, they must wash themselves, as if they had intermixed themselves with the company of a foreigner." Josephus, *The War of the Jews*, vol. 1, book 2, chap. 8, verse 10.

3. Dolores Cannon, *Jesus and the Essenes* (Bath, UK: Gateway Books, 1992), pp. 84, 97, 101, 117, 162, 170, 176, 179, 180, and 185; also Stuart Wilson and Joanna Prentis, *The Essenes: Children of the Light* (Wheaton, IL: Ozark Publishing, 2005), pp. 21–36, 299.

4. Past-life researchers Dolores Cannon, Stuart Wilson, and Joanna Prentis all have clients who claim to have interacted with the mysterious Kaloo, the priestly remnants of the Atlantean continent that sank beneath the sea some 9000 years before Jesus was born. The Dead Sea Scrolls appear to reveal only a tiny glimpse into the Essenes' true depth of knowledge.

5. Christian Ginsburg, *The Essenes and the Kabbala* (London: Routledge and Kegan Paul, 1869), p. 141.

6. Josephus, *The Wars of the Jews*, vol. 1, book 2, chap. 8, verses 6–7.

7. Wilson and Prentis, *Children of the Light*, pp. 319–320.

8. Wilson and Prentis, *Children of the Light*, p. 320.

9. Josephus, *Antiquities of the Jews*, vol. 3, book 13, chap. 5, verse 9.

10. Since the 19th century, attempts have been made to connect early Christianity and Pythagoreanism with the Essenes. According to Martin A. Larson, author of more than twenty books, including *The Essene Heritage* (1967), the Essenes were really Jewish Pythagoreans who lived as monks. They preached a coming war with the Sons of Darkness and saw themselves as the "Sons of Light." This reveals yet another influence from Zoroastrianism. According to Larson, both the Essenes and Pythagoreans resembled the cults of the Greek

Orphic mysteries called the *thiasoi*, who believed in life, death, and rebirth. See also Wilson and Prentis, *Children of the Light*, pp. 112–113.

11. Wilson and Prentis, *Children of the Light*, pp. 84–85.

12. Barbara Thiering, *Jesus the Man* (New York: Atria Books, 1992), p. 32.

13. Bentley Layton, *The Gnostic Scriptures* (London: SCM Press, 1987), p. 20.

14. Victoria LaPage, *Mysteries of the Bridechamber* (Rochester, VT: Inner Traditions, 2007), p. 93.

15. LaPage, *Mysteries of the Bridechamber*, p. 93.

16. LaPage, *Mysteries of the Bridechamber*, p. 96.

17. LaPage, *Mysteries of the Bridechamber*, p. 98.

18. LaPage, *Mysteries of the Bridechamber*, p. 94–96.

19. Gaalyah Cornfield and David Noel Freedman, *The Archaeology of the Bible: Book by Book* (New York: Harper and Row, 1976), p. 141.

20. *The Habakkuk Commentary*, parts 4 and 5 of the *Book of Enoch*, and various statements found in *The Testaments of the Twelve Patriarchs*, the original portions of which were composed while Hyracanus was king. See Michael A. Larson, "Whatever Happened to the Dead Sea Scrolls?" *The Journal of Historical Review*, vol. 3, no. 2, pp. 119–128. www.vho.org/GB/Journals/ JHR/3/2/Larson119-128.html (accessed: January 4, 2009).

21. "For John truly baptized with water, but you shall be baptized with the Holy Spirit not many days from now" (Acts 1:5).

22. Some have surmised that James, Jesus' older brother, was a member of the Zealots. James was Jesus' successor to the bloodline, but he never had Jesus' years of training in the Mystery Schools or his vision. If he was a Zealot, James seems to have had a change of heart after the Crucifixion, deliberately allowing himself to be martyred rather than to refute his brother's teachings.

23. Michael Baigent, *The Jesus Papers* (San Francisco: Harper San Francisco, 2006), p. 37.

24. This idea had been presented in the Rule of the Community, one of the first scrolls found among the Dead Sea Scrolls in 1947.

25. John the Baptist was thought to have been the reincarnation of one of the last of the great Jewish prophets, Elijah.

Chapter 14

1. William Blake, "Jerusalem," in *Milton* (Princeton, NJ: Princeton University Press, 1998).

2. Cyril C. Dobson, *Did Our Lord Visit Britain as they say in Cornwall and Somerset?* 8th ed. (self-published, June, 1947).

3. Reverend Baring Gould composed the hymn "Onward Christian Soldiers," and authored over 1000 books and publications.

4. Lionel Smithett Lewis, *St. Joseph of Arimathea at Glastonbury or the Apostolic Church of Britain* 1st ed. (London: James Clarke & Company, Ltd., 1955; Cambridge, U.K.: Lutterworth Press, 2004), p. 66.

5. Stuart Wilson and Joanna Prentis, *The Essenes: Children of the Light* (Wheaton, IL: Ozark Publishing, 2005), p. 135.

6. Smithett Lewis, *St. Joseph of Arimathea at Glastonbury*, p. 52. Tyre was an island city founded in the third millennium B.C.E. that reached her Golden Age in the last millennium before Christ. The city fell to Alexander the Great in 332 B.C.E., after a seven-month siege, and by 64 B.C.E., it was under Roman rule. Tyre was an important port for naval vessels traveling the ancient shipping routes of the sea-faring Phoenicians. These would have been used by Joseph of Arimathea in the exportation of his tin from Britain and to Rome. "Countries: Tyre," *Middle East* website, http://www.middleeast.com/tyre.htm (accessed: February 14, 2009).

7. Hamish Miller and Paul Broadhurst, *The Sun and the Serpent* (Cornwall, U.K.: Pendragon Press, 1989), p. 79; Barry Dunford, *The Holy Land of Scotland: Jesus in Scotland and the Gospel of the Grail* (Glenlyon, Perthshire, Scotland: Sacred Connections, 2002), p. 2.

8. Dobson *Did Our Lord Visit Britain*, p. 3.

9. Dobson *Did Our Lord Visit Britain*, p. 1.

10. Dobson *Did Our Lord Visit Britain*, pp. 2, 12.

11. Dobson, *Did Our Lord Visit Britain*, p. 1.

12. Dunford, *The Holy Land of Scotland*, p. 81.

13. Dobson, *Did Our Lord Visit Britain*, p. 7.

14. A full course of study among the Druids could take as long as twenty years and included natural philosophy, astronomy, geometry, medicine, poetry, jurisprudence, arithmetic, and oration.

15. George F. Jowett, *The Drama of the Lost Disciples* (London: Covenant Publishing, 1972), p. 138.

16. Dunford, *The Holy Land of Scotland*, p. 109.

17. Dobson, *Did Our Lord Visit Britain*, pp. 84–90.

18. Wilson and Prentis, *Children of the Light*, p. 101.

19. Manly P. Hall, *The Secret Teachings of All Ages* (New York: Jeremy P. Tarcher/Penguin, 1929/2003), pp. 191–205.

20. Dunford, *The Holy Land of Scotland*, p. 112; Michell, *The New View Over Atlantis* (New York: Thames and Hudson, 1983), p. 203.

21. Michell, *The New View Over Atlantis*, p. 198.

22. Dunford, *The Holy Land of Scotland*, p. 32.

23. This included the sea-going Phoenicians, said to have been remnants of that mighty lost civilization.

24. According to the 11th-century Irish chronicle the *Book of Invasions*, or *Lebor Gabála Érenn*, the famous British queen, Queen Scota, was the daughter of Egyptian Pharaoh Necho II. Scota bore a son who was destined to become the ancestor of the Gaels. Her granddaughter, also named Queen Scota, was the daughter of the Egyptian pharaoh Neferhotep I. She migrated to Ireland with her eight sons. "Celtic Mythology: Milesians," *Answers* website, http://www.answers.com/topic/milesians (accessed: February 12, 2009).

25. Dunford, *The Holy Land of Scotland*, pp. 37-39.

26. There are some interesting works that support this theory, among them Dr. Adam Rutherford, *Israel Britain: An Explanation of the Origin, Function and Destiny of the Anglo-Celto-Saxon Race in the British Empire and U.S.A.* (Muskogee, OK:Artisan Publishers, 1934); W. H. Bennett, *Symbols of Our Celto-Saxon Heritage* (London: Covenant Books, 1976); and W. M. H. Milner, *The Royal House of Britain: An Enduring Dynasty*, (London: Covenant House, 1902), http://www.originofnations.org/books,%20papers/throne1.pdf (accessed: February 13, 2009).

27. Dunford, *The Holy Land of Scotland*, p. 40.

28. Dunford, *The Holy Land of Scotland*, p. 91.

29. *Beli* is derived from the root word *Bel*, or light, as in the word Beltane, an ancient name for the May Day festival, which celebrated the return of the light after the winter. Beli could also have been associated with a particular deity, such as Zeus, Shamash, Ra, or Horus in the Greek, Sumerian, or Egyptian pantheons. As a god of light, this deity was also called Bel, Bal, and Baal in Mesopotamia. *Taran* probably derives from the ancient Druid name for Earth, *Tara*, and thus means "the sons of Earth" or those who are in control of their own destinies. See Zecharia Sitchin and his ten-book *Earth Chronicles* series.

30. Dunford, *The Holy Land of Scotland*, p. 91.

31. Also called Rama, Ramallah, and Ramah.

32. E. Raymond Capt, *The Traditions of Glastonbury* (Thousand Oaks, CA: Artisan Sales, 1983), p. 19. In a 1534 account from the records of Glastonbury Abbey's library, John Leland, Henry the VIII's official historian, writes: "The Isle of Avalon greedy of burials… received thousands of sleepers, among whom Joseph de Marmore from Arimathea by name, entered his perpetual sleep. And he lies in a bifurcated line next to the southern angle of the oratory made of circular wattles by thirteen inhabitants of the place over the powerful adorable Virgin." Smithett Lewis, *St. Joseph of Arimathea at Glastonbury*, p. 94.

33. Smithett Lewis, *St. Joseph of Arimathea at Glastonbury*, pp. 56, 73.

34. Smithett Lewis, *St. Joseph of Arimathea at Glastonbury*, pp. 11, 32, 213.

35. Dobson, *Did Our Lord Visit Britain*, p. 10.

36. Dobson, *Did Our Lord Visit Britain*, pp. 229–232.

37. Smithett Lewis, *St. Joseph of Arimathea at Glastonbury*, p. 63.

38. Wilson and Prentis, *Children of the Light*, pp. 229, 232.

39. The community of Lammana sits on a hill overlooking the English bay and the small island of Looe that is also referred to as Lammana. Because of its associations with Jesus and Anna, a monastic community grew up there around the tenth century that was affiliated with Glastonbury Abbey. "Lammana: Place of Mystery and Peace," *Looe Old Cornwall Society* website, http://looeoldcornwallsoc.com/lamana.aspx (accessed: February 21, 2009).

40. Lewis, *St. Joseph of Arimathea at Glastonbury*, pp. 63–64.

41. Mary Caine, *The Glastonbury Zodiac: Key to the Mysteries of Britain* (Surrey, England: Kingstone Press, 1978), p. 150.

42. Lisa Sarasohn, "Find Your Center, Discover Your Power," *Sage Woman Magazine*, Volume 74: Visions of the Goddess: The Queen (2008), p. 11.

43. Dunford, *The Holy Land of Scotland*, p. 1.

44. Venerable Narada Mahathera, "The Buddha on the So Called Creator God," *Parabola Magazine*, Volume 33, Summer - 2008, p. 80.

45. The British monk and historian Venerable Bede tells us that the Gewissae or Gewissaw family became the rulers of Wessex in the upper Thames region around 470 C.E., and were considered one of the seven major Celtic tribal groups that ruled Britain. *Ecclesiastical History of the English People* (London: Penguin Classics, 1990), pp. 153, 230.

46. *The Lost Books of the Bible*, Protevangelion, chapter IV, (Surrey, England: Alpha House, 1927), p. 1.

47. Victoria LaPage, *Mysteries of the Bridechamber* (Rochester, VT: Inner Traditions, 2007), p. 24.

48. *The Lost Books of the Bible*, p. 30.

49. Wilson and Prentis, *Children of the Light*, p. 131.

CHAPTER 15

1. William Blake, "Jerusalem" in Ross Nichols, *The Book of Druidry* (London: Thorsons, 1992), p. 19. Blake was Chief of the British Druid Order from 1799 to his death in 1827.

2. Barry Dunford, *The Holy Land of Scotland: Jesus in Scotland and the Gospel of the Grail* (Glenlyon, Perthshire, Scotland: Sacred Connections, 2002), p. 59.

3. Dunford, *The Holy Land of Scotland*, p. 59.

4. John and Caitlin Matthews, *The Encyclopedia of Celtic Wisdom* (Shaftsbury, Dorset, England: Element Press, 1994), p. 183.

5. Matthews, *The Encyclopedia of Celtic Wisdom*, p. 186.

6. Liz and Colin Murray, *The Celtic Tree Oracle* (New York: St. Martin's Press, 1988), pp. 85–86.

7. "Eye of God," *Religion Facts: Just the Facts on the World's Religions* website, http://www.religionfacts.com/christianity/symbols/eye_of_god.htm (accessed: February 22, 2009).

8. Ross Nichols, *Book of Druidry* (London: Harper Collins, 1992), p. 24.

9. Nichols, *Book of Druidry*, p. 51; Dunford, *The Holy Land of Scotland*, p. 91.

10. James Freeman Clarke, *Ten Great Religions* (n.p.: Eliot C. Clarke, Project Gugenberg, 1871).

11. Manly P. Hall, *The Secret Teachings of All Ages* (New York: Jeremy P. Tarcher/Penguin), originally published in 1928 and reissued 2003, pp. 40–43.

12. Glenn Kimball, Marshall Masters and Janice Manning, eds., *The Kolbrin Bible* (Carson City, NV: Your Own World Books, Inc., 2005), p. 516.

13. Hall, *Secret Teachings*, p. 47.

14. Peter James and Nick Thorpe, *Ancient Mysteries* (New York: Ballantine Books, 1999), p. 293.

15. Jeremy Narby, *The Cosmic Serpent: DNA and the Origins of Knowledge* (New York: Jeremy P. Tarcher/Putnam, 1999), p. 123.

16. "Grace Cathedral: An Episcopal Cathedral," *Grace Cathedral* website, http://www.gracecathedral.org/community/labyrinths/ (accessed: February 23, 2009).

17. Hall, *Secret Teachings*, pp. 44–45.

18. C. W. Leadbeater, *Ancient Mystic Rites* (Wheaton, IL: Theosophical Heritage Classics, Quest Books, 1985), p. 121.

19. Leadbeater, *Ancient Mystic Rites*, p. 43.

20. *The Kolbrin Bible; The Britain Book*, p. 516. Abri is derived from the Egyptian words *Ibri, Abari* or *Abri*, meaning "wise ones."

21. Hall, *Secret Teachings*, p. 45.

22. Eugene Whitworth, *The Nine Faces of Christ* (Marina Del Rey, CA: DeVorss & Co, 1980), p. 168.

23. Hall, *Secret Teachings*, pp. 43–45.

24. Leadbeater, *Ancient Mystic Rites*, p. 121.

25. Whitworth, *Nine Faces of Christ*, pp. 173–189.

26. "Which Cubit was Used?" *Catholic Planet* website, http://www.catholicplanet.com/Tabernacle/which-cubit.htm (accessed: February 23, 2009).

27. Leadbeater, *Ancient Mystic Rites*, pp. 42–52.

28. For Egyptian influence in the Celtic landscape, see Hamish Miller and Paul Broadhurst, *The Sun and the Serpent* (Cornwall, U.K.: Pendragon Press, 1989), p. 71; John Michell, *The New View Over Atlantis*, (New York: Thames and Hudson, 1983), p. 198; Peter James and Nick Thorpe, *Ancient Mysteries* (New York: Ballantine Books, 1999), p. 529.

29. Christopher L.C.E. Witcombe, "Archaeoastronomy and Stonehenge," *Earth Mysteries* Web site, http://witcombe.sbc.edu/earthmysteries/EMStonehenge-

aerial.html (accessed: February 14, 2009). See also British astronomer Gerald Hawkins, *Stonehenge Decoded*.

30. Arianrhod was the Celtic Moon goddess, called Queen of the Wheel. She was the Welsh Goddess of the Wheeling Stars, also known as the Goddess of Fate, telling us that she was intricately linked to the turning of the heavens, the pole star, and the precession of the equinoxes. "Arianrhod, Welsh Goddess," *A Musing Grace Gallery: The Magical Art of Thalia* website, http://www.thaliatook.com/AMGG/arianrhod.html (accessed: February 20, 2009).

31. Nicholas R. Mann, *The Isle of Avalon* (St. Paul, MN: Llewellyn Publications, 1996), pp. 51, 105.

32. *The Kolbrin Bible: The Britain Book*, p. 516.

CHAPTER 16

1. Ross Nichols, "The Universal Druid Prayer" in *The Book of Druidry* (London: Thorsons, 1992), p. 286.

2. *The Kolbrin Bible: The Britain Book*, p. 429.

3. John and Caitlin Matthews, *The Encyclopedia of Celtic Wisdom* (Shaftsbury, Dorset, England: Element Press, 1994), pp. 22, 51.

4. Willis Barnstone, ed., *The Other Bible* (San Francisco: Harper San Francisco, 1984), p. 489.

5. Manly P. Hall, *The Secret Teachings of All Ages* (New York: Jeremy P. Tarcher/ Penguin, originally published in 1928 and reissued 2003), pp. 296-297.

6. Matthews, *Encyclopedia of Celtic Wisdom*, pp. 44-46, 296.

7. Barnstone, *The Other Bible*, p. 352.

8. Victoria LaPage, *Mysteries of the Bridechamber* (Rochester, VT: Inner Traditions, 2007), pp. 60-63.

9. Liz and Colin Murray, *The Celtic Tree Oracle* (New York: St. Martin's Press, 1988), pp. 32-33.

10. "Xache, The Mayan Tree of Life," *Buried Mirror: Mesoamerica and Mayan World* website, http://www.buriedmirror.com/yaxche.htm (accessed: February 14, 2009).

11. Ed Eagle Man McGaa, *Mother Earth Spirituality: Native American Paths to Healing Ourselves and Our World* (San Francisco: Harper San Francisco, 1990), p. 86.

12. Thomas E. Mails, *Secret Native American Pathways: A Guide to Inner Peace* (Tulsa, OK: Council Oak Books, 1988), p. 188.

13. Hall, *Secret Teachings*, pp. 297-298.

14. Ross Nichols, *Book of Druidry* (London: Harper Collins, 1992), p. 128.

15. "Hu Gadarn: a Cymric Pseudo Deity—HU the Mighty," *Nemeton, The Sacred Grove* website, http://www.celtnet.org.uk/gods_h/hu_gadarn.html (accessed: February 19, 2009).

16. Nichols, *Book of Druidry*, p. 124.

17. In Revelation 22:16, Jesus says, "I, Jesus... am the root and the offspring of David, the Bright and Morning Star." Venus, the planet of love, known as the Morning Star, rises in the east.

18. Herman L. Hoeh, *Compendium of World History* Vol. II, (USA: A Dissertation Presented to the Faculty of Ambassador College Graduate School of Education in Partial Fulfillment of the Degree of Doctor of Theology, 1969), pp. 49-50.

19. "Joshua and the Israelites in Britain and Ireland," *Cry Aloud: the Cybermagazine that Dares to Discuss Religion, Race, Sex and Politics* website, http://www.cryaloud.com/joshua_hu_gadarn_druids.htm (accessed: February 20, 2009).

20. Eleanor Merry, *The Flaming Door: A Preliminary Study of the Mission of the Celtic Folk-Soul by Means of Legends and Myths* (London: Rider & Co.), pp. 137, 153-165.

21. Nichols, *Book of Druidry*, pp. 124, 128.

22. Morgan Le Fey, "Sacred Trees, Oghams and Celtic Symbolism," *Geocities* website, http://www.geocities.com/Area51/Shire/3951/dryadart.html (accessed: February 14, 2009).

CHAPTER 17

1. William Blake, "Milton," in *Milton a Poem*, copy C, c. 1811 (New York Public Library) object 16 (Bentley 14, Erdman 15 [17], Keynes 14.

2. Smithett Lewis, *Glastonbury, Mother of all Saints* (Bristol, England: St. Stephen's Press, 1925), p. 4.

3. Also spelled *Ynys Witrin*. Eugene Whitworth, *The Nine Faces of Christ* (Marina Del Rey, CA: DeVorss & Co. 1980), p. 165.

4. Lionel Smithett Lewis, *St. Joseph of Arimathea at Glastonbury, or the Apostolic Church of Britain*, 1st ed. (Cambridge, U.K.: Lutterworth Press, 2004), p. 13.

5. The Ceryneian Hind of Wisdom was driven to Hyperborea (Britain) by Herakles in his third labor, and he followed it to seek wisdom. This gentle creature, long associated with the sign of Capricorn, the winter solstice, and the birth of the Lord of Light on December 25th, sheltered under an apple tree, the Celtic Tree of Paradise. Ross Nichols, *Book of Druidry* (London: Harper Collins, 1992), p. 46.

6. Nicholas Mann, *The Isle of Avalon* (St. Paul, MN: Llewellyn Publishing, 1996), p. 35.

7. Mann, *The Isle of Avalon*, p. 19.

8. Hamish Miller and Paul Broadhurst, *The Sun and the Serpent* (Cornwall, U.K.: Pendragon Press, 1989), p. 294.

9. The term *omphalos* means "navel," the center of the Goddess' body, the source of all things. The Romans placed it in the temple of Vesta, the Virgin;

the Greeks at Delphi, the "Temple of the Womb." The Jews located it at the Temple of Zion, and the Christians at Jerusalem. Barbara Walker, *The Women's Encyclopedia of Myths and Secrets* (New York: Harper San Francisco, 1983), pp. 740-741.

10. Ward Rutherford, *Celtic Mythology* (New York: Sterling Publishing Co, Inc., 1990), p. 103.

11. Nichols, *Book of Druidry*, p. 43.

12. Frances Howard-Gordon, *Glastonbury, Maker of Myths* (Glastonbury: Gothic Image Publications, 1982), p. 12.

13. Smithett Lewis, *St. Joseph of Arimathea at Glastonbury*, p. 54.

14. Mann, *The Isle of Avalon*, pp. 9-10.

15. Whitworth, *Nine Faces of Christ*, p. 165.

16. Mann, *The Isle of Avalon*, p. 12; Peter James and Nick Thorpe, *Ancient Mysteries* (New York: Ballantine Books, 1999), p. 284.

17. Mann, *The Isle of Avalon*, p. 15.

18. Mann tells us: "We can be certain that water-worn caves do exist in the limestone under the Tor. The legends imply that they are there... A spring would be capable of cutting tunnels through the soft limestone and provide the potential for sizeable chambers to form... At the same time the calcium carbonate in the limestone will crystallize in the right conditions and has undoubtedly formed beautiful stalagmite and stalactite formations under the Tor...The terraces of the Tor soak up water like a sponge and convey it through the fissures in the sandstone to the limestone strata below. Somewhere in this there is a geological formation capable of holding water, impregnating it with minerals, and then—at least in the case of Chalice Well—releasing it at a constant rate of flow regardless of the fluctuations in rainfall." *The Isle of Avalon*, pp. 142 and 169.

19. Howard-Gordon, *Glastonbury, Maker of Myths*, p. 17.

20. In the stone carving of the tower, Brigit is shown milking a cow, reminiscent of the Egyptian Hathor, long known as the "Celestial Cow of milk and honey." The Celtic Brighde was said to have presided over the lactation of domestic animals, and like Hathor, she was the goddess of childbirth.

21. Howard-Gordon, *Glastonbury, Maker of Myths*, p. 17.

22. Gwyn's name means "the White One of Night," a clear reference to Osiris, the Lord of Light who sits in the Halls of the Dead. Gwyn was well known from Welsh folklore as a Celtic deity, and was worshipped in southwest Britain in Roman times.

23. John Michell, *The New View Over Atlantis*, (New York: Thames and Hudson, 1983), p. 80.

24. Manly P. Hall, *The Secret Teachings of All Ages* (New York: Jeremy P. Tarcher/Penguin), originally published in 1928 and reissued 2003, p. 47.

25. Nichols, *Book of Druidry*, p. 119.

26. Michell, *The New View Over Atlantis*, p. 51.

27. Michell, *The New View Over Atlantis*, p. 80.

28. Diodorus is quoting from the famed geographer Hecataeus, of the fourth century B.C.E., who writes that Britain was the land of the Hyperboreans, meaning "those who live beyond the North Wind."

29. James and Thorpe, *Ancient Mysteries*, p. 193.

30. Sesha protects the Egg or lotus flower of Vishnu and Lakshmi, where the eternal Father and Mother of the universe reside. Jeremy Narby, *The Cosmic Serpent: DNA and the Origins of Knowledge* (New York: Jeremy P. Tarcher/Penguin, 1999), pp. 85-86.

31. In Indian cosmology, this World Axis is called Mount Mandara. Jill Purce, *The Mystic Spiral: Journey of the Soul* (London: Thames and Hudson, 1974), pp. 18, 37.

32. Srila Visvanatha Chakravarti, *Rupa Chintamani: A Guided Meditation in 32 Sanskrit Verses*, (Epworth, GA: Nectar Books,), p. 4.

33. Alan Jacobs, ed. *The Gnostic Gospels* (London: Watkins Publishing, 2006), p. 173.

34. George Oliver, *History of Initiation* (n.p., Kessinger Publishers, 1997).

35. Philip Gardiner, *Gnosis: The Secret of Solomon's Temple Revealed* (New Jersey: Career Press, 2006), p. 29.

36. Lauren Artress, *Walking a Sacred Path: Rediscovering the Labyrinth as a Spiritual Tool* (New York: Riverhead Books, 1995), pp. 96-97.

37. James and Thorpe, *Ancient Mysteries*, p. 291.

38. Purce, *Mystic Spiral*, pp. 105, 110.

39. Howard-Gordon, *Glastonbury, Maker of Myths*, p. 22.

40. "Labyrinth," *Greek Mythology* website, http://www.mlahanas.de/Greeks/Mythology/Labyrinth.html (accessed: March 10, 2009).

41. Purce, *Mystic Spiral*, p. 111.

42. Hugh MacGregor Ross, *Gospel of Thomas* (London: Watkins Publishing, 1987), pp. 10–11.

43. "Labyrinth," *Greek Mythology* website, (accessed: March 10, 2009).

44. Purce, *Mystic Spiral*, p. 99.

45. This was in At Hadrumentum in North Africa. Karl Kereny, *Dionysus: Archetypal Image of Indestructible Life* (Princeton, NJ: Princeton University Press, 1976), p. 31.

46. For example, we see the spiral painted into the ninth-century minaret of the mosque of Samarra, Iraq.

47. Purce, *Mystic Spirals*, pp. 31, 49, 56–57.

CHAPTER 18

1. Robert Stephen Hawker, *The Quest of the San Graal* (London: Thorsons an imprint of HarperCollins Publishing, *The Book of Druidry*, Ross Nichols, 1975), p. 138.

2. John Michell, *The New View Over Atlantis* (New York: Thames and Hudson, 1983), pp. 53–54.

3. Peter James and Nick Thorpe, *Ancient Mysteries* (New York: Ballantine Books, 1999), p. 197.

4. These fields, known as torsion fields, have been measured and studied by leading scientists like Prabhat Poddar, Dee J. Nelson, and Alexey Dmitriev. Poddar indentifies two kinds of phenomena that can be measured at such a site: the energy passing through the vertical axis of the mound, and the spiral energy moving up the pyramid's apex in a helical column toward the heavens. See David Wilcock, "A Scientific Blueprint for Ascension," *The Spirit of Ma'at* website, http://netmar.com/~maat/archive/sep2/wilcock.htm (accessed: February 18, 2009). Also Philip Gardiner, *Gnosis: The Secret of Solomon's Temple Revealed* (New Jersey: Career Press, 2006), pp. 162, 166.

5. James and Thorpe, *Ancient Mysteries*, p. 71.

6. John Michell, *Twelve Tribe Nations and the Science of Enchanting the Landscape* (Grand Rapids, MI: Phanes Press, 1991), p. 90.

7. Nicholas Mann, *The Isle of Avalon* (St. Paul, MN: Llewellyn Publications, 1996), p. 104.

8. Michell, *Twelve Tribe Nations*, p. 74.

9. Key among them are Hamish Miller, Paul Broadhurst, Graham Hancock, Robert Bauval, C.E. Street, and historian John Michell, who are all involved with the research, reporting, and rediscovery of the ancient science of geomancy.

10. Mann, *The Isle of Avalon*, p. 69, 150.

11. Hamish Miller and Paul Broadhurst, *The Sun and the Serpent* (Cornwall, U.K.: Pendragon Press, 1989), pp. 89–90.

12. Michell, *The New View Over Atlantis*, pp. 188-189.

13. Catherine Maltwood, *Glastonbury's Temple of the Stars* (London: Watkins Publishing, 1935), Since then, other investigators have followed, including Mary Caine, *The Glastonbury Zodiac: Keys to the Mysteries of Britain* (Surrey, England: Kingstone Press, 1978) .

14. This may well have to do with the "Boat of a Million Years," in which it was said each soul must journey to reach heaven. There is also a thirteenth sign in the Glastonbury Zodiac, set apart from the larger circle on the land as its guardian; it is called the great dog of Langport who guards the abode of

Annwn. This figure is five miles wide, and reminds us of Anubis, the protective dog, whose Egyptian title was the "Opener of the Ways."

15. The circle's northern end encompasses Avalon, forming a perfect triangle to two other sites: Cadbury Castle, some twelve miles to the southeast, thought to have once been the site of Camelot; and Alfred Burrow, Athelney, twelve miles to the southwest, where another terraced hill similar to the Tor now stands. Maltwood, *Glastonbury's Temple of the Stars*, p. 21.

16. Frances Howard-Gordon, *Glastonbury, Maker of Myths* (Glastonbury: Gothic Image Publications, 1982), pp. 29, 130.

17. Caine, *Glastonbury Zodiac*, pp. 20-23, 32, 39.

18. Howard-Gordon, *Glastonbury, Maker of Myths*, pp. 15, 22, 27.

Chapter 19

1. Robert Stephen Hawker, *The Quest of the San San Graal,* Ross Nichols, *The Book of Druidry* (London: Thorsons Publishers), pp. 13, 138.

2. Lionel Smithett Lewis, *St. Joseph of Arimathea at Glastonbury or the Apostolic Church of Britain* (Cambridge, U.K.: Lutterworth Press, 2004), p. 31.

3. Ross Nichols, *Book of Druidry* (London: Harper Collins, 1992), pp. 38, 151-152, 158. This is mentioned some fifty times in the Old Testament.

4. Smithett Lewis, *St. Joseph of Arimathea at Glastonbury*, p. 29.

5. Frances Howard-Gordon, *Glastonbury, Maker of Myths* (Glastonbury: Gothic Image Publications, 1982), p. 36.

6. E. Rayond Capt, *The Traditions of Glastonbury* (Thousand Oaks, CA: AArtisan Sales, 1983), p. 43.

7. C. E. Street, *Earthstar's Visionary Landscape: London, City of Revelation* (London: Hermitage Publishing, 2000), p. 295.

8. Street, *Earthstar's Visionary Landscape*, p. 43.

9. "The Final Exile of Joseph of Arimathea from Israel to the Isle of Avalon," *Bible Searchers* website, http://biblesearchers.com/hebrewchurch/primitive/primitive6.shtml#Magdalene (accessed: February 19, 2009).

10. John Michell, *Twelve Tribe Nations and the Science of Enchanting the Landscape* (Grand Rapids, MI: Phanes Press, 1991), pp. 102–104.

11. Capt, *Traditions of Glastonbury*, p. 45, 47.

12. Cardinal Baronius, *Ecclesiastical Annals*, volume 1, section 35.

13. "The Final Exile of Joseph of Arimathea from Israel to the Isle of Avalon," *Bible Searchers* website, www.biblesearchers.com (accessed: February 20, 2009).The date for Joseph of Arimathea's death is recorded as July 27, 82 c.e., and even today his feast is held in the early days of August. Lewis, *St. Joseph of Arimathea at Glastonbury*, p. 111.

14. Stuart Wilson and Joanna Prentis, *The Essenes: Children of the Light* (Wheaton, IL: Ozark Publishing, 2005), p. 215.

15. "Places of Peace and Power: Saintes Marie de la Mer, France," *The Church of the Tree Saints* website, http://www.sacredsites.com/europe/france/church_of_three_saints.html (accessed: February 19, 2009).

16. "Britain, Phoenicia's Secret Treasure," *Encyclopedia Phoenician* website, http://phoenicia.org/britmines.html (accessed: March 14, 2009).

17. William of Malmesbury's date is slightly askew, since Joseph's landing is elsewhere noted as 36 or 37 C.E., only a year or so after Jesus' Crucifixion. But we must remember that William of Malmesbury is writing some 1100 years after the events.

18. John W. Taylor, *The Coming of the Saints* (Muskogee, OK: Artisan Sales/Hoffman Printing, 1985), pp. 151–152.

19. Lewis, *St. Joseph of Arimathea at Glastonbury*, p. 86.

20. This name contains the two words *Mary* and *Zion*, which together mean "new Mary," perhaps a reference to Mary the Mother or Mary Magdalene.

21. Lewis, *St. Joseph of Arimathea at Glastonbury*, p. 29.

22. R. W. Morgan, *St. Paul in Britain* (1860; reprinted Thousand Oaks, CA: Artisan Sales/Hoffman Printing, 1984), p. 73.

23. Arviragus was the son of Cunobelinus, one of the Pendragons, keepers of the electro-magnetic ley lines that flowed across the land. The Pendragons were the ancestors of King Arthur and his father, Uther, and the Tudor kings and queens of England eventually claimed their descent from this royal line. Henry W. Stough, *Dedicated Disciples* (Muskogee, OK: Artisan Sales, Hoffman Printing, 1987), p. 87.

24. *The Kolbrin Bible: The Britain Book*, chapter 5, verse 21, 517.

25. *The Kolbrin Bible: The Britain Book*, chapter 1, verses 7–8, 503.

26. Others say a hide is 160 acres, making a total of 1920 acres given by the Silurian royal family.

27. *The Domesday Book*, the written record of a census and survey of English landowners and their property made by order of William the Conqueror in 1085–1086.

28. *The Kolbrin Bible: The Britain Book*, 516.

29. The many stories in *The Kolbrin Bible* are a collection of first-hand accounts ranging from those who lived after the Great Flood, to events contiguous with those of the Old and New Testaments.

30. This is an interesting reference to the Eye of God, which was well known in most esoteric circles, but was specifically linked with the wisdom of Egypt as the Eye of Ra or the Eye of Horus.

31. Here the Druid is speaking about the multi-dimensional nature of reality and the planes that are nested one inside the other like the layers of an onion.

32. *The Kolbrin Bible: The Britain Book*, chapter four, "The Writings of Aristolas," verses 6–20.

33. These illnesses were endemic to the region and the fact that those in Joseph's party avoided them indicated they were spiritually protected from them.

34. *The Kolbrin Bible: The Britain Book*, chapter 1, verse 9.

35. Eugene Whitworth, *The Nine Faces of Christ* (Marina Del Rey, CA: DeVorss & Co, 1980), p. 80.

36. *The Kolbrin: The Britain Book*, chapter 1, verses 11–21.

37. Howard-Gordon, *Glastonbury, Maker of Myths*, p. 51.

38. Quoted in Howard-Gordon, *Glastonbury, Maker of Myths*, p. 51–52.

39. This seems to imply that Jesus himself appeared in Britain to bless this chapel, perhaps even seeding it with a holy egg. Just such an ancient stone, or *omphalos*, has been found at this site, with one side inscribed with a cross. Howard-Gordon, *Glastonbury, Maker of Myths*, pp. 41, 43.

40. Lewis, *Glastonbury, the Mother of Saints*, p. 4.

41. William of Malmsbury, quoted in Lewis, *Glastonbury, the Mother of Saints*. pp. 10-11.

42. Howard-Gordon, *Glastonbury, Maker of Myths*, pp. 43–45.

43. Michell, *The New View Over Atlantis*, p. 168.

44. Hamish Miller and Paul Broadhurst, *The Sun and the Serpent* (Cornwall, U.K.: Pendragon Press, 1989), p. 83.

45. Peter James and Nick Thorpe, *Ancient Mysteries* (New York: Ballantine Books, 1999), p. 529. The presence of two pyramids marking the spot of a Celtic king is significant. Egyptian emblems litter the English countryside. See John Michell, *The Dimensions of Paradise* (London: Harper & Row, 1988), p. 15.

46. Howard-Gordon, *Glastonbury, Maker of Myths*, p. 49.

47. The coffin contained two bodies: one of an enormously tall, armored man conforming to the descriptions of King Arthur, who appeared to have died from a blow to the head; the other of a blonde-haired woman that he held in his arms. The inscription read: "Here in Avalon lies buried the renowned King Arthur, with Guinevere, his Second Wife." James and Thorpe, *Ancient Mysteries*, pp. 529–530.

48. Lewis, *Saint Joseph of Arimathea at Glastonbury*, p. 153.

49. Lewis, *Saint Joseph of Arimathea at Glastonbury*, p. 606.

50. Nicholas Mann, *The Isle of Avalon*, p. 3.

CHAPTER 20

1. *The Sophia of Jesus Christ* in Alan Jacobs, ed., *The Gnostic Gospels*, (London: Watkins Publishing, 2006).

2. Manly P. Hall, *The Secret Teachings of All Ages* (New York: Jeremy P. Tarcher/ Penguin), originally published in 1928 and reissued 2003, p. 582.

3. The name derives from the Sanskrit word for "knowledge" or "wisdom" (veda). The Vedas are believed to be more than 5000 years old. They were

"passed down faithfully by special families within the Brahman communities of India." Other references to these seven sacred Rishis appear in the Edfu Building Texts of Egypt. Hancock and Faii, *Heaven's Mirror: Quest for the Lost Civilization* (New York: Crown Publishers, 1996), p. 139. See also Lockamanya Bal Gangadhar Tilak, *The Arctic Home in the Vedas: Being Also a Key to the Interpretation of Many Vedic texts and Legends*, originally self-published in 1903 and 1925, then republished by Messrs. Tilak Brothers, Poona City, 1956, p. 420.

4. Edward Martin, *King of Travelers: Jesus' Lost Years in India* (Lampasas, TX: Jonah Publishing, 1999), pp. 148–149.

5. Confirmation of Jesus' return to Palestine in his later twenties comes from the *Acts of Pilate*. If this account is true, then Jesus returned to Judea for perhaps even a year or two before leaving again for Britain. This would have allowed him to reconnect with friends and family, and renew his connections with the Essene community. W. D. Mahan, *The Acts of Pilate* (Kirkfield, MO: Impact Christian Books, 1997), p. 63.

6. Eugene Whitworth, *The Nine Faces of Christ* (Marina Del Rey, CA: DeVorss & Co, 1980), pp. 192-194.

7. The *siddhis* are considered inherent human abilities that show up when the consciousness has reached a certain level of spiritual development. In Hindu belief, a Siddha is a perfected master who has transcended the ego and subdued the mind, transforming the body through constant meditation into a body of purity.

8. Whitworth, *Nine Faces of Christ*, pp. 47–64, 196-197.

9. Nicolas Notovitch, *The Unknown Life of Jesus Christ* (originally published in Chicago: Rand McNally, 1894, current publisher: Joshua Tree, CA: Tree of Life Publications, 1996), pp. 11-12, 15.

10. Swami Abhedananda, *Journey into Kashmir and Tibet* (Bengali: Ramakrishna Vedanta Math Publications, Demy Octavo, 1922), p. 119.

11. Elizabeth Clare Prophet, *The Lost Years of Jesus* (Livingston, MT: Summit University Press, 1984), p. 54.

12. Elizabeth Clare Prophet, *The Lost Years of Jesus* (Livingston, MT: Summit University Press, 1984), pp. 16–17.

13. Notovitch, *The Unknown Life of Jesus Christ*, p. 32.

14. Notovitch, *The Unknown Life of Jesus Christ*, pp. 10–11.

15. Robert Siblerud, *The Unknown Life of Jesus: Correcting the Church Myth* (Wellington, CO: New Science Publications, 2003), p. 128.

16. Willis Barnstone, *The Other Bible* (San Francisco: Harper SanFrancisco, 1984), p. 465.

17. Notovitch, *The Unknown Life of Jesus Christ*, p. 35.

18. Siblerud, *The Unknown Life of Jesus*, p. 128.

19. Notovitch, *The Unknown Life of Jesus Christ*, p. 35.
20. The Acts of Thomas were written in Edessa around 225 C.E.
21. Notovitch, *The Unknown Life of Jesus Christ*, p. 129.
22. Whitworth, *Nine Faces of Christ*, pp. 194–180. See also Jean-Yves Leloup, *The Gospel of Mary Magdalene* (Rochester, VT: Inner Traditions, 2002), pp. vii, 35. These are considered the Five Passions of the Mind.
23. Leloup, *The Gospel of Mary Magdalene*, pp. 194–204.
24. This triumvirate in the Hindu pantheon would be Brahma, Vishnu, and Shiva, the Creator, Maintainer, and Destroyer. See Alan Jacobs, ed., *The Gnostic Gospels* (London: Watkins Publishing, 2006), pp. 171–172, 181.
25. Notovitch, *The Unknown Life of Jesus Christ*, pp. 40–41.
26. Notovitch, *The Unknown Life of Jesus Christ*, p. 202.
27. Notovitch, *The Unknown Life of Jesus Christ*, p. 38.
28. Notovitch, *The Unknown Life of Jesus Christ*, p. 38.
29. Elizabeth Clare Prophet, *The Lost Years of Jesus* (Livingston, MT: Summit University Press, 1984), p. 17.
30. Whitworth, *The Nine Faces of Christ*, pp. 213–214.
31. Notovitch, *The Unknown Life of Jesus Christ*, p. 35.
32. Whitworth, *The Nine Faces of Christ*, pp. 212–220.
33. Elizabeth Clare Prophet, *The Lost Years of Jesus* (Livingston, MT: Summit University Press, 1984), p. 17.

CHAPTER 21

1. From the Teachings of the Buddha, Digha Nikaya 26:25. Marcus Borg, *Jesus and Buddha: The Parallel Sayings* (Berkeley, CA: Ulysses Press, 1997), p. 141.
2. H. Spencer Lewis, PhD, *The Mystical Life of Jesus*, (CA: Grand Lodge of the English Language Jurisdiction, AMORC, 1997), p. 134.
3. Over the centuries, the teachings of the Buddha have been preserved in many forms: *Samyutta Nikaya*, the short Connected Discourses; *Majjhima Nikaya*, The Middle Length Discourses; and *Digha Nikaya*, the Long Discourses. Like our modern day Bible, these discourses are codified by using chapter and verse designations, such as 2:22. The *Digha Nikaya* ("Collection of Long Discourses") is the first of the five nikayas (collections) in the *Sutta Pitaka*.
4. From the Digha Nikaya 26: 25. Marcus Borg, *Jesus and Buddha: The Parallel Sayings* (Berkeley, CA: Ulysses Press, 1997), p. 141.
5. Jayaram V, "Purusha, the Universal Cosmic Male and Prakiti, the Mother Nature," *Hindu* Web site, www.hinduwebsite.com/prakriti.asp (accessed: January 19, 2009).
6. Jayaram V, "Purusha" website, (accessed: January 19, 2009).

7. Daniel Pinchbeck and Ken Jordan, *Towards 2012: Perspectives on the New Age* (New York: Jeremy P. Tarcher/Penguin, 2008), pp. 116, 123.

8. "The Avatars of Vishnu: The Buddha and the Maha-Purusha," *Takoda's Book of Shadows: Return to the Ancient Ways*, www.geocities.com/takoda_Magick/hinduavatars.html (accessed: January 16, 2009).

9. "The Avatars of Vishnu" *Takoda's Book of Shadows* website (accessed: January 16, 2009).

10. Jayaram V, "Purusha" website. (accessed: January 19, 2009).

11. Jayaram V, "Purusha" website. (accessed: January 19, 2009).

12. Ralph Thomas Hotchkin Griffith, originally trans. in 1889, *The Rigveda*, Book 10, HYMN XC, Purusha, the Purusha Sukta (1896), *Sacred Texts* website, www.sacred-texts.com/hin/rigveda/rv10090.htm (accessed: January 16, 2009).

13. Hugh McGregor Ross, ed., *The Gospel of Thomas* (London: Watkins Publishing, 1987), p. 53

14. Ross, *The Gospel of Thomas*, p. vii.

15. W. D. Mahan, *Acts of Pilate* (Kirkfield, MO: Impact Christian Books, 1997), pp. 119–120.

16. Nicolas Notovitch, *The Unknown Life of Jesus Christ* (originally published in Chicago: Rand McNally, 1894, current publisher: Joshua Tree, California: Tree of Life Publications, 1996), pp. 20-21.

17. Here the lama seems to be calling both the Jews and the Romans pagans. Perhaps all civilizations presume their way is better and call "the others" pagans. Notovitch, *The Unknown Life of Jesus Christ*, p. 21.

18. Clement of Alexandria, *Stomata* (or *Miscellanies*), Andover-Harvard University Library, (Edinburgh, Scotland: T. and T. Clark Publishing, 1871), book I, chapter XV, verse 21, quoted in Alexander Roberts, Sir James Donaldson, and Allan Menzies, *Ante-Nicene Christian Library: Translations of the Writings of the Fathers down to A.D. 325,* vol. II, *Early Christian Writings* website, www.earlychristianwritings.com/clement.html (accessed: January 19, 2009).

19. C. Vercellonis and J. Cozza, *Bibliorum Sacrorum Graecus Codex Vaticanus*, (Roma 1868). "Origen's Commentary on Ezekiel," is one of many commentaries written by Origen on the Bible. While many of Origen's prolific writings did not survive, Origen's Commentary on Ezekiel can be found within the *Codex Vaticanus*, a collection of the early books of Christianity that is currently housed within the Vatican Library. T. C. Skeat, a paleographer at the British Museum, first argued that *Codex Vaticanus* was among the first fifty Bibles that the Emperor Constantine I (275-337 c.e.) ordered Eusebius of Caesarea to produce, making this collection nearly 1700 years old.

CHAPTER 22

1. The Upanishads.

2. Swami Abhedananda, *Journey into Kashmir and Tibet* (Bengali: Ramakrishna Vedanta Math Publications, Demy Octavo, 1922), p. 236. Nicolas Notovitch, *The Unknown Life of Jesus Christ* (originally published in Chicago: Rand McNally, 1894, current publisher: Joshua Tree, CA: Tree of Life Publications, 1996), p. 38.

3. Eugene Whitworth's claims may be based on actual records that have been preserved about Jesus' time in the Far East. *The Nine Faces of Christ* (Marina Del Rey, CA: DeVorss & Co. 1980), pp. 217–218.

4. "Bukhoro," *Answers Online* website, www.answers.com/topic/bukhara (accessed: January 16, 2009).

5. Nestorius was the patriarch of Constantinople (modern Istanbul) from 428 to 431 C.E. His doctrine alleges two persons (one divine, one human) in Jesus Christ. Later the Nestorians became known as the Assyrian Church of the East. They used the Aramaic language spoken by the Jews in Judea and Galilee at the time that Jesus lived.

6. "Bokhara," *The Jewish Encyclopedia* website, www.jewishencyclopedia.com/view.jsp?artid=1243&letter=B (accessed: January 17, 2009).

7. Some believe Zoroaster was born around 1000 B.C.E.; others say far earlier. It is possible that a line of Zoroastrian high priests carried his message into various centuries.

8. Edmond Bordeaux Szekely, *The Essenes by Josephus and His Contemporaries*, from Philo's text about the Essenes called the *Quod Omnis Probus Liber*, meaning "that all men are free" (Los Angeles: International Biogenic Society, 1981), pp. xii–xiii , 37.

9. Adrian G. Gilbert, *Magi: The Quest for a Secret Mystical Tradition* (London: Bloomsbury Publishing, 1996), p. 54.

10. Whitworth, *The Nine Faces of Christ*, p. 219.

11. Timothy Freke and Peter Gandy, *The Jesus Mysteries* (New York: Three Rivers Press, 1999), p. 265.

12. Szekely, *The Essenes by Josephus and His Contemporaries*, p. 55.

13. LaPage, Victoria, *Mysteries of the Bridechamber* (Rochester, VT: Inner Tradition, 2007), p. 154.

14. Andrew Welburn, *The Beginnings of Christianity* (Edinburgh, Scotland: Floris Books, 1995), p. 19.

15. David Ulansey, *The Mithraic Mysteries: Cosmology and Salvation in the Ancient World* (New York: Oxford University Press, 1989), pp. 59, 107.

16. David Fideler, *Jesus Christ, Sun of God: Ancient Cosmology and Early Christian Symbolism* (Wheaton, IL: Quest Books, 1961), pp. 143–156.

17. Manly P. Hall, *The Secret Teachings of All Ages* (New York: Jeremy P. Tarcher/ Penguin), originally published in 1928 and reissued 2003, p. 597.

18. Caves were considered sacred to Mother Earth. Entering them is like entering the womb of Creation itself. Many Native American tribes enact this same ritual in sweat lodges, where one learns to be still and listen to Mother Earth and Father Sky. The Essenes also met in caves, and both John of Patmos and Mary Magdalene were said to have spent their last years in caves in meditation and prayer.

19. John P. Lundy, *Monumental Christianity or The Art and Symbolism of the Primitive Church*, 1st ed. (New York: J. W. Bouton, 1876; Reprinted by Kessinger Publishing, LLC, 2003).

20. I call these beings Rigel and Auriel, which are still other names for the Eagle and the Dove, or the primordial and divine presences of the Divine Father and Mother, Truth and Love, that create, sustain, and maintain the universe.

21. Gilbert, *Magi*, p. 54.

22. Brian Swimme, *The Hidden Heart of the Cosmos* (New York: Orbis Books, 2000), pp. 93, 109–110.

23. Swimme, *Hidden Heart of the Cosmos*, pp. 110–111.

24. Joseph Campbell, *Masks of the Gods III* (New York: Viking Penguin Books, 1964, reissued by Arkana, 1991), p. 261.

25. Hall, *Secret Teachings*, p. 59.

26. Hall, *Secret Teachings*, p. 51.

27. Hall, *Secret Teachings*, p. 51.

28. Campbell, *Masks of the Gods*, p. 255.

29. The great persecution of Christians officially ended in April of 311 c.e., when Galerius, then senior emperor of the Tetrarchy, issued an edict of toleration that granted Christians the right to practice their religion. In 313, Constantine I and Licinius announced toleration of Christianity in the Edict of Milan, which removed penalties for professing the faith. Fordham University Center for Medieval Studies, *Internet Medieval Sourcebook: The End of the Classical World*, www.fordham.edu/halsall/sbook1b.html#Persecution%20 of%20Christians (accessed: January 22, 2009).

30. Freke and Gandy, *The Jesus Mysteries*, pp. 1-3.

31. Josceyln Godwin, *Mystery Religions of the Ancient World* (San Francisco: Harper & Row, 1981), p. 28.

32. Nima Sadjadi, "Mithraism – The God Eternal Time," *Farvardyn* website, www.farvardyn.com/mithras5.php (accessed: January 22, 2009).

33. Ulansey, *The Mithraic Mysteries*, p. 117.

34. Fideler, *Jesus Christ, Sun of God*, p. 258.

35. LaPage, *Mysteries of the Bridechamber*, pp. 152–153.

36. Ulansey, *Mithraic Mysteries*, p. 125.

CHAPTER 23

1. John Anthony West, *The Serpent in the Sky: the High Wisdom of Ancient Egypt* (Wheaton, IL: Quest Books, 1993), p. 127.

2. G. R. S. Mead, *Thrice Greatest Hermes*, vol. III (London: John M. Watkins, 1964), p. 99.

3. Adrian G. Gilbert, *Magi: The Quest for a Secret Mystical Tradition* (London: Bloomsbury, 1996), p. 13.

4. Delores Devore, *I Am the Beloved Mastery of the Self,* website, www.iamthebeloved.com (accessed: January 18, 2009).

5. Antioch was the capital of ancient Syria until 64 B.C.E., and one of the early centers of Christianity.

6. W. D. Mahan, *The Acts of Pilate* (Kirkfield, MO: Impact Christian Books, 1997), p. 120.

7. Stuart Wilson and Joanna Prentis, *The Essenes: Children of the Light* (Wheaton, IL: Ozark Publishing, 2005), pp. 37–38.

8. Gilbert, *Magi*, p. 217.

9. "Parchment of the Sarmoung Brotherhood," www.mystae.com/restricted/streams/scripts/sarman.html (accessed: January 18, 2009).

10. Gilbert, *Magi*, p. 45.

11. Gilbert, *Magi*, p. 259.

12. John G. Bennett, *Gurdjieff: Making of A New World* (New York: Harper and Row, 1973), p. 54.

13. Jonnie Hill, "The Traveling Masons," available at *Masonic Light* website, www.masoniclight.com/papers/13Traveling%20Mason.txt (accessed: January 18, 2009).

14. Subhuti Dharmananda, "Myrrh and Frankincense," *The Institute for Traditional Medicine* website, www.itmonline.org/arts/myrrh.htm (accessed: January 22, 2009).

15. The term *Saoshyant* means "the helper who will come to deliver the Earth from the fetters of Anramainya, the dark force."

16. "Zoroaster ~ Zarathrustra," *The Seeker* website, www:personalpages.tds.net/~theseeker/ZOROAS~1.HTM (accessed: January 18, 2009).

17. Gilbert, *Magi*, p. 297.

18. "Zoroaster," *Search* website, www.search.com/reference/Zoroaster (accessed: January 21, 2009).

19. J. G. Bennett, *The Masters of Wisdom* (Santa Fe: Bennett Books, 1995), p. 51.

20. This epic poem was written by the Persian poet Ferdowsi around 1000 C.E. and is called the *Shahnama*. It tells the mythical and historical past of Iran from the creation of the world up until the Islamic conquest of Iran in the 7th century. "Ferdowsi's Shahnameh," *Life is Beautiful and Free* website,

http://my.opera.com/iceage_2098/blog/2008/02/07/ferdow (accessed: January 20, 2009).

21. Abd-run-shin, *Zoroaster: Life and Work of the Forerunner in Persia* (Stuttgart, Germany: Stiftung Gralsbotschaft Publishing Company, 1993), p. 248.

22. Gilbert, *Magi*, p. 57.

23. Herodotus, *Persian War*, Book II (London: Penguin Books, 1954, revised 1972 and 1996), p. 114.

24. Herodotus, *Persian War*, Book II (London: Penguin Books, 1954, revised 1972 and 1996), pp. 114, 122–125.

25. Ahriman is also called Angra Mainyu.

26. James R. Lewis and Evelyn Dorothy Oliver, *Angels A to Z* (Canton, MI: Visible Ink Press, 1996), p. 14.

27. Tim Wallace-Murphy and Marilyn Hopkins, *Custodians of the Truth* (Boston: Weiser Books, 2005), p. 87.

28. Mystics like Edgar Cayce tell us that this battle actually took place in the final days before the sinking of Atlantis, when "the Sons of Light and the Sons of Beliel" fought over Earth's resources.

29. Alan Jacobs, ed., *The Gnostic Gospels* (London: Watkins Publishing, 2006), pp. 75–76.

30. Nicholas Notovitch, *The Unknown Life of Jesus Christ* (originally published in Chicago: Rand McNally, 1894, current publisher: Joshua Tree, CA: Tree of Life Publications, 1996), p. 37.

Chapter 24

1. John Anthony West, *The Serpent in the Sky: the High Wisdom of Ancient Egypt* (Wheaton, IL: Quest Books, 1993), p. 1.

2. The ten visible sephiroths represent the archetypal qualities of the planets. The eleventh, Daath, represents the distant planet Pluto. Pluto, along with Jupiter, the radiant planet of light, represents the archetypal energies of Osiris, the Lord of the Dead.

3. Tim Wallace Murphy and Marilyn Hopkins, *Custodians of Truth* (Boston: Weiser Books 2005), pp. 19–33.

4. Graham Hancock and Robert Bauval, *The Message of the Sphinx: A Quest for the Hidden Legacy of Mankind* (New York: Crown Publishers, 1996), p. 213.

5. The word *Zep* means "time"; *Tepi* means "first," but can also relate to the "commencement or beginning of a thing," as well as the concept of one's ancestors, revealing that Egypt's true legacy of wisdom may lay in a time far more remote than traditional Egyptologists previously have been willing to admit. See Wallace-Murphy, *Custodians*, pp. 206–207.

6. Wallace-Murphy, *Custodians*, p. 32.

7. Wallace-Murphy, *Custodians*, p. 33.

8. Glen Kimball and David Stirland, *Hidden Politics of the Crucifixion* (Salt Lake City, UT: Ancient Manuscripts Publishing, 1998), p. 67.

9. The Great White Brotherhood's headquarters may have been in the Himalayas, in the Valley of Timir. Only students who have learned out-of-body travel and can travel there in their *Nuri Sarup*, or light bodies, can reach it. At the time of Jesus, the Brotherhood's accessible headquarters was in Egypt.

10. H. Spencer Lewis, *The Mystical Life of Jesus* (Los Angeles: Rosicrucian Press, 1929), p. 92.

11. C. W. Leadbeater, *Ancient Mystic Rites* (Wheaton, IL: Theosophical Heritage Classics, Quest Books, 1985), p. 25.

12. Kimball and Stirland, *Hidden Politics of the Crucifixion*, p. 35.

13. Hall, *The Secret Teachings of All Ages*, p. 581.

14. Kimball and Stirland, *Hidden Politics of the Crucifixion*, p. 142.

15. Michael Baigent, *The Jesus Papers* (San Francisco: Harper San Francisco, 2006), p. 52.

16. This is one of many places in the Bible where it appears that Jesus was able to make himself invisible to the crowds when he needed.

17. Baigent, *Jesus Papers*, p. 14.

18. W. D. Mahan, *The Acts of Pilate* (Kirkfield, MO: Impact Books, 1997), pp. 87, 92–93. Thaumaturgy is the performance of miracles or Magic. Necromancy is the practice of talking with spirits—either the spirits of the dead or higher dimensional forces—in order to predict or influence the future.

19. Mahan, *Acts of Pilate*, pp. 132–136.

20. Ahmed Osman, *Jesus in the House of the Pharaohs*, (Rochester, VT: Bear and Company, 1991), pp. 28–29.

21. Pilate tells us that, at the time of the Crucifixion, Jesus had around 4000 followers, and Caiaphas writes that there were at least 100,000 people present during the Passover crucifixion. See Mahan, *Acts of Pilate*, pp. 108–125.

22. Mahan, *Acts of Pilate*, pp. 107–108.

23. John Marc Allegro, *The Official Website of John Marc Allegro* website, http://johnallegro.org/main/index.php?module=pagemaster&PAGE_user_op=view_printable&PAGE_id=1&lay_quiet=1 (accessed: January 26, 2009).

24. "Two New Gospels," *Subtle Energies* website: Articles and Art about Subtle Energy and Its Manifestation, http://www.subtleenergies.com/ormus/jesus/new.htm (accessed: February 10, 2009).

25. "The Essene Humane Gospel of Christ," *Essene* website, www.essene.com/TheEsseneHumaneGospel/index.html (accessed: February 1, 2009).

26. Since we know that Moses was trained as a priest in the temples of Heliopolis, this statement is most significant.

27. This "Holy Name" is linked to the master Thoth, who was known as a master of sacred geometry and sound. It was then transmitted to Isis, who had the power of the Word through which she worked miracles.

28. "The Essene Humane Gospel of Christ," *Essene* website (accessed: February 1, 2009).

29. "The Essene Humane Gospel of Christ," *Essene* website (accessed: February 10, 2009).

30. "The Gospel of the Holy Twelve," translated from the original Aramaic and edited by Gideon Jasper Richard Ouseley in 1892, *Essene* website (accessed: February 10, 2009).

31. "The Gospel of the Holy Twelve," *Essene* website (accessed: February 10, 2009).

32. "The Gospel of the Holy Twelve," *Essene* website (accessed: February 10, 2009).

33. Levi Dowling, *The Aquarian Gospel of Jesus the Christ in the Piscean Age*, (Santa Monica, CA: DeVors Publishing Co., 1907), p. 88.

CHAPTER 25

1. Bhagavad-Gita, Barbara Stolea Miller, (NY: Quality Paperback Book Club, 1988), p. 31.

2. E. A. Wallis Budge, *The Gods of the Egyptians* (New York: Dover Publications, 1969), p. 119.

3. Tablets discovered in the temple at Nineveh tell us that these gods and goddesses were tall (nine to fifteen feet) and exceedingly long-lived human beings who came to our planet some 435,000 years ago. They were responsible for seeding our planet's culture and nurturing mankind's earliest civilizations. They taught monotheism, since they themselves saw the universe as an ever-unfolding expression of the One.

4. John Anthony West, *The Traveler's Key to Ancient Egypt* (Wheaton, IL: Quest Books, 1995), pp. 46–47.

5. Manly P. Hall, *The Lost Keys to Freemasonry* includes the classic works *Freemasonry of the Ancient Egyptians* and *Masonic Orders of Fraternity* (New York: Jeremy P. Tarcher/Penguin, 2006), pp. 114-115.

6. Hall, *The Lost Keys to Freemasonry*, p. 9.

7. Hall, *The Lost Keys to Freemasonry*, p. 101.

8. Hall, *The Lost Keys to Freemasonry*, pp. xii-xii.

9. West, *The Traveler's Key to Ancient Egypt*, p. 42.

10. The chakras represent the Merkaba field, the light bodies that must be activated to generate mastery. The Nile, a perfect symbol of our inner nervous system, even branches outward like the ganglia of the brain into the northern

delta basin, creating the shape of the flowering lotus, a symbol long associated with the thousand-petal lotus of the crown chakra, which resides at the top of head. A similar symbolism was carved into the tops of all Egyptian columns as the emblems of the lily and the lotus, two flowers that represented the Flower of Life.

11. John Anthony West, *The Serpent in the Sky: the High Wisdom of Ancient Egypt* (Wheaton, IL: Quest Books, 1993), pp. 127–128.

12. *The Ancient Egypt Site: An Interactive Book of the History, Monuments, Language and Culture of Ancient Egypt* website, www.ancient-egypt.org/index. html (accessed: January 27, 2009).

13. West, *The Traveler's Key to Ancient Egypt*, p. 194.

14. The *ka* was the life force, the difference between a living and a dead person. Death occurred when the ka left the body. The ka was created by Khnum on a potter's wheel, and passed on to children via their father's semen. The Egyptians also believed that the ka was sustained through food and drink. For this reason, food and drink offerings were presented to the dead. The ka was often represented in Egyptian iconography as a second image of the individual, leading early translators to translate the word as "double."

15. Zecharia Sitchin, *The Lost Book of Enki* (Rochester, VT: Bear & Company, 2002), pp. 128–145. Sumerian records tell us that, along with his son, Ningishzidda (Thoth), and Enki's half-sister, Ninharsag (Hathor), Enki genetically enhanced Cro-Magnon man, and thus created modern-day homo sapiens.

16. David Fideler, *Jesus Christ, Sun of God: Ancient Cosmology and Early Christian Symbolism* (Wheaton, IL: Quest Books, 1961), p. 254.

17. In Greece, these teachings were expressed in the first levels of the Mysteries, which were centered around the great mother, Demeter, and her lost daughter, Kore, who descended to the Underworld. Demeter was but another name for Isis; Kore represented the tiny seed of the great creatrix who had fallen to Earth and must return to heaven. Kore's other names are Persephone and Kernel.

18. West, *The Serpent in the Sky*, p. viii.

19. West, *The Traveler's Key to Ancient Egypt*, p. 45.

20. West, *The Traveler's Key to Ancient Egypt*, p. 9.

21. Victoria LaPage, *Mysteries of the Bridechamber* (Rochester, VT: Inner Traditions, 2007), pp. xxiv–xxv.

22. R. A. Schwaller de Lubicz, *Sacred Science: The King of Pharaonic Theocracy* (Rochester, VT: Inner Traditions, 1988), pp. 235–236. The lions represent Aker, a hermetic symbol that means "yesterday" and "tomorrow." They are a reference not only to the Sphinx, with its lion's body, but to the Lord Osiris. "Yesterday" and "tomorrow" refer to the great passages of time that mark the precession of the equinoxes and the eternal leadership of Horus and Osiris,

with whom the new Pharaoh was always identified. Notice the solar significance of the twelve princes around the pharaoh, like the twelve signs of the Zodiac.

23. Schwaller de Lubicz, *Sacred Science*, p. 236.

24. This process was traditionally believed to take place inside the Pyramid of Unas at Saqqara, close to the Giza plateau, beneath a canopy of painted stars that represented the heavens. This was a symbol of the pharaoh's journey into the Duat, or the Great Beyond. We know that the actual king-making initiation began at sunset and continued until dawn, and that its purpose was to link the incoming pharaoh directly with Osiris, making him the next Horus, or rightful heir of Egypt.

25. Christopher Knight and Robert Lomas, *The Hiram Key* (New York: Barnes and Noble, 1996), p. 107.

26. Knight, *The Hiram Key*, p. 11. "The bright and morning star" was used as one of the spiritual names for the Horus king in both Egyptian and Freemasonry rituals to signify allegiance to the Christ.

27. Jose Argüelles, *Surfers of the Zuvuya: Tales of Inter-dimensional Travel* (Santa Fe, NM: Bear & Company, 1988). In the Mayan tradition, this process of soul travel is called "surfing the Zuvuya;" in Sufi traditions, it is "riding the Shabda." In the wisdom of the Vairagi masters, who teach the esoteric science of soul travel, this tone is called the Audible Life Stream, the Sound Current behind every living thing. One uses the powers of light and sound to access this Word, and thus the initiate traveled into the heart of Creation itself, all the way to the seat of the great central Sun.

28. Edmond Bordeaux Szekely, *The Essene Gospel of Peace: Book Four, the Teachings of the Elect* (California: International Biogenic Society, 1981), pp. 7, 42.

29. Hugh McGregor Ross, ed., *The Gospel of Thomas* (London: Watkins Publishing, 1987), p. 65.

30. Schwaller De Lubicz, *Sacred Science*, pp. 24, 237–238.

31. Ross, *Gospel of Thomas*, p. 24.

32. West, *The Traveler's Key to Ancient Egypt*, p. 273.

33. C. W. Leadbeater, *Ancient Mystic Rites* (Wheaton, IL: Theosophical Heritage Classics, Quest Books, 1985), p. 45.

34. Joscelyn Godwin, *Mystery Religions in the Ancient World* (San Francisco: Harper & Row Publishers, 1981) pp. 34–35.

35. Leadbeater, *Ancient Mystic Rites*, p. 98.

CHAPTER 26

1. E. A. Wallis Budge, The Papyrus of Ani, XLII, *The Egyptian Book of the Dead*, (New York: Dover Publications, 1967), p. 356.

2. Philip Gardiner, *Gnosis: The Secret of Solomon's Temple Revealed* (New Jersey: Career Press, 2006), p. 50. "Anu was the pole star, the axis [of the world]… and it was from Anu… that the kings of the earth derived their power—they were kings by the powers of the Otherworld," writes Gardiner in his 2007 book *Gateway to the Otherworld*.

3. The name *Awen* in the Celtic world was the name of the lord of the dead. Thoth and Horus/Apollo were known in Britain long before the Druids began.

4. Graham Hancock and Robert Bauval, *The Message of the Sphinx: A Quest for the Hidden Legacy of Mankind* (New York: Crown, 1996), p. 155.

5. Zecharia Sitchin, *The Lost Book of Enki* (Rochester, VT: Bear & Company, 2002), pp. 285–286.

6. E. A. Wallis Budge, *The Gods of the Egyptians* (New York: Dover Publications, 1969), p. 328.

7. Graham Hancock and Santha Faiia, *Heaven's Mirror: Quest for the Lost Civilization* (London: Michael Joseph, 1998), p. x.

8. The enormous temple of Karnak measures 480 by 550 meters (less than half the size of Heliopolis), and its walls are not even twelve meters thick. Jimmy Dunn, "The Area of Ancient Heliopolis," *Tour Egypt* website, http://www.touregypt.net/featurestories/on.htm (accessed: January 27, 2009).

9. David Fideler, *Jesus Christ, Sun of God* (Wheaton, IL: Quest Books, 1961), pp. 54–55.

10. Diodorus Siculus, *The Historical Library of Diodorus the Sicilian in Fifteen Books*, translated by George Booth. Vol. I & II. (London: W. McDowall, 1814), Book 1, chap. 4,

11. From Plato, *The Laws*. See Fideler, *Jesus Christ, Sun of God*, p. 54 and Paul Brunton, *A Search in Secret Egypt* (York Beach, ME: Samuel Weiser), 1977), p. 28.

12. Robert Bauval and Adrian G. Gilbert, *The Orion Mystery* (New York: Three Rivers Press, 2004), p. 196.

13. "The Secret of the Great Pyramids," *Master Mason* website, www.mastermason.com/hiramdiscovered/Pyramid3.html (accessed: January 27, 2009).

14. Tim Wallace-Murphy and Marilyn Hopkins, *Custodians of Truth* (Boston: Weiser Books 2005), pp. 14-15.

15. Wallace-Murphy, *Custodians*, pp. 14–15.

16. M. and R. Sabbah, *Les Secrets de L'Expode* (Paris: Godefroy, 2000), p. 99.

17. Herodotus (London: Penguin Books, 2003), p. 635.

18. Ralph Ellis, *Jesus, Last of the Pharaohs* (Cheshire, UK: EDFU Books, 1998), p. 116. See also Zecharia Sitchin, *The Wars of Gods and Men* (New York: Avon Books, 1985), pp. 33–35.

19. Hancock and Faiia, *Heaven's Mirror*, p. 66.

20. Stansbury Hagar, "The Zodiacal Temples of Uxmal," *Popular Astronomy Magazine*, vol. 79 (1921), p. 96.

21. Their names were Shu, Tefnut, Geb, Nuit, Osiris, Isis, Set, Nephthys, and Ra.

22. Budge, *The Egyptian Book of the Dead*, pp. liii–liv.

23. Egypt was called *Khemit*, meaning "the black lands," a reference to the rich soil that rose from the annual inundation of the Nile River.

24. Wallace-Murphy, *Custodians*, p. 6.

25. Tony Bushby, *The Secret in the Bible* (Queensland, Australia: Stanford Publishing Company and Joshua Books, 2003), pp. 33-35.

26. Bushby, *The Secret in the Bible*, p. 34.

27. David Ulansey, *The Mithraic Mysteries: Cosmology and Salvation in the Ancient World* (New York: Oxford University Press, 1989), p. 107.

28. Bushby, *The Secret in the Bible*, p. 100.

29. Bushby, *The Secret in the Bible*, p. 35.

30. The winged lion of Saint Mark was also adopted by the city of Venice in 828 C.E. when Saint Mark became its patron saint.

31. Gerald Massey, *The Egyptian Book of the Dead and the Ancient Mysteries of Amenta* (New York: A&B Publishers Group, 1939), pp. 62–65.

32. Richard Russell Cassaro, "The Osiris Connection," *Atlantis Rising Magazine*, no. 27, (May-June 2001), pp. 42–43.

33. Eugene Whitworth, *The Nine Faces of Christ* (Marina Del Rey, CA: DeVorss & Co, 1980), p. 275.

34. E. A. Wallis Budge, *Osiris and the Egyptian Resurrection* (New York: Dover Publications, 1973), p. 17.

35. C. W. Leadbeater, *Ancient Mystic Rites* (Wheaton, IL: Theosophical Heritage Classics, Quest Books, 1985), p. 17.

36. Alan Jacobs, *Sophia of Jesus Christ* (London: Watkins Publishing, 2006), p. 175.

37. Hugh McGregor Ross, ed., *The Gospel of Thomas* (London: Watkins Publishing, 1987), p. 53.

CHAPTER 27

1. E. A. Wallis Budge, The Papyrus of Ani, chapter LXXVII, (*The Egyptian Book of the Dead*, (New York: Dover Publications, 1967), p. 332.

2. Graham Hancock and Santha Faiia, *Heaven's Mirror: Quest for the Lost Civilization* (London: Michael Joseph, 1998), p. 321.

3. Herodotus *The Histories (Book II)* (London: Penguin Books, 2003), p. 124.

4. Venus may be the Morning Star, or it may refer to the periodic rotation of the planet Niburu, said to pass through our solar system every 3600 years. Or it may be a periodic conjunction of two or more planets rising in the east.

5. Herodotus, *The Histories (Book II)* (London: Penguin Books, 2003), p. 137.

6. Herodotus, *The Histories (Book II)* (London: Penguin Books, 2003), p. 137.

7. Robert Bauval and Adrian G. Gilbert, *The Orion Mystery* (New York: Three Rivers Press, 2004), p. 225.

8. Hancock and Faiia, *Heaven's Mirror*, p. 107. See also Tony Bushby, *The Secret in the Bible* (Queensland, Australia: Joshua Books, 2003), p. 78.

9. The falcon god of Hierakonpolis-Nekhen, representing Horus the Elder, or Divine Father principle, and Min, representing the Horus aspect in every pharaoh, also wore these feathers.

10. E. A. Wallis Budge, *Osiris and the Egyptian Resurrection* (New York: Dover Publications, 1973), p. xi.

11. Budge, *Osiris and Egyptian Resurrection*, pp. xi, liii, 339–342.

12. Budge, *The Egyptian Book of the Dead*, pp. xix, liv.

13. Henri Frankfort, *Kingship and the Gods* (Chicago: University of Chicago Press, 1948), p. 209.

14. Budge, *Osiris and the Egyptian Resurrection*, p. 80.

15. John 19:38–40 says: "After this, Joseph of Arimathea, being a disciple of Jesus, but secretly, for fear of the Jews, asked Pilate that he might take away the body of Jesus; and Pilate gave him permission. So he came and took the body of Jesus. And Nicodemus, who at first came to Jesus by night, also came, bringing a mixture of myrrh and aloes, about a hundred pounds. Then they took the body of Jesus and bound it in strips of linen with the spices, as the custom of the Jews is to bury."

16. Richard Russell Cassaro, "The Osiris Connection," *Atlantis Rising* Magazine, no. 27, (May-June 2001), p. 42.

17. Budge, *The Egyptian Book of the Dead*, pp. 332–340.

18. Budge, *The Egyptian Book of the Dead*, pp. 339–343.

19. E. A. Wallis Budge, *The Gods of the Egyptians,* (New York: Dover Publications, 1969), p. 332.

20. *Tour Net* website, http://www.touregypt.net/featurestories/heliopolis.htm (accessed: January 28, 2009).

21. Alexander Trevi, "Moving the Vatican Obelisk," http://pruned.blogspot.com/2007/05/moving-vatican-obelisk.html (accessed: January 28, 2009).

22. If we calculate Jesus' birthday as 6, 7 or 8 B.C.E., and his public ministry in Palestine beginning after John's (29 C.E.), this would mean that Jesus' ministry started between 30 to 33 C.E. From the beginning date of his ministry, subtract seven years to take him back to Egypt to begin this phase of his training. By this calculation, Jesus would have arrived in Egypt somewhere between 23 and 25 C.E.

23. David Fideler, *Jesus Christ, Sun of God: Ancient Cosmology and Early Christian Symbolism* (Wheaton, IL: Quest Books, 1961), p. 197.

CHAPTER 28

1. The Egyptian Coffin Texts.
2. Eugene Whitworth, *The Nine Faces of Christ* (Marina Del Rey, CA: DeVorss & Co. 1980), pp. 251–252.
3. Whitworth, *Nine Faces of Christ*, p. 252.
4. The jaguar priests of the Caribes were once highly respected in the ancient world. They may have come, along with the Phoenicians, from Atlantis.
5. The Adam Cadmon (or Adam Kadmon) can be defined as "the first being to emerge with the creation of the cosmos" and is common to a number of religious and philosophical traditions. The Upanishads describe a primal man composed of the very elements which were to become the world. According to the Upanishads this "gigantic divine being" is both infinitely far from and deposited near the innermost recesses of the human heart. In Hindu tradition, the Primordial Man is identified both with the entire Universe and the soul or essence of all things. This figure is similar to Mithra, Osiris, and Jesus, who emerges from the Cosmic Egg. See Sanford L. Drob, "The Lurianic Kabbalah," *New Kabbalah* website, www.newkabbalah.com/adam.html (accessed: January 28, 2009).
6. Jeremy Naydler, *Temple of the Cosmos* (Rochester, VT: Inner Traditions, 1996), p. 197.
7. Whitworth, *Nine Faces of Christ*, p. 253.
8. Whitworth, *Nine Faces of Christ*, p. 253–254.
9. Daniel Beresniak, *Symbols of Freemasonry* (New York: Barnes and Noble Books, 2003), p. 11.
10. Beresniak, *Symbols of Freemasonry*, p. 11.
11. Willis Barnstone, *The Other Bible* (San Francisco: Harper SanFrancisco, 1984), pp. 419-420.
12. Whitworth, *Nine Faces of Christ*, p. 263. A fuller delineation of these subtle bodies can be found in Naydler's *Temple of the Cosmos*.
13. Paramahansa Yogananda, *The Yoga of Jesus* (Los Angeles: Self Realization Fellowship, 2007), p. 35.
14. This is a reference to the nine bodies of man that allowed Jesus to learn how to completely re-alchemicalize his flesh. See Whitworth, *Nine Faces of Christ*, p. 263.
15. Paramahansa Yogananda, *The Yoga of Jesus*, pp. 35–36.
16. Heru is the higher aspect of Horus and was considered the masculine aspect of the eternal divine.
17. Pyramid Text 1.325-335 taken from the Unas Pyramid. The Pyramid Texts are a collection of about 4000 hymns and formulae from the Vth and VIth Dynasties found inscribed in the ceilings and walls of various pyramids in

the vicinity of Sakkara. They were first discovered in 1879 and finally explored in 1881. The texts describe events, histories, weather conditions, and theological concepts that predate everything we had previously known of Egyptian history. See Tim Wallace-Murphy and Marilyn Hopkins, *Custodians of Truth* (Boston: Weiser Books 2005), p. 10.

18. Ra's symbol was also a ram, as well as a hawk, like Horus and Osiris.

19. Lucie Lamy, *Egyptian Mysteries* (London: Thames & Hudson, 1981), pp. 56–57.

20. Lamy, *Egyptian Mysteries*, p. 57.

21. Yogananda, *The Yoga of Jesus*, pp. 36–37.

22. Ross Nichols, *Book of Druidry* (London: Harper Collins, 1992), p. 24.

23. These texts include the *Book of the Two Ways, the Book of Knowing What is in the Duat, the Egyptian Book of the Dead, the Coffin Texts, the Papyrus of Ani,* and the *Pyramid Texts.*

24. Tony Bushby, *The Secret in the Bible* (Queensland, Australia: Standford Publishing Group and Joshua Books, 2003), pp. 23-25.

25. Bushby, *The Secret in the Bible*, pp. 23–26.

26. Bushby, *The Secret in the Bible*, pp. 26–27. There are seven major halls described, containing twenty-one columns or pylons, all of which were believed to have existed both in the heavens and in the landscape below the Giza plateau. This celestial theology was also studied by the Gnostics, and can be found in the Books of Enoch, which describe the journey of the soul through the various heavenly spheres. See also David Ulansey, *The Mithraic Mysteries: Cosmology and Salvation in the Ancient World* (New York: Oxford University Press, 1989), p. 87.

27. Budge, *The Egyptian Book of the Dead*, p. v.

28. Naydler, *Temple of the Cosmos*, p. 215.

29. Naydler, *Temple of the Cosmos*, p. 219.

30. Naydler, *Temple of the Cosmos*, p. 259.

31. Gerald Benedict, *The Mayan Prophecies for 2012* (London: Watkins Publishing, 2008), pp. 153–154.

32. Lamy, *Egyptian Mysteries*, p.31.

33. Naydler, *Temple of the Cosmos*, p.257.

34. Naydler, *Temple of the Cosmos*, p. 258.

35. Lamy, *Egyptian Mysteries*, p. 30–31.

36. Hugh MacGregor Ross, ed. *The Gospel of Thomas* (London: Watkins Publishing, 1987), p. 24.

37. Lamy, *Egyptian Mysteries*, p. 58.

38. The first section includes the three coccyx bones at the base of the spine. The second includes the five sacral bones. The five lumbar bones and nerves

make up the third section. The fourth section comprises the twelve thoracic bones and nerves that give rotational movement. The fifth section is the seven cervical bones and the eight nerves that control the head, neck, and shoulders and attach to the brain.

39. The pineal gland, located in the middle of the brain, is important for the production of various hormones that regulate the activity of certain glands.
40. Lamy, *Egyptian Mysteries*, p. 58.
41. Whitworth, *Nine Faces of Christ*, p. 262. These words, which are direct quotes from Thoth, are attributed to Jesus.

Chapter 29

1. Gerald Massey, *The Egyptian Book of the Dead and the Ancient Mysteries of Amenta* (New York: A&B Publishers Group, 1939).
2. Philip Gardiner, *Gnosis: The Secret of Solomon's Temple Revealed* (New Jersey: Career Press, 2006), p. 161.
3. John Anthony West, *The Traveler's Key to Ancient Egypt* (Wheaton, IL: Quest Books, 1995), p. 123.
4. C. W. Leadbeater, *Ancient Mystic Rites* (Wheaton, IL: Theosophical Heritage Classics, Quest Books, 1985), p. 25.
5. Tony Bushby, *The Secret in the Bible* (Queensland, Australia: The Stanford Publishing Group and Joshua Books, 2003), p. 135.
6. "Evidence that the upper section of the Great Pyramid was once painted was established when chunks of casing stones with a rusty colored surface were found around its base early in the 19th Century. Through careful chemical and spectrographic analysis at the Sorbonne in Paris, it was determined that the stones had once been covered with a layer of paint made from iron oxide." See Bushby, *The Secret in the Bible*, p. 132.
7. Bushby, *The Secret in the Bible*, p. 135.
8. Bushby, *The Secret in the Bible*, p. 154.
9. The merger of these two elements reflects the perennial principle of balance of the two alchemical currents, male and female, merged for enlightenment.
10. Gardiner, *Gnosis*, p. 70. Rostau can also be translated as "gateway to the Duat."
11. W. Max Muller, *Egyptian Mythology* (New York: Dover Publications, 2004), p. 43.
12. A Sumerian cylinder seal speaks of "a vast underground palace… entered through a tunnel, its entrance hidden by sand and by what they call Huwana… his teeth as the teeth of a dragon, his face, the face of a lion." Bushby, *The Secret in the Bible*, p. 164.
13. Henri Frankfort, *Kingship and the Gods* (Chicago: University of Chicago Press, 1948), p. 61.

14. *Heru* means "the face of heaven," the head of the otherwise unknown and invisible god. E. A. Wallis Budge, *The Gods of the Egyptians* (New York: Dover Publications, 1969), pp. 466–470. Hawk-headed lion statues have been found in other archaeological digs, most notably at the mythical city of Troy. They were known throughout the ancient world, and connected with the legends of more ancient civilizations like Lemuria and Atlantis. Bushby, *The Secret in the Bible*, pp. 148–149, 164.

15. The historical records of Manetho name the Egyptian rulers going back some 35,000 years, including a 12,000-year span when Egypt was ruled only by the gods, an 18,000-year span when Egypt was ruled by the demigods (half mortal, half Anunnaki, or shining ones), and a 3,000-year span when mortal men and women took power. The last is the beginning of our history, approximately 3100 B.C.E. It was at the end of the first phase that the followers of Horus, or the Shemsa-Hor, helped him regain his throne, and thus, in the time of the demigods, they became the rulers of the land. See Tim Wallace-Murphy and Marilyn Hopkins, *Custodians of Truth* (Boston: Weiser Books 2005), pp. 12–15.

16. Graham Hancock and Robert Bauval, *The Message of the Sphinx: A Quest for the Hidden Legacy of Mankind* (New York: Crown Publishers, 1996), p. 162.

17. John Anthony West, *The Traveler's Key to Ancient Egypt* (Wheaton, IL: Quest Books, 1995), p. 137.

18. Thothmes IV ruled for nine years, from 1447 B.C.E. to 1438 B.C.E.

19. "The Stele of Thothmes IV," translation by D. Mallet, www.dabar.org/RecordsOfThePast/Vol2/SteleThothmes-4.html (accessed: January 28, 2009).

20. Bushby, *The Secret in the Bible*, pp. 148-149.

21. Cheops lived from 2551 to 2528 B.C.E. See West, *The Traveler's Key to Ancient Egypt*, p. 139.

22. John Anthony West, *The Serpent in the Sky: the High Wisdom of Ancient Egypt* (Wheaton, IL: Quest Books, 1993), p. xv.

23. West, *Serpent in the Sky*, p. 163.

24. Herodotus also tells us that the body of the pharaoh Cheops was placed deep beneath the Great Pyramid, in an underground sepulcher on an island fed by the Nile. See West, *The Traveler's Key to Ancient Egypt*, p. 102.

25. Herodotus, *The Histories*, trans. by Aubrey de Selincourt, Revised with Introduction and Notes by John Marincola (New York: Penguin, 2003) pp. 156–157.

26. Herodotus, *The Histories*, p. 163.

27. West, *The Traveler's Key to Ancient Egypt*, p. 97.

28. David H. Lewis, "Hidden Enormous Chambers Deep Under Giza," *Secrets of the Pyramid* website, http://www.galactic.to/rune/pyrmyst.html (accessed: February 1, 2009). Egyptian headlines read: "Mystery Tunnel in Sphinx."

29. Tony Bushby, "The Lost History of the Pyramids," From the book: *The Secret in the Bible*, Queensland, Australia: Stanford Publishing and Joshua Books, 2003, p. 150.

30. Christian Rosenkreuz, or Father C.R.C., was born in Germany in 1378 and was responsible for the formation of the Secret Society of the Rose Cross. See Manly P. Hall, *The Secret Teachings of All Ages* (New York: Jeremy P. Tarcher/ Penguin), originally published in 1928 and reissued 2003, pp. 442–458.

31. Hall, *The Secret Teachings of All Ages*, pp. 441–446.

32. Bushby, *Lost History of the Pyramids*, p. 167.

33. "Deep Hidden Enormous Chambers, Deep Under Giza," *Secrets of the Pyramid* (accessed: February 1, 2009).

34. West, *The Traveler's Key to Ancient Egypt*, pp. 448-449.

35. "Egyptian Civilization Lover," *Egypt State Information: Your Gateway to Egypt* website, www.sis.gov.eg/En/Pub/magazin/winter2004/110229000000000004. htm (accessed: February 10, 2009).

36. Bushby, *The Secret in the Bible*, pp. 168-169, 171. See also "Egyptian Civilization Lover," *Egypt State Information: Your Gateway to Egypt* website, Dr. Hassan was later to write a sixteen volume, 12,000-word set of books entitled *Ancient Egypt*, as well as a two-book set called *Pharonic Literature* and a book about the history and secrets of the Sphinx.

37. Bushby, *The Secret in the Bible*, p. 169.

38. Bushby, *The Secret in the Bible*, pp. 169–170.

39. Bushby, *The Secret in the Bible*, pp. 169–170.

40. Daniel Beresniak, *Symbols of Freemasonry* (New York: Barnes & Noble Books, 2003), p. 30.

41. Bushby, *The Secret in the Bible*, p. 170.

42. Bushby, *The Secret in the Bible*, p. 171.

43. Photographs of these discoveries were revealed by the Government Press in Cairo in 1944 in a ten-volume report entitled *Excavations at Giza*, written by Dr. Selim Hassan.

44. Manly P. Hall, *The Lost Keys to Freemasonry* includes the classic works *Freemasonry of the Ancient Egyptians* and *Masonic Orders of Fraternity* (New York: Jeremy P. Tarcher/Penguin, 2006), p. 128. See also Bushby, *Secrets in the Bible*, pp. 42–43, 91–95.

45. Bushby, *The Secret in the Bible*, p. 43.

46. Bushby, *The Secret in the Bible*, pp. 44–46.

47. Jeremy Harwood, *The Freemasons* (London: Hermes House, 2006), pp. 56–57.

48. Leadbeater, *Ancient Mystic Rites*, pp. 45-46.

49. The *Crata Repo* or *Initiations to the Ancient Mysteries of the Priests of Egypt* is a book composed of dozens of first-hand reports from ancient initiates

that allow us to piece together some of the sequences of its major initiations. These accounts come from such respected sources as Plutarch, Cicero, Iamblichus, Porphyry, Herodotus, Apuleius, Tertullian, Plato, and Rufinus. The book first made its appearance in a German edition of 1770, and was published without either the name of the author or the printer. A second edition was published in Berlin in 1778 by the librarian Stahlbaum, who declared that the author of the work was unknown, and that an ineffectual search had been made for him in every corner of Germany. See Hall, *The Lost Keys to Freemasonry*, pp. 157–163, 311.

50. Hall, *The Lost Keys to Freemasonry*, p. 45.

51. Hall, *The Lost Keys to Freemasonry*, pp. 166–167. The Scottish Rite Freemasons also include the cave in their ninth degree, linking it to the nine sacred principles (neters) that sprang forth from the cosmic womb. Today, Masonic lodges still use such rooms. They often contain objects of contemplation; a human skull and bones for mortality; a lump of bread and flask of water for sustenance; and an hourglass for the fleeting passage of time.

52. Hall, *The Lost Keys to Freemasonry*.

53. Beresniak, *Symbols of Freemasonry*, p.22

54. According to the French author Jamblique, who wrote *de Mysteriis*, Pausanias, the famous Greek travel writer of the second century of our common era, expressly states that these columns were found in the subterranean chambers near the temples of Thebes. Hall, *The Lost Keys to Freemasonry*, p. 166.

55. Hall, *The Lost Keys to Freemasonry*, p. 167.

56. Metempsychosis was a teaching of the Pythagoreans, made popular in our own times by the famous psychologist Carl Jung. It taught that the soul, which is immortal and reincarnates many times, drinks from Lethe, the River of Forgetfulness, before coming into each lifetime, and thus forgets its true self as it journeys down into the lower worlds. Metempsychosis concerns the changing states of psyche, commonly translated as "soul," but better envisaged as "soul stuff," a divisible substance released at death from its bond with the body. See Joscelyn Godwin, *The Golden Thread: The Ageless Wisdom of the Western Mystery Traditions* (Wheaton, IL: Quest Books, 2007), p. 160.

57. Hall, *The Lost Keys to Freemasonry*, pp. 169–170.

58. Hall, *The Lost Keys to Freemasonry*, pp. 170–172.

59. Whitworth, *Nine Faces of Christ*, pp. 283–289.

60. Whitworth, *Nine Faces of Christ*, pp. 286–289.

61. Leadbeater, *Ancient Mystic Rites*, p. 47.

Conclusion

1. Charles Upton, "He Is that He Is," *Parabola Magazine*, Summer 2008.
2. Ross, p. 55.
3. *Krishna Art* (NY: Ganga Publishing, n.d.), plate 4.
4. Ross, p. 65.

Afterword

1. Wilson and Prentis, pp. 144–145.

Appendix

1. Marcus Borg, *Jesus and Buddha: The Parallel Sayings* (Berkeley, CA: Ulysses Press, 1997). Used with permission.
2. *Dhamma Web* website dedicated to the teachings and scriptures of Buddha, www.dhammaweb.net/dhamma.html (accessed: January 17, 2009).

INDEX

About the Author

Tricia McCannon is a renowned American clairvoyant, historian, author, and teacher who has traveled the world in search of answers to the greatest Mysteries of the Ages. As a dedicated researcher, and mystical symbologist trained in many ancient paths of wisdom, she is known as "the Mysteries Expert." She has appeared on over 150 radio and TV shows worldwide, including *Unsolved Mysteries, Strange Universe,* and a number of international documentaries. Ms. McCannon speaks on a variety of subjects, from *Connecting with Your Spirit Guides,* to the *Nine Orders of the Angels;*  the *Wisdom of King Solomon* to the *Return of the Shepherd Kings;* the *Coming Age of Aquarius* to the *Quest for the Philosopher's Stone.*

Ms. McCannon is also the author of the acclaimed book *Dialogues with the Angels,* and for the past two decades, she has been a Headliner at Conferences in Europe and America. Trained as an initiate of many ancient streams of knowledge, including mystical Christianity, Native American wisdom, the Shabda teachings of the Masters of the Far East, and the Goddess teachings, she has led workshops in transformation for thousands around the world. Ordained as a Reverend in the International Assembly of Spiritual Healers, and a Bishop in the Madonna Ministries, her interactive workshops and visually stunning lectures create a powerful synthesis of grounded and mystical wisdom. As the Director of the Phoenix Fire Lodge Mystery School, she is also the author of a score of audio, video and online classes, and has given Soul Matrix readings for over 6000 people around the world in her continuing commitment to human dignity, personal empowerment, inner awakening, and world unity. She can be reached through her website: www.triciamccannonspeaks.com

ACKNOWLEDGMENTS

I could never have written this book without the unflagging devotion of so many other exceptional scholars, researchers, and enlightened teachers throughout the centuries—dedicated truth seekers who have gone before me, not only in the Christian arena, but also in the wise civilizations of the past. To all of you, masters and scholars alike, I am deeply indebted.

The first two years of research on this book were supported by students in my Earth Revelations and Alchemist Dream teaching classes, and finally in the last year by the Phoenix Fire Lodge Mystery School, all of whose wonderful members encouraged me to persevere in this task. Thank you all for your love of the Mysteries and your support as this book was being birthed.

At a more personal level, I want to dearly thank my spiritual initiate friends Ron Yanda, Tamara Rowe, and Ellie Leal, who've had my back in countless ways; inspirational angels Tony and Mary Lang, Duane Oxley and Lynn Clements who brought me the rare, hidden documents of *The Britain Book*, *The Koelbrin Bible*, and *The Acts of Pilate*; Dr. Cindy Gale and Stephanie Copeland, who read the first draft of the book and loved it; my encouraging writer friends Burge Smith, Debbie Unterman, David Ryback, and Leslie Sherman; and my old friend Angel Terrazas, who held my hand through the last harried days of production. Thank you each for your heartfelt friendship, and your dedication to the spiritual quest for truth.

I wish to also thank my wonderful illustrator, Sylvia Laurens, whose profound conversations about Jesus and the Great Spiritual Hierarchy sustained me in the last long year of production. It was through the grace of Spirit that

Sylvia became my constant soul companion in the very practical matter of producing the many wonderful original illustrations in this book, even though we had not yet met except over the phone.

I also wish to give grateful thanks to my long-term friends who have produced me through the years in countless speaking engagements across the world: In California, Robert Perala, Marilyn Crockett, Osha and Robert Quicksilver, Shima Moore, Pamela Millar, Joan Handgarter, Paul Andrews, Tim Gunns, Carey Williams, and Betty Binder; in New York, Aldee Filey, Trudy Beers, Andy Kaen, Alan Steinfield, Phil Gruber, Glenn Pruitt, and Lynn Rivers; in the UK, James Parsons, Amma Prema Grace, Sally Arnold, and Linda Rauch; and scattered around the world, Mel Minatour, Jim Marrs, Zayna Ravenheart, Mina Weber, Shasta Zaring, Tom Chaudoin, Claudia Thompson, Donna Sessler, and Lauren and Bruce Starr.

Also, a great thanks to my amazing publisher Greg Brandenburg, and to the terrific staff at Hampton Roads and Red Wheel/Weiser/Conari. Greg knew from the moment we met that this book had to be brought to the world, and throughout its long birthing process, he continued to campaign for it. And I am unfailingly grateful to my wonderful agent Cynthia Cannell in New York, who never ceased to believe in me or the book.

Finally, I must give deep and humble thanks to my incredible mother, Carolyn McCannon, who has long held the torch of unconditional love in our family, knowing that where there is love, there is always the possibility of a miracle of healing. Mom, you are one of the greatest lights of my life. Thank you for seeing past the cultural differences in the various forms of religion, to the wisdom of the heart. This is the true path of Jesus, for it leads us to the Kingdom of Heaven within.

HAMPTON ROADS PUBLISHING COMPANY

. . . FOR THE EVOLVING HUMAN SPIRIT

Hampton Roads Publishing Company publishes books on a variety of subjects, including spirituality, health, and other related topics.

For a copy of our latest trade catalog, call 978-465-0504, or visit our website www.hrpub.com